The
Conservative Tradition
in American Thought

AN ANTHOLOGY

SELECTED AND EDITED BY

Jay A. Sigler

G. P. PUTNAM'S SONS
NEW YORK

CONTENTS

FOREWORD

Some scholars claim that ours is an age of ideological consensus. They claim that the days of struggle among divergent interpretations of America's political future are over. This book argues that the contrary is true. America is a nation whose whole history has been enlivened by political debate between liberals and conservatives. The conservatives have often received scant attention from liberal historians and political scientists who have thereby often projected their own attitudes rather than portraying the real political world.

This book is not intended to serve as a rallying cry for conservatives and potential converts. It is, instead, an intellectual summary of where they have been, age by age, in American political thought. The book is intended to demonstrate the intellectual debt which all Americans, regardless of contemporary political outlook, owe to the tradition of American conservative political thought. As such, both liberals and conservatives should find it of value, so that they may identify their own positions more clearly.

American conservative thinkers have not formed a single school or shared in a continuous tradition. They have had to survive in a somewhat hostile atmosphere and to accommodate themselves to the leveling tendencies of political democracy. On the whole, they have done this well. They have shifted their concerns and anxieties in each generation to that issue which seemed most threatened by the rampant liberalism of the time. This has created a discontinuity in American conservatism, but the careful reader should be able to sort out the various strands of conservative thought with the aid of the organization of materials provided here.

Several words of caution are in order. First, it must be emphasized that many writers, just as many individuals, have shared both the liberal and the conservative traditions. Few pure types of either can be found at any time. Second, the dichotomy between liberals and conservatives is not to be taken too literally. On many particular issues they would agree, on a few issues there may be minor disagreement, and only rarely will sharp contrasts be visible. Certainly it is unreasonable to regard liberalism and conservatism as mirror images of each other. That kind of ideological cleavage has been almost unknown in America, for reasons that will become clear.

In preparing this book it was surprising to the author to find that this sort of collection has never appeared before. The tendency has been to pile all American political thinkers into one heap, requiring the reader to struggle to find the patterns among the pieces. It is hoped that the approach adopted here will permit a fresh and penetrating overview of American conservatism for that generation of Americans who have become numbed by liberal rhetoric or appalled by primitive, quasi-conservative dogma.

The assembling of these writings was a difficult mechanical task. Some of the books are rare and hard to find. Among the institutions which aided me were the Rutgers University Libraries, the University of Pennsylvania Library, Haverford College Library, and the Library Company of Pennsylvania. The assistance of Miss Melva Sanzon and Miss Janet Williams were invaluable in the physical task and in some of the intellectual labor. I deeply appreciate the editorial suggestions which Walter Volkomer gave me. Finally, my wife, Margaret, must be given credit for her patient criticism.

This book is intended to be a mere beginning. A wise, informed conservative will want to peruse the bibliography and to reread the classic works from which these selections are taken. But even the fair-minded liberal will, I expect, come away from these readings with respect for his historic adversaries who have played, by their honest opposition, so honorable a role in the development of American political ideas.

JAY A. SIGLER

Rutgers University
Camden, New Jersey

INTRODUCTION

American Conservatism—An Interpretation

Most conservatives, an English writer observed, prefer fox hunting to politics. In this country golf, baseball, or fishing would be better choices, not because the foxes are fewer but because the hunting of foxes is considered an aristocratic, and therefore disreputable, pursuit. Yet the point remains the same. Most conservatives do not place a high premium on political discussion, because they do not expect that the political order can change much in their personal lives. Instead, their thoughts turn to sports, the family, religion, the home, and the enjoyment of perennial pleasures, which are never free and which are worth preserving.

Consequently, there are not many simple conservative political doctrines. Conservative beliefs are not a prepacked, plastic, ready-to-assemble kit. Instead they involve a mood of suspicion, a doubt about all government, and a distrust of all Utopian schemes.

Today many people claim to espouse the ideas of conservatism. Once the word itself was tainted, but now it is acceptable, particularly when tempered by some qualifying adjective, such as "moderate" or "dynamic."

There must be some common threads which can be followed through the labyrinth of political terminology, similar assumptions and shared sources. To grasp the nature of the so-called new American conservatism, one must know what went before and then appraise the novelty of the movement. Inconsistencies appear in the development of American conservatism, but the pattern of the conservative mood can be discerned throughout. It is an American and a democratic pattern.

1

It is possible, however, to trace conservative ideas far back into history. Aristotle, the father of political science, was deeply concerned with the preservation of social balance, civic virtue, private property, the truth of common sense, and the way of moderation. Aristotle (*c.* 384–322 B.C.) wrote the *Politics* to counteract the aristocratic doctrines of his mentor, Plato (*c.* 427–347 B.C.). Aristotle was unconvinced by the airy abstractions of the ideal autocratic state in Plato's *Republic.* In the name of common sense and Greek experience Aristotle attempted to preserve the best aspects of Greek life at a time when these were under challenge by barbarian ideals and practices. Yet it was Plato who was the radical, because he sought to model Athens after its enemy, Sparta. Aristotle, a democrat, recognized the necessary stabilizing effect of a virtuous middle class. Aristotle favored an avoidance of the extremes of democracy, including mob rule and tyranny.

The origin of modern conservatism is a matter of considerable debate, but there is no doubt that conservatism as a modern movement is a response to the excesses of rationalistic zeal let loose by eighteenth-century French radicals such as Jean-Jacques Rousseau (1712–1778). Indeed, the word "conservatism" was coined from the French word *conservateur,* a name given to certain French writers who wished to return to the conditions existing prior to the rise of Napoleon I (1769–1821) and the French Revolution. As a doctrine, modern conservatism is usually traced to Edmund Burke, whose *Reflections on the Revolution in France* (1790) is the first attack upon the seemingly boundless arrogance of those who would destroy every vestige of established society, replacing it with idolatrous monuments to the anthropomorphic, man-created Goddess of Reason.

Conservatism continues to retain significance because the claims of naked reason, abstract theory, pure science, statism, and inevitably managed progress continue to be made. Conservatism is perhaps best understood by comparing it with its half brother, liberalism, since both are attempts to meet the needs of mass government in an age of dawning industrialism.

On the European Continent the reaction to the French Revolution took rather extreme forms. Joseph de Maistre (1754–1821), a French philosopher, called for a complete rejection of modernism and a retreat to the outworn authoritarian French monarchy. Klemens Metternich (1773–1859), an Austrian statesman, attempted to preserve the legitimate rule of European kings. In the German and Italian states similar antidemocratic reactions set in. Monarchial, oligarchic, and aristocratic opinions are still held by some in Western Europe today.

In most European nations the political spectrum includes all sorts of beliefs, ranging from Communism and Fascism to anarchy; but in England and the United States the democratic ideology is accepted by most members of society. Political debate takes the form of differing views of democracy and of the best way to realize its potential. In this debate there is a natural, although not always perceptible, division between conservatives and liberals. It should be apparent, then, that conservatives are democrats.

There are many reactionaries and radicals who pose as conservatives in hopes of gaining respectability. To claim as a motto that the United States "is a republic not a democracy" places the John Birch Society outside the pale of democratic discussion. The Ku Klux Klan, the Native American Party, the Minutemen, and the American Nazi Party each represent departures from the norm of democratic politics. Since these are radical rightist groups, whose discourse is violent, as are at times their deeds, their abuses cannot be blamed upon the practicing democratic conservative, no more than the misdeeds of the Communists, the Maoists, the Trotskyites, and other leftist perversions can be credited to the liberals. American liberals and conservatives were both taken in by Senator Joseph McCarthy, just as some liberals were misled by Joseph Stalin, Fidel Castro, and others.

Radical right groups are often gripped by a morbid fear of Communism. In the name of the defense of the United States, they would suppress the very liberties the nation now sustains. The sense of a secret, dangerous conspiracy which plays a hidden but vital role in history has long marked the paranoid vision of reactionaries. Adolf Hitler believed a Jewish–Marxist conspiracy on the one hand and a Jewish–capitalist conspiracy on the other to be motive forces in recent history. This hysterical view of modern life does not fit the reasonable, commonsense mood of conservatism. The true conservative does not maintain that all liberals are Communist conspirators, merely that they are misguided, confused, or vainglorious.

In order to perceive the nature of conservatism in America it is necessary to start with a completely fresh view, or else risk becoming entrapped in a quicksand of words. We must discard the European meanings of the words "liberal" and "conservative" and adopt a native

American view of these ideological approaches to politics. If we can do this, we can avoid the intellectual errors of Allen Guttmann and other frail critics of American conservatism who have set up a conservative straw man in eighteenth-century garb and attacked the poor chap for believing in old-fashioned ideas. Guttmann will only admit into his conservative camp a few aristocratic novelists and poets, thus consigning Mr. Buckley and Mr. Goldwater into intellectual no–man's land, together with other self-deluded "conservatives," who do not realize that they are really liberals.*

American conservatism can best be understood as a changing group of interpretations of problems set up by English political theorist John Locke (1632–1704). Although Locke died seventy-two years prior to our Revolution, the principles he formulated, the rights he cherished, and the institutions he described were more relevant to America than to any other nation.

Locke wrote his works primarily to justify the Glorious Revolution, which brought William and Mary to the throne of England in 1688. He devoted only one minor book to conditions in colonial America. Nonetheless his views converted most thoughtful American colonials. This conversion was so complete that Locke's writings form a mine of ideas for both liberals and conservatives in America. It is possible for the staunchest conservative or the most militant liberal to find some statement in Locke which can be used to attack the position of the opposition. It is this fact which makes it so difficult for foreigners, and the more superficial observers in America, to separate the liberals from the conservatives. We are all Lockeans, and Locke was both a liberal and a conservative.

Locke assumed that all men are, by birth, free, equal, and independent and that no one could ever be subjected to political power without his consent. Men formed a social compact in which a single community was formed. After this, a political body was also created by the mutual consent of the members of the new community. Those who entered the social contract also agreed that the majority had the right to act for the whole of the people, because the society will move naturally as "the greater force carries it, which is the consent of the majority."

---

* Allen Guttmann, *The Conservative Tradition in America* (New York: Oxford University Press, 1967), pp. 167–68, depicts William F. Buckley and Barry Goldwater as nineteenth-century liberals.

Most conservatives and liberals would subscribe to the principles just listed. They would differ over the meaning of majority rule, the role of the individual against the majority, the way in which the majority should be represented, and the proper interpretations to be given our written social compact—the national Constitution. These differences echo down the corridors of American history.

Even more fundamentally, conservatives and liberals would disagree about the relative importance of the natural rights of man, which are also mentioned by Locke. Life, liberty, and property are sacred to each individual, but what if there be a conflict among these rights? Which would prevail? Liberals and conservatives have shifted position, although both agree that capitalism is the economic system best able to protect individual rights.

Locke introduced many ideas into the American conservative tradition. The ideas of limited government, individualism, the rights of property, government by consent, representative government, and legislative supremacy are examples of Locke's influence on conservatism. Liberals, on the contrary, choose to emphasize majority rule, the right of rebellion, natural rights, the right to resist authority, and popular sovereignty. Indeed, there are many inconsistencies in the writings of Locke which support either view. Both the democratic and the capitalist traditions were nourished by Locke, and he wrote to defend the rights established by the English Bill of Rights of 1689 which served as a model for the American Bill of Rights in 1790. Lockeanism is enshrined in the American Constitution itself, which most scholars regard as a conservative document.

Edmund Burke (1729–1797) was another defender of the English settlement of 1689. Burke's writings did not have the popularity of Locke's in early America. Although Burke has always been important in English political thought, the revival of interest in his work is a rather new and welcome phenomenon in the development of American conservative thought. John Adams studied Burke, but until the twentieth century very few other American conservatives have done so. As a member of Parliament, Burke's major concerns were the preservation of the English constitution against the designs of the King and the defense of the Americans, Indians, and Irish against abusive colonial rule. Burke favored war against Jacobin France, and it was only in this enterprise that his policies were adopted. His political career and his intellectual growth were intimately interwoven, as one would expect of a philosopher committed to practical experience.

Burke was deeply committed to the principle of order. God, he believed, is the author of a divine scheme which is orderly and intelligible. The universal moral law is an exemplification of God's plan. The moral law is embodied in the laws and governments found in the various nations of the world. This moral law operates through the institutions of government, not through single individuals.

Individual rights, according to Burke, arise out of society and are dependent upon society. A man's individual rights cannot be separated from the society of which he is a part and from which his rights derive. Liberty in the abstract does not exist but is a dangerous, unsettling concept lacking in limitation because it lacks specific historical content. Neither are all men equal in liberty, but each is entitled to the rights accorded his station in life.

There is no single best form of government in Burke's view, but he warned that in a democracy the oppression of the minority by the majority can be worse than in a monarchy. There is no simple method to construct a commonwealth, and men cannot change governments as they change their coats. Only the experience and wisdom of many generations can be a reliable guide to good government. Revolution should be a last resort, as peaceful as possible and for the purpose of preserving the best traditions.

Burke distrusted the voice of the people and denied the principle of majority rule. Government was to be the business of a ruling class of ability, property, and birth. The propertied classes must be protected against the jealousy of the masses. The ruling class is not bound to provide direct representation to the voters but only an indirect determination of the public good.

As can be seen, many of these Burkean views are at odds with Locke and with the American experience. Obviously, then, there must be other ways in which Burke may be regarded as the best intellectual proponent of conservatism; this is to be found in the emphasis Burke placed on conserving. Established governments, laws, classes, customs, religions, and traditions are worthy of respect because they embody the wisdom of the past. Not only are these part of God's plan for man, but they are also a product of prescription. The particular rights, duties, titles, and institutions which have existed for many generations are the inherited product of millions of our ancestors who passed these benefits on to the current generation. As Burke explained his theory of prescription:

> It is a presumption in favour of any settled scheme of government against any untried project, that a nation has long existed and flourished under it . . . because a nation is not an idea only of local extent, and individual monetary aggregation; but it is an idea of continuity, which extends in time as well as in numbers and in space. And this is a choice not of one day, or one set of people, not a tumultary and giddy choice; it is a deliberate election of ages and of generations.

When Burke said in this same paragraph that both the fortunate individual and the multitude "is foolish when they act without deliberation" but that the species is wise, he said a hard truth which few have so pungently expressed. It is the essence of conservatism. Reason, sentiment, and experience are combined to combat unaided, abstract "reasoning." Burke provides a starting point for a modern definition of conservatism.

Although Locke's influence pervades the eighteenth, nineteenth, and twentieth centuries, and Burke has been rediscovered in recent decades, American political thought antedates both of these giants, and some of the notions of the pre-Revolutionary period linger on and mingle with the dominant themes of John Locke.

This nation was first settled by Puritans who came to America not to establish democracy but to form a society in which they could worship God as they pleased. The freedom they valued was religious, not political, in character. They attempted to construct a perfect Christian community in the New World, one in which politics was subservient to theology.

In the Puritan colonies God was Sovereign and the Bible was His law. A strict theocracy, following the principles of John Calvin (1509–1564), was established in Massachusetts Bay. Governor John Winthrop barred nonchurch members from government positions; a small circle of the "elect," who were foreordained for salvation, ruled the colony. Obviously, a theocracy is likely to be authoritarian; strict government control of private life is necessary. In Massachusetts Bay individualism and resistance to government were severely discouraged.

The political thought of John Winthrop and John Cotton, two eminent leaders of the Puritans, was not conservative in the post-Lockean sense. Both men opposed the idea of democracy, which Cotton condemned as unfit in God's ordinance "either in church or common-wealth." Nonetheless, from these great founders of the Massachusetts colony we may gain a gleam of that moral fervor and sense of social order which is shared by modern American conservatives.

The Revolution which came one hundred and forty-six years after the landing at Plymouth Rock was no startling event. The gradual movement toward separatism from England was apparent to many in the early part of the eighteenth century. Some of the Englishmen who could not adjust to the strange new society emerging in America departed for Canada and England. Many of these loyalists were conservatives in the European sense. With their departure before and after the Revolution the bonds between American and European conservatism were severed. Nearly 100,000 loyalists left America. Most of them were drawn from the top strata of American society. Merchants, professional men, and officials—they were horrified by the version of John Locke's philosophy which aided the disloyalty of the rebels.

One of these loyalists, Jonathan Boucher, provides a good example of the maladjustment of these Old World conservatives. Boucher was born in England and came to America as a young Anglican priest. Serving in Maryland and Virginia in the 1770's, Boucher called for submission to royal authority and acceptance of the wisdom of the past, as commanded by the Bible. In order to defend these views Boucher had to preach with a pair of loaded pistols lying on the pulpit cushion. He, and many others of the old conservative temperament, were driven out of the country upon the outbreak of the war with Great Britain.

The American Revolution was, to some extent, a conservative event. Primarily a war for independence from colonial status, the American Revolution was also less drastic in its social effects than the French Revolution would be a few years later. The changes wrought by the French Revolution reached the inner order of society itself; social and class distinctions were overturned. The American Revolution was less disturbing to the ordinary relationships among men. The society itself was not greatly altered. It is true that some people lost their property, some families were ruptured, some respected individuals lost prestige, and some fled to Canada. But these effects were largely unintentional. It was never the object of our revolutionary leaders to create a new social order or to disturb the customary order of American life, except for the severed connection with Britain.

Compared to later revolutionary movements, the American Revolution was relatively free from rabble-rousing, demagogic ideological slogans. The demand for self-government did not include appeals for radical leveling. The democratic ideals expressed by American leaders were mild, even by the standards of the time. The American Revolution is a better example of early nationalism than it is of democratic radicalism.

On a spectrum of revolutions the American Revolution was relatively conservative. Its aims were limited and were soon attained after the withdrawal of British troops. The reforms demanded, even at the most emotional moments, were essentially political, not social or economic, in nature. The Revolution was an orderly step in the development of the idea of self-government under constitutional restraints. Historian Robert Brown has demonstrated that in Massachusetts, at least, the Revolution was regarded almost entirely as a war of independence and not as a great political, social, or economic revolt.

The contrast between the writings of the British loyalists and the Federalists of the post-Revolutionary period is quite remarkable, demonstrating the gap existing between Old World conservatism and conservatism in America. Even the cautious authors of the *Federalist Papers* admitted the existence of a right of revolution, and they also subscribed to the idea of constructing a new and progressive society in America. Such beliefs were quite foreign to the conservatism of the prewar loyalists.

The new republican government was not created by a band of radical conspirators driven by mass frenzy but by a body of distinguished, well-educated, propertied men of stable and conservative backgrounds. The Constitution was not constructed by the same men who signed the liberal Declaration of Independence but by sober men of means who feared the excess of popular government.

The Constitution was not a conservative document in terms of the prevailing attitudes of Europe in the eighteenth century. But if we consider the first American government under the Articles of Confederation, the Constitution is far more conservative by comparison. The Articles had turned over most political power to the states. The small amount of national power was in the hands of a legislative assembly which operated on instructions received from the states. Commerce, finance, and trade were left to the none too tender care of the states.

It was primarily to allow for national control over commerce, finance, and trade that the movement to create a replacement for the Articles of Confederation began. Regularity in commerce, protection of the currency, and stability in finance motivated many of the founding fathers. Jefferson, writing to John Adams from Paris, said it was "an assembly of demi-gods." It was not that, but it was composed of the most talented and constructive men available in the country, and it did not contain representatives of the more radical political views to be found in the country. Neither Patrick Henry nor Samuel Adams, for example, attended the Convention. The leaders of the Revolution generally declined to attend because they feared a conservative triumph.

The Constitution itself created a republican form of government with only indirect popular control. Originally, none of the federal officers was elected by the people. The President was to be chosen by a group of select individuals known as the electoral college. The Senate was to be elected by state legislatures. The judges, rather than elected as was the case in many of the states, were appointed by the President. The terms of office, except for members of the House, were long. Separation of powers and checks and balances were built into the system in order to limit the growth of power in any branch of government. The Constitution also contained many provisions which served to restrain state invasions of property rights. The states were, for example, enjoined from interfering with the provisions of contracts.

Ever since 1789 the Constitution has been a shield for American conservatives, and they have found in it a source for most of their important values. The national judiciary has often, for example, supported conservative views of the proper scope of national and state power. Periodically, conservative writers call for a return to the original spirit of the Constitution, indicating that the Constitution plays the role in America which European conservatives discover in the ancient customs and habits of their nations.

In the American South the development of conservatism was retarded somewhat by a backward economic and social system. Some Southerners regarded themselves as descendants of the English gentry. A romantic conception of European aristocracy often supported an outmoded style of democracy. Only a few Southern writers were able to express their opposition to the dominant political concepts to be found in American political thought. In the decades prior to the Civil War George Fitzhugh, for example, openly challenged the fundamental viewpoint of John Locke, and John C. Calhoun questioned many particular Lockean assumptions. The defense of inequality, never a popular theme in America, is developed to its fullest by these Southern writers. In its brief life-span pre-Civil War Southern conservatism has shown that non-Lockean conservatism has no audience in America.

Even since the breakdown of proslavery attitudes, American conservatives have learned to accept and support the capitalist, industrial economic system. The ideal figure became the Horatio Alger hero, who by hard work and good luck rose from rags to riches. Locke's idea of limited government was easily blended with the idea of restricted government activity in the economic system. The conservative accepted the necessity of a marriage between capitalism and democracy, regarding a threat to the former as a danger to the latter. Locke's philosophy, formulated in a society which had not yet felt the impact of industrialism, was amended to meet the needs of contemporary life.

Modern conservatism is largely an English product, with peculiar American variations. Burkean views and Toryism are deeply rooted in English history and tradition and lack the dogmatic fervor of Continental parties on the right. The inspiration for English conservatism is quite parochial. It rests upon a society which has recently been feudal, remains royal, and possesses a special relationship to Christianity. The principle of hierarchy, of degree and social position, is a profound part of this kind of conservatism. The strict relationship of class to class, with the monarchy at the apex, and other nobility trailing not far below, is well suited to a conserving attitude. Europe was made, said Burke, by Christianity and the spirit of a gentleman. One must be cautious in applying the lessons of English experience to America, however, where the religious tradition is different and the word "gentleman" does not have a special connotation.

After the American Revolution, British conservatism took paths other than those of American conservatism. Benjamin Disraeli (1804–1881), the shining conservative light of the nineteenth century, pursued policies unlike those called conservative on this side of the Atlantic. Disraeli opposed the liberal free enterprise, competitive, exploitative practices of the first decades of the Industrial Revolution. By forging an alliance between the aristocrats and the working class under the banner of Tory democracy, Disraeli sought to protect the lower orders from the evils of rampant industrial capitalism. Conservative reformism proceeded in the name of the best English traditions under the leadership of the old families and the landed gentry. At the same time, however, Disraeli attached the practice of imperialism to the traditions of English conservatism, a characteristic which survives to a limited extent even in the Conservative Party today. Although brilliant American conservatives, such as Russell Kirk (1918–   ), have expressed admiration for Disraeli, they have not shown the significance of his ideas for the American situation.

Indeed, the existence of a valid American conservative tradition has been questioned by some historians. They point to the fact that the American Revolution itself was primarily a liberal movement and that the ideas which nourished it are the common liberal heritage of all Americans. The claims of inherited privilege, an established aristocracy of ancient lineage, have never existed on these shores. Rigid class structure, established churches, hallowed customs, and ritualized behavior have all been largely absent from the American experience. The leveling influence of American egalitarianism has gone too far, say some, to support a genuine American conservatism.

Certainly it is true that there is no American conservative Golden Age. There is no ancient, harmonic American society with which to criticize and compare the contemporary scene. There are not even conservative Utopias, ideal models of a perfectly ordered, dignified society which could re-create the best of what has passed.

But this criticism is essentially unfair. It taunts the American conservative for not being a European. It oversimplifies the American past by not allowing for the variations of more than three centuries of native political thought. It neglects to emphasize the conscious borrowings of Alexander Hamilton and John Adams from the writings of Harrington, Burke, and others. Finally, these critics fail to account for the deep, sometimes passionate cleavages which have existed in American political history. Some have been based on economic motives, some on class motives, but regardless of cause, they have revealed the fundamental gulf between liberal and conservative persuasion.

In selecting representative figures of American conservative thought, it was necessary to search the history of American thought for individuals who exemplify the conservatism of their period in the clearest fashion. Many writers have some conservative and some liberal beliefs, but to choose typical thinkers it is necessary to apply a rigorous test to each in order to determine the degree of conservatism or the variety.

Some conservatives, like Friedrich von Hayek (1899–   ), insist on calling themselves "liberal." Others, like Russell Kirk, are more interested in English conservatism. Some, like Walter Lippmann (1889–   ) and Peter Viereck (1916–   ), are at times strictly conservative, but both vacillate between liberalism and conservatism. The selection process was greatly aided by certain assumptions made about American conservatism, many of which were gleaned from a rereading of Burke and Locke.

Conservatives do not have a rosy view of human nature. They are impressed by the frailty and weakness of man. The restraint of the evil tendencies of man is a proper object of government, but conservatives feel that the improvement of man is more the result of individual effort than it is of anything the state may do. Men do not change rapidly or easily. Governments and laws are not capable of making fundamental changes in the nature of man. The conservative accepts the mysterious uniqueness of man.

The conservative suspicion of government flows from the same doubt about the good motives of men. Rulers, too, are fallible beings. Their plans and schemes may be motivated by selfishness, pride, or glory rather than by the common good.

The conservative prefers to emphasize the moral equality of men more than their legal, social, or economic equality. These latter equalities may be more superficial than moral equality and may also be antithetical to it.

The conservative accepts as natural the differences which separate men. Class, intelligence, nationality, and race make men different. Difference does not imply superiority or inferiority; it merely states an observable fact.

Conservatives have ingrained respect for talent and birth. The preference for the best man, rather than the most popular man, is a typical attitude. The aristocratic reformer is a familiar figure in American politics, especially in state and local politics. Open aristocratic preferences are rarely stated.

The conservative does not oppose change, but he does resist it. In the interest of social stability it is safer to retain a known constellation of relationships than blindly to seek new ones. Change must come, as it always has, but it can be guided by experience and fitted into the already existing patterns.

Since government is to be distrusted, power must be diffused.

Political power is inherently dangerous, so it must be controlled by dividing up responsibility, reducing authority. Arbitrary power is particularly odious, especially when wielded by an insensitive bureaucrat.

Government may promote morality, but it cannot produce universal prosperity. The government may assist the helpless, but only when they cannot help themselves, for to do so might destroy their individual self-respect.

Freedom is not absolute or unconditional. Society creates duties as well as rights. Excessive selfishness is fed by insistence on personal rights at the cost of society itself. Men must learn to serve as well as to be served.

The Constitution provides the best guide to political action. It is an expression of the higher law which restricts arbitrary government. It is the symbol of the nation and the source of its stability.

Property has its rights, though these are not unlimited. The possession of private property is an asset for the society as well as for the possessors. Stability, work, and responsibility are encouraged by the system of private property.

The vision of conservatism is one of common sense, practicality, and realism. It is concerned with the possible and the feasible. Reform is desirable, but only when it can succeed and when it really improves.

As can be seen, conservatism cannot be expressed in a set of programs, in a religious tract, or as a set of specific moral or political guides. In American politics it is a style rather than a creed. There is neither a monarchy nor an established religion to defend; only a Constitution and a historical method of practical, gradual change. Conservatism is a way of thinking and a way of speaking. The conservative is not sure that tomorrow will always be an improvement upon today or that "progress is our most important product." He doubts the wisdom of the current majority style, which happens to be liberalism. He offers the evidence of the history texts. There has been no Utopia in the past, and there will not be one in the future. In a phrase, the conservative is the man who is sure that he doesn't know the answers and doubts that you do.

There are weaknesses in the practice of the conservative and the liberal style. If the besetting sin of the liberal is his romantic self-image as the savior of the poor and downtrodden, the conservative sometimes falls victim to the mythic image. Rather than glorifying himself, he creates a heroic stereotype of the founding fathers and of other men and women of patriotic fame. There is no reason for believing that men are no longer as great as once they were, for all men are fallible, even the nation's past heroes. This attitude at least instills the social value of patriotism, although it can also lend itself to parody and ridicule by the irreverent.

Clinton Rossiter has pointed out that in a nation founded by a liberal revolution the only tradition worthy of preservation is a liberal one. For this reason he doubts that conservatism can survive in America unless it is attuned to American conditions. He has called for a new conservatism which would be "less individualistic, dogmatic, optimistic and materialistic, and even more traditionalist and conservative, than the conservatism of today." To some extent that plea has not been met. American conservative theorists today have yet to match the intellectual power of James Madison, John Adams, or John Calhoun. There is much to be learned from these men. Yet conservatives cannot expect merely to repeat the formulas of the past but must continually reinterpret the past to the heirs of the present day.

The liberals are no better off. They are less optimistic about eliminating poverty, reviving the city, and controlling crime and are for the first time in a generation fearful of broad executive power. A disillusionment has set in, although there is no disarray. There is a decline in liberal purpose as the shallowness of many liberal programs has become apparent. Even some intellectuals are deserting the liberal ranks as the realization dawns that intellectuals are themselves an elite. The time seems ripe for reappraisal, not only of ends but of means. An examination of the liberal and conservative traditions in America will provide a start for many. The liberal majority needs the corrective of thoughtful conservatism. The conservatives may hope to convert the majority to traditional values. American society cannot help but benefit by such a development.

I

The Colonial
Experience

One hundred and sixty-nine years span the period between the founding of Jamestown in 1607 and the signing of the Declaration of Independence. Our history as an independent nation is only a few decades longer. During the long colonial era a number of different governments existed under the English flag, but despite their dissimilarities they shared the common bond of their English heritage and the experience of building a new society.

The most remarkable of the early colonies was founded at Plymouth by religious Separatists who, though English, came to these shores in 1620 from Holland. They had expressed their political hopes in the Mayflower Compact, signed in May of that year. In 1630 the Company of Massachusetts Bay moved to the new land, gradually expanding to the north and south of Massachusetts Bay. By 1635 a group of settlers moved into what is now Connecticut, while in the following year Roger Williams and his followers fled the Massachusetts Bay colony to form their own settlement based on a conflicting set of religious and political principles.

From the very beginning the founders of the Plymouth and Massachusetts Bay colonies concerned themselves with the nature of secular society and the proper relationship between their religion and the state. Men like John Cotton (1584–1652), John Winthrop (1588–1649), Thomas Hooker (1586–1647), Increase Mather (1639–1723), and Cotton Mather (1663–1728) were protesters against the established Church of England and followers of Protestant theologian John Calvin.

Massachusetts Calvinists were strict believers in the supremacy of the church over the state. They claimed that the church was an expression of the divine will of God, and the state its servant. The church was composed of the "elect," who were admitted by the elders upon sufficient examination. The state included the elect and the unelect, controlling all persons within its jurisdiction. But all were not to be allowed the right of participation.

The system established in Massachusetts was essentially oligarchical and undemocratic. Emphasis was placed upon the Christian duty of obedience. Yet contained within the concept of individual salvation was the germ of the idea of political individualism, which is so much a part of American conservatism, though little else remains of Puritan political thought.

In the South of the new land the first settlements took place in the Carolinas in 1670. The year before, English writer and philosopher John Locke had attempted to draw up the Fundamental Constitutions of Carolina, a feudal document which was not appropriate to the new colony. As a practical matter Locke's scheme was useless in America, but as a man of ideas Locke became a pervasive influence in the colonies, even providing a justification for revolution from the mother country.

America never possessed a class of hereditary noblemen. Feudalism never took root here. The Puritan doctrine of the elect was eventually rejected in Massachusetts. Locke had reserved to the people the right of revolution when the social contract with the government had been broken by "a long train of abuses." In a new nation in which social differences were not great, Locke's doctrines of equality, self-government, and natural rights were bound to become popular. When the time was ripe, his revolutionary ideas were accepted by many. However, in spite of this radical aspect of his thought, Locke also expressed ideas which are still appealing for conservatives, so that it can be seen that all Americans are followers of John Locke, although we may choose to emphasize one or another feature of his writings. In this section the ideas of pre-Lockean conservatives are to be found, but their words sound strange and almost foreign. Our natural vocabulary of political belief is drawn from John Locke.

1. COTTON

The Sovereignty of God

John Cotton (1584–1652) was the Puritan minister whose spiritual leadership supported the Massachusetts Bay Company in the first decade of its existence in America. Cotton preached a farewell sermon to the Massachusetts Bay Company as it prepared to leave for the New World. In this sermon, "God's Promise to His Plantation," from which this selection* is taken, can be found the essence of the Puritan motive—the religious force which caused them to attempt to create a new Calvinist society in the New World. The divine source of authority for the formation of the new colony is made apparent by frequent Biblical references; Cotton and his Calvinist followers believed that political authority ultimately came from God.

2 SAM. 7. 10.

Moreover I will appoint a place for my people Israell, and I will plant them, that they may dwell in a place of their owne, and move no more.

In the beginning of this chapter we reade of *Davids* purpose to build God an house, who thereupon consulted with *Nathan* about it, one Prophet standing in neede of anothers help in such waightie matters. *Nathan* incourageth the King unto this worke, verse 3. God the same night meetes *Nathan* and tells him a contrary purpose of his: Wherein God refuseth *Davids* offer, with some kind of earnest and vehement dislike, *verse* 4, 5: Secondly, he refuseth the reason of *Davids* offer, from his long silence. For foure hundred yeares together he spake of

---

* *Old South Leaflets*, No. 53, published in Boston by the Old South Church in 1890.

no such thing, unto any of the Tribes of *Israel* saying, *Why build you not me an house?* in 6, 7, verses.

Now lest *David* should be discouraged with this answer, the Lord bids *Nathan* to shut up his speech with words of encouragement, and so he removes his discouragement two wayes:

First, by recounting his former favours dispensed unto *David*. Secondly, by promising the continuance of the like or greater: and the rather, because of this purpose of his. And five blessings God promiseth unto *David*, and his, for his sake.

The first is in the 10. verse: *I will appoint a place for my people Israell*.

Secondly, seeing it was in his heart to build him an house, God would therefore, *build him an house renowned forever*, verse 11.

Thirdly, that he would accept of an house from *Solomon*, verse 12.

Fourthly, hee will be a Father to his sonne, vers. 14, 15.

Fifthly, that he will *establish the throne of his house for ever*.

In this 10 verse is a double blessing promised:

First, the designment of a place for his people.

Secondly, a plantation of them in that place, from whence is promised a threefold blessing.

First, they shall dwell there like Free-holders in a place of their owne.

Secondly, hee promiseth them firme and durable possession, they shall move no more.

Thirdly, they shall have peaceable and quiet resting there, The sonnes of wickedness shall afflict them no more: which is amplified by their former troubles, as before time.

From the appointment of a place for them, which is the first blessing, you may observe this note,

The placing of a people in this or that Countrey is from the appointment of the Lord.

This is evident in the Text, and the Apostle speakes of it as grounded in nature, *Acts* 17. 26. *God hath determined the times before appointed, and the bounds of our habitation. Dut. 2 chap. 5. 9.* God would not have the *Israelites* meddle with the *Edomites*, or the *Moabites*, because he had given them their land for a possession. God assigned out such a land for such a posterity, and for such a time.

Quest. Wherein doth this worke of God stand in appointing a place for a people?

Answ. First, when God espies or discovers a land for a people, as in *Ezek*. 20. 6. he brought them into a land that he had espied for them: And that is, when either he gives them to discover it themselves, or heare of it discovered by others, and fitting them.

Secondly, after he hath espied it, when he carrieth them along to it, so that they plainly see a providence of God leading them from one Country to another: As in *Exod*. 19. 4. *You have seene how I have borne you as on Eagles wings, and brought you unto my selfe.* So that though they met with many difficulties, yet hee carried them high above them all, like an eagle, flying over seas and rockes, and all hindrances.

Thirdly, when he makes roome for a people to dwell there, as in *Psal*. 80. 9. *Thou preparedst roome for them.* When *Isaac* sojourned among the *Philistines*, he digged one well, and the *Philistines* strove for it, and he called it *Esek.* and he digged another well, and for that they strove also, therefore he called it *Sitnah:* and he removed thence, and digged an other well, and for that they strove not, and he called it *Rohoboth*, and said, *For now the Lord hath made roomee for us, and we shall be fruitfull in the Land.* Now no *Esek*, no *Sitnah*, no quarrel or contention, but now he sits downe in *Rohoboth* in a peaceable roome. . . .

This placeing of people in this or that Countrey, is from Gods soveraignty over all the earth, and the inhabitants thereof: as in *Psal*. 24. 1. *The earth is the Lords, and the fulnesse thereof.* And in *Ier*. 10. 7. God is there called, *The King of Nations:* and in *Deut*. 10. 14. Therefore it is meete he should provide a place for all Nations to inhabite, and haue all the earth replenished. Onely in the Text here is meant some more speciall appointment, because God tells them it by his owne mouth; he doth not so with other people, he doth not tell the children of *Sier*, that hee hath appointed a place for them: that is, He gives them the land by promise; others take the land by his providence, but Gods people take the land by promise: And therefore the land of *Canaan* is called a land of promise. Which they discerne, first, by discerning themselves to be in Christ, in whom all the promises are yea, and amen.

Secondly, by finding his holy presence with them, to wit, when he plants them in the holy Mountaine of his Inheritance: *Exodus*. 15. 17. And that is when he giveth them the liberty and purity of his Ordinances. It is a land of promise, where they have provision for soule as well as for body. *Ruth* dwelt well for outward respects while shee dwelt in *Moab*, but when shee cometh to dwell in *Israel*, shee is said to come under the wings of God: *Ruth* 2. 12. When God wrappes us

Thirdly, though this promise was made that others should not wrong them, yet it followes not but that they might wrong themselves by trespassing against God, and so expose themselves to affliction. Whilst they continued Gods plantation, they were a noble Vine, a right seede, but if *Israel* will destroy themselves, the fault is in themselves. And yet even in their captivity the good amongst them God graciously provided for: The *Basket of good figges* God sent into the land of *Caldea* for their good: *Jer.* 24. 5. But if you rebell against God, the same God that planted you will also roote you out againe, for all the evill which you shall doe against your selves: *Jer.* 11. 17. When the Israelites liked not the soile, grew weary of the Ordinances, and forsooke the worship of God, and said, *What part have we in David?* after this they never got so good a King, nor any settled rest in the good land wherein God had planted them. As they waxed weary of God, so hee waxed wearie of them, and cast them out of his sight.

Vse 1. To exhort all that are planted at home, or intend to plant abroad, to looke well to your plantation, as you desire that the sonnes of wickedness may not afflict you at home, nor enemies abroad, looke that you be right planted, and then you need not to feare, you are safe enough: God hath spoken it, I will plant them, and they shall not be moved, neither shall the sonnes of wickedness afflict them any more.

Quest. What course would you have us take?

Answ. Have speciall care that you ever have the Ordinances planted amongst you, or else never looke for security. As soone as Gods Ordinances cease, your security ceaseth likewise; but if God plant his Ordinances among you, feare not, he will maintaine them. *Isay* 4. 5, 6. *Upon all their glory there shall be a defence;* that is, upon all Gods Ordinances: for so was the Arke called *the Glory of Israel,* 1 *Sam.* 4. 22.

Secondly, have a care to be implanted into the Ordinances, that the word may be ingrafted into you, and you into it: If you take rooting in the ordinances, grow up thereby, bring forth much fruite, continue and abide therein, then you are a vineyard of red wine, and the Lord will keepe you, *Isay* 27. 2. 3. that no sonnes of violence shall destroy you. Looke into all the stories whether divine or humane, and you shall never finde that God ever rooted out a people that had the Ordinances planted amongst them, and themselves planted into the Ordinances: never did God suffer such plants to be plucked up; on all their glory shall be a defence.

Thirdly, be not unmindfull of our *Ierusalem* at home, whether you leave us, or stay at home with us. *Oh pray for the peace of Ierusalem, they shall prosper that love her, Psal.* 122. 6. *They shall all be confounded and turned backe that hate Sion, Psal.* 129. 5. As God continueth his presence with us, (blessed be his name) so be ye present in spirit with us, though absent in body: Forget not the wombe that bare you and the brest that gave you sucke. Even ducklings hatched under an henne, though they take the water, yet will still have recourse to the wing that hatched them: how much more should chickens of the same feather, and yolke? In the amity and unity of brethren, the Lord hath not onely promised, but commanded a blessing, even life forevermore: *Psal.* 133. 1, 2.

Fourthly, goe forth, every man that goeth, with a publick spirit, looking not on your owne things onely, but also on the things of others: *Phil.* 2. 4. This care of universall helpfullnesse was the prosperity of the first Plantation of the Primitive Church, *Acts* 4. 32.

Fifthly, have a tender care that you looke well to the plants that spring from you, that is, to your children, that they doe not degenerate as the Israelites did; after which they were vexed with afflictions on every hand. How came this to passe? *Ier.* 2. 21. *I planted them a noble Vine, holy, a right seede, how then art thou degenerate into a strange Vine before mee?* Your Ancestours were of a noble divine spirit, but if they suffer their children to degenerate, to take loose courses, then God will surely plucke you up: Otherwise if men have a care to propagate the Ordinances and Religion to their children after them, God will plant them and not roote them up. For want of this, the seede of the repenting *Ninivites* was rooted out.

Sixthly, and lastly, offend not the poore Natives, but as you partake in their land, so make them partakers of your precious faith: as you reape their temporalls, so feede them with your spiritualls: winne them to the love of Christ, for whom Christ died. They never yet refused the Gospell, and therefore more hope they will now receive it. Who knoweth whether God have reared this whole Plantation for such an end:

Vse 2. Secondly, for consolation to them that are planted by God in any place, that finde rooting and establishing from God, this is a cause of much encouragement unto you, that what hee hath planted he will maintaine, every plantation his right hand hath not planted shalbe rooted up, but his owne plantation shall prosper, & flourish.

When he promiseth peace and safety, what enemies shalstbe able to make the promise of God of none effect? Neglect not walls, and bulwarkes, and fortifications for your owne defence; but

ever let the name of the Lord be your strong

Tower; and the word of his Promise the

Rocke of your refuge. His word

that made heaven and earth

will not faile, till hea-

ven and earth be

no more

Amen.

2.   WINTHROP

Obedience to God's Law

John Winthrop (1588–1649) was one of the founders of Puritan Massachusetts, serving as lieutenant governor and governor for twenty years. The Puritan settlers did not come to the New World to enjoy private pleasures but to fulfill a holy mission. Winthrop, the first secular leader of the Massachusetts Bay colony, maintained that the bond between church and state was one of "brotherly affection." The public interest required that the Lord be the absolute ruler of the colony and the people be led by a mixed government elected by the people which would, once elected, rule by divine decree. The authority of the government came from God. Winthrop's sermon "A Modell of Christian Charity," from which this selection* is taken, was written in 1620 while he was on shipboard approaching the New World. In it he made clear his opposition to a "mere democracy," which, he said, was the "meanest and worst of all forms of Government." The essence of Puritan political thought was conservative, in the sense that it distrusted the masses, relied on the leadership to make wise decisions, and rested on divine rather than merely man-made principles.

A MODELL OF CHRISTIAN CHARITY.

Written
On Boarde the Arrabella,
On the Atlantick Ocean.
By the Honorable JOHN WINTHROP Esquire.

In His passage, (with the great Company of Religious people, of which Christian Tribes he was the Brave Leader and famous Governor;) from the Island of Great Brittaine, to New-England in the North America. Anno 1630.

* From *Winthrop Papers*, Vol. II (Boston: Massachusetts Historical Society, 1931), pp. 282, 292–95.

CHRISTIAN CHARITIE.
A MODELL HEREOF.

God Almightie in his most holy and wise providence hath soe disposed of the Condicion of mankinde, as in all times some must be rich some poore, some highe and eminent in power and dignitie; others meane and in subjeccion. . . .

. . . Conclusions.

1 First, This love among Christians is a reall thing not Imaginarie.

2ly. This love is as absolutely necessary to the being of the body of Christ, as the sinewes and other ligaments of a naturall body are to the being of that body.

3ly. This love is a divine spirituall nature free, active strong Couragious permanent under valueing all things beneathe its propper object, and of all the graces this makes us nearer to resemble the virtues of our heavenly father.

4ly, It restes in the love and wellfare of its beloved, for the full and certaine knowledge of these truthes concerning the nature use, [and] excellency of this grace, that which the holy ghost hath left recorded 1. Cor. 13. may give full satisfaccion which is needfull for every true member of this lovely body of the Lord Jesus, to worke upon theire heartes, by prayer meditacion continuall exercise at least of the speciall [power] of this grace till Christ be formed in them and they in him all in eache other knitt together by this bond of love.

It rests now to make some applicacion of this discourse by the present designe which gave the occasion of writeing of it. Herein are 4 things to be propounded: first the persons, 2ly, the worke, 3ly, the end, 4ly the meanes.

1. For the persons, wee are a Company professing our selves fellow members of Christ, In which respect onely though wee were absent from eache other many miles, and had our imploymentes as farre distant, yet wee ought to account our selves knitt together by this bond of love, and live in the excercise of it, if wee would have comforte of our being in Christ, this was notorious in the practise of the Christians in former times, as is testified of the Waldenses from the mouth of one of the adversaries Aeneas Sylvius, mutuo [solent amare] penè antequam norint, they use to love any of theire owne religion even before they were acquainted with them.

2ly. for the worke wee have in hand, it is by a mutuall consent through a speciall overruleing providence, and a more then an ordinary approbation of the Churches of Christ to seeke out a place of Cohabitation and Consorteshipp under a due forme of Goverment both civill and ecclesiasticall. In such cases as this the care of the publique must oversway all private respects, by which not onely conscience, but meare Civill pollicy doth binde us; for it is a true rule that perticuler estates cannott subsist in the ruine of the publique.

3ly. The end is to improve our lives to doe more service to the Lord the comforte and encrease of the body of Christe whereof wee are members that our selves and posterity may be the better preserved from the Common corrupcions of this evill world to serve the Lord and worke out our Salvacion under the power and purity of his holy Ordinances.

4ly for the meanes whereby this must bee effected, they are 2fold, a Conformity with the worke and end wee aime at, these wee see are extraordinary, therefore wee must not content our selves with usuall ordinary meanes whatsoever wee did or ought to have done when wee lived in England, the same must wee doe and more allsoe where wee goe: That which the most in theire Churches maineteine as a truthe in profession onely, wee must bring into familiar and constant practise, as in this duty of love wee must love brotherly without dissimulation, wee must love one another with a pure hearte fervently wee must beare one anothers burthens, wee must not looke onely on our owne things, but allsoe on the things of our brethren, neither must wee think that the lord will beare with such faileings at our hands as hee dothe from those among whome wee have lived, and that for 3 Reasons.

1. In regard of the more neare bond of mariage, betweene him and us, wherein he hath taken us to be his after a most strickt and peculiar manner which will make him the more Jealous of our love and obedience soe he tells the people of Israell, you onely have I knowne of all the families of the Earthe therefore will I punishe you for your Transgressions.

2ly, because the lord will be sanctified in them that come neare him. Wee know that there were many that corrupted the service of the Lord some setting upp Alters before his owne, others offering both strange fire and strange Sacrifices allsoe; yet there came noe fire from heaven, or other sudden Judgement upon them as did upon Nadab and Abihu whoe yet wee may thinke did not sinne presumptuously.

3ly When God gives a speciall Commission he lookes to have it stricktly observed in every Article, when hee gave Saule a Commission to destroy Amaleck hee indented with him upon certaine Articles and because hee failed in one of the least, and that upon a faire pretence, it lost him the kingdome, which should have beene his reward, if hee had observed his Commission: Thus stands the cause betweene God and us, wee are entered into Covenant with him for this worke, wee have taken out a Commission, the Lord hath given us leave to drawe our owne Articles wee have professed to enterprise these Accions upon these and these ends, wee have hereupon besought him of favour and blessing: Now if the Lord shall please to heare us, and bring us in peace to the place we desire, then hath hee ratified this Covenant and sealed our Commission, [and] will expect a strickt performance of the Articles contained in it, but if wee shall neglect the observacion of these Articles which are the ends wee have propounded, and dissembling with our God, shall fall to embrace this present world and prosecute our carnall intencions, seekeing greate things for our selves and our posterity, the Lord will surely breake out in wrathe against us be revenged of such a perjured people and make us knowe the price of the breache of such a Covenant.

Now the onely way to avoyde this shipwracke and to provide for our posterity is to followe the Counsell of Micah, to doe Justly, to love mercy, to walke humbly with our God, for this end, wee must be knitt together in this worke as one man, wee must entertaine each other in brotherly Affeccion, wee must be willing to abridge our selves of our superfluities, for the supply of others necessities, wee must uphold a familiar Commerce together in all meekness, gentlenes, patience and liberallity, wee must delight in eache other, make others Condicions our owne rejoyce together, mourne together, labour, and suffer together, allwayes haveing before our eyes our Commission and Community in the worke, our Community as members of the same body, soe shall wee keepe the unitie of the spirit in the bond of peace, the Lord will be our God and delight to dwell among us, as his owne people and wlil commaund a blessing upon us in all our wayes, soe that wee shall see much more of his wisdome power goodnes and truthe then formerly wee have beene acquainted with, wee shall finde that the God of Israell is among us, when tenn of us shall be able to resist a thousand of our enemies, when hee shall make us a prayse and glory, that men shall say of succeeding plantacions: the lord make it like that of New England: for wee must Consider that wee shall be as a Citty upon a Hill, the eies of all people are uppon us; soe that if wee shall deale

falsely with our god in this worke wee have undertaken and soe cause
him to withdrawe his present help from us, wee shall be made a story
and a by-word through the world, wee shall open the mouthes of
enemies to speak evill of the wayes of god and all professours for Gods
sake; wee shall shame the faces of many of gods worthy servants, and
cause theire prayers to be turned into Cursses upon us till wee be
consumed out of the good land whether wee are goeing: And to shutt
upp this discourse with that exhortacion of Moses that faithfull servant
of the Lord in his last farewell to Israell Deut. 30. Beloved there is now
sett before us life, and good, deathe and evill in that wee are Com-
maunded this day to love the Lord our God, and to love one another
to walke in his wayes and to keepe his Commaundements and his
Ordinance, and his lawes, and the Articles of our Covenant with him
that wee may live and be multiplyed, and that the Lord our God may
blesse us in the land whether wee goe to possesse it: But if our heartes
shall turne away soe that wee will not obey, but shall be seduced and
worshipp other Gods our pleasures, and proffitts, and serve them; it
is propounded unto us this day, wee shall surely perishe out of the good
Land whether wee passe over this vast Sea to possesse it;

Therefore lett us choose life,
that wee, and our Seede,
may live; by obeyeing his
voyce, and cleaveing to him,
for hee is our life, and
our prosperity.

3. SEABURY
Against Disloyalty to the King

Samuel Seabury (1729–1796), a New York clergyman, was an American loyalist who opposed the American Revolution. He was a conservative in that he sought to preserve the ties which bound America to England and preferred the institutions of monarchy to those of untried republicanism. The following selection* was originally written in 1774 in reply to Alexander Hamilton's arguments for independence made at the Continental Congress in that year. Seabury, a follower of the philosopher Thomas Hobbes, maintained that sovereignty was indivisible. The English King alone possessed sovereignty, and if the colonists declared their independence, they risked returning to a chaotic state of nature, without a common authority to maintain the necessary peace and security.

Sir,

You have done me the honour "to bestow some notice upon" a little pamphlet which I lately published, entitled, *Free Thoughts on the Proceedings of the Continental Congress,* in a Piece which you call, *A full Vindication of the Measures of the Congress, from the Calumnies of their Enemies.* My present business shall be to examine your Vindication, and see whether it *fully* exculpates *the measures of the Congress,* from the charges brought against them by the friends of order and good government. This task I shall endeavour to perform, with all that freedom of thought and expression, which, as an *Englishman* I have a right to; and which never shall be wrested from me, either by *yourself* or the *Congress.*

I freely own, that I wrote and published the *Free Thoughts* with a design to "diminish the influence, and prevent the effects of the

* The selection is taken from "A View of the Controversy, &c. in A Letter to the Author of *A full Vindication, &c.,*" in *Letters of a Westchester Farmer* (London: Richardson and Urquhart, 1775), pp. 103–12.

decisions" of the Congress. You speak of the *impotence* of such attempts; of the general *indignation* with which they are treated; you say "that no material ill consequences (i.e. to your party) can be dreaded from them." Why then did you take the pains to write so long, so elaborate a pamphlet, to justify decisions against whose influence none but impotent attempts had been made?—to prevent ill consequences which were not to be dreaded?—You felt, Sir, the force of the stubborn facts exhibited to the view of the public in the *Free Thoughts*: You perceived the ground on which the decrees of the Congress were founded, to be hollow and ready to fall in: you was willing to prop it up at any rate. You knew, that at the bar of *impartial* reason, and *common* sense, the conduct of the Congress must be condemned. You was too much interested, too deeply engaged in party views and party heats, to bear this with patience. You had no remedy but *artifice, sophistry, misrepresentation* and *abuse*: These are your weapons, and these you wield like an old experienced practitioner.

Is this *too* heavy a charge? Can you lay your hand upon your heart, and upon your honour plead *not guilty*?—Was it then vanity that led you to combat *ill consequences that were not to be dreaded*? To prevent *impotent efforts* from succeeding, which, you knew, were not likely to succeed? to make *that* the object of general indignation, which already *was* so?—Was it purely to shine as a *patriotic writer*? To give a specimen of your abilities?—To shew us, in short, what you *can* do, that gave birth to the Vindication?—Probably, you had better have repressed these emotions: for though your pamphlet may please your party,—and I dare say, would have pleased them just as well with half its real merit,— though they may praise and extol it, as a matchless, inimitable performance; yet, Sir, in a literary way, good judges will consider it only as the effort of a genius that never can rise above mediocrity. If you seldom *sink* into meanness of diction, you never *soar* into that *briliancy* of thought; nor, even with the help of Johnson's Dictionary, into that *classical elegance* of expression which is absolutely necessary for the arduous attempt of *ridiculing wit*.

I, who am a plain Farmer, though of some education, have no manner of inclination to dispute the prize of *Wit* and *Ridicule*, with the panegyrist of the late *all-accomplished* Congress. You, Sir, shall bear off the palm, unrivalled, unenvied by me.—I, also, congratulate you on the discovery of "a seeming contradiction" in the Free Thoughts. I could point out to you a dozen more of its errors in diction and grammar; one of which you have quoted more than once, but you had two much generosity of temper to animadvert upon it. I wrote the Free Thoughts, as I write now, without much regard to stile, or grammatical accuracy. My business was not to *please* or *amuse*, but to *convince* my countrymen and fellow-subjects of the evil tendency of the measures of the Congress, and to give all the obstruction in my power to their being carried into execution. This I did from a principle of conscience, from a sense of duty, from a love of *liberty*, of *order*, of *good* government, and of *America* my native country: Nor have my endeavours been without success. The *Free Thoughts* have answered my utmost expectation: They have been rapidly purchased, and eagerly read; and notwithstanding the *general indignation* of which you speak, I have had the satisfaction of hearing them commended and approved by many, very many sensible people, in the city, as well as in the country: And I doubt not they will contribute, among other causes, to the restoration of that order and peace in this province, which is the earnest wish of every *real* friend to America. I cannot but hope, that the time of this event is fast approaching. I see the influence of the Congress daily diminishing. Few committees are chosen in the country to carry their *decrees* into execution. The committee of New-York has been obliged to recede from an *exact* compliance with their *edicts*, that even the appearance of a compliance might be preserved: Why else do they permit the owners of goods imported, and which were ordered to be sold for the benefit of the Boston poor, to bid for their own goods, and have them struck off at an under rate? Why are they obliged to permit the very best regulation the Congress did make, to be continually infringed, by the importation of Tea, Gin, &c. from Holland. These relaxations were necessary to cajole and take in the merchants, and therefore the committee complied: You thought it necessary to cajole and take in the Farmers, and therefore you wrote your pamphlet. But have a care, "sweet Sir,"—pray was you in the nursery where the whole conversation turned on *sweeties* and *goodies*, when you luckily hit on this expression? Or did you find it in Johnson's Dictionary?— Have a care, I say, or we honest supporters of the laws and liberties of our country, shall finally get the better; reduce you and your party to peace and order, and make you good subjects in spite of your teeth. I, for my part, shall exert my little influence to accomplish so benevolent a purpose; and shall exercise my *pen* and hiccory *cudgel* in such a manner as I shall think most likely to effect it: And while I wield these weapons in defence of the laws of my country, and in such a way as they permit and will warrant, I fear neither your *answers* nor your *threats*. The first committee-man that comes to rob me of my Tea, or my wine, or molasses, shall feel the weight of my arm; and should you be the man, however lightly you may think of it, a stroke of my cudgel would make you reel, notwithstanding the thickness of your skull.

You begin your vindication with such an air of importance, and such pomposity of expression, as I scarce ever met with before.—"It was hardly to be expected that any man *could* be so *presumptuous*, as *openly* to controvert the *equity, wisdom* and *authority* of the measures adopted by the Congress: an assembly truly respectable on *every* account!—whether we consider the characters of the men, who composed it; the number and dignity of their constituents, or the important ends for which they were appointed."—Mere explosions of the wind of vanity! Three grains of consideration would have prevented such a sentence from ever seeing the light.

It has ever been esteemed the privilege of Englishmen to canvass freely, the proceedings of every branch of the legislature; to examine into all public measures; to point out the errors that are committed in the administration of the government, and to censure without fear the conduct of all persons in public stations, whose conduct shall appear to deserve it. The exercise of this right has always been considered as one of the grand pillars which support our present happy constitution. The liberty taken with the *King, Lords* and *Commons* in many late publications in England, must convince every man, that the English nation retains, unimpaired, this right of bringing the most respectable characters before the tribunal of the public: and is an incontestible proof that the nation is not enslaved. Nor is this privilege exercised with less freedom in America than England. Did not the Congress? Do not you yourself? Does not every pidler in politics, who calls himself a *son of liberty*, take the licence of censuring and condemning the conduct of the *King*, the *Lords*, and the *Commons*, the supreme sovereign authority of the whole British Empire? Blush then at your own effrontery, in endeavouring to intimidate your countrymen from exercising this Right with regard to the Congress.

The Congress, Sir, was founded in sedition; its decisions are supported by tyranny; and is it *presumption* to controvert its *authority*? In your opinion, they "are *restless spirits*,"—"enemies to the natural rights of mankind" who shall dare to speak against the *Congress*, or attempt to "diminish the influence of *their* decisions:" while *they* are friends to America, and to the natural rights of mankind, who shall traduce and slander the sovereign authority of the nation; contravene and trample under foot the laws of their country.

I have no inclination to scrutinize the characters of men, who composed the Congress. It is not the dignity of their private characters, but their public conduct as *Delegates* that comes under my examination. The manner in which they were chosen was subversive of all law, and of the very constitution of the province. After they had met they were only a popular assembly, without check or controul, and therefore unqualified to make laws, or to pass ordinances. Upon supposition that they had been chosen by all the people with one voice, they could be only the servants of the people; and every individual must have had a right to animadvert on their conduct, and to have censured it where he thought it wrong. *We* think, Sir, that we have a double right to do so, seeing they were chosen by a party only, and have endeavoured to tyrannize over the whole people.

You seem to think it very wrong that the Delegates should be called to any account, because "we did not, especially in this province, circumscribe them by any fixed boundary, and therefore as they cannot be said to have exceeded the limits of their authority, their act must be esteemed the act of their constituents."—Above you had said that "their decrees are binding upon all, and demand a religious observance." A little below you make them their *own judges*, whether they have done right or not. And you represent it as no small degree of *arrogance* and *self-sufficiency* for *any* individual to oppose his *private sentiments* to their *united counsels*.

I have looked at this paragraph at least ten times, and every time with astonishment. It is so superlatively arrogant and impudent, that I confess myself at a loss what to say to it. And here, least I should grow angry and forget it, I must observe once for all, that I verily believe the New-York Delegates were some of the very best who attended the Congress. I have been informed that they, for a long time, opposed the violent measures that were in agitation. I honour them for this opposition; and should almost have adored them, had they preserved their integrity to the end.—But evil communications corrupt good manners. Let no honest man hereafter trust himself at a Philadelphia Congress!

Not a hundredth part of the people of this province, Sir, had any vote in sending the Delegates, and do you imagine that they would take the trouble to *circumscribe* them, when they did not chuse to have any thing to do with them? The *juntos* indeed who sent them, acted the same foolish part in not *circumscribing* them, that they did in chusing them. But supposing all the people in the province had joined in sending them *uncircumscribed*: Were the Delegates at liberty to do as they pleased? To pursue the most violent measures? To stop up every avenue of accommodation with Great-Britain? And render our state ten times worse than they found it? Must all the province *religiously* observe their *wicked* decrees? And take all their *mad pranks* upon themselves, whether they will or not? To be sure they must: The Delegates were their *uncircumscribed* representatives.—I have heard often that the privileges of our representatives, were the privileges of the people, but never till now that any absurd measures they might adopt were chargeable to their constituents.

Do you think, Sir, that because the Delegates were chosen by a party, that therefore they are accountable only to the *party* who chose them? You deceive yourself if you do. Every day will produce more *Free Thoughts*, and *Canvassings*, and *Examinations*, till their influence is totally destroyed, and their tyranny at an end.

The epithet of *restless spirits* you must take back to yourself and your party. The next time you write, bestow it where it is due;—on those who have wantonly employed themselves in fomenting disturbances in the colony, in creating and widening the disunion between the mother country and us, in order to advance their favorite republican plan.

I wish you had explicitly declared to the public your ideas of the *natural rights of mankind*. Man in a *state of nature* may be considered as perfectly free from all restraints of law and government: And then the *weak* must submit to the *strong*. From such a state, I confess, I have a violent aversion. I think the form of government we lately enjoyed a much more eligible state to live in: And cannot help regretting our having *lost* it, by the *equity*, *wisdom*, and *authority* of the Congress, who have introduced in the room of it, confusion and violence; where all must submit to the power of a mob.

You have taken some pains to prove what would readily have been granted you—that *liberty* is a very *good* thing, and *slavery* a very *bad* thing. But then I must think that liberty under a *King, Lords* and

Commons is as good as liberty under a republican Congress: And that slavery under a republican Congress is as bad, at least, as slavery under a *King*, *Lords* and *Commons:* And upon the whole, that *liberty* under the supreme authority and protection of Great-Britain, is infinitely preferable to *slavery* under an American Congress. I will also agree with you, "that Americans are intitled to freedom." I will go further: I will own and acknowledge that not only *Americans*, but *Africans*, *Europeans*, *Asiaticks*, all men, of all countries and degrees, of all sizes and complexions, have a right to as much freedom as is consistent with the security of civil society: And I hope you will not think me an "enemy to the *natural* rights of mankind" because I cannot wish them more. We must however remember, that more liberty may, without inconvenience, be allowed to individuals in a small government, than can be admitted of in a large empire.

But when you assert that "since Americans have not by any act of theirs impowered the British parliament to make laws for them, it follows they can have no just authority to do it," you advance a position subversive of that dependence which all colonies must, from their very nature, have on the mother country.—By the British parliament, I suppose you mean the supreme legislative authority, the King, Lords and Commons, because no other authority in England has a right to make laws to bind the kingdom, and consequently no authority to make laws to bind the colonies. In this sense I shall understand, and use the phrase *British parliament*.

Now the dependence of the colonies on the mother-country has ever been acknowledged. It is an impropriety of speech to talk of an independent colony. The words *independency* and *colony*, convey contradictory ideas: much like *killing* and *sparing*. As soon as a colony becomes independent on its parent state, it ceases to be any longer a colony; just as when you *kill* a sheep, you cease to *spare* him. The British colonies make a part of the British Empire. As parts of the body they must be subject to the general laws of the body. To talk of a colony independent of the mother-country, is no better sense than to talk of a limb independent of the body to which it belongs.

In every government there must be a supreme, absolute authority lodged somewhere. In arbitrary governments this power is in the monarch; in aristocratical governments, in the nobles; in democratical, in the people; or the deputies of their electing. Our own government being a mixture of all these kinds, the supreme authority is vested in the King, Nobles and People, i.e. the King, House of Lords, and House of Commons elected by the people. This supreme authority extends as far as the British dominions extend. To suppose a part of the British dominions which is not subject to the power of the British legislature, is no better sense than to suppose a country, at one and the same time, to be, and not to be a part of the British dominions. If therefore the colony of New-York be a part of the British dominions, the colony of New-York is subject, and dependent on the supreme legislative authority of Great-Britain.

Legislation is not an inherent right in the colonies. Many colonies have been established, and subsisted long without it. The Roman colonies had no legislative authority. It was not till the later period of their republic that the privileges of Roman citizens, among which that of voting in the assemblies of the people at Rome was a principal one, were extended to the inhabitants of Italy. All the laws of the empire were enacted at Rome. Neither their colonies, nor conquered countries had any thing to do with legislation.

The position that we are bound by no laws to which we have not consented, either by ourselves, or our representatives, is a novel position, unsupported by any authoratative record of the British constitution, ancient or modern. It is republican in its very nature, and tends to the utter subversion of the English monarchy.

This position has arisen from an artful change of terms. To say that an Englishman is not bound by any laws, but those to which the representatives of the nation have given their consent, is to say what is true: But to say that an Englishman is bound by no laws but those to which *he* hath consented in person, or by *his* representative, is saying what never was true, and never can be true. A great part of the people in England have no vote in the choice of representatives, and therefore are governed by laws to which they never consented either by *themselves* or by *their* representatives.

The right of colonists to exercise a legislative power, is no natural right. They derive it not from nature, but from the indulgence or grant of the parent state, whose subjects they were when the colony was settled, and by whose permission and assistance they made the settlement.

Upon supposition that every English colony enjoyed a legislative power independent of the parliament; and that the parliament has no just authority to make laws to bind them, this absurdity will follow—

that there is no power in the British empire, which has authority to make laws for the whole empire; i.e. we have an empire, without government; or which amounts to the same thing, we have a government which has no supreme power. All our colonies are independent of each other: Suppose them independent of the British parliament,—what power do you leave to govern the whole? None at all. You split and divide the empire into a number of petty insignificant states. This is the direct, the necessary tendency of refusing submission to acts of parliament. Every man who can see one inch beyond his nose, must see this consequence. And every man who endeavours to accelerate the independency of the colonies on the British parliament, endeavours to accelerate the ruin of the British empire.

To talk of being liege subjects to King George, while we disavow the authority of parliament is another piece of whiggish nonsense. I love my King as well as any whig in America or England either, and am as ready to yield him all lawful submission: But while I submit to the King, I submit to the authority of the laws of the state, whose guardian the King is. The difference between a good and a bad subject, is only this, that the one obeys, the other transgresses the law. The difference between a loyal subject and a rebel, is, that the one yields obedience to, and faithfully supports the supreme authority of the state, and the other endeavours to overthrow it. If we obey the laws of the King, we obey the laws of the parliament. If we disown the authority of the parliament, we disown the authority of the King. There is no medium without ascribing powers to the King which the constitution knows nothing of:—without making him superior to the laws, and setting him above all restraint. These are some of the ridiculous absurdities of American whiggism. . . .

4. BOUCHER
Liberty in Civil Society

The Reverend Jonathan Boucher (1738–1804), an extreme British loyalist, was chased out of the colonies in 1775. Before leaving he delivered sermons which bitterly attacked the Lockean scheme of natural rights, social contract, and the right of revolution. Boucher, like the Puritans, turned to the Bible and Divine Will as a source of political authority. He attacked the idea of majority rule and agreed that there existed no absolute liberty for each individual to do as he wished. Boucher was an intelligent and effective critic of John Locke's political theory. He pointed to the inconsistencies between majority rule and the right of a minority to engage in revolution, and he perceived that Locke's concept of equality was undermined by the theory of a social contract which created political inequality. In addition, Boucher pointed to the conflict in Locke's thought between individual rights and majority rule. The selection is taken from his *A View of the Causes and Consequences of the American Revolution*.

Stand fast in the liberty wherewith Christ hath made you free.

As the liberty here spoken of respected the Jews, it denoted an exemption from the burthensome services of the ceremonial law: as it respected the Gentiles, it meant a manumission from bondage under the *weak and beggarly elements of the world*, and an admission into the covenant of grace: and as it respected both in common, it meant a freedom from the servitude of sin. Every sinner is, literally, a slave; for, *his servants ye are, to whom ye obey:*—and the only true liberty is the liberty of being the servants of God; for, *his service is perfect freedom*. The passage cannot, without infinite perversion and torture, be made to refer to any other kind of liberty; much less to that liberty of which every man now talks, though few understand it. However common this term has been, or is, in the mouths chiefly of those persons who are as little distinguished for the accuracy as they are for the paucity of their words; and whatever influence it has had on the affairs of the world, it is remarkable that it is never used (at least not in any such sense as it is elsewhere used) in any of the laws either of God or men. Let a minister of God, then, stand excused if (taught by him who knoweth what is fit and good for us better than we ourselves, and is *wont also to give us more than either we desire or deserve*) he seeks not to amuse you by any flowery panegyrics on liberty. Such panegyrics are the productions of ancient heathens and modern patriots: nothing of the kind is to be met with in the Bible, nor in the Statute Book. The word *liberty*, as meaning civil liberty, does not, I believe, occur in all the Scriptures. With the aid of a concordance I find only two or three passages, in two apocryphal writers, that look at all like it. In the xivth chapter and 26th verse of the 1st of Maccabees, the people are said to owe much gratitude to Simon, the high-priest, for having renewed a friendship and league with the Lacedemonians, confirmed the league with the Romans, established Israel, and *confirmed their liberty*. But it is evident that this expression means, not that the Jews were then to be exempted from any injunctions, or any restraints, imposed upon them by their own lawful government; but only that they were delivered from a foreign jurisdiction and from tributary payments, and left free to live under the law of Moses. The only circumstance relative to government, for which the Scriptures seem to be particularly solicitous, is in inculcating obedience to lawful governors, as well knowing where the true danger lies. Nevertheless, as occasion has lately been taken from this text, on which I am now to discourse, to treat largely on civil liberty and government, (though for no other reason that appears but that the word *liberty* happens to stand in the text,) I entreat your indulgence, whilst, without too nicely scrutinizing the propriety of deducing from a text a doctrine which it clearly does not suggest, I once more adopt a plan already chalked out for me, and deliver to you what occurs to me as proper for a Christian audience to attend to on the subject of Liberty.

It has just been observed, that the liberty inculcated in the Scriptures, (and which alone the Apostle had in view in this text,) is wholly of the spiritual or religious kind. This liberty was the natural result of the new religion in which mankind were then instructed; which certainly gave them no new civil privileges. They remained subject to the governments under which they lived, just as they had been before they became

Christians, and just as others were who never became Christians; with this difference only, that the duty of submission and obedience to Government was enjoined on the converts to Christianity with new and stronger sanctions. The doctrines of the Gospel make no manner of alteration in the nature or form of Civil Government; but enforce afresh, upon all Christians, that obedience which is due to the respective Constitutions of every nation in which they may happen to live. Be the supreme power lodged in one or in many, be the kind of government established in any country absolute or limited, this is not the concern of the Gospel. It's single object, with respect to these public duties, is to enjoin obedience to the laws of every country, in every kind or form of government.

The only liberty or freedom which converts to Christianity could hope to gain by becoming Christians, was the being exempted from sundry burthensome and servile Jewish ordinances, on the one hand; and, on the other, from Gentile blindness and superstitution. They were also in some measure perhaps made more *free* in the *inner man*; by being endowed with greater firmness of mind in the cause of truth, against the terrors and the allurements of the world; and with such additional strength and vigour as enabled them more effectually to resist the natural violence of their lusts and passions. On all these accounts it was that our Saviour so emphatically told the Jews, that *the truth* (of which himself was now the preacher) would *make them* free. And on the same principle St. James terms the Gospel *the perfect law of liberty*.

In the infancy of Christianity, it would seem that some rumour had been spread (probably by Judas of Galilee, who is mentioned in the Acts) that the Gospel was designed to undermine kingdoms and commonwealths; as if the intention of our Saviour's first coming had been the same with that which is reserved for the second, viz. to *put down all rule, and all authority, and all power*. On this supposition the apparent solicitude of our Saviour and his Apostles, in their frequent and earnest recommendation of submission to *the higher powers*, is easily and naturally accounted for. Obedience to Government is every man's duty, because it is every man's interest: but it is particularly incumbent on Christians, because (in addition to it's moral fitness) it is enjoined by the positive commands of God: and therefore, when Christians are disobedient to human ordinances, they are also disobedient to God. If the form of government under which the good providence of God has been pleased to place us be mild and free, it is our duty to enjoy it with gratitude and with thankfulness; and, in particular, to be careful not to abuse it by licentiousness. If it be less indulgent and less liberal than in reason it ought to be, still it is our duty not to disturb and destroy the peace of the community, by becoming refractory and rebellious subjects, and *resisting the ordinances of God*. However humiliating such acquiescence may seem to men of warm and eager minds, the wisdom of God in having made it our duty is manifest. For, as it is the natural temper and bias of the human mind to be impatient under restraint, it was wise and merciful in the blessed Author of our religion not to add any new impulse to the natural force of this prevailing propensity, but, with the whole weight of his authority, altogether to discountenance every tendency to disobedience.

If it were necessary to vindicate the Scriptures for this their total unconcern about a principle which so many other writings seem to regard as the first of all human considerations, it might be observed, that, avoiding the vague and declamatory manner of such writings, and avoiding also the useless and impracticable subtleties of metaphysical definitions, these Scriptures have better consulted the great general interest of mankind, by summarily recommending and enjoining a conscientious reverence for law whether human or divine. To respect the laws, is to respect liberty in the only rational sense in which the term can be used; for liberty consists in a subserviency to law. "Where there is no law," says Mr. Locke, "there is no freedom." The mere man of nature (if such an one there ever was) has no freedom: *all his lifetime he is subject to bondage*. It is by being included within the pale of civil polity and government that he takes his rank in society as a free man.

Hence it follows, that we are free, or otherwise, as we are governed by law, or by the mere arbitrary will, or wills, of any individual, or any number of individuals. And liberty is not the setting at nought and despising established laws—much less the making our own wills the rule of our own actions, or the actions of others—and not bearing (whilst yet we dictate to others) the being dictated to, even by the laws of the land; but it is the being governed by law, and by law only. The Greeks described Eleutheria, or Liberty, as the daughter of Jupiter, the supreme fountain of power and law. And the Romans, in like manner, always drew her with the pretor's wand, (the emblem of legal power and authority,) as well as with the cap. Their idea, no doubt, was, that liberty was the fair fruit of just authority, and that it consisted in men's being subjected to law. The more carefully well-devised restraints of law are enacted, and the more rigorously they are executed in any country, the greater degree of civil liberty does that country enjoy. To pursue liberty, then, in a manner not warranted by law, whatever the pretence may be, is clearly to be hostile to liberty: and those persons who thus *promise you liberty*, are themselves *the servants of corruption*. . . .

True liberty, then, is a liberty to do every thing that is right, and the being restrained from doing any thing that is wrong. So far from our having a right to do every thing that we please, under a notion of liberty, liberty itself is limited and confined—but limited and confined only by laws which are at the same time both it's foundation and it's support. It can, however, hardly be necessary to inform you, that ideas and notions respecting liberty, very different from these, are daily suggested in the speeches and the writings of the times; and also that some opinions on the subject of government at large, which appear to me to be particularly loose and dangerous, are advanced in the sermon now under consideration; and that, therefore, you will acknowledge the propriety of my bestowing some farther notice on them both.

It is laid down in this sermon, as a settled maxim, that the end of government is "the common good of mankind." I am not sure that the position itself is indisputable; but, if it were, it would by no means follow that, "this common good being matter of common feeling, government must therefore have been instituted by common consent." There is an appearance of logical accuracy and precision in this state-ment; but it is only an appearance. The position is vague and loose; and the assertion is made without an attempt to prove it. If by men's "common feelings" we are to understand that principle in the human mind called common sense, the assertion is either unmeaning and insignificant, or it is false. In no instance have mankind ever yet agreed as to what is, or is not, "the common good." A form or mode of government cannot be named, which these "common feelings" and "common consent," the sole arbiters, as it seems, of "common good," have not, at one time or another, set up and established, and again pulled down and reprobated. What one people in one age have con-curred in establishing as the "common good," another in another age have voted to be mischievous and big with ruin. The premises, therefore, that "the common good is matter of common feeling," being false, the consequence drawn from it, viz. that government was instituted by "common consent," is of course equally false.

This popular notion, that government was originally formed by the consent or by a compact of the people, rests on, and is supported by, another similar notion, not less popular, nor better founded. This other notion is, that the whole human race is born equal; and that no man is naturally inferior, or, in any respect, subjected to another; and that he can be made subject to another only by his own consent. The position is equally ill-founded and false both in it's premises and conclusions. In hardly any sense that can be imagined is the position strictly true; but, as applied to the case under consideration, it is demonstrably not true. Man differs from man in every thing that can be supposed to lead to supremacy and subjection, *as one star differs from another star in glory*. It was the purpose of the Creator, that man should be social: but, without government, there can be no society; nor, without some relative inferiority and superiority, can there be any government. A musical instrument composed of chords, keys, or pipes, all perfectly equal in size and power, might as well be expected to produce harmony, as a society composed of members all perfectly equal to be productive of order and peace. If (according to the idea of the advocates of this chimerical scheme of equality) no man could rightfully *be compelled to come in* and be a member even of a government to be formed by a regular compact, but by his own individual consent; it clearly follows, from the same principles, that neither could he rightfully be made or compelled to submit to the ordinances of any government already formed, to which he has not individually or actually consented. On the principle of equality, neither his parents, nor even the vote of a majority of the society, (however virtuously and honourably that vote might be obtained,) can have any such authority over any man. Neither can it be maintained that acquiescence implies consent; because acquiescence may have been extorted from impotence or incapacity. Even an explicit consent can bind a man no longer than he chooses to be bound. The same principle of equality that exempts him from being governed without his own consent, clearly entitles him to recall and resume that consent whenever he sees fit; and he alone has a right to judge when and for what reasons it may be resumed.

Any attempt, therefore, to introduce this fantastic system into practice, would reduce the whole business of social life to the wearisome, confused, and useless task of mankind's first expressing, and then withdrawing, their consent to an endless succession of schemes of government. Governments, though always forming, would never be completely formed: for, the majority to-day, might be the minority tomorrow; and, of course, that which is now fixed might and would be soon unfixed. Mr. Locke indeed says, that, "by consenting with others to make one body-politic under government, a man puts himself under an obligation to every one of that society to submit to the determination of the majority, and to be concluded by it." For the sake of the peace of society, it is undoubtedly reasonable and necessary that this should be the case: but, on the principles of the system now under consideration, before Mr. Locke or any of his followers can have authority to say that it actually is the case, it must be stated and proved that every individual man, on entering into the social compact, did first consent, and declare his consent, to be concluded and bound in all cases by the vote of the majority. In making such a declaration, he would certainly consult both his interest and his duty; but at the same time he would also completely relinquish the principle of equality, and eventually subject himself to the possibility of being governed by ignorant and corrupt tyrants. Mr. Locke himself afterwards disproves his own position respecting the supposed obligation to submit to the "determination of the majority," when he argues that a right of resistance still exists in the governed: for, what is resistance but a recalling and resuming the consent heretofore supposed to have been given, and in fact refusing to submit to the "determination of the majority?" It does not clearly appear what Mr. Locke exactly meant by what he calls "the determination of the majority:" but the only rational and practical public manner of declaring "the determination of the majority," is by law: the laws, therefore, in all countries, even in those that are despotically governed, are to be regarded as the declared "determination of a majority" of the members of that community; because, in such cases, even acquiescence only must be looked upon as equivalent to a declaration. A right of resistance, therefore, for which Mr. Locke contends, is incompatible with the duty of submitting to the determination of "the majority," for which he also contends.

It is indeed impossible to carry into effect any government which, even by compact, might be framed with this reserved right of resistance. Accordingly there is no record that any such government ever was so formed. If there had, it must have carried the seeds of it's decay in it's very constitution. For, as those men who make a government (certain that they have the power) can have no hesitation to vote that they also have the right to unmake it; and as the people, in all circumstances, but more especially when trained to make and unmake governments, are at least as well disposed to do the latter as the former, it is morally impossible that there should be any thing like permanency or stability in a government so formed. Such a system, therefore, can produce only perpetual dissensions and contests, and bring back mankind to a supposed state of nature; arming every man's hand, like Ishmael's, against every man, and rendering the world an *aceldama*, or field of blood.—Such theories of government seem to give something like plausibility to the notions of those other modern theorists, who regard all governments as invasions of the natural rights of men, usurpations, and tyranny. On this principle it would follow, and could not be denied, that government was indeed fundamentally, as our people are sedulously taught it still is, an evil. Yet it is to government that mankind owe their having, after their fall and corruption, been again reclaimed, from a state of barbarity and war, to the conveniency and the safety of the social state: and it is by means of government that society is still preserved, the weak protected from the strong, and the artless and innocent from the wrongs of proud oppressors. It was not without reason, then, that Mr. Locke asserted, that a greater wrong cannot be done to prince and people, than is done by "propagating wrong notions concerning government."

Ashamed of this shallow device, that government originated in superior strength and violence, another party, hardly less numerous, and certainly not less confident than the former, fondly deduce it from some imaginary compact. They suppose that, in the decline perhaps of some fabulous age of gold, a multitude of human beings, who, like their brother beasts, had hitherto ranged the forests, *without guide, overseer, or ruler*—at length convinced, by experience, of the impossibility of living either alone with any degree of comfort or security, or together in society, with peace, without government, had (in some lucid interval of reason and reflection) met together in a spacious plain, for the express purpose of framing a government. Their first step must have been the transferring to some individual, or individuals, some of those rights which are supposed to have been inherent in each of them: of these it is essential to government that they should be divested; yet can they not, rightfully, be deprived of them, otherwise than by their own consent. Now, admitting this whole supposed assembly to be perfectly equal as to rights, yet all agreed as to the propriety of ceding some of them, on what principles of equality is it possible to determine, either who shall relinquish such a portion of his rights, or who shall be invested with such new accessory rights? By asking another to exercise jurisdiction over me, I clearly confess that I do not think myself his equal; and by his consenting to exercise such authority, he also virtually declares that he thinks himself superior. And, to establish this hypothesis of a compact, it is farther necessary that the whole assembly should concur in this opinion—a concurrence so extremely improbable, that it seems to be barely possible. The supposition that a large concourse of people, in a rude and imperfect state of society, or even a majority of them, should thus rationally and unanimously concur to subject themselves to various restrictions, many of them irksome and unpleasant, and all of them contrary to all their former habits, is to suppose them possessed of more wisdom and virtue than multitudes in any instance in real life have ever shewn. Another difficulty respecting this notion may yet be mentioned. Without a power of life and death, it will, I presume, be readily admitted that there could be no government. Now, admitting it to be possible that men, from motives of public and private utility, may be induced to submit to many heavy penalties, and even to corporal punishment, inflicted by the sentence of the law, there is an insuperable objection to any man's giving to another a power over his life: this objection is, that no man has such a power over his own life; and cannot therefore transfer to another, or to others, be they few or many, on any conditions, a right which he does not himself possess. He only who gave life, can give the authority to take it away: and as such authority is essential to government, this argument seems very decidedly to prove, not only that government did not originate in any compact, but also that it was originally from God. . . .

It is from other passages of Scripture, from the nature of the thing, from the practice of Adam, and from the practice of all nations (derived from and founded on this precedent) that we infer that Adam had and exercised sovereign power over all his issue. But the first instance of power exercised by one human being over another is in the subjection of Eve to her husband. This circumstance suggests sundry reflections, of some moment in this argument. In the first place, it shews that power is not a natural right. Adam could not have assumed, nor could Eve have submitted to it, had it not been so ordained of God. It is, therefore, equally an argument against the domineering claims of despotism, and the fantastic notion of a compact. It proves too, that there is a sense in which it may, with truth, be asserted, that government was originally founded in weakness and in guilt: that it may and must be submitted to by a fallen creature, even when exercised by a fallen creature, lost both to wisdom and goodness. The equality of nature (which, merely as it respects an ability to govern, may be admitted, only because God, had he so seen fit, might have ordained that the man should be subjected to the woman) was superseded by the actual interference of the Almighty, to whom alone original underived power can be said to belong.

Even where the Scriptures are silent, they instruct: for, in general, whatever is not therein commanded is actually forbidden. Now, it is certain that mankind are no where in the Scriptures commanded to resist authority; and no less certain that, either by direct injunction, or clear implication, they are commanded to *be subject to the higher powers:* and this subjection is said to be enjoined, not for our sakes only, but also *for the Lord's sake.* The glory of God is much concerned, that there should be good government in the world: it is, therefore, the uniform doctrine of the Scriptures, that it is under the deputation and authority of God alone that *kings reign and princes decree justice.* Kings and princes (which are only other words for supreme magistrates) were doubtless created and appointed, not so much for their own sakes, as for the sake of the people committed to their charge: yet are they not, therefore, the creatures of the people. So far from deriving their authority from any supposed consent or suffrage of men, they receive their commission from Heaven; they receive it from God, the source and original of all power. However obsolete, therefore, either the sentiment or the language may now be deemed, it is with the most perfect propriety that the supreme magistrate, whether consisting of one or of many, and whether denominated an emperor, a king, an archon, a dictator, a consul, or a senate, is to be regarded and venerated as the vicegerent of God. . . .

II

Federalism and Constitutionalism

Many of the men who fought and led the Revolution were recognized conservatives. This was certainly true of George Washington, John Adams, William Livingston, and Charles Carroll. These men hoped to prevent mob rule, although they supported the idea of separation from England. They hoped to form an orderly society with rule by the responsible, the educated, and the propertied elements. In many respects their conservatism was triumphant, and their ultimate victory, the American Constitution, is a notable conservative instrument.

For a dozen years prior to the Philadelphia Convention which drew up the Constitution, the Americans had experimented with new forms of government. The newly freed states first formed a weak central government in 1781 under the Articles of Confederation. This government left all vital powers in the hands of the states and denied to the central government the power to levy taxes, regulate commerce, or act directly upon the citizens.

Distrust of state government also existed at the time. Early state constitutions created a weak executive and, in many cases, a system of annual elections. Even in the states, however, the emphasis was upon liberty rather than equality, upon the protection of property above most other rights.

Lockean philosophy suggested the adoption of a constitution to serve as evidence of the social contract—the contract which would create limited government responsible to the people. Americans put Locke into literal practice by creating written constitutions. Constitutions, however, may be conservative, liberal, or radical, and the American framers of the 1789 Constitution wrote a clearly conservative document.

The framers themselves were men drawn from the better-educated, wealthier, and more influential groups of the day. Many of them feared a drift toward radical Lockeanism by state governments. They were dismayed by the disruption of commerce brought about by state tariff wars. They wished to create a government for the people, but not necessarily of or by the people, so they constructed a scheme of indirect representation in a strengthened national government which would have greatly expanded powers over the states. Rights like the obligation of contract were protected against state action.

The distrust of mass rule is evident in the Constitution. Only the House of Representatives was directly elected by the people. The President was to be selected by specially chosen electors and the Senators chosen by the state legislatures. The appointed judges were to serve for life.

French philosopher Baron de Montesquieu (1689–1755) had suggested a theory of separating the functions of government into different spheres of activity as a protection for the liberties of the people. The separation of powers into three separate categories—legislative, executive, and judicial—is found, as a reflection of his ideas, in the 1789 Constitution. Added to it, in the interest of the conservative view of government as a dangerous force needing limitation, was James Madison's idea of checks and balances which set the branches of government in direct competition with each other as a means of creating a mutuality of restraint.

The Federalist conservative looked to the judiciary as the ultimate guarantor of the Constitution. In the arena of the courts the concepts of national supremacy and judicial review were expounded by Federalist judges, and especially by John Marshall as Chief Justice of the United States from 1801 to 1835.

In economics, the forward-looking Alexander Hamilton devoted himself to the building of a strong new nation by encouraging the use of national power to support new industries. In addition, Hamilton instituted the adoption of a national program to promote and defend the public credit.

While Hamilton and John Adams both yearned for an aristocratic government in which the best could rule as they saw fit, they did make some compromises with the growing belief in popular government. Nonetheless, they and the other Federalists put America upon a course of conservatism from which it has only gradually departed. Suspicious of democracy, they did not favor direct self-government. Later even Jeffersonians agreed that self-government was dangerous. In order to preserve the best of Locke, which they held to be his views of property, limited government, and republicanism, the Federalists forged a new system of government.

5.   MADISON

The Principles of Republicanism

The Constitution of the United States was drafted in 1787 to replace the original form of government under the Articles of Confederation. However, the popular endorsement of the new Constitution was among the most bitter controversies in American history. In the state of New York a series of eighty-five lengthy articles signed "Publius" appeared in the press in defense of the Constitution. The articles were a product of the joint effort of Alexander Hamilton, John Jay, and James Madison. Ever since their appearance in book form as *The Federalist*, these articles have been generally regarded as the finest expression of American political thought. The following three selections* present some of the most important points of these essays. The first (No. 10—this selection) describes the correct principles of Republican government; the second (No. 46—Selection 6) indicates the nature of American federalism; the third (No. 78—Selection 7) discusses the role of the judiciary.

To the People of the State of New York:

Among the numerous advantages promised by a well-constructed Union, none deserves to be more accurately developed than its tendency to break and control the violence of faction. The friend of popular governments never finds himself so much alarmed for their character and fate, as when he contemplates their propensity to this dangerous vice. He will not fail, therefore, to set a due value on any plan which, without violating the principles to which he is attached, provides a proper cure for it. The instability, injustice, and confusion introduced into the public councils, have, in truth, been the mortal diseases under

* No. 10 (Madison); No. 46 (Madison); No. 78 (Hamilton), in *The Federalist*.

which popular governments have everywhere perished; as they continue to be the favorite and fruitful topics from which the adversaries to liberty derive their most specious declamations. The valuable improvements made by the American constitutions on the popular models, both ancient and modern, cannot certainly be too much admired; but it would be an unwarrantable partiality, to contend that they have as effectually obviated the danger on this side, as was wished and expected. Complaints are everywhere heard from our most considerate and virtuous citizens, equally the friends of public and private faith, and of public and personal liberty, that our governments are too unstable, that the public good is disregarded in the conflicts of rival parties, and that measures are too often decided, not according to the rules of justice and the rights of the minor party, but by the superior force of an interested and overbearing majority. However anxiously we may wish that these complaints had no foundation, the evidence of known facts will not permit us to deny that they are in some degree true. It will be found, indeed, on a candid review of our situation, that some of the distresses under which we labor have been erroneously charged on the operation of our governments; but it will be found, at the same time, that other causes will not alone account for many of our heaviest misfortunes; and, particularly, for that prevailing and increasing distrust of public engagements, and alarm for private rights, which are echoed from one end of the continent to the other. These must be chiefly, if not wholly, effects of the unsteadiness and injustice with which a factious spirit has tainted our public administrations.

By a faction, I understand a number of citizens, whether amounting to a majority or minority of the whole, who are united and actuated by some common impulse of passion, or of interest, adverse to the rights of other citizens, or to the permanent and aggregate interests of the community.

There are two methods of curing the mischiefs of faction: the one, by removing its causes; the other, by controlling its effects.

There are again two methods of removing the causes of faction: the one, by destroying the liberty which is essential to its existence; the other, by giving to every citizen the same opinions, the same passions, and the same interests.

It could never be more truly said than of the first remedy, that it was worse than the disease. Liberty is to faction what air is to fire, an aliment without which it instantly expires. But it could not be less folly to abolish liberty, which is essential to political life, because it nourishes faction, than it would be to wish the annihilation of air, which is essential to animal life, because it imparts to fire its destructive agency.

The second expedient is as impracticable as the first would be unwise. As long as the reason of man continues fallible, and he is at liberty to exercise it, different opinions will be formed. As long as the connection subsists between his reason and his self-love, his opinions and his passions will have a reciprocal influence on each other; and the former will be objects to which the latter will attach themselves. The diversity in the faculties of men, from which the rights of property originate, is not less an insuperable obstacle to a uniformity of interests. The protection of these faculties is the first object of government. From the protection of different and unequal faculties of acquiring property, the possession of different degrees and kinds of property immediately results; and from the influence of these on the sentiments and views of the respective proprietors, ensues a division of the society into different interests and parties.

The latent causes of faction are thus sown in the nature of man; and we see them everywhere brought into different degrees of activity, according to the different circumstances of civil society. A zeal for different opinions concerning religion, concerning government, and many other points, as well of speculation as of practice; an attachment to different leaders ambitiously contending for pre-eminence and power; or to persons of other descriptions whose fortunes have been interesting to the human passions, have, in turn, divided mankind into parties, inflamed them with mutual animosity, and rendered them much more disposed to vex and oppress each other than to co-operate for their common good. So strong is this propensity of mankind to fall into mutual animosities, that where no substantial occasion presents itself, the most frivolous and fanciful distinctions have been sufficient to kindle their unfriendly passions and excite their most violent conflicts. But the most common and durable source of factions has been the various and unequal distribution of property. Those who hold and those who are without property have ever formed distinct interests in society. Those who are creditors, and those who are debtors, fall under a like discrimination. A landed interest, a manufacturing interest, a mercantile interest, a moneyed interest, with many lesser interests, grow up of necessity in civilized nations, and divide them into different classes, actuated by different sentiments and views. The regulation of these various and interfering interests forms the principal task of modern legislation, and involves the spirit of party and faction in the necessary and ordinary operations of the government.

No man is allowed to be a judge in his own cause, because his interest would certainly bias his judgment, and, not improbably, corrupt his integrity. With equal, nay with greater reason, a body of men are unfit to be both judges and parties at the same time; yet what are many of the most important acts of legislation, but so many judicial determinations, not indeed concerning the rights of single persons, but concerning the rights of large bodies of citizens? And what are the different classes of legislators but advocates and parties to the causes which they determine? Is a law proposed concerning private debts? It is a question to which the creditors are parties on one side and the debtors on the other. Justice ought to hold the balance between them. Yet the parties are, and must be, themselves the judges; and the most numerous party, or, in other words, the most powerful faction must be expected to prevail. Shall domestic manufactures be encouraged, and in what degree, by restrictions on foreign manufactures? are questions which would be differently decided by the landed and the manufacturing classes, and probably by neither with a sole regard to justice and the public good. The apportionment of taxes on the various descriptions of property is an act which seems to require the most exact impartiality; yet there is, perhaps, no legislative act in which greater opportunity and temptation are given to a predominant party to trample on the rules of justice. Every shilling with which they overburden the inferior number, is a shilling saved to their own pockets.

It is in vain to say that enlightened statesmen will be able to adjust these clashing interests, and render them all subservient to the public good. Enlightened statesmen will not always be at the helm. Nor, in many cases, can such an adjustment be made at all without taking into view, indirect and remote considerations, which will rarely prevail over the immediate interest which one party may find in disregarding the rights of another or the good of the whole.

The inference to which we are brought is, that the *causes* of faction cannot be removed, and that relief is only to be sought in the means of controlling its *effects*.

If a faction consists of less than a majority, relief is supplied by the republican principle, which enables the majority to defeat its sinister views by regular vote. It may clog the administration, it may convulse the society; but it will be unable to execute and mask its violence under the forms of the Constitution. When a majority is included in a faction, the form of popular government, on the other hand, enables it to sacrifice to its ruling passion or interest both the public good and the rights of other citizens. To secure the public good and private rights against the danger of such a faction, and at the same time to preserve the spirit and the form of popular government, is then the great object to which our inquiries are directed. Let me add that it is the great desideratum by which this form of government can be rescued from the opprobrium under which it has so long labored, and be recommended to the esteem and adoption of mankind.

By what means is this object attainable? Evidently by one of two only. Either the existence of the same passion or interest in a majority, having such coexistent passion or interest, must be rendered, by their number and local situation, unable to concert and carry into effect schemes of oppression. If the impulse and the opportunity be suffered to coincide, we well know that neither moral nor religious motives can be relied on as an adequate control. They are not found to be such on the injustice and violence of individuals, and lose their efficacy in proportion to the number combined together, that is, in proportion as their efficacy becomes needful.

From this view of the subject it may be concluded that a pure democracy, by which I mean a society consisting of a small number of citizens, who assemble and administer the government in person, can admit of no cure for the mischiefs of faction. A common passion or interest will, in almost every case, be felt by a majority of the whole; a communication and concert result from the form of government itself; and there is nothing to check the inducements to sacrifice the weaker party or an obnoxious individual. Hence it is that such democracies have ever been spectacles of turbulence and contention; have ever been found incompatible with personal security or the rights of property; and have in general been as short in their lives as they have been violent in their deaths. Theoretic politicians, who have patronized this species of government, have erroneously supposed that by reducing mankind to a perfect equality in their political rights, they would, at the same time, be perfectly equalized and assimilated in their possessions, their opinions, and their passions.

A republic, by which I mean a government in which the scheme of representation takes place, opens a different prospect, and promises the cure for which we are seeking. Let us examine the points in which it varies from pure democracy, and we shall comprehend both the nature of the cure and the efficacy which it must derive from the Union.

The two great points of difference between a democracy and a republic are: first, the delegation of the government, in the latter, to a small number of citizens elected by the rest; secondly, the greater number of citizens, and greater sphere of country, over which the latter may be extended.

The effect of the first difference is, on the one hand, to refine and enlarge the public views, by passing them through the medium of a chosen body of citizens, whose wisdom may best discern the true interest of their country, and whose patriotism and love of justice will be least likely to sacrifice it to temporary or partial considerations. Under such a regulation, it may well happen that the public voice, pronounced by the representatives of the people, will be more consonant to the public good than if pronounced by the people themselves, convened for the purpose. On the other hand, the effect may be inverted. Men of factious tempers, of local prejudices, or of sinister designs, may, by intrigue, by corruption, or by other means, first obtain the suffrages, and then betray the interests, of the people. The question resulting is, whether small or extensive republics are more favorable to the election of proper guardians of the public weal; and it is clearly decided in favor of the latter by two obvious considerations:

In the first place, it is to be remarked that, however small the republic may be, the representatives must be raised to a certain number, in order to guard against the cabals of a few; and that, however large it may be, they must be limited to a certain number, in order to guard against the confusion of a multitude. Hence, the number of representatives in the two cases not being in proportion to that of the two constituents, and being proportionally greater in the small republic, it follows that, if the proportion of fit characters be not less in the large than in the small republic, the former will present a greater option, and consequently a greater probability of a fit choice.

In the next place, as each representative will be chosen by a greater number of citizens in the large than in the small republic, it will be more difficult for unworthy candidates to practise with success the vicious arts by which elections are too often carried; and the suffrages of the people being more free, will be more likely to centre in men who possess the most attractive merit and the most diffusive and established characters.

It must be confessed that in this, as in most other cases, there is a mean, on both sides of which inconveniences will be found to lie. By enlarging too much the number of electors, you render the representative too little acquainted with all their local circumstances and lesser interests; as by reducing it too much, you render him unduly attached to these, and too little fit to comprehend and pursue great and national objects. The federal Constitution forms a happy combination in this respect; the great and aggregate interests being referred to the national, the local and particular to the State legislatures.

The other point of difference is, the greater number of citizens and extent of territory which may be brought within the compass of republican than of democratic government; and it is this circumstance principally which renders factious combinations less to be dreaded in the former than in the latter. The smaller the society, the fewer probably will be the distinct parties and interests composing it; the fewer the distinct parties and interests, the more frequently will a majority be found of the same party; and the smaller the number of individuals composing a majority, and the smaller the compass within which they are placed, the more easily will they concert and execute their plans of oppression. Extend the sphere and you take in a greater variety of parties and interests; you make it less probable that a majority of the whole will have a common motive to invade the rights of other citizens; or if such a common motive exists, it will be more difficult for all who feel it to discover their own strength, and to act in unison with each other. Besides other impediments, it may be remarked that, where there is a consciousness of unjust or dishonorable purposes, communication is always checked by distrust in proportion to the number whose concurrence is necessary.

Hence, it clearly appears, that the same advantage which a republic has over a democracy, in controlling the effects of faction, is enjoyed by a large over a small republic,—is enjoyed by the Union over the States composing it. Does the advantage consist in the substitution of representatives whose enlightened views and virtuous sentiments render them superior to local prejudices and to schemes of injustice? It will not be denied that the representation of the Union will be most likely to possess these requisite endowments. Does it consist in the greater security afforded by a greater variety of parties, against the event of any one party being able to outnumber and oppress the rest? In an equal degree does the increased variety of parties comprised within the Union, increase this security. Does it, in fine, consist in the greater obstacles opposed to the concert and accomplishment of the secret wishes of an unjust and interested majority? Here, again, the extent of the Union gives it the most palpable advantage.

The influence of factious leaders may kindle a flame within their particular States, but will be unable to spread a general conflagration through the other States. A religious sect may degenerate into a political faction in a part of the Confederacy; but the variety of sects dispersed over the entire face of it must secure the national councils against any danger from that source. A rage for paper money, for an abolition of debts, for an equal division of property, or for any other improper or wicked project, will be less apt to pervade the whole body of the Union than a particular member of it; in the same proportion as such a malady is more likely to taint a particular county or district, than an entire State.

In the extent and proper structure of the Union, therefore, we behold a republican remedy for the diseases most incident to republican government. And according to the degree of pleasure and pride we feel in being republicans, ought to be our zeal in cherishing the spirit and supporting the character of Federalists.

PUBLIUS

6. MADISON

The Nature of American Federalism*

To the People of the State of New York:

Resuming the subject of the last paper, I proceed to inquire whether the federal government or the State governments will have the advantage with regard to the predilection and support of the people. Notwithstanding the different modes in which they are appointed, we must consider both of them as substantially dependent on the great body of the citizens of the United States. I assume this position here as it respects the first, reserving the proofs for another place. The federal and State governments are in fact but different agents and trustees of the people, constituted with different powers, and designed for different purposes. The adversaries of the Constitution seem to have lost sight of the people altogether in their reasonings on this subject; and to have viewed these different establishments, not only as mutual rivals and enemies, but as uncontrolled by any common superior in their efforts to usurp the authorities of each other. These gentlemen must here be reminded of their error. They must be told that the ultimate authority, wherever the derivative may be found, resides in the people alone, and that it will not depend merely on the comparative ambition or address of the different governments, whether either, or which of them, will be able to enlarge its sphere of jurisdiction at the expense of the other. Truth, no less than decency, requires that the event in every case should be supposed to depend on the sentiments and sanction of their common constituents.

Many considerations, besides those suggested on a former occasion, seem to place it beyond doubt that the first and most natural attachment of the people will be to the governments of their respective States. Into

* See introduction to Selection 5.

the administration of these a greater number of individuals will expect to rise. From the gift of these a greater number of offices and emoluments will flow. By the superintending care of these, all the more domestic and personal interests of the people will be regulated and provided for. With the affairs of these, the people will be more familiarly and minutely conversant. And with the members of these, will a greater proportion of the people have the ties of personal acquaintance and friendship, and of family and party attachments; on the side of these, therefore, the popular bias may well be expected most strongly to incline.

Experience speaks the same language in this case. The federal administration, though hitherto very defective in comparison with what may be hoped under a better system, had, during the war, and particularly whilst the independent fund of paper emissions was in credit, an activity and importance as great as it can well have in any future circumstances whatever. It was engaged, too, in a course of measures which had for their object the protection of every thing that was dear, and the acquisition of every thing that could be desirable to the people at large. It was, nevertheless, invariably found, after the transient enthusiasm for the early Congresses was over, that the attention and attachment of the people were turned anew to their own particular governments; that the federal council was at no time the idol of popular favor; and that opposition to proposed enlargements of its powers and importance was the side usually taken by the men who wished to build their political consequence on the prepossessions of their fellow-citizens.

If, therefore, as has been elsewhere remarked, the people should in future become more partial to the federal than to the State governments, the change can only result from such manifest and irresistible proofs of a better administration, as will overcome all their antecedent propensities. And in that case, the people ought not surely to be precluded from giving most of their confidence where they may discover it to be most due; but even in that case the State governments could have little to apprehend, because it is only within a certain sphere that the federal power can, in the nature of things, be advantageously administered.

The remaining points on which I propose to compare the federal and State governments, are the disposition and the faculty they may respectively possess, to resist and frustrate the measures of each other.

It has been already proved that the members of the federal will be more dependent on the members of the State governments, than the latter will be on the former. It has appeared also, that the prepossessions of the people, on whom both will depend, will be more on the side of the State governments, than of the federal government. So far as the disposition of each towards the other may be influenced by these causes, the State governments must clearly have the advantage. But in a distinct and very important point of view, the advantage will lie on the same side. The prepossessions, which the members themselves will carry into the federal government, will generally be favorable to the States; whilst it will rarely happen, that the members of the State governments will carry into the public councils a bias in favor of the general government. A local spirit will infallibly prevail much more in the members of Congress, than a national spirit will prevail in the legislatures of the particular States. Every one knows that a great proportion of the errors committed by the State legislatures proceeds from the disposition of the members to sacrifice the comprehensive and permanent interest of the State, to the particular and separate views of the counties or districts in which they reside. And if they do not sufficiently enlarge their policy to embrace the collective welfare of their particular State, how can it be imagined that they will make the aggregate prosperity of the Union, and the dignity and respectability of its government, the objects of their affections and consultations? For the same reason that the members of the State legislatures will be unlikely to attach themselves sufficiently to national objects, the members of the federal legislature will be likely to attach themselves too much to local objects. The States will be to the latter what counties and towns are to the former. Measures will too often be decided according to their probable effect, not on the national prosperity and happiness, but on the prejudices, interests, and pursuits of the governments and people of the individual States. What is the spirit that has in general characterized the proceedings of Congress? A perusal of their journals, as well as the candid acknowledgments of such as have had a seat in that assembly, will inform us, that the members have but too frequently displayed the character, rather of partisans of their respective States, than of impartial guardians of a common interest; that where on one occasion improper sacrifices have been made of local considerations, to the aggrandizement of the federal government, the great interests of the nation have suffered on a hundred, from an undue attention to the local prejudices, interests, and views of the particular States. I mean not by these reflections to insinuate, that the new federal government will not embrace a more enlarged plan of policy than the existing government may have pursued; much less, that its views will be as confined as those of the State legislatures; but only that it will partake sufficiently of the spirit of both, to be disinclined to invade the rights of the individual States, or the prerogatives of their governments. The motives on the part of the State governments, to augment their prerogatives by defalcations from the federal government, will be overruled by no reciprocal predispositions in the members.

Were it admitted, however, that the Federal government may feel an equal disposition with the State governments to extend its power beyond the due limits, the latter would still have the advantage in the means of defeating such encroachments. If an act of a particular State, though unfriendly to the national government, be generally popular in that State, and should not too grossly violate the oaths of the State officers, it is executed immediately and, of course, by means on the spot and depending on the State alone. The opposition of the federal government, or the interposition of federal officers, would but inflame the zeal of all parties on the side of the State, and the evil could not be prevented or repaired, if at all, without the employment of means which must always be resorted to with reluctance and difficulty. On the other hand, should an unwarrantable measure of the federal government be unpopular in particular States, which would seldom fail to be the case, or even a warrantable measure be so, which may sometimes be the case, the means of opposition to it are powerful and at hand. The disquietude of the people; their repugnance and, perhaps, refusal to coöperate with the officers of the Union; the frowns of the executive magistracy of the State; the embarrassments created by legislative devices, which would often be added on such occasions, would oppose, in any State, difficulties not to be despised; would form, in a large State, very serious impediments; and where the sentiments of several adjoining States happened to be in unison, would present obstructions which the federal government would hardly be willing to encounter.

But ambitious encroachments of the federal government, on the authority of the State governments, would not excite the opposition of a single State, or of a few States only. They would be signals of general alarm. Every government would espouse the common cause. A correspondence would be opened. Plans of resistance would be concerted. One spirit would animate and conduct the whole. The same combinations, in short, would result from an apprehension of the federal, as was produced by the dread of a foreign, yoke; and unless the projected innovations should be voluntarily renounced, the same appeal to a trial of force would be made in the one case as was made in the other. But what degree of madness could ever drive the federal government to such an extremity. In the contest with Great Britain, one part of the empire was employed against the other. The more numerous part invaded the rights of the less numerous part. The attempt was unjust and unwise; but it was not in speculation absolutely chimerical. But what would be the contest in the case we are supposing? Who would be the parties? A few representatives of the people would be opposed to the people themselves; or rather one set of representatives would be contending against thirteen sets of representatives, with the whole body of their common constituents on the side of the latter.

The only refuge left for those who prophesy the downfall of the State governments is the visionary supposition that the federal government may previously accumulate a military force for the projects of ambition. The reasonings contained in these papers must have been employed to little purpose indeed, if it could be necessary now to disprove the reality of this danger. That the people and the States should, for a sufficient period of time, elect an uninterrupted succession of men ready to betray both; that the traitors should, throughout this period, uniformly and systematically pursue some fixed plan for the extension of the military establishment; that the governments and the people of the States should silently and patiently behold the gathering storm, and continue to supply the materials, until it should be prepared to burst on their own heads, must appear to every one more like the incoherent dreams of a delirious jealousy, or the misjudged exaggerations of a counterfeit zeal, than like the sober apprehensions of genuine patriotism. Extravagant as the supposition is, let it however be made. Let a regular army, fully equal to the resources of the country, be formed; and let it be entirely at the devotion of the federal government: still it would not be going too far to say, that the State governments, with the people on their side, would be able to repel the danger. The highest number to which, according to the best computation, a standing army can be carried in any country, does not exceed one hundredth part of the whole number of souls; or one twenty-fifth part of the number able to bear arms. This proportion would not yield, in the United States, an army of more than twenty-five or thirty thousand men. To these would be opposed a militia amounting to near half a million of citizens with arms in their hands, officered by men chosen from among themselves, fighting for their common liberties, and united and conducted by governments possessing their affections and confidence. It may well be doubted, whether a militia thus circumstanced could ever be conquered by such a proportion of regular troops. Those who are best acquainted with the last successful resistance of this country against the British arms, will be most inclined to deny the possibility of it. Besides the advantage of being armed, which the Americans possess over the people of almost every other nation, the existence of subordinate governments, to which the people are attached, and by which the militia officers are appointed, forms a barrier against the enterprises of ambition, more insurmountable than any which a simple government of any form can admit of. Notwithstanding the military establishments in the several kingdoms of Europe, which are carried as far as the public resources will bear, the governments are afraid to trust the people with arms. And it is not certain, that with this aid alone they would not be able to shake off their yokes. But were the people to possess the additional advantages of local governments chosen by themselves, who could collect the national will and direct the national force, and of officers appointed out of the militia, by these governments, and attached both to them and to the militia, it may be affirmed with the greatest assurance, that the throne of every tyranny in Europe would be speedily overturned in spite of the legions which surround it. Let us not insult the free and gallant citizens of America with the suspicion, that they would be less able to defend the rights of which they would be in actual possession, than the debased subjects of arbitrary power would be to rescue theirs from the hands of their oppressors. Let us rather no longer insult them with the supposition that they can ever reduce themselves to the necessity of making the experiment, by a blind and tame submission to the long train of insidious measures which must precede and produce it.

The argument under the present head may be put into a very concise form, which appears altogether conclusive. Either the mode in which the federal government is to be constructed will render it sufficiently dependent on the people, or it will not. On the first supposition, it will be restrained by that dependence from forming schemes obnoxious to their constituents. On the other supposition, it will not possess the confidence of the people, and its schemes of usurpation will be easily defeated by the State governments, who will be supported by the people.

On summing up the considerations stated in this and the last paper, they seem to amount to the most convincing evidence, that the powers proposed to be lodged in the federal government are as little formidable to those reserved to the individual States, as they are indispensably necessary to accomplish the purposes of the Union; and that all those alarms which have been sounded, of a meditated and consequential annihilation of the State governments, must, on the most favorable interpretation, be ascribed to the chimerical fears of the authors of them.

PUBLIUS

7.   HAMILTON

The Role of the Judiciary*

To the People of the State of New York:

We proceed now to an examination of the judiciary department of
the proposed government.

In unfolding the defects of the existing Confederation the utility and
necessity of a federal judicature have been clearly pointed out. It is the
less necessary to recapitulate the considerations there urged, as the
propriety of the institution in the abstract is not disputed; the only
questions which have been raised being relative to the manner of
constituting it, and to its extent. To these points, therefore, our observations shall be confined.

The manner of constituting it seems to embrace these several objects:
1st. The mode of appointing the judges. 2d. The tenure by which they
are to hold their places. 3d. The partition of the judiciary authority
between different courts, and their relations to each other.

First. As to the mode of appointing the judges; this is the same with
that of appointing the officers of the Union in general, and has been
so fully discussed in the two last numbers, that nothing can be said
here which would not be useless repetition.

Second. As to the tenure by which the judges are to hold their places:
this chiefly concerns their duration in office; the provisions for their
support; the precautions for their responsibility.

According to the plan of the convention, all judges who may be
appointed by the United States are to hold their offices *during good
behavior;* which is conformable to the most approved of the State
constitutions, and among the rest, to that of this State. Its propriety
having been drawn into question by the adversaries of that plan, is

* See introduction to Selection 5.

no light symptom of the rage for objection, which disorders their imaginations and judgments. The standard of good behavior for the continuance in office of the judicial magistracy, is certainly one of the most valuable of the modern improvements in the practice of government. In a monarchy it is an excellent barrier to the despotism of the prince; in a republic it is a no less excellent barrier to the encroachments and oppressions of the representative body. And it is the best expedient which can be devised in any government, to secure a steady, upright, and impartial administration of the laws.

Whoever attentively considers the different departments of power must perceive, that, in a government in which they are separated from each other, the judiciary from the nature of its functions, will always be the least dangerous to the political rights of the Constitution; because it will be least in a capacity to annoy or injure them. The Executive not only dispenses the honors, but holds the sword of the community. The legislature not only commands the purse, but prescribes the rules by which the duties and rights of every citizen are to be regulated. The judiciary, on the contrary, has no influence over either the sword or the purse; no direction either of the strength or of the wealth of the society; and can take no active resolution whatever. It may truly be said to have neither FORCE nor WILL, but merely judgment; and must ultimately depend upon the aid of the executive arm even for the efficacy of its judgments.

This simple view of the matter suggests several important consequences. It proves incontestably, that the judiciary is beyond comparison the weakest of the three departments of power*; that it can never attack with success either of the other two; and that all possible care is requisite to enable it to defend itself against their attacks. It equally proves, that though individual oppression may now and then proceed from the courts of justice, the general liberty of the people can never be endangered from that quarter; I mean so long as the judiciary remains truly distinct from both the legislature and the Executive. For I agree, that "there is no liberty, if the power of judging be not separated from the legislative and executive powers."† And it proves, in the last place, that as liberty can have nothing to fear from

---

* The celebrated Montesquieu, speaking of them, says: "Of the three powers above mentioned, the judiciary is next to nothing."—"Spirit of Laws," vol. i., page 186. —PUBLIUS.

† *Idem*, page 181.—PUBLIUS.

the judiciary alone, but would have every thing to fear from its union with either of the other departments; that as all the effects of such a union must ensue from a dependence of the former on the latter, notwithstanding a nominal and apparent separation; that as, from the natural feebleness of the judiciary, it is in continual jeopardy of being overpowered, awed, or influenced by its coördinate branches; and that as nothing can contribute so much to its firmness and independence as permanency in office, this quality may therefore be justly regarded as an indispensable ingredient in its constitution, and, in a great measure, as the citadel of the public justice and the public security.

The complete independence of the courts of justice is peculiarly essential in a limited Constitution. By a limited Constitution, I understand one which contains certain specified exceptions to the legislative authority; such, for instance, as that it shall pass no bills of attainder, no *ex-post-facto* laws, and the like. Limitations of this kind can be preserved in practice no other way than through the medium of courts of justice, whose duty it must be to declare all acts contrary to the manifest tenor of the Constitution void. Without this, all the reservations of particular rights or privileges would amount to nothing.

Some perplexity respecting the rights of the courts to pronounce legislative acts void, because contrary to the constitution, has arisen from an imagination that the doctrine would imply a superiority of the judiciary to the legislative power. It is urged that the authority which can declare the acts of another void, must necessarily be superior to the one whose acts may be declared void. As this doctrine is of great importance in all the American constitutions, a brief discussion of the ground on which it rests cannot be unacceptable.

There is no position which depends on clearer principles, than that every act of a delegated authority, contrary to the tenor of the commission under which it is exercised, is void. No legislative act, therefore, contrary to the Constitution, can be valid. To deny this, would be to affirm, that the deputy is greater than his principal; that the servant is above his master; that the representatives of the people are superior to the people themselves; that men acting by virtue of powers, may do not only what their powers do not authorize, but what they forbid.

If it be said that the legislative body are themselves the constitutional judges of their own powers, and that the construction they put upon them is conclusive upon the other departments, it may be answered, that this cannot be the natural presumption, where it is not to be collected from any particular provisions in the Constitution. It is not otherwise to be supposed, that the Constitution could intend to enable the representatives of the people to substitute their *will* to that of their constituents. It is far more rational to suppose, that the courts were designed to be an intermediate body between the people and the legislature, in order, among other things, to keep the latter within the limits assigned to their authority. The interpretation of the laws is the proper and peculiar province of the courts. A constitution is, in fact, and must be regarded by the judges, as a fundamental law. It therefore belongs to them to ascertain its meaning, as well as the meaning of any particular act proceeding from the legislative body. If there should happen to be an irreconcilable variance between the two, that which has the superior obligation and validity ought, of course, to be preferred; or, in other words, the Constitution ought to be preferred to the statute, the intention of the people to the intention of their agents.

Nor does this conclusion by any means suppose a superiority of the judicial to the legislative power. It only supposes that the power of the people is superior to both; and that where the will of the legislature, declared in its statutes, stands in opposition to that of the people, declared in the Constitution, the judges ought to be governed by the latter rather than the former. They ought to regulate their decisions by the fundamental laws, rather than by those which are not fundamental.

This exercise of judicial discretion, in determining between two contradictory laws, is exemplified in a familiar instance. It not uncommonly happens, that there are two statutes existing at one time, clashing in whole or in part with each other, and neither of them containing any repealing clause or expression. In such a case, it is the province of the courts to liquidate and fix their meaning and operation. So far as they can, by any fair construction, be reconciled to each other, reason and law conspire to dictate that this should be done; where this is impracticable, it becomes a matter of necessity to give effect to one, in exclusion of the other. The rule which has obtained in the courts for determining their relative validity is, that the last in order of time shall be preferred to the first. But this is a mere rule of construction, not derived from any positive law, but from the nature and reason of the thing. It is a rule not enjoined upon the courts by legislative provision, but adopted by themselves, as consonant to truth and propriety, for the direction of their conduct as interpreters of the law. They thought it reasonable, that between the interfering acts of an *equal* authority, that which was the last indication of its will should have the preference.

But in regard to the interfering acts of a superior and subordinate authority, of an original and derivative power, the nature and reason of the thing indicate the converse of that rule as proper to be followed. They teach us that the prior act of a superior ought to be preferred to the subsequent act of an inferior and subordinate authority; and that accordingly, whenever a particular statute contravenes the Constitution, it will be the duty of the judicial tribunals to adhere to the latter and disregard the former.

It can be of no weight to say that the courts, on the pretence of a repugnancy, may substitute their own pleasure to the constitutional intentions of the legislature. This might as well happen in the case of two contradictory statutes; or it might as well happen in every adjudication upon any single statute. The courts must declare the sense of the law; and if they should be disposed to exercise WILL instead of JUDGMENT, the consequence would equally be the substitution of their pleasure to that of the legislative body. The observation, if it prove any thing, would prove that there ought to be no judges distinct from that body.

If, then, the courts of justice are to be considered as the bulwarks of a limited Constitution against legislative encroachments, this consideration will afford a strong argument for the permanent tenure of judicial offices, since nothing will contribute so much as this to that independent spirit in the judges which must be essential to the faithful performance of so arduous a duty.

This independence of the judges is equally requisite to guard the Constitution and the rights of individuals from the effects of those ill humors, which the arts of designing men, or the influence of particular conjunctures, sometimes disseminate among the people themselves, and which, though they speedily give place to better information, and more deliberate reflection, have a tendency, in the meantime, to occasion dangerous innovations in the government, and serious oppressions of the minor party in the community. Though I trust the friends of the proposed Constitution will never concur with its enemies,* in questioning that fundamental principle of republican government, which admits the right of the people to alter or abolish the established Constitution,

* *Vide* "Protest of the Minority of the Convention of Pennsylvania," Martin's Speech, etc.—PUBLIUS.

whenever they find it inconsistent with their happiness, yet it is not to be inferred from this principle, that the representatives of the people, whenever a momentary inclination happens to lay hold of a majority of their constituents, incompatible with the provisions in the existing Constitution, would, on that account, be justifiable in a violation of those provisions; or that the courts would be under a greater obligation to connive at infractions in this shape, than when they had proceeded wholly from the cabals of the representative body. Until the people have, by some solemn and authoritative act, annulled or changed the established form, it is binding upon themselves collectively, as well as individually; and no presumption, or even knowledge, of their sentiments, can warrant their representatives in a departure from it, prior to such an act. But it is easy to see, that it would require an uncommon portion of fortitude in the judges to do their duty as faithful guardians of the Constitution, where legislative invasions of it had been instigated by the major voice of the community.

But it is not with a view to infractions of the Constitution only, that the independence of the judges may be an essential safeguard against the effects of occasional ill humors in the society. These sometimes extend no farther than to the injury of the private rights of particular classes of citizens, by unjust and partial laws. Here also the firmness of the judicial magistracy is of vast importance in mitigating the severity and confining the operation of such laws. It not only serves to moderate the immediate mischiefs of those which may have been passed, but it operates as a check upon the legislative body in passing them; who, perceiving that obstacles to the success of iniquitous intention are to be expected from the scruples of the courts, are in a manner compelled, by the very motives of the injustice they meditate, to qualify their attempts. This is a circumstance calculated to have more influence upon the character of our governments, than but few may be aware of. The benefits of the integrity and moderation of the judiciary have already been felt in more States than one; and though they may have displeased those whose sinister expectations they may have disappointed, they must have commanded the esteem and applause of all the virtuous and disinterested. Considerate men, of every description, ought to prize whatever will tend to beget or fortify that temper in the courts; as no man can be sure that he may not be to-morrow the victim of a spirit of injustice, by which he may be a gainer to-day. And every man must now feel, that the inevitable tendency of such a spirit is to sap the foundations of public and private confidence, and to introduce in its stead universal distrust and distress.

That inflexible and uniform adherence to the rights of the Constitution, and of individuals, which we perceive to be indispensable in the courts of justice, can certainly not be expected from judges who hold their offices by a temporary commission. Periodical appointments, however regulated, or by whomsoever made, would, in some way or other, be fatal to their necessary independence. If the power of making them was committed either to the Executive or legislature, there would be danger of an improper complaisance to the branch which possessed it; if to both, there would be an unwillingness to hazard the displeasure of either; if to the people, or to persons chosen by them for the special purpose, there would be too great a disposition to consult popularity, to justify a reliance that nothing would be consulted but the Constitution and the laws.

There is yet a further and a weightier reason for the permanency of the judicial offices, which is deducible from the nature of the qualifications they require. It has been frequently remarked, with great propriety, that a voluminous code of laws is one of the inconveniences necessarily connected with the advantages of a free government. To avoid an arbitrary discretion in the courts, it is indispensable that they should be bound down by strict rules and precedents, which serve to define and point out their duty in every particular case that comes before them; and it will readily be conceived from the variety of controversies which grow out of the folly and wickedness of mankind, that the records of those precedents must unavoidably swell to a very considerable bulk, and must demand long and laborious study to acquire a competent knowledge of them. Hence it is, that there can be but few men in the society who will have sufficient skill in the laws to qualify them for the stations of judges. And making the proper deductions for the ordinary depravity of human nature, the number must be still smaller of those who unite the requisite integrity with the requisite knowledge. These considerations apprise us, that the government can have no great option between fit character; and that a temporary duration in office, which would naturally discourage such characters from quitting a lucrative line of practice to accept a seat on the bench, would have a tendency to throw the administration of justice into hands less able, and less well qualified, to conduct it with utility and dignity. In the present circumstances of this country, and in those in which it is likely to be for a long time to come, the disadvantages on this score would be greater than they may at first sight appear; but it must be confessed, that they are far inferior to those which present themselves under the other aspects of the subject.

Upon the whole, there can be no room to doubt that the convention acted wisely in copying from the models of those constitutions which have established *good behavior* as the tenure of their judicial offices, in point of duration; and that so far from being blamable on this account, their plan would have been inexcusably defective, if it had wanted this important feature of good government. The experience of Great Britain affords an illustrious comment on the excellence of the institution.

PUBLIUS

8.   ADAMS
Distrust of Democracy

John Adams (1735–1826), second President of the United States, although an active supporter of the American Revolution, defended the rights of property and the role of aristocrats in American society. Adams favored strong national government and stood opposed to excessive localism in American political affairs. He further believed in the natural inequality of men but allowed that the people must have a voice in their own government. In this selection from the *Discourses on Davila* (1790)* Adams suggests the difficulties of both excessive representation and insufficient representation and indicates his distrust of extreme forms of democratic government.

. . . There is a voice within us which seems to intimate that real merit should govern the world, and that men ought to be respected only in proportion to their talents, virtues, and services. But the question always has been, how can this arrangement be accomplished? How shall the men of merit be discovered? How shall the proportions of merit be ascertained and graduated? Who shall be the judge? When the government of a great nation is in question, shall the whole nation choose? Will such a choice be better than chance? Shall the whole nation vote for senators? Thirty millions of votes, for example, for each senator in France! It is obvious that this would be a lottery of millions of blanks to one prize, and that the chance of having wisdom and integrity in a senator by hereditary descent would be far better. There is no individual personally known to an hundredth part of the nation. The voters, then, must be exposed to deception from intrigues and maneuvers without number, that is to say, from all the chicanery, impostures, and falsehoods imaginable, with scarce a possibility of preferring real merit. Will you divide the nation into districts and let

---

* From Charles Francis Adams, ed., *The Works of John Adams*, Vol. VI (Boston, 1856), pp. 249–52.

each district choose a senator? This is giving up the idea of national merit and annexing the honor and the trust to an accident, that of living on a particular spot. A hundred or a thousand men of the first merit in a nation may live in one city, and none at all of this description in several whole provinces. Real merit is so remote from the knowledge of whole nations that, were magistrates to be chosen by that criterion alone and by a universal suffrage, dissensions and venality would be endless. The difficulties arising from this source are so obvious and universal that nations have tried all sorts of experiments to avoid them.

As no appetite in human nature is more universal than that for honor, and real merit is confined to a very few, the numbers who thirst for respect are out of all proportion to those who seek it only by merit. The great majority trouble themselves little about merit but apply themselves to seek for honor by means which they see will more easily and certainly obtain it by displaying their taste and address, their wealth and magnificence, their ancient parchments, pictures, and statues, and the virtues of their ancestors, and if these fail, as they seldom have done, they have recourse to artifice, dissimulation, hypocrisy, flattery, imposture, empiricism, quackery, and bribery. What chance has humble, modest, obscure, and poor merit in such a scramble? Nations, perceiving that the still small voice of merit was drowned in the insolent roar of such dupes of impudence and knavery in national elections without a possibility of a remedy, have sought for something more permanent than the popular voice to designate honor. Many nations have attempted to annex it to land, presuming that a good estate would at least furnish means of a good education, and have resolved that those who should possess certain territories should have certain legislative, executive, and judicial powers over the people. Other nations have endeavored to connect honor with offices; and the names and ideas at least of certain moral virtues and intellectual qualities have been by law annexed to certain offices, as veneration, grace, excellence, honor, serenity, majesty. Other nations have attempted to annex honor to families without regard to lands or offices. The Romans allowed none but those who had possessed curule offices to have statues or portraits. He who had images or pictures of his ancestors was called noble. He who had no statue or pictures but his own was called a new man. Those who had none at all were ignoble. Other nations have united all those institutions—connected lands, offices,

and families, made them all descend together and honor, public attention, consideration, and congratulation along with them.

This has been the policy of Europe; and it is to this institution she
owes her superiority in war and peace, in legislation and commerce,
in agriculture, navigation, arts, sciences, and manufactures, to Asia
and Africa.* These families, thus distinguished by property, honors,
and privileges, by defending themselves have been obliged to defend
the people against the encroachments of despotism. They have been
a civil and political militia, constantly watching the designs of the
standing armies and courts; and by defending their own rights, liberties,
properties, and privileges, they have been obliged in some degree to
defend those of the people by making a common cause with them. But
there were several essential defects in this policy; one was that the
people took no rational measures to defend themselves, either against
these great families or the courts. They had no adequate representation
of themselves in the sovereignty. Another was that it never was determined where the sovereignty resided. Generally it was claimed by
kings, but not admitted by the nobles. Sometimes every baron pretended
to be sovereign in his own territory; at other times the sovereignty was
claimed by an assembly of nobles, under the name of States or Cortes.
Sometimes the united authority of the king and states was called the
sovereignty. The common people had no adequate and independent
share in the legislatures and found themselves harassed to discover
who was the sovereign and whom they ought to obey as much as they
ever had been or could be to determine who had the most merit. A
thousand years of barons' wars, causing universal darkness, ignorance,
and barbarity, ended at last in simple monarchy, not by express
stipulation but by tacit acquiescence, in almost all Europe—the people
preferring a certain sovereignty in a single person to endless disputes
about merit and sovereignty, which never did and never will produce
anything but aristocratical anarchy; and the nobles contenting themselves with a security of their property and privileges by a government
of fixed laws, registered and interpreted by a judicial power, which they
called sovereign tribunals, though the legislation and execution were
in a single person.

In this system to control the nobles, the church joined the kings and

* This is a truth, but by no means a justification of the system of nobility in
France, nor in other parts of Europe. Not even in England without a more
equitable representation of the Commons in the legislature. J. A. 1812.

common people. The progress of reason, letters, and science has weakened the church and strengthened the common people, who, if they are honestly and prudently conducted by those who have their confidence, will most infallibly obtain a share in every legislature. But if the common people are advised to aim at collecting the whole sovereignty in single national assemblies, as they are by the Duke de la Rochefoucauld and the Marquis of Condorcet, or at the abolition of the regal executive authority, or at a division of the executive power, as they are by a posthumous publication of the Abbé de Mably—they will fail of their desired liberty as certainly as emulation and rivalry are founded in human nature and inseparable from civil affairs. It is not to flatter the passions of the people, to be sure, nor is it the way to obtain a present enthusiastic popularity, to tell them that in a single assembly they will act as arbitrarily and tyrannically as any despot, but it is a sacred truth, and as demonstrable as any proposition whatever, that a sovereignty in a single assembly must necessarily and will certainly be exercised by a majority as tyrannically as any sovereignty was ever exercised by kings or nobles. And if a balance of passions and interests is not scientifically concerted, the present struggle in Europe will be little beneficial to mankind and produce nothing but another thousand years of feudal fanaticism under new and strange names.

9. HAMILTON

The Development of American Industry

Alexander Hamilton (1757–1804) was born on the island of Nevis in the British West Indies. Abandoned by his father, Hamilton made his own way in life by the force of his personality, his quick intelligence, and his literary skill. Hamilton was an ardent revolutionary, participating in numerous military skirmishes before 1776. He distinguished himself at the Battle of Princeton (Jan. 3, 1777) and was made an aide-de-camp on General Washington's staff. In peacetime he was worried about the political drift of the new nation and worked on plans to strengthen it. At the Constitutional Convention in 1787 Hamilton was a strong nationalist, but most of his ideas were not accepted by the drafters. Nonetheless, Hamilton was a strong defender of the Constitution and later, as Secretary of the Treasury (1789–1795), contributed economic insights which were intended to develop America's industrial capacities and strengthen its financial foundation. While serving as Secretary of the Treasury, Hamilton authored a number of important studies for President Washington. These included: "First Report on the Public Credit" (1790), "Opinion on the Constitutionality of the Bank of the United States" (1791), "Report on the Establishment of a Mint" (1791), and "Report on Manufactures" (1791), from which this selection* is taken.

MANUFACTURES

Communicated to the House of Representatives, December 5, 1791.

The Secretary of the Treasury, in obedience to the order of the House of Representatives, of the 15th day of January, 1790, has applied his attention, at as early a period as his other duties would permit, to

* From *The Works of Alexander Hamilton*, Henry Cabot Lodge, ed. (New York: G. P. Putnam's Sons, 1904), Vol. IV., pp. 70–86.

the subject of Manufactures, and particularly to the means of promoting such as will tend to render the United States independent on foreign nations for military and other essential supplies; and he thereupon respectfully submits the following report:

The expediency of encouraging manufactures in the United States, which was not long since deemed very questionable, appears at this time to be pretty generally admitted. The embarrassments which have obstructed the progress of our external trade, have led to serious reflections on the necessity of enlarging the sphere of our domestic commerce. The restrictive regulations, which, in foreign markets, abridge the vent of the increasing surplus of our agricultural produce, serve to beget an earnest desire that a more extensive demand for that surplus may be created at home; and the complete success which has rewarded manufacturing enterprise in some valuable branches, conspiring with the promising symptoms which attend some less mature essays in others, justify a hope that the obstacles to the growth of this species of industry are less formidable than they were apprehended to be, and that it is not difficult to find, in its further extension, a full indemnification for any external disadvantages, which are or may be experienced, as well as an accession of resources, favorable to national independence and safety.

There are still, nevertheless, respectable patrons of opinions unfriendly to the encouragement of manufactures. The following are, substantially, the arguments by which these opinions are defended:

"In every country (say those who entertain them) agriculture is the most beneficial and productive object of human industry. This position, generally if not universally true, applies with peculiar emphasis to the United States, on account of their immense tracts of fertile territory, uninhabited and unimproved. Nothing can afford so advantageous an employment for capital and labor, as the conversion of this extensive wilderness into cultivated farms. Nothing, equally with this, can contribute to the population, strength, and real riches of the country.

"To endeavor, by the extraordinary patronage of government, to accelerate the growth of manufactures, is, in fact, to endeavor, by force and art, to transfer the natural current of industry from a more to a less beneficial channel. Whatever has such a tendency, must necessarily be unwise; indeed, it can hardly ever be wise in a government to attempt to give a direction to the industry of its citizens. This, under the quick-sighted guidance of private interest, will, if left to itself, infallibly find its own way to the most profitable employment; and it is by such employment, that the public prosperity will be most effectually promoted. To leave industry to itself, therefore, is, in almost every case, the soundest as well as the simplest policy.

"This policy is not only recommended to the United States, by considerations which affect all nations; it is, in a manner, dictated to them by the imperious force of a very peculiar situation. The smallness of their population compared with their territory; the constant allurements to emigration from the settled to the unsettled parts of the country; the facility with which the less independent condition of an artisan can be exchanged for the more independent condition of a farmer;—these, and similar causes, conspire to produce, and, for a length of time, must continue to occasion, a scarcity of hands for manufacturing occupation, and dearness of labor generally. To these disadvantages for the prosecution of manufactures, a deficiency of pecuniary capital being added, the prospect of a successful competition with the manufactures of Europe, must be regarded as little less than desperate. Extensive manufactures can only be the offspring of a redundant, at least of a full, population. Till the latter shall characterize the situation of this country, 't is vain to hope for the former.

"If, contrary to the natural course of things, an unseasonable and premature spring can be given to certain fabrics, by heavy duties, prohibitions, bounties, or by other forced expedients, this will only be to sacrifice the interests of the community to those of particular classes. Besides the misdirection of labor, a virtual monopoly will be given to the persons employed on such fabrics; and an enhancement of price, the inevitable consequence of every monopoly, must be defrayed at the expense of the other parts of society. It is far preferable, that those persons should be engaged in the cultivation of the earth, and that we should procure, in exchange for its productions, the commodities with which foreigners are able to supply us in greater perfection and upon better terms."

This mode of reasoning is founded upon facts and principles which have certainly respectable pretensions. If it had governed the conduct of nations more generally than it has done, there is room to suppose that it might have carried them faster to prosperity and greatness than they have attained by the pursuit of maxims too widely opposite. Most general theories, however, admit of numerous exceptions, and there are few, if any, of the political kind, which do not blend a considerable portion of error with the truths they inculcate.

I. In order to make an accurate judgment how far that which has been just stated ought to be deemed liable to a similar imputation, it is necessary to advert carefully to the considerations which plead in favor of manufactures, and which appear to recommend the special and positive encouragement of them in certain cases and under certain reasonable limitations.

It ought readily be conceded that the cultivation of the earth, as the primary and most certain source of national supply, as the immediate and chief source of subsistence to a man, as the principal source of those materials which constitute the nutriment of other kinds of labor, as including a state most favorable to the freedom and independence of the human mind—one, perhaps, most conducive to the multiplication of the human species, has intrinsically a strong claim to pre-eminence over every other kind of industry.

But, that it has a title to any thing like an exclusive predilection, in any country, ought to be admitted with great caution; that it is even more productive than every other branch of industry, requires more evidence than has yet been given in support of the position. That its real interests, precious and important as, without the help of exaggeration, they truly are, will be advanced, rather than injured, by the due encouragement of manufactures, may, it is believed, be satisfactorily demonstrated. And it is also believed that the expediency of such encouragement, in a general view, may be shown to be recommended by the most cogent and persuasive motives of national policy.

It has been maintained that agriculture is not only the most productive, but the only productive, species of industry. The reality of this suggestion in either respect, has, however, not been verified by any accurate detail of facts and calculations; and the general arguments which are adduced to prove it, are rather subtle and paradoxical, than solid or convincing.

Those which maintain its exclusive productiveness are to this effect:

Labor bestowed upon the cultivation of land produces enough not only to replace all the necessary expenses incurred in the business, and to maintain the persons who are employed in it, but to afford, together with the ordinary profit on the stock or capital of the farmer, a net surplus or rent for the landlord or proprietor of the soil. But the labor of artificers does nothing more than to replace the stock which employs them (or which furnishes materials, tools, and wages), and yields the ordinary profit upon that stock. It yields nothing equivalent to the rent of land; neither does it add any thing to the total value of the whole annual produce of the land and labor of the country. The additional value given to those parts of the produce of land which are wrought into manufactures, is counterbalanced by the value of those other parts of that produce which are consumed by the manufacturers. It can, therefore, only be by saving or parsimony, not by the positive productiveness of their labor, that the classes of artificers can, in any degree, augment the revenue of the society.

To this it has been answered:

1. "That, inasmuch as it is acknowledged that manufacturing labor re-produces a value equal to that which is expended or consumed in carrying it on, and continues in existence the original stock or capital employed, it ought, on that account, alone, to escape being considered as wholly unproductive. That, though it should be admitted, as alleged, that the consumption of the produce of the soil, by the classes of artificers or manufacturers, is exactly equal to the value added by their labor to the materials upon which it is exerted, yet it would not thence follow that it added nothing to the revenue of the society, or to the aggregate value of the annual produce of its land and labor. If the consumption, for any given period, amounted to a given sum, and the increased value of the produce manufactured, in the same period, to a like sum, the total amount of the consumption and production, during that period, would be equal to the two sums, and consequently double the value of the agricultural produce consumed; and though the increment of value produced by the classes of artificers should, at no time, exceed the value of the produce of the land consumed by them, yet there would be, at every moment, in consequence of their labor, a greater value of goods in the market than would exist independent of it."

2. "That the position, that artificers can augment the revenue of a society only by parsimony, is true in no other sense than in one which is equally applicable to husbandmen or cultivators. It may be alike affirmed of all these classes, that the fund acquired by their labor, and destined for their support, is not, in an ordinary way, more than equal to it. And hence it will follow that augmentations of the wealth or capital of the community (except in the instances of some extra-

ordinary dexterity or skill) can only proceed, with respect to any of them, from the savings of the more thrifty and parsimonious."

3. "That the annual produce of the land and labor of a country can only be increased in two ways—by some improvement in the productive powers of the useful labor which actually exists within it, or by some increase in the quantity of such labor. That, with regard to the first, the labor of artificers being capable of greater subdivision and simplicity of operation than that of cultivators, it is susceptible, in a proportionable greater degree of improvement in its productive powers whether to be derived from an accession of skill or from the application of ingenious machinery, in which particular, therefore, the labor employed in the culture of land can pretend to no advantage over that engaged in manufactures. That, with regard to an augmentation of the quantity of useful labor, this, excluding adventitious circumstances, must depend essentially upon an increase of capital, which again must depend upon the savings made out of the revenues of those who furnish or manage that which is at any time employed, whether in agriculture or in manufactures, or in any other way."

But while the exclusive productiveness of agricultural labor has been denied and refuted, the superiority of its productiveness has been conceded without hesitation. As this concession involves a point of considerable magnitude, in relation to maxims of public administration, the grounds on which it rests are worthy of a distinct and particular examination.

One of the arguments made use of in support of the idea may be pronounced both quaint and superficial. It amounts to this: That in the productions of the soil, nature cooperates with man, and that the effect of their joint labor must be greater than that of the labor of man alone.

This, however, is far from being a necessary inference. It is very conceivable that the labor of man alone, laid out upon a work requiring great skill and art to bring it to perfection, may be more productive, in value, than the labor of nature and man combined, when directed towards more simple operations and objects; and when it is recollected to what an extent the agency of nature, in the application of the mechanical powers, is made auxiliary to the prosecution of manufactures, the suggestion which has been noticed loses even the appearance of plausibility.

It might also be observed, with a contrary view, that the labor employed in agriculture is, in a great measure, periodical and occasional, depending on seasons, and liable to various and long intermissions; while that occupied in many manufactures is constant and regular, extending through the year, embracing, in some instances, night as well as day. It is also probable that there are, among the cultivators of land, more examples of remissness than among artificers. The farmer, from the peculiar fertility of his land, or some other favorable circumstance, may frequently obtain a livelihood, even with a considerable degree of carelessness in the mode of cultivation; but the artisan can with difficulty effect the same object, without exerting himself pretty equally with all those who are engaged in the same pursuit. And if it may likewise be assumed as a fact, that manufactures open a wider field to exertions of ingenuity than agriculture, it would not be a strained conjecture, that the labor employed in the former, being at once more constant, more uniform, and more ingenious, than that which is employed in the latter, will be found, at the same time, more productive.

But it is not meant to lay stress on observations of this nature; they ought only to serve as a counterbalance to those of a similar complexion. Circumstances so vague and general, as well as so abstract, can afford little instruction in a matter of this kind.

Another, and that which seems to be the principal argument offered for the superior productiveness of agricultural labor, turns upon the allegation, that labor employed on manufactures yields nothing equivalent to the rent of land, or to that net surplus, as it is called, which accrues to the proprietor of the soil.

But this distinction, important as it has been deemed, appears rather verbal than substantial.

It is easily discernable, that what, in the first instance, is divided into two parts, under the denominations of the ordinary profit of the stock of the farmer and rent to the landlord, is, in the second instance united under the general appellation of the ordinary profit on the stock of the undertaker; and that this formal or verbal distribution constitutes the whole difference in the two cases. It seems to have been overlooked, that the land is itself a stock or capital, advanced or lent by its owner to the occupier or tenant, and that the rent he receives is only the ordinary profit of a certain stock in land, not managed by the proprietor himself, but by another, to whom he lends or lets it, and who, on his part, advances a second capital, to stock and improve the land, upon which he also receives the usual profit. The rent of the landlord and the profit of the farmer are, therefore, nothing more than the ordinary profits of two capitals belonging to two different persons, and united in the cultivation of a farm; as, in the other case, the surplus which arises upon any manufactory, after replacing the expenses of carrying it on, answers to the ordinary profits of one or more capitals engaged in the prosecution of such manufactory. It is said one or more capitals, because, in fact, the same thing which is contemplated in the case of the farm, sometimes happens in that of a manufactory. There is one who furnishes a part of the capital or lends a part of the money by which it is carried on, and another who carries it on with the addition of his own capital. Out of the surplus which remains after defraying expenses, an interest is paid to the money-lender, for the portion of the capital furnished by him, which exactly agrees with the rent paid to the landlord; and the residue of that surplus constitutes the profit of the undertaker or manufacturer, and agrees with what is denominated the ordinary profits on the stock of the farmer. Both together make the ordinary profits of two capitals employed in a manufactory; as, in the other case, the rent of the landlord and the revenue of the farmer compose the ordinary profits of two capitals employed in the cultivation of a farm.

The rent, therefore, accruing to the proprietor of the land, far from being a criterion of exclusive productiveness, as has been argued, is no criterion even of superior productiveness. The question must still be, whether the surplus, after defraying expenses, of a given capital, employed in the purchase and improvement of a piece of land, is greater or less than that of a like capital, employed in the prosecution of a manufactory; or whether the whole value produced from a given capital and a given quantity of labor, employed in one way, be greater or less than the whole value produced from an equal capital and an equal quantity of labor, employed in the other way; or rather, perhaps, whether the business of agriculture, or that of manufactures, will yield the greater product, according to a compound ratio of the quantity of the capital and the quantity of labor which are employed in the one or in the other.

The solution of either of these questions is not easy; it involves numerous and complicated details, depending on an accurate knowledge of the objects to be compared. It is not known that the comparison has ever yet been made upon sufficient data, properly ascertained and analyzed. To be able to make it, on the present occasion, with satisfactory precision, would demand more previous inquiry and investigation than there has been hitherto either leisure or opportunity to accomplish.

Some essays, however, have been made towards acquiring the requisite information, which have rather served to throw doubt upon, than to confirm, the hypothesis under examination. But it ought to be acknowledged that they have been too little diversified, and are too imperfect to authorize a definite conclusion either way; leading rather to probable conjecture than to certain deduction. They render it probable that there are various branches of manufactures, in which a given capital will yield a greater total product, and a considerably greater net product, than an equal capital invested in the purchase and improvement of lands; and that there are also some branches, in which both the gross and the net product will exceed that of the agricultural industry, according to a compound ratio of capital and labor. But it is on this last point that there appears to be the greatest room for doubt. It is far less difficult to infer generally, that the net produce of capital engaged in manufacturing enterprises is greater than that of capital engaged in agriculture.

The foregoing suggestions are not designed to inculcate an opinion that manufacturing industry is more productive than that of agriculture. They are intended rather to show that the reverse of this proposition is not ascertained; that the general arguments which are brought to establish it are not satisfactory; and, consequently, that a supposition of the superior productiveness of tillage ought to be no obstacle to listening to any substantial inducements to the encouragement of manufactures, which may be otherwise perceived to exist, through an apprehension that they may have a tendency to divert labor from a more to a less profitable employment.

It is extremely probable that, on a full and accurate development of the matter, on the ground of fact and calculation, it would be discovered that there is no material difference between the aggregate productiveness of the one and of the other kind of industry; and that the propriety of the encouragements which may, in any case, be proposed to be given to either, ought to be determined upon considerations irrelative to any comparison of that nature.

II. But, without contending for the superior productiveness of manufacturing industry, it may conduce to a better judgment of the policy which ought to be pursued respecting its encouragement, to contemplate the subject under some additional aspects, tending not only to confirm the idea that this kind of industry has been improperly represented as unproductive in itself, but to evince, in addition, that the establishment and diffusion of manufactures have the effect of rendering the total mass of useful and productive labor, in a community, greater than it would otherwise be. In prosecuting this discussion, it may be necessary briefly to resumé and review some of the topics which have been already touched.

To affirm that the labor of the manufacturer is unproductive, because he consumes as much of the produce of land as he adds value to the raw material which he manufactures, is not better founded than it would be to affirm that the labor of the farmer, which furnishes materials to the manufacturer, is unproductive, because he consumes an equal value of manufactured articles. Each furnishes a certain portion of the produce of his labor to the other, and each destroys a corresponding portion of the produce of the labor of the other. In the meantime, the maintenance of two citizens, instead of one, is going on; the State has two members instead of one; and they, together, consume twice the value of what is produced from the land.

If, instead of a farmer and artificer, there were a farmer only, he would be under the necessity of devoting a part of his labor to the fabrication of clothing and other articles, which he would procure of the artificer, in the case of there being such a person; and of course he would be able to devote less labor to the cultivation of his farm, and would draw from it a proportionately less product. The whole quantity of production, in this state of things, in provisions, raw materials, and manufactures, would certainly not exceed in value the amount of what would be produced in provisions and raw materials only, if there were an artificer as well as a farmer.

Again, if there were both an artificer and a farmer, the latter would be left at liberty to pursue exclusively the cultivation of his farm. A greater quantity of provisions and raw materials would, of course, be produced, equal, at least, as has been already observed, to the whole amount of the provisions, raw materials, and manufactures, which would exist on a contrary supposition. The artificer, at the same time, would be going on in the production of manufactured commodities, to an amount sufficient, not only to repay the farmer, in those commodities, for the provisions and materials which were procured from him, but to furnish the artificer himself with a supply of similar commodities for his own use. Thus, then, there would be two quantities or values in existence, instead of one; and the revenue and consumption would be double, in one case, what it would be in the other.

If, in place of both of these suppositions, there were supposed to be two farmers and no artificer, each of whom applied a part of his labor to the culture of land and another part to the fabrication of manufactures; in this case, the portion of the labor of both, bestowed upon land, would produce the same quantity of provisions and raw materials only, as would be produced by the entire sum of the labor of one, applied in the same manner; and the portion of the labor of both, bestowed upon manufactures, would produce the same quantity of manufactures only, as would be produced by the entire sum of the labor of one, applied in the same manner. Hence, the produce of the labor of the two farmers would not be greater than the produce of the labor of the farmer and artificer; and hence it results, that the labor of the artificer is as positively productive as that of the farmer, and as positively augments the revenue of the society.

The labor of the artificer replaces to the farmer that portion of his labor with which he provides the materials of exchange with the artificer, and which he would otherwise have been compelled to apply to manufactures; and while the artificer thus enables the farmer to enlarge his stock of agricultural industry, a portion of which he purchases for his own use, he also supplies himself with the manufactured articles of which he stands in need. He does still more. Besides this equivalent, which he gives for the portion of agricultural labor consumed by him, and this supply of manufactured commodities for his own consumption, he furnishes still a surplus which compensates for the use of the capital advanced, either by himself or some other person, for carrying on the business. This is the ordinary profit of the stock employed in the manufactory, and is, in every sense, as effective an addition to the income of the society as the rent of land.

The produce of the labor of the artificer, consequently, may be regarded as composed of three parts: one, by which the provisions for his subsistence and the materials for his work are purchased of the farmer; one, by which he supplies himself with manufactured necessaries; and a third, which constitutes the profit on the stock employed. The two last portions seem to have been overlooked in the system which represents manufacturing industry as barren and unproductive.

In the course of the preceding illustrations, the products of equal quantities of the labor of the farmer and artificer have been treated as if equal to each other. But this is not to be understood as intending to assert any such precise equality. It is merely a manner of expression, adopted for the sake of simplicity and perspicuity. Whether the value of the produce of the labor of the farmer be somewhat more or less than that of the artificer, is not material to the main scope of the argument, which, hitherto, has only aimed at showing that the one, as well as the other, occasions a positive augmentation of the total produce and revenue of the society. . . .

10. MARSHALL
Judicial Review of National Laws

John Marshall (1755–1835), fourth Chief Justice of the United States, was appointed by President John Adams in 1801, in the waning days of the outgoing Adams administration. The Supreme Court had been a minor part of the national government until Marshall arrived to take its leadership. No jurist has left so deep an imprint on American law. During his lengthy term (1801–1835) most of the major Constitutional questions which were decided by the Marshall Court favored the nation over the states and private property against its detractors. Marshall had also served as special envoy to France, Congressman from Virginia, and President Adams' Secretary of State. At his death on July 6, 1835, the Liberty Bell inexplicably cracked as it was being rung in mourning.

William Marbury was appointed justice of the peace for the District of Columbia in 1801 as a last-minute gesture by President John Adams, who sought to place members of the defeated Federalist Party in the federal courts. Marbury's commission to the post had been signed and sealed but not delivered, and the incoming Secretary of State, James Madison, refused to deliver his commission. As a result, Marbury sued under Section 13 of the Judiciary Act of 1789, applying to the Supreme Court for a writ of mandamus, which would have required Madison to deliver Marbury's commission. John Marshall, as Chief Justice of the Supreme Court, wrote an opinion in which Marbury's claim was denied but a greater victory was subtly obtained—the assertion for the first time by the Court of its possession of the power to declare an act of Congress unconstitutional. Careful reading is necessary to grasp the ingenious reasoning of Chief Justice Marshall.*

. . . This, then, is a plain case for a *mandamus*, either to deliver the commission, or a copy of it from the record; and it only remains to be inquired, whether it can issue from this court?

The act to establish the judicial courts of the United States authorizes

---

* Marbury v. Madison 1 Cranch 137, 173–80 (1803).

the supreme court, "to issue writs of *mandamus*, in cases warranted by the principles and usages of law, to any courts appointed or persons holding office, under the authority of the United States." The secretary of state, being a person holding an office under the authority of the United States, is precisely within the letter of this description; and if this court is not authorized to issue a writ of *mandamus* to such an officer, it must be because the law is unconstitutional, and therefore, absolutely incapable of conferring the authority, and assigning the duties which its words purport to confer and assign.

The constitution vests the whole judicial power of the United States in one supreme court, and such inferior courts as congress shall, from time to time, ordain and establish. This power is expressly extended to all cases arising under the laws of the United States; and consequently, in some form, may be exercised over the present case; because the right claimed is given by a law of the United States.

In the distribution of this power, it is declared, that "the supreme court shall have original jurisdiction, in all cases affecting ambassadors, other public ministers and consuls, and those in which a state shall be a party. In all other cases, the supreme court shall have appellate jurisdiction." It has been insisted, at the bar, that as the original grant of jurisdiction to the supreme and inferior courts, is general, and the clause, assigning original jurisdiction to the supreme court, contains no negative or restrictive words, the power remains to the legislature, to assign original jurisdiction to that court, in other cases than those specified in the article which has been recited; provided those cases belong to the judicial power of the United States.

If it had been intended to leave it in the discretion of the legislature, to apportion the judicial power between the supreme and inferior courts, according to the will of that body, it would certainly have been useless to have proceeded further than to have defined the judicial power, and the tribunals in which it should be vested. The subsequent part of the section is mere surplusage—is entirely without meaning, if such is to be the construction. If congress remains at liberty to give this court appellate jurisdiction, where the constitution has declared their jurisdiction shall be original; and original jurisdiction where the constitution has declared it shall be appellate; the distribution of jurisdiction, made in the constitution, is form without substance. Affirmative words are often, in their operation, negative of other objects than those affirmed;

and in this case, a negative or exclusive sense must be given to them, or they have no operation at all.

It cannot be presumed, that any clause in the constitution is intended to be without effect; and therefore, such a construction is inadmissible, unless the words require it. If the solicitude of the convention, respecting our peace with foreign powers, induced a provision that the supreme court should take original jurisdiction in cases which might be supposed to affect them; yet the clause would have proceeded no further than to provide for such cases, if no further restriction on the powers of congress had been intended. That they should have appellate jurisdiction in all other cases, with such exceptions as congress might make, is no restriction; unless the words be deemed exclusive of original jurisdiction.

When an instrument organizing, fundamentally, a judicial system, divides it into one supreme, and so many inferior courts as the legislature may ordain and establish; then enumerates its powers, and proceeds so far to distribute them, as to define the jurisdiction of the supreme court, by declaring the cases in which it shall take original jurisdiction, and that in others it shall take appellate jurisdiction, the plain import of the words seems to be, that in one class of cases, its jurisdiction is original, and not appellate; in the other, it is appellate, and not original. If any other construction would render the clause inoperative, that is an additional reason for rejecting such other construction, and for adhering to their obvious meaning. To enable this court, then, to issue a *mandamus*, it must be shown to be an exercise of appellate jurisdiction, or to be necessary to enable them to exercise appellate jurisdiction.

It has been stated at the bar, that the appellate jurisdiction may be exercised in a variety of forms, and that if it be the will of the legislature that a *mandamus* should be used for that purpose, that will must be obeyed. This is true, yet the jurisdiction must be appellate, not original. It is the essential criterion of appellate jurisdiction, that it revises and corrects the proceedings in a cause already instituted, and does not create that cause. Although, therefore, a *mandamus* may be directed to courts, yet to issue such a writ to an officer, for the delivery of a paper, is, in effect, the same as to sustain an original action for that paper, and therefore, seems not to belong to appellate, but to original jurisdiction. Neither is it necessary in such a case as this, to enable the court to exercise its appellate jurisdiction. The authority, therefore, given to the supreme court by the act establishing the judicial courts of the United States, to issue writs of *mandamus* to public officers, appears not to be warranted by the constitution; and it becomes necessary to inquire, whether a jurisdiction so conferred can be exercised.

The question, whether an act, repugnant to the constitution, can become the law of the land, is a question deeply interesting to the United States; but, happily, not of an intricacy proportioned to its interest. It seems only necessary to recognise certain principles, supposed to have been long and well established, to decide it. That the people have an original right to establish, for their future government, such principles as, in their opinion, shall most conduce to their own happiness, is the basis on which the whole American fabric has been erected. The exercise of this original right is a very great exertion; nor can it, nor ought it, to be frequently repeated. The principles, therefore, so established, are deemed fundamental: and as the authority from which they proceed is supreme, and can seldom act, they are designed to be permanent.

This original and supreme will organizes the government, and assigns to different departments their respective powers. It may either stop here, or establish certain limits not to be transcended by those departments. The government of the United States is of the latter description. The powers of the legislature are defined and limited; and that those limits may not be mistaken or forgotten, the constitution is written. To what purpose are powers limited, and to what purpose is that limitation committed to writing, if these limits may, at any time, be passed by those intended to be restrained? The distinction between a government with limited and unlimited powers is abolished, if those limits do not confine the persons on whom they are imposed, and if acts prohibited and acts allowed, are of equal obligation. It is a proposition too plain to be contested, that the constitution controls any legislative act repugnant to it; or that the legislature may alter the constitution by an ordinary act.

Between these alternatives, there is no middle ground. The constitution is either a superior paramount law, unchangeable by ordinary means, or it is on a level with ordinary legislative acts, and, like other acts, is alterable when the legislature shall please to alter it. If the former part of the alternative be true, then a legislative act, contrary to the constitution, is not law: if the latter part be true, then written constitutions are absurd attempts, on the part of the people, to limit a power, in its own nature, illimitable.

Certainly, all those who have framed written constitutions contemplate them as forming the fundamental and paramount law of the nation, and consequently, the theory of every such government must be, that an act of the legislature, repugnant to the constitution, is void. This theory is essentially attached to a written constitution, and is, consequently, to be considered, by this court, as one of the fundamental principles of our society. It is not, therefore, to be lost sight of, in the further consideration of this subject.

If an act of the legislature, repugnant to the constitution, is void, does it, notwithstanding its invalidity, bind the courts, and oblige them to give it effect? Or, in other words, though it be not law, does it constitute a rule as operative as if it was a law? This would be to overthrow, in fact, what was established in theory; and would seem, at first view, an absurdity too gross to be insisted on. It shall, however, receive a more attentive consideration.

It is, emphatically, the province and duty of the judicial department, to say what the law is. Those who apply the rule to particular cases, must of necessity expound and interpret that rule. If two laws conflict with each other, the courts must decide on the operation of each. So, if a law be in opposition to the constitution; if both the law and the constitution apply to a particular case, so that the court must either decide that case, conformable to the law, disregarding the constitution; or conformable to the constitution, disregarding the law; the court must determine which of these conflicting rules govern the case: this is of the very essence of judicial duty. If then, the courts are to regard the constitution, and the constitution is superior to any ordinary act of the legislature, the constitution, and not such ordinary act, must govern the case to which they both apply.

Those, then, who controvert the principle, that the constitution is to be considered, in court, as a paramount law, are reduced to the necessity of maintaining that courts must close their eyes on the constitution, and see only the law. This doctrine would subvert the very foundation of all written constitutions. It would declare that an act which, according to the principles and theory of our government, is entirely void, is yet, in practice, completely obligatory. It would declare, that if the legislature shall do what is expressly forbidden, such act, notwithstanding the express prohibition, is in reality effectual.

It would be giving to the legislature a practical and real omnipotence, with the same breath which professes to restrict their powers within narrow limits. It is prescribing limits, and declaring that those limits may be passed at pleasure. That it thus reduces to nothing, what we have deemed the greatest improvement on political institutions, a written constitution, would, of itself, be sufficient, in America, where written constitutions have been viewed with so much reverence, for rejecting the construction. But the peculiar expressions of the constitution of the United States furnish additional arguments in favor of its rejection. The judicial power of the United States is extended to all cases arising under the constitution. Could it be the intention of those who gave this power, to say, that in using it, the constitution should not be looked into? That a case arising under the constitution should be decided, without examining the instrument under which it arises? This is too extravagant to be maintained. In some cases, then, the constitution must be looked into by the judges. And if they can open it at all, what part of it are they forbidden to read or to obey?

There are many other parts of the constitution which serve to illustrate this subject. It is declared, that "no tax or duty shall be laid on articles exported from any state." Suppose, a duty on the export of cotton, of tobacco or of flour; and a suit instituted to recover it. Ought judgment to be rendered in such a case? ought the judges to close their eyes on the constitution, and only see the law?

The constitution declares "that no bill of attainder or *ex post facto* law shall be passed." If, however, such a bill should be passed, and a person should be prosecuted under it; must the court condemn to death those victims whom the constitution endeavors to preserve?

"No person," says the constitution, "shall be convicted of treason, unless on the testimony of two witnesses to the same *overt* act, or on confession in open court." Here, the language of the constitution is addressed especially to the courts. It prescribes, directly for them, a rule of evidence not to be departed from. If the legislature should change that rule, and declare one witness, or a confession out of court, sufficient for conviction, must the constitutional principle yield to the legislative act?

From these, and many other selections which might be made, it is apparent, that the framers of the constitution contemplated that instrument as a rule for the government of courts, as well as of the legislature. Why otherwise does it direct the judges to take an oath to support it? This oath certainly applies in an especial manner, to their conduct in their official character. How immoral to impose it on them, if they were to be used as the instruments, and the knowing instruments, for violating what they swear to support!

The oath of office, too, imposed by the legislature, is completely demonstrative of the legislative opinion on this subject. It is in these words: "I do solemnly swear, that I will administer justice, without respect to persons, and do equal right to the poor and to the rich; and I will faithfully and impartially discharge all the duties incumbent on me as ———, according to the best of my abilities and understanding, agreeably to the constitution and laws of the United States." Why does a judge swear to discharge his duties agreeably to the constitution of the United States, if that constitution forms no rule for his government? if it is closed upon him, and cannot be inspected by him? If such be the real state of things, this is worse than solemn mockery. To prescribe, or to take this oath, becomes equally a crime.

It is also not entirely unworthy of observation, that in declaring what shall be the supreme law of the land, the constitution itself is first mentioned; and not the laws of the United States, generally, but those only which shall be made in pursuance of the constitution, have that rank.

Thus, the particular phraseology of the constitution of the United States confirms and strengthens the principle, supposed to be essential to all written constitutions, that a law repugnant to the constitution is void; and that courts, as well as other departments, are bound by that instrument.

The rule must be discharged.

11. MARSHALL

Judicial Review and the States

A Virginia state statute forbade the selling of lottery tickets. The defendants claimed the protection of an act of Congress which authorized a lottery for the District of Columbia. After being convicted in a state court, the defendants appealed to the Supreme Court of the United States under the Judiciary Act of 1789. Counsel for the State of Virginia denied that the Supreme Court had a right to review decisions of state courts. In this important 1821 case, John Marshall carefully defined the extent of federal judicial power and ably defended the right of the Supreme Court to review decisions of state tribunals.*

. . . 2d. The second objection to the jurisdiction of the court is, that its appellate power cannot be exercised, in any case, over the judgment of a state court.

This objection is sustained chiefly by arguments drawn from the supposed total separation of the judiciary of a state from that of the Union, and their entire independence of each other. The argument considers the federal judiciary as completely foreign to that of a state; and as being no more connected with it, in any respect whatever, than the court of a foreign state. If this hypothesis be just, the argument founded on it is equally so; but if the hypothesis be not supported by the constitution, the argument fails with it.

This hypothesis is not founded on any words in the constitution, which might seem to countenance it, but on the unreasonableness of giving a contrary construction to words which seem to require it; and on the incompatibility of the application of the appellate juris-diction to the judgments of state courts, with that constitutional relation which subsists between the government of the Union and the governments of those states which compose it.

* Cohens v. Virginia, 6 Wheaton 264, 413–23 (1821).

Let this unreasonableness, this total incompatibility, be examined.

That the United States form, for many, and for most important purposes, a single nation, has not yet been denied. In war, we are one people. In making peace, we are one people. In all commercial regulations, we are one and the same people. In many other respects, the American people are one; and the government which is alone capable of controlling and managing their interests in all these respects, is the government of the Union. It is their government, and in that character they have no other. America has chosen to be, in many respects, and to many purposes, a nation; and for all these purposes, her government is complete; to all these objects, it is competent. The people have declared, that in the exercise of all powers given for these objects it is supreme. It can, then, in effecting these objects, legitimately control all individuals or governments within the American territory. The constitution and laws of a state, so far as they are repugnant to the constitution and laws of the United States, are absolutely void. These states are constituent parts of the United States. They are members of one great empire—for some purposes sovereign, for some purposes subordinate.

In a government so constituted, is it unreasonable that the judicial power should be competent to give efficacy to the constitutional laws of the legislature? That department can decide on the validity of the constitution or law of a state, if it be repugnant to the constitution or to a law of the United States. Is it unreasonable that it should also be empowered to decide on the judgment of a state tribunal enforcing such unconstitutional law? Is it so very unreasonable as to furnish a justification for controlling the words of the constitution?

We think it is not. We think that in a government acknowledgedly supreme, with respect to objects of vital interest to the nation, there is nothing inconsistent with sound reason, nothing incompatible with the nature of government, in making all its departments supreme, so far as respects those objects, and so far as is necessary to their attainment. The exercise of the appellate power over those judgments of the state tribunals which may contravene the constitution or laws of the United States, is, we believe, essential to the attainment of those objects.

The propriety of entrusting the construction of the constitution, and laws made in pursuance thereof, to the judiciary of the Union, has not, we believe, as yet, been drawn into question. It seems to be a corollary from this political axiom, that the federal courts should either possess exclusive jurisdiction in such cases, or a power to revise the judgment rendered in them, by the state tribunals. If the federal and state courts have concurrent jurisdiction in all cases arising under the constitution, laws, and treaties of the United States; and if a case of this description brought in a state court cannot be removed before judgment, nor revised after judgment, then the construction of the constitution, laws, and treaties of the United States, is not confided particularly to their judicial department, but is confided equally to that department and to the state courts, however they may be constituted. "Thirteen independent courts," says a very celebrated statesman (and we have now more than twenty such courts), "of final jurisdiction over the same causes, arising upon the same laws, is a hydra in government, from which nothing but contradiction and confusion can proceed."

Dismissing the unpleasant suggestion, that any motives which may not be fairly avowed, or which ought not to exist, can ever influence a state or its courts, the necessity of uniformity, as well as correctness in expounding the constitution and laws of the United States, would itself suggest the propriety of vesting in some single tribunal the power of deciding, in the last resort, all cases in which they are involved.

We are not restrained, then, by the political relations between the general and state governments, from construing the words of the constitution, defining the judicial power, in their true sense. We are not bound to construe them more restrictively than they naturally import.

They give to the Supreme Court appellate jurisdiction in all cases arising under the constitution, laws, and treaties of the United States. The words are broad enough to comprehend all cases of this description, in whatever court they may be decided. In expounding them, we may be permitted to take into view those considerations to which courts have always allowed great weight in the exposition of laws.

The framers of the constitution would naturally examine the state of things existing at the time; and their work sufficiently attests that they did so. All acknowledge that they were convened for the purpose of strengthening the confederation by enlarging the powers of the government, and by giving efficacy to those which it before possessed, but could not exercise. They inform us themselves, in the instrument they presented to the American public, that one of its objects was to form a more perfect union. Under such circumstances, we certainly should not expect to find, in that instrument, a diminution of the powers of the actual government.

Previous to the adoption of the confederation, Congress established courts which received appeals in prize causes decided in the courts of the respective states. This power of the government, to establish tribunals for these appeals, was thought consistent with, and was founded on, its political relations with the states. These courts did exercise appellate jurisdiction over those cases decided in the state courts, to which the judicial power of the federal government extended.

The confederation gave to Congress the power "of establishing courts for receiving and determining finally appeals in all cases of captures."

This power was uniformly construed to authorize these courts to receive appeals from the sentences of state courts, and to affirm or reverse them. State tribunals are not mentioned; but this clause in the confederation necessarily comprises them. Yet the relation between the general and state governments was much weaker, much more lax, under the confederation than under the present constitution; and the states being much more completely sovereign, their institutions were much more independent.

The convention which framed the constitution, on turning their attention to the judicial power, found it limited to a few objects, but exercised, with respect to some of those objects, in its appellate form, over the judgments of the state courts. They extend it, among other objects, to all cases arising under the constitution, laws, and treaties of the United States; and in a subsequent clause declare, that in such cases, the Supreme Court shall exercise appellate jurisdiction. Nothing seems to be given which would justify the withdrawal of a judgment rendered in a state court, on the constitution, laws, or treaties of the United States, from this appellate jurisdiction.

Great weight has always been attached, and very rightly attached, to contemporaneous exposition. No question, it is believed, has arisen to which this principle applies more unequivocally than to that now under consideration.

The opinion of the Federalist has always been considered as of great authority. It is a complete commentary on our constitution; and is appealed to by all parties in the questions to which that instrument has given birth. Its intrinsic merit entitles it to this high rank; and the part two of its authors performed in framing the constitution, put it very much in their power to explain the views with which it was framed. These essays having been published while the constitution was before the nation for adoption or rejection, and having been written in answer to objections founded entirely on the extent of its powers, and on its diminution of state sovereignty, are entitled to the more consideration where they frankly avow that the power objected to is given, and defend it.

In discussing the extent of the judicial power, the Federalist says: "Here another question occurs: what relation would subsist between the national and state courts in these instances of concurrent jurisdiction? I answer, that an appeal would certainly lie from the latter to the Supreme Court of the United States. The constitution in direct terms gives an appellate jurisdiction to the Supreme Court in all the enumerated cases of federal cognizance in which it is not to have an original one, without a single expression to confine its operation to the inferior federal courts. The objects of appeal, not the tribunals from which it is to be made, are alone contemplated. From this circumstance, and from the reason of the thing, it ought to be construed to extend to the state tribunals. Either this must be the case, or the local courts must be excluded from a concurrent jurisdiction in matters of national concern, else the judicial authority of the Union may be eluded at the pleasure of every plaintiff or prosecutor. Neither of these consequences ought, without evident necessity, to be involved; the latter would be entirely inadmissible, as it would defeat some of the most important and avowed purposes of the proposed government, and would essentially embarrass its measures. Nor do I perceive any foundation for such a supposition. Agreeably to the remark already made, the national and state systems are to be regarded as one whole. The courts of the latter will of course be natural auxiliaries to the execution of the laws of the Union, and an appeal from them will as naturally lie to that tribunal which is destined to unite and assimilate the principles of natural justice, and the rules of national decision. The evident aim of the plan of the national convention is, that all the causes of the specified classes shall, for weighty public reasons, receive their original or final determination in the courts of the Union. To confine, therefore, the general expressions which give appellate jurisdiction to the Supreme Court, to appeals from the subordinate federal courts, instead of allowing their extension to the state courts, would be to abridge the latitude of the terms, in subversion of the intent, contrary to every sound rule of interpretation."

A contemporaneous exposition of the constitution, certainly of not less authority than that which has been just cited, is the judiciary act itself. We know that in the Congress which passed that act were many eminent members of the convention which formed the constitution. Not a single individual, so far as is known, supposed that part of the act which gives the Supreme Court appellate jurisdiction over the judgments of the state courts in the cases therein specified, to be unauthorized by the constitution.

While on this part of the argument, it may be also material to observe that the uniform decisions of this court on the point now under consideration, have been assented to, with a single exception, by the courts of every state in the Union whose judgments have been revised. It has been the unwelcome duty of this tribunal to reverse the judgments of many state courts in cases in which the strongest state feelings were engaged. Judges, whose talent and character would grace any bench, to whom a disposition to submit to jurisdiction that is usurped, or to surrender their legitimate powers, will certainly not be imputed, have yielded without hesitation to the authority by which their judgments were reversed, while they, perhaps, disapproved the judgment of reversal.

This concurrence of statesmen, of legislators, and of judges, in the same construction of the constitution, may justly inspire some confidence in that construction.

In opposition to it, the counsel who made this point has presented in a great variety of forms, the idea already noticed, that the federal and state courts must, of necessity, and from the nature of the constitution, be in all things totally distinct and independent of each other. If this court can correct the errors of the courts of Virginia, he says it makes them courts of the United States, or becomes itself a part of the judiciary of Virginia.

But, it has been already shown that neither of these consequences necessarily follows. The American people may certainly give to a national tribunal a supervising power over those judgments of the state courts, which may conflict with the constitution, laws, or treaties of the United States, without converting them into federal courts, or converting the national into a state tribunal. The one court still derives its authority from the state, the other still derives its authority from the nation.

If it shall be established, he says, that this court has appellate jurisdiction over the state courts in all cases enumerated in the 3d article of the constitution, a complete consolidation of the states, so far as respects judicial power, is produced.

But, certainly, the mind of the gentleman who urged this argument is too accurate not to perceive that he has carried it too far; that the premises by no means justify the conclusion. "A complete consolidation of the states, so far as respects the judicial power," would authorize the legislature to confer on the federal courts appellate jurisdiction from the state courts in all cases whatsoever. The distinction between such a power, and that of giving appellate jurisdiction in a few specified cases in the decision of which the nation takes an interest, is too obvious not to be perceived by all.

This opinion has been already drawn out to too great a length to admit of entering into a particular consideration of the various forms in which the counsel who made this point has, with much ingenuity, presented his argument to the court. The argument in all its forms is essentially the same. It is founded, not on the words of the constitution, but on its spirit, a spirit extracted, not from the words of the instrument, but from his view of the nature of our Union, and of the great fundamental principles on which the fabric stands.

To this argument, in all its forms, the same answer may be given. Let the nature and objects of our Union be considered; let the great fundamental principles, on which the fabric stands, be examined; and we think the result must be, that there is nothing so extravagantly absurd in giving to the court of the nation the power of revising the decisions of local tribunals on questions which affect the nation, as to require that words which import this power should be restricted by a forced construction. . . .

III

Opposition to
Jacksonian Democracy

The theme of equality which Lockean liberals prefer to emphasize has periodically been reasserted by those who profess dislike for the leadership of the privileged or the propertied. The Jeffersonians had raised that cry against the Federalists, and it was revived with a vengeance by Andrew Jackson and his followers as they ushered in an age of the common man in the 1820's and 1830's.

The Jacksonian democracy came almost of necessity out of the broadening of the suffrage in the early decades of the nineteenth century. As more and more people were allowed to vote and as property qualifications were modified or eliminated, a large group of citizens came to expect a direct voice in government.

The word "democracy," which had been almost equivalent to "mob rule" in the previous century, now gained respectability. Yet leading conservatives like Daniel Webster of Massachusetts, Supreme Court Justice Joseph Story, Chancellor James Kent of New York, and John Randolph of Virginia questioned whether the extension of the right of suffrage might not endanger the Lockean right of property and insisted that in a balanced government at least one branch should represent property.

The question of whether the common man could be trusted with the voting privilege was often avoided by conclusions that the suffrage was a right, although neither Locke nor the Constitution had recognized such a claim. The conservatives were, however, fighting a losing battle, although this does not mean that their contention that all men are not entitled to equal political power is invalid.

The fear that extension of the vote would bring with it an assault upon property, and unbalance the delicate mechanism of the Constitution, was soon borne out in Jacksonian practice. The Bank of the United States was destroyed. The political party, an institution unknown to the Constitution and feared by the founding fathers, arose as a vote-catching mechanism. Experienced public servants were cast out of office to be replaced by political appointees indebted to President Jackson, and as has been true of most liberal Presidents, the office of the

Presidency was exalted far above that of the competing branches. Jackson even proposed a constitutional amendment to abolish the electoral college and favored extending the Presidential tenure to one term of six years.

Clearly, the conservatives of the day were placed on the defensive. Many of them lost their positions of eminence in politics. The conservatives who always had preferred a rule by the accomplished minority on behalf of the majority were forced to reexamine their doctrines. Many Northern conservatives turned to the Supreme Court to defend the interests of property. Some retreated from the field in aristocratic distaste for Jackson and his followers, as did literary figures like Ralph Waldo Emerson. Others continued to fight from their safe political bastions—Daniel Webster in the Senate, for example. Southern conservatives tended to retreat into a narrow sectionalism.

The age of Jackson was the first low tide of American conservatism. The formulas of the Federalist period had to be readjusted. In fact, the laissez-faire view of economics which Jackson espoused was later captured by conservatives in their political resurgence after the Civil War.

Alexander Hamilton had envisaged a government which would actively promote the interests of business during the Federalist period. Conservatives of that day accepted government as an active partner in developing the nation. Andrew Jackson, as a President in the liberal tradition of Thomas Jefferson, attacked the alliance of business and government, but, partly as a result of his success, conservatives were converted to the virtues of a laissez-faire policy.

12. KENT

The Argument Against
Universal Suffrage

James Kent (1763–1847) was one of the most famous legal scholars and jurists of the nineteenth century. His *Commentaries on American Law* (1830) is still an outstanding American legal treatise and once was an essential part of all American legal training. Kent was also chancellor of the courts of New York State and a lecturer at Columbia College.

As a politician, James Kent was three times elected to the New York State Assembly. In the legislature and in the New York State Constitutional Convention of 1821 Kent's strong conservatism made him many enemies. He opposed, for example, the abolition of the property qualification for voting in New York. As one friend wrote, Kent fought always "for the rights of the individual as distinguished from those of the people." The following selection* shows Kent's opposition to extension of the suffrage, which he felt should be held only by property owners.

. . . This state has existed for forty-four years under our present constitution, which was formed by those illustrious sages and patriots who adorned the revolution. It has wonderfully fulfilled all the great ends of civil government. During that long period, we have enjoyed in an eminent degree, the blessings of civil and religious liberty. We have had our lives, our privileges, and our property, protected. We have had a succession of wise and temperate legislatures. The code of our statute law has been again and again revised and corrected, and it may proudly bear a comparison with that of any other people. We have

* *Reports of the Proceedings and Debates of the Convention of 1821* (Albany, 1821), pp. 219–22.

had during that period, (though I am, perhaps, not the fittest person to say it) a regular, stable, honest, and enlightened administration of justice. All the peaceable pursuits of industry, and all the important interests of education and science, have been fostered and encouraged. We have trebled our numbers within the last twenty-five years, have displayed mighty resources, and have made unexampled progress in the career of prosperity and greatness.

Our financial credit stands at an enviable height; and we are now successfully engaged in connecting the great lakes with the ocean by stupendous canals, which excite the admiration of our neighbours, and will make a conspicuous figure even upon the map of the United States.

These are some of the fruits of our present government; and yet we seem to be dissatisfied with our condition, and we are engaged in the bold and hazardous experiment of remodelling the constitution. Is it not fit and discreet: I speak as to wise men; is it not fit and proper that we should pause in our career, and reflect well on the immensity of the innovation in contemplation? Discontent in the midst of so much prosperity, and with such abundant means of happiness, looks like ingratitude, and as if we were disposed to arraign the goodness of Providence. Do we not expose ourselves to the danger of being deprived of the blessings we have enjoyed?—When the husbandman has gathered in his harvest, and has filled his barns and his granaries with the fruits of his industry, if he should then become discontented and unthankful, would he not have reason to apprehend, that the Lord of the harvest might come in his wrath, and with his lightning destroy them?

The senate has hitherto been elected by the farmers of the state—by the free and independent lords of the soil, worth at least $250 in freehold estate over and above all debts charged thereon. The governor has been chosen by the same electors, and we have hitherto elected citizens of elevated rank and character. Our assembly has been chosen by free-holders, possessing a freehold of the value of $50, or by persons renting a tenement of the yearly value of $5, and who have been rated and actually paid taxes to the state. By the report before us, we propose to annihilate, at one stroke, all those property distinctions and to bow before the idol of universal suffrage. That extreme democratic principle, when applied to the legislative and executive departments of govern-ment, has been regarded with terror, by the wise men of every age, because in every European republic, ancient and modern, in which it has been tried, it has terminated disastrously, and been productive of corruption, injustice, violence, and tyranny. And dare we flatter ourselves that we are a peculiar people, who can run the career of history, exempted from the passions which have disturbed and corrupted the rest of mankind? If we are like other races of men, with similar follies and vices, then I greatly fear that our posterity will have reason to deplore in sackcloth and ashes, the delusion of the day.

It is not my purpose at present to interfere with the report of the committee, so far as respects the qualifications of electors for governor and members of assembly. I shall feel grateful if we may be permitted to retain the stability and security of a senate, bottomed upon the freehold property of the state. Such a body, so constituted, may prove a sheet anchor amidst the future factions and storms of the republic. The great leading and governing interest of this state, is, at present, the agricultural; and what madness would it be to commit that interest to the winds. The great body of the people, are now the owners and actual cultivators of the soil. With that wholesome population we always expect to find moderation, frugality, order, honesty, and a due sense of independence, liberty, and justice. It is impossible that any people can lose their liberties by internal fraud or violence, so long as the country is parcelled out among freeholders of moderate possessions, and those freeholders have a sure and efficient control in the affairs of the government. Their habits, sympathies, and employments, necessarily inspire them with a correct spirit of freedom and justice; they are the safest guardians of property and the laws. . . .

I wish those who have an interest in the soil, to retain the exclusive possession of a branch in the legislature, as a strong hold in which they may find safety through all the vicissitudes which the state may be destined, in the course of Providence, to experience. I wish them to be always enabled to say that their freeholds cannot be taxed without their consent. The men of no property, together with the crowds of dependents connected with great manufacturing and commercial establishments, and the motley and undefinable population of crowded ports, may, perhaps, at some future day, under skilful management, predominate in the assembly, and yet we should be perfectly safe if no laws could pass without the free consent of the owners of the soil. That security we at present enjoy; and it is that security which I wish to retain.

The apprehended danger from the experiment of universal suffrage

applied to the whole legislative department, is no dream of the imagination. It is too mighty an excitement for the moral constitution of men
to endure. The tendency of universal suffrage, is to jeopardize the
rights of property, and the principles of liberty. There is a constant
tendency in human society, and the history of every age proves it;
there is a tendency in the poor to covet and to share the plunder of the
rich; in the debtor to relax or avoid the obligation of contracts; in the
majority to tyrannize over the minority, and trample down their rights;
in the indolent and the profligate, to cast the whole burthens of society
upon the industrious and the virtuous; and *there is a tendency in
ambitious and wicked men, to inflame these combustible materials.* It
requires a vigilant government, and a firm administration of justice,
to counteract that tendency. . . . Who can undertake to calculate with
any precision, how many millions of people, this great state will contain
in the course of this and the next century, and who can estimate the
future extent and magnitude of our commercial ports? The dispro-
portion between the men of property, and the men of no property, will
be in every society in a ratio to its commerce, wealth, and population.
We are no longer to remain plain and simple republics of farmers, like
the New-England colonists, or the Dutch settlements on the Hudson.
We are fast becoming a great nation, with great commerce, manufactures, population, wealth, luxuries, and with the vices and miseries
that they engender. One seventh of the population of the city of Paris
at this day subsists on charity, and one third of the inhabitants of that
city die in the hospitals; what would become of such a city with universal
suffrage? France has upwards of four, and England upwards of five
millions of manufacturing and commercial labourers without property.
Could these kingdoms sustain the weight of universal suffrage? The
radicals in England, with the force of that mighty engine, would at
once sweep away the property, the laws, and the liberties of that island
like a deluge.

The growth of the city of New-York is enough to startle and awaken
those who are pursuing the *ignis fatuus* of universal suffrage. . . .

It is rapidly swelling into the unwieldy population, and with the
burdensome pauperism, of an European metropolis. New-York is
destined to become the future London of America; and in less than a
century, that city, with the operation of universal suffrage, and under
skilful direction, will govern this state.

The notion that every man that works a day on the road, or serves an idle hour in the militia, is entitled as of right to an equal participation in the whole power of the government, is most unreasonable, and has no foundation in justice. We had better at once discard from the report such a nominal test of merit. If such persons have an equal share in one branch of the legislature, it is surely as much as they can in justice or policy demand. Society is an association for the protection of property as well as of life, and the individual who contributes only one cent to the common stock, ought not to have the same power and influence in directing the property concerns of the partnership, as he who contributes his thousands. He will not have the same inducements to care, and diligence, and fidelity. His inducements and his temptation would be to divide the whole capital upon the principles of an agrarian law.

Liberty, rightly understood, is an inestimable blessing, but liberty without wisdom, and without justice, is no better than wild and savage licentiousness. The danger which we have hereafter to apprehend, is not the want, but the abuse, of liberty. We have to apprehend the oppression of minorities, and a disposition to encroach on private right—to disturb chartered privileges—and to weaken, degrade, and overawe the administration of justice; we have to apprehend the establishment of unequal, and consequently, unjust systems of taxation, and all the mischiefs of a crude and mutable legislation. A stable senate, exempted from the influence of universal suffrage, will powerfully check these dangerous propensities, and such a check becomes the more necessary, since this Convention has already determined to withdraw the watchful eye of the judicial department from the passage of laws. . . .

Universal suffrage once granted, is granted forever, and never can be recalled. There is no retrograde step in the rear of democracy. However mischievous the precedent may be in its consequences, or however fatal in its effects, universal suffrage never can be recalled or checked, but by the strength of the bayonet. We stand, therefore, this moment, on the brink of fate, on the very edge of the precipice. If we let go our present hold on the senate, we commit our proudest hopes and our most precious interests to the waves. . . .

13. WEBSTER

The Principles of the Whig Party

Daniel Webster (1782–1852) is well known for his nationalist and conservative views of the Constitution and for his opposition to the asserted right of the states to resist national laws. He is also interesting, however, because of his attempt to adopt the new style of popular democracy which developed during the era of Jacksonian democracy. The conservative Webster, although obviously an ally of the upper economic classes and of the new merchant class in particular, nevertheless sought to make the Whigs a popular party in the election of 1840. Had it not been for the slavery issue, the Whigs might have survived as a legitimate conservative party with broad popular appeal, but the problem was soon to divide and destroy the party.

The following speech* concerning the principles and purposes of the Whig Party was delivered by Webster on September 10, 1840. The occasion was a general convention of the Whigs of New England, of which Webster was the president.

When men pause from their ordinary occupations, and assemble in great numbers, a proper respect for the judgment of the country and of the age requires that they should clearly set forth the grave causes which have brought them together, and the purposes which they seek to promote.

Feeling the force of this obligation, fifty thousand of the free electors of the New England States, honored also by the presence of like free electors from nearly every other State in the Union, having assembled on Bunker Hill, on this 10th day of September, 1840, proceed to set forth a declaration of their principles, and of the occasion and objects of their meeting.

In the first place, we declare our unalterable attachment to that public liberty, the purchase of so much blood and treasure, in the acquisition

* *The Works of Daniel Webster*, Vol. II (Boston: Charles C. Little and James Brown, 1851), pp. 41–51.

of which the field whereon we stand obtained early and imperishable renown. Bunker Hill is not a spot on which we shall forget the principles of our fathers, or suffer any thing to quench within our own bosoms the love of freedom which we have inherited from them.

In the next place, we declare our warm and hearty devotion to the Constitution of the country, and to that Union of the States which it has so happily cemented, and so long and so prosperously preserved. We call ourselves by no local names, we recognize no geographical divisions, while we give utterance to our sentiments on high constitutional and political subjects. We are Americans, citizens of the United States, knowing no other country, and desiring to be distinguished by no other appellation. We believe the Constitution, while administered wisely and in its proper spirit, to be capable of protecting all parts of the country, securing all interests, and perpetuating a national brotherhood among all the States. We believe that to foment local jealousies, to attempt to prove the existence of opposite interests between one part of the country and another, and thus to disseminate feelings of distrust and alienation, while it is in contemptuous disregard of the counsels of the great father of his country, is but one form in which irregular ambition, destitute of all true patriotism, and a love of power, reckless of the means of its gratification, exhibit their unsubdued and burning desire.

We believe, too, that party spirit, however natural or unavoidable it may be in free republics, yet, when it gains such an ascendancy in men's minds as leads them to substitute party for country, to seek no ends but party ends, no approbation but party approbation, and to fear no reproach or contumely so that there be no party dissatisfaction, not only alloys the true enjoyment of such institutions, but weakens, every day, the foundations on which they stand.

We are in favor of the liberty of speech and of the press; we are friends of free discussion; we espouse the cause of popular education; we believe in man's capacity for self-government; we desire to see the freest and widest dissemination of knowledge and of truth; and we believe, especially, in the benign influence of religious feeling and moral instruction on the social, as well as on the individual, happiness of man.

Holding these general sentiments and opinions, we have come together to declare that, under the present administration of the general government, a course of measures has been adopted and pursued, in our judgments, disastrous to the best interests of the country, threatening the accumulation of still greater evils, utterly hostile to the true spirit of the Constitution and to the principles of civil liberty, and calling upon all men of honest purpose, disinterested patriotism, and unbiased intelligence, to put forth their utmost constitutional efforts in order to effect a change.

General Andrew Jackson was elected President of the United States, and took the oaths of office on the 4th of March, 1829; and we readily admit that, under his administration, certain portions of the public affairs were conducted with ability. But we have to lament that he was not proof against the insinuations and influences of civil counsellors, or perhaps against his own passions, when moved and excited. Hence, in one most important branch of the public interest, in that essential part of commercial regulation which respects the money, the currency, the circulation, and the internal changes of the country, accidental occurrences, acting on his characteristic love of rule, and uneasiness under opposition, led him to depart from all that was expected from him, and to enter upon measures which plunged both him and the country in greater and greater difficulties at every step, so that, in this respect, his whole course of administration was but a series of ill-fated experiments, and of projects framed in disregard of prudence and precedent, and bursting in rapid succession; the final explosion taking place a few months after his retirement from office.

General Jackson was not elected with any desire or expectation, on the part of any of his supporters, that he would interfere with the currency of the country. We affirm this as the truth of history. It is incapable of refutation or denial. It is as certain as that the American Revolution was not undertaken to destroy the rights of property, or overthrow the obligation of morals.

But, unhappily, he became involved in a controversy with the then existing Bank of the United States. He manifested a desire, how originating or by whom inspired is immaterial, to exercise a political influence over that institution, and to cause that institution to exercise, in turn, a political influence over the community. Published documents prove this, as plainly as they prove any other act of his administration. In this desire he was resisted, thwarted, and finally defeated. But what he could not govern, he supposed he could destroy; and the event showed that he did not overrate his popularity and his power. He pursued the bank to the death, and achieved his triumph by the veto of 1832. The accustomed means of maintaining a sound and a uniform currency, for the use of the whole country, having been thus trampled down and destroyed, recourse was had to those new modes of experimental administration, to which we have already adverted, and which terminated so disastrously, both for the reputation of his administration and for the welfare of the country.

But General Jackson did not deny his constitutional obligations, nor seek to escape from their force. He never professedly abandoned all care over the general currency. His whole conduct shows that he admitted, throughout, the duty of the general government to maintain a supervision over the currency of the country, both metallic and paper, for the general good and use of the people; and he congratulated both himself and the nation, that, by the measures adopted by him, the currency and the exchanges of the country were placed on a better footing than they ever had been under the operation of a Bank of the United States. This confidence in his own experiments, we know, proved most illusory. But the frequency with which he repeated this and similar declarations establishes incontestably his own sense of the duty of government.

In all the measures of General Jackson upon the currency, the present chief magistrate is known to have concurred. Like him, he was opposed to the Bank of the United States; like him, he was in favor of the State deposit banks; and, like him, he insisted that, by the aid of such banks, the administration had accomplished all that could be desired on the great subjects of the currency and the exchange.

But the catastrophe of May, 1837, produced a new crisis, by overthrowing the last in the series of experiments, and creating an absolute necessity, either of returning to that policy of the government which General Jackson had repudiated, or of renouncing altogether the constitutional duty which it had been the object of that policy to perform. The latter branch of the alternative was adopted. Refuge was sought in escape. A duty, up to that moment admitted by all, was suddenly denied, and the fearful resolution announced, that government would hereafter provide for its own revenues, and that, for the rest, the people must take care of themselves.

Assembled here to-day, and feeling, in common with the whole country, the evil consequences of these principles and these measures, we pronounce against them all, from first to last, our deep and solemn sentence of condemnation. We condemn the early departure of General

Jackson from that line of policy which he was expected to pursue. We deplore the temper which led him to his original quarrel with the bank. We deplore the headstrong spirit which instigated him to pursue that institution to its destruction. We deplore the timidity of some, the acquiescence of others, and the subserviency of all of his party, which enabled him to carry its whole, unbroken phalanx to the support of measures, and the accomplishment of purposes, which we know to have been against the wishes, the remonstrances, and the consciences of many of the most respectable and intelligent. We deplore his abandonment of those means for assuring a good currency, which had been successfully tried for forty years; his rash experiments with great interests; and the perseverance with which he persisted in them, when men of different temperament must have been satisfied of their uselessness and impotence.

But General Jackson's administration, authority, and influence are now historical. They belong to the past, while we have to do, to-day, with the serious evils, and the still more alarming portents, of the present. We remonstrate, therefore, most earnestly and emphatically, against the policy of the present administration upon this subject. We protest against the truth of its principles. We deny the propriety and justice of its measures. We are constrained to have too little respect for its objects, and we desire to rouse the country, so far as we can, to the evils which oppress and the dangers that surround us.

We insist that the present administration has consulted its own party ends, and the preservation of its own power, to the manifest neglect of great objects of public interest. We think there is no liberality, no political comprehension, no just or enlarged policy, in its leading measures. We look upon its abandonment of the currency as fatal; and we regard its system of sub-treasuries as but a poor device to avoid a high obligation, or as the first in a new series of ruthless experiments. We believe its professions in favor of a hard-money currency to be insincere; because we do not believe that any person of common information and ordinary understanding can suppose that the use of paper, as a circulating medium, will be discontinued, even if such discontinuance were desirable, unless the government shall break down the acknowledged authority of the State governments to establish banks. We believe the clamor against State banks, State bonds, and State credits, to have been raised by the friends of the administration to divert public attention from its own mismanagement and to throw on others the consequence of its own conduct. We heard nothing of all this in the early part of General Jackson's administration, nor until his measures had brought the currency of the country into the utmost disorder. We know that, in times past, the present chief magistrate has, of all men, had most to do with the systems of State banks, the most faith in their usefulness, and no very severely chastened desire to profit by their influence. We believe that the purpose of exercising a money influence over the community has never departed from the administration. What it could not accomplish by an attempt to bend the Bank of the United States to its purposes, we believe it has sought, and now seeks, to effect by its project of the sub-treasury. We believe that, in order to maintain the principles upon which the system of the sub-treasury is founded, the friends of the administration have been led to espouse opinions destructive of the internal commerce of the country, paralyzing to its whole industry, tending to sink its labor, both in price and in character, to the degraded standard of the uninformed, the ignorant, the suffering labor of the worst parts of Europe. Led by the same necessity, or pushing the same principles still farther, and with a kind of revolutionary rapidity, we have seen the rights of property not only assailed, but denied; the boldest agrarian notions put forth; the power of transmission from father to son openly denounced; the right of one to participate in the earnings of another, to the rejection of the natural claims of his own children asserted as a fundamental principle of the new democracy;—and all this by those who are in the pay of government, receiving large salaries, and whose offices would be nearly sinecures but for the labor performed in the attempt to give currency to these principles and these opinions. We believe that the general tone of the measures of the administration, the manner in which it confers favors, its apparent preference for partisans of extreme opinions, and the readiness with which it bestows its confidence on the boldest and most violent, are producing serious injuries upon the political morals and general sentiments of the country. We believe that to this cause is fairly to be attributed the most lamentable change which has taken place in the temper, the sobriety, and the wisdom with which the high public counsels have been hitherto conducted. We look with alarm to the existing state of things, in this respect; and we would most earnestly, and with all our hearts, as well for the honor of the country as for its interests, beseech all good men to unite with us in an attempt to bring back the deliberative age of the government, to restore to the collected bodies of the people's representatives that self-respect, decorum, and dignity, without which the business of legislation can make no regular progress, and is always in danger either of accomplishing nothing, or of reaching its ends by unjustifiable and violent means.

We believe the conduct of the administration respecting the public revenue to be highly reprehensible. It has expended twenty millions, previously accumulated, besides all the accruing income since it came into power; and there seems at this moment to be no doubt, that it will leave to its successors a public debt of from five to ten millions of dollars. It has shrunk from its proper responsibilities. With the immediate prospect of an empty treasury, it has yet not had the manliness to recommend to Congress any adequate provision. It has constantly spoken of the excess of receipts over expenditures, until this excess has finally manifested itself in an absolute necessity for loans, and in a power conferred on the President, altogether new, and in our judgment hostile to the whole spirit of the Constitution, to meet the event of want of resources by withholding, out of certain classes of appropriations made by Congress, such as he chooses to think may be best spared. It lives by shifts and contrivances, by shallow artifices and delusive names, by what it calls "facilities," and the "exchange of treasury notes for specie"; while in truth, it has been fast contracting a public debt, in the midst of all its boasting, without daring to lay the plain and naked truth of the case before the people.

We protest against the conduct of the House of Representatives in the case of the New Jersey election. This is not a local, but a general question. In the union of the States, on whatever link the blow of injustice or usurpation falls, it is felt, and ought to be felt, through the whole chain. The cause of New Jersey is the cause of every State, and every State is therefore bound to vindicate it.

That the regular commission, or certificate of return, signed by the chief magistrate of the State, according to the provisions of law, entitles those who produce it to be sworn in as members of Congress, to vote in the organization of the House, and to hold their seats until their right be disturbed by regular petition and proof, is a proposition of constitutional law, of such universal extent and universal acknowledgment, that it cannot be strengthened by argument or by analogy. There is nothing clearer, and nothing better settled. No legislative body could ever be organized without the adoption of this principle. Yet, in the case of the New Jersey members of Congress, it was entirely disregarded. And it is of awful portent, that on such a question,—a question in its nature strictly judicial,—the domination of party should lead men thus flagrantly to violate first principles. It is the first step that costs. After this open disregard of the elementary rules of law and justice, it should create no surprise that, pending the labors of a committee especially appointed to ascertain who were duly elected, a set of men calling themselves representatives of the people of New Jersey, who had no certificates from the chief magistrate of the State or according to the laws of the State, were voted into their seats, under silence imposed by the previous question, and afterwards gave their votes for the passage of the sub-treasury law. We call most solemnly upon all who, with us, believe that these proceedings alike invade the rights of the States, and dishonor the cause of popular government and free institutions, to supply an efficient and decisive remedy, by the unsparing application of the elective franchise.

We protest against the plan of the administration respecting the training and disciplining of the militia. The President now admits it to be unconstitutional; and it is plainly so, on the face of it, for the training of the militia is by the Constitution expressly reserved to the States. If it were not unconstitutional, it would yet be unnecessary, burdensome, entailing enormous expenses, and placing dangerous powers in executive hands. It belongs to the prolific family of executive projects, and it is a consolation to find that at least one of its projects has been so scorched by public rebuke and reprobation, that no man raises his hand or opens his mouth in its favor.

It was during the progress of the late administration, and under the well-known auspices of the present chief magistrate, that the declaration was made in the Senate, that, in regard to public office, the spoils of victory belong to the conquerors; thus boldly proclaiming, as the creed of the party, that political contests are rightfully struggles for office and emolument. We protest against doctrines which thus regard offices as created for the sake of incumbents, and stimulate the basest passions to the pursuit of high public trusts.

We protest against the repeated instances of disregarding judicial decisions by officers of government, and others enjoying its countenance; thus setting up executive interpretation over the solemn adjudications of courts and juries, and showing marked disrespect for the usual and constitutional interpretation and execution of the laws.

This misgovernment and maladministration would have been the more tolerable, if they had not been committed, in most instances, in direct contradiction to the warmest professions and the most solemn assurances. Promises of a better currency, for example, have ended in the destruction of all national and uniform currency; assurances of the strictest economy have been but preludes to the most wasteful excess; even the Florida war has been conducted under loud pretences of severe frugality; and the most open, unblushing, and notorious interference with State elections has been systematically practised by the paid agents of an administration, which, in the full freshness of its oath of office, declared that one of its leading objects should be, *to accomplish that task of reform which particularly required the correction of those abuses by which the patronage of the federal government was brought into conflict with the freedom of elections.*

In the teeth of this solemn assurance, it has been proved that United States officers have been assessed, in sums bearing proportion to the whole amount they receive from the treasury, for the purpose of supporting their partisans even in State and municipal elections.

Whatever, in short, has been most professed, has been least practised; and it seems to have been taken for granted, that the American people would be satisfied with pretence, and a full-toned assurance of patriotic purpose. The history of the last twelve years has been but the history of broken promises and disappointed hopes. At every successive period of this history, an enchanting, rose-colored futurity has been spread out before the people, especially in regard to the great concerns of revenue, finance, and currency. But these colors have faded, as the object has been approached. Prospects of abundant revenue have resulted in the necessity of borrowing; the brilliant hopes of a better currency end in general derangement, stagnation, and distress; and while the whole country is roused to an unprecedented excitement by the pressure of the times, every state paper from the Cabinet at Washington comes forth fraught with congratulations on that happy state of things which the judicious policy of the administration is alleged to have brought about! Judged by the tone of these papers, every present movement of the people is quite unreasonable, and all attempts at change are only so many ungrateful returns for the wise and successful administration of public affairs!

There is yet another subject of complaint to which we feel bound to advert, by our veneration for the illustrious dead, by our respect for truth, by our love for the honor of our country, and by our own wounded pride as American citizens. We feel that the country has been dishonored, and we desire to free ourselves from all imputation of acquiescence in the parricidal act. The late President, in a communication to Congress, more than intimates that some of the earliest and most important measures of Washington's administration were the offspring of personal motives and private interests. His successor has repeated and extended this accusation, and given to it, we are compelled to say, a greater degree of offensiveness and grossness. No man, with an American heart in his bosom, can endure this without feeling the deepest humiliation, as well as the most burning scorn. The fame of Washington and his immediate associates is one of the richest treasures of the country. His is that name which an American may utter with pride in every part of the world, and which, wherever uttered, is shouted to the skies by the voices of all true lovers of human liberty. Imputations which assail his measures so rudely, while they are abominable violations of the truth of history, are an insult to the country, and an offence against the moral sentiments of civilized mankind. Miserable, miserable indeed, must be that cause which cannot support its party predominance, its ruinous schemes and senseless experiments, without thus attempting to poison the fountains of truth, and prove the government of our country disgracefully corrupt, even in its very cradle. Our hearts would sink within us, if we believed that such efforts could succeed; but they must be impotent. Neither the recent nor the present President was born to cast a shade on the character of Washington or his associates. The destiny of both has been, rather, to illustrate, by contrast, that wisdom and those virtues which they have not imitated, and to hurl blows, which the affectionate veneration of American citizens and the general justice of the civilized world, will render harmless to others, and powerful only in their recoil upon themselves. If this language be strong, so also is that feeling of indignation which has suggested it; and, on an occasion like this, we could not leave this consecrated spot without the consciousness of having omitted an indispensable duty, had we not thus given utterance to the fulness of our hearts, and marked with our severest rebuke and most thorough reprobation and scorn, a labored effort to fix a deep and enduring stain on the early history of the government.

Finally, on this spot, the fame of which began with our liberty, and can only end with it, in the presence of these multitudes, of the whole country, and of the world, we declare our conscientious convictions, that the present administration has proved itself incapable of conducting the public affairs of the nation in such a manner as shall preserve the Constitution, maintain the public liberty, and secure general prosperity. We declare, with the utmost sincerity, that we believe its main purpose to have been, to continue its own power, influence, and popularity; that to this end it has abandoned indispensable, but highly responsible, constitutional duties; that it has trifled with the great concerns of finance and currency; that it has used the most reprehensible means for influencing public opinion; that it has countenanced the application of public money to party purposes; that it endeavors to consolidate and strengthen party by every form of public patronage; that it laboriously seeks to conceal the truth from the people on subjects of great interest; that it has shown itself to be selfish in its ends, and corrupt in its means; and that, if it should be able to maintain itself in power through another term, there is the most imminent danger that it will plunge the country in still further difficulty, bring on still greater disorder and distress, and undermine at once the foundations of the public prosperity and the institutions of the country.

Men thus false to their own professions, false to the principles of the Constitution, false to the interests of the people, and false to the highest honor of their country, are unfit to be the rulers of this republic.

The people of the United States have a right to good government. They have a right to an honest and faithful exercise of all the powers of the Constitution, as understood and practised in the best days of the republic for the general good. They have an inalienable right to all the blessings of that *Liberty* which their fathers achieved, and all the benefits of that *Union* which their fathers established.

And standing here, this day, with the memory of these fathers fresh on our hearts, and with the fields of their glory and the monuments of their fame full in our view, with Bunker Hill beneath us, and Concord, and Lexington, and Dorchester Heights, and Faneuil Hall all around us, we here, as a part of the people, pledge ourselves to each other, and to our country to spare no lawful and honorable efforts to vindicate and maintain these rights, and to remove from the high places of the nation men who have thus contemned and violated them.

And we earnestly and solemnly invoke all good men and true patriots throughout the Union, foregoing all consideration of party, and forgetting all distinction of State or section, to rally once more, as our fathers did in 1775, against the common oppressors of our country, and to unite with us in restoring our glorious Constitution to its true interpretation, its practical administration, and its just supremacy.

In such a cause, principles are every thing; individuals nothing. Yet we cannot forget that we have worthy, honest, capable candidates for the offices from which we hope to remove the present incumbents.

Those who desire a change, throughout the whole country, have agreed, with extraordinary unanimity, to support General William Henry Harrison for the office of President. We believe him to be an honest and faithful citizen, who has served his country successfully, in divers civil trusts; and we believe him a veteran soldier, whose honor and bravery cannot be questioned. We give him our unhesitating confidence; and in that confidence we shall support him, and the distinguished citizen of Virginia who has been nominated for the Vice-Presidency, with all our efforts and all our hearts, through the present contest; convinced that by their election the true spirit of the Constitution will be restored, the prosperity of the people revived, the stability of our free institutions reassured, and the blessings of union and liberty secured to ourselves and our posterity.

14. WEBSTER
Defense of the Protective Tariff

On December 2, 1846, Webster was honored at a public dinner in Philadelphia. In his address, from which this selection* is taken, he expressed opposition to President Polk's politics on the Mexican War and the tariff.

Another great subject of public interest at the present time is the recent tariff, which I discussed when it was established, and about which I have nothing new to say. My object is, and has been, in every thing connected with the protective policy, the true policy of the United States, to see that the labor of the country, the industry of the country, is properly provided for. I am looking, not for a law such as will benefit capitalists,—they can take care of themselves,—but for a law that shall induce capitalists to invest their capital in such a manner as to occupy and employ American labor. I am for such laws as shall induce capitalists not to withhold their capital from actual operations, which give employment to thousands of hands. I look to capital, therefore, in no other view than as I wish it drawn out and used for the public good, and the employment of the labor of the country. . . .

I will only say, that I am for protection, ample, permanent, founded on just principles; and that, in my judgment, the principles of the act of 1842 are the true principles,—*specific* duties, and not *ad valorem* assessment; just discrimination, and, in that just discrimination, great care not to tax the raw material so high as to be a bounty to the foreign manufacturer and an oppression on our own. Discrimination and specific duties, and such duties as are full and adequate to the purposes of protection,—these are the principles of the act of 1842. Whenever there is presented to me any proposition, from any quarter, which

* *The Works of Daniel Webster*, Vol. II (Boston: Charles C. Little and James Brown, 1851), pp. 349–54.

contains adequate protection, founded on those indispensable principles, I shall take it. My object is to obtain in the best way I can, and when I can, and as I can, full and adequate and thorough protection to the domestic industry of the country, upon just principles.

In the next place, I have to say that I will take no part in any tinkering of the present law, while its vicious principles remain. As far as depends upon me, the administration shall not escape its just responsibility, by any pretended amendments of the recent law with a view to particular political interests. Allow me to say, frankly, ye iron men and ye coal men of Pennsylvania, that I know you are incapable of compromising in such a case; but if you were, and any inducements were held out to you to make your iron a little softer, and your coal burn a little clearer, while you left the hand-loom weaver—(The vociferous cheering which burst forth drowned the remainder of the sentence.)

I understand there are seven thousand hand-loom weavers in the city and county of Philadelphia; that their wages have hitherto averaged five dollars a week; that the *ad valorem* duty, as applied to cottons, affects them very injuriously, in its tendency to reduce wages and earnings; especially as the wages of a hand-loom weaver in Scotland hardly exceed one dollar and seventy-five cents or two dollars per week. What the precise result may be, remains to be seen. The carpet-weavers, it is said, may find some indemnity in the reduced price of wool. If this be so, it only shows that the loss is shifted from the weaver to the wool-grower. Washington County, Fayette County, and other counties in this State, will probably learn how this is. In the aggregate it has been estimated that the value of manufactures in the city and county of Philadelphia scarcely falls short of the value of those at Lowell; and their production, it is supposed, employs more hands here than are employed in Lowell.

Gentlemen, on the tariff I have spoken so often and so much, that I am sure no gentleman wishes me to utter the word again. There are some things, however, which cannot be too often repeated. Of all countries in the world, England, for centuries, was the most tenacious in adhering to her protective principles, both in matters of commerce and manufacture. She has of late years relaxed, having found that her position could afford somewhat of free trade. She has the skill acquired by long experience, she has vast machinery, and vast capital, she has a dense population; a cheaply working, because a badly fed and badly clothed, population. She can run her career, therefore, in free trade.

We cannot, unless willing to become badly fed and badly clothed also. Gentlemen, for the gymnastic exercises, men strip themselves naked and for this strife and competition in free trade, our laborers, it seems, must strip themselves naked also.

It is, after all, an insidious system, in a country of diversified arts and attainments, of varied pursuits of labor, and different occupations of life. If all men in a country were merely agricultural producers, free trade would be very well. But where divers employments and pursuits have sprung up and exist together, it is necessary that they should succor and support one another, and defend all against dangerous foreign competition.

We may see, at this moment, what consequences result from the doctrines of free trade carried to extremes. Ireland is a signal example. The failure of a potato crop half starves a population of eight millions. The people have no employment which enables them to purchase food. Government itself is already absolutely obliged to furnish employment, often on works of little or no value, to keep the people from positive famine. And yet there are able men,—able I admit them to be, but theoretic men I think them to be; distinguished men, nevertheless,— who maintain that Ireland now is no worse off than if all the great landholders owning estates in Ireland, instead of living in England and spending there the rents of their Irish estates, lived in Ireland, and supported Irish labor on their farms, and about their establishments, and in the workshops.

This opinion is maintained by theoretical economists, notwithstanding the cry of Ireland for employment, employment! And has it not come even to that pass, that the government is obliged to employ hundreds and thousands of the people and pay them, and put them on works of very little utility, merely to give them bread? I wish that every Irishman in the State of Pennsylvania could be here to-night, so that I could ask him to remember the condition of the people of his own country, who are starving for the want of employment, and compare that condition with his own, here in Pennsylvania, where he has good employment and fair wages.

Gentlemen, this notion of free trade, which goes to cut off the employment of large portions and classes of the population, on the ground that it is best to buy where you can buy cheapest, is a folly, in a country like ours. The case of England is not analogous. What is the cry of free trade in England? Why, it is for cheap bread. In England the deficiency is in bread. Labor is limited in its reward. It can earn but so much, and we have Mr. Cobden's authority for saying that there is a disposition to reduce its earnings still lower. It has, accordingly, a vital interest in reducing the price of food. Therefore free trade in England is but another name for cheap bread. It is not so with us. What we desire for our laboring population is employment. We do not expect food to be cheaper in this country; our object is to make it dear; that is to say, our agricultural interests desire to raise the price of grain; and the laboring classes can stand this, if their employments are protected and the price of labor kept up. Our hope, and let all rejoice in it, is, that the price of our agricultural productions may rise for the benefit of the farmer. Manufacturers and operators, so long as they get steady employment and good wages, can buy at any reasonable rate.

These views are confirmed by the practice of most of the civilized governments of the world. Who of all Europe imitates England? Nobody, as far as I know, except Holland and Turkey. Austria, Russia, Spain, and France adhere to what I call the common-sense doctrine of protecting their own labor. M. Dupin, in the French Chamber of Deputies, said, last year, that the instincts of France were in favor of the protection of French labor. Our American instincts from the first have been very much of the same character. Whence arose all those non-importation agreements, soon after the Revolutionary war, but from an instinct, or feeling that the interests of our own industrious population ought to be consulted and promoted? I happen to have a very important document here, which one of your fellow-citizens caused to be copied and printed in a very handsome manner. It is a non-importation agreement, entered into in this city as early as 1765. That was an American instinct! Here are names to be for ever remembered! I perceive amongst them Robert Morris, the financier of the Revolution, Charles Thompson, the Secretary of Congress, and other illustrious names, whose representatives are still amongst us.

There is one imputation that honest men ought to resist, which is, that the protective policy aids capitalists, and is meant to do so, exclusively. We hear every day of the great capitalists and rich corporations of New England. A word dissipates all this. A corporation in New England is a form of partnership. Any body enters into it that chooses. Where individuals invest their property to build a mill, they do it in the form of a corporation, for the sake of convenience in transacting the business of the concern, their private responsibility still remaining in a qualified sense. The talk about rich and exclusive corporations is idle and delusive. There is not one of them into which men of moderate means may not enter, and many such men do enter, and are interested in them to a considerable extent.

Gentlemen, I have already alluded to the great importance of the protective policy, in this State and in other States, to the handicrafts. That was the original specific aim and design of the policy. At the time of the adoption of the Constitution, large manufacturing corporations were not known. No great works existed, though sagacious and far-seeing men perceived that the application of water-power must one day greatly advance the manufacturing interests. At that day, the handicrafts, the mechanics, and artisans in the city were looked upon as those whose labor it was desirable to protect. Will you pardon me, Gentlemen, for recalling to the recollection of your older fellow-citizens an interesting celebration which took place in this city, on the 4th day of July, 1788. On that day the citizens of Philadelphia celebrated the Declaration of Independence made by the thirteen United States of America on the 4th of July, 1776, and the establishment of the Constitution or frame of government, then recently adopted by ten States. A procession was formed. The military and companies of the various trades and professions united in it. It was organized and commanded by Generals Mifflin and Stewart, and some other well-known personages. The various companies displayed their flags and banners with appropriate devices and mottos. Richard Bache, Esq., on horseback, as a herald, attended by a trumpet, proclaimed a "New Era." The Hon. Peter Muhlenberg carried a blue flag, with the words "17th of September, 1787," in silver letters. Chief Justice McKean, and his associates, in their robes of office, were seated in a lofty car, shaped like an eagle, and drawn by six white horses. The Chief Justice supported a tall staff, on the top of which was the Cap of Liberty; under the cap the "New Constitution," framed and ornamented, and immediately under the Constitution the words "The People," in large gold letters. Next followed various corps and troops and associations, consuls, collectors, judges, and others. Then came the Agricultural Society, with its flag and motto, "Venerate the Plough." Then the Manufacturing Society, with their spinning and carding machines, looms, and other machinery and implements. Mr. Gallaudet carried the flag, the device on which was a Beehive, standing in the beams of the sun, bees issuing from the hive; the flag a blue silk; motto, "In its rays we shall feel new vigor." This was followed by a carriage holding men weaving and printing. A lady and her four daughters sat upon it, pencilling a piece of chintz, all dressed in cotton of their own manufacture, and over them all, on a lofty staff, was a flag with this motto, "May the Union Government protect the Manufactures of America." The federal ship "Union" followed next, and after her, boat-builders, sail-makers, merchants, and others interested in commerce. Then other trades, such as cabinet and chair-makers, with a flag and motto, "By Unity we support Society." Next bricklayers, with a flag on which there was a brickyard and kiln burning; hands at work; and in the distance a federal city building, with this motto, "It was hard in Egypt, but this prospect makes it easy." Then came the porters, bearing on their flag the motto, "May Industry ever be encouraged." After them various trades again, and then whip and cane-makers, with the motto, "Let us encourage our own Manufactures." After them still others, and amongst the last the brewers, with a flag with this motto, "Home-brewed is best."

I now ask you, Gentlemen, whether these sentiments and banners indicated that government was to lay duties only for revenue, and without respect to home industry? Do you believe the doctrines of Mr. Polk, or those of the citizens of Philadelphia in 1788? (Loud shouts of "Eighty-eight," and long-continued cheering.) . . .

15.   WEBSTER
The Constitution and Slavery

On March 7, 1850, Daniel Webster delivered a historic speech in the United States Senate. A packed gallery witnessed Webster's dramatic defense of the Constitution and of the principle of federalism against those Senators preferring states' rights and the institution of slavery. The following selection* is taken from this Senate address.

. . . Mr. President, in the excited times in which we live, there is found to exist a state of crimination and recrimination between the North and South. There are lists of grievances produced by each; and those grievances, real or supposed, alienate the minds of one portion of the country from the other, exasperate the feelings, and subdue the sense of fraternal affection, patriotic love, and mutual regard. I shall bestow a little attention, Sir, upon these various grievances existing on the one side and on the other. I begin with complaints of the South. I will not answer, further than I have, the general statements of the honorable Senator from South Carolina, that the North has prospered at the expense of the South in consequence of the manner of administering this government, in the collecting of its revenues, and so forth. These are disputed topics, and I have no inclination to enter into them. But I will allude to other complaints of the South, and especially to one which has in my opinion just foundation; and that is, that there has been found at the North, among individuals and among legislators, a disinclination to perform fully their constitutional duties in regard to the return of persons bound to service who have escaped into the free States. In that respect, the South, in my judgment, is right, and the North is wrong. Every member of every Northern legislature is bound by oath, like every other officer in the country, to support the Con-

* *The Works of Daniel Webster*, Vol. V (Boston: Charles C. Little and James Brown, 1851), pp. 53–66.

stitution of the United States; and the article of the Constitution which
says to these States that they shall deliver up fugitives from service
is as binding in honor and conscience as any other article. No man
fulfils his duty in any legislature who sets himself to find excuses,
evasions, escapes from this constitutional obligation. I have always
thought that the Constitution addressed itself to the legislatures of the
States or to the States themselves. It says that those persons escaping
to other States "shall be delivered up," and I confess I have always
been of the opinion that it was an injunction upon the States themselves. When it is said that a person escaping into another State, and
coming therefore within the jurisdiction of that State, shall be delivered
up, it seems to me the import of the clause is, that the State, itself, in
obedience to the Constitution, shall cause him to be delivered up.
That is my judgment. I have always entertained that opinion, and I
entertain it now. But when the subject, some years ago, was before the
Supreme Court of the United States, the majority of the judges held
that the power to cause fugitives from service to be delivered up was
a power to be exercised under the authority of this government. I do
not know, on the whole, that it may not have been a fortunate decision.
My habit is to respect the result of judicial deliberations and the
solemnity of judicial decisions. As it now stands, the business of seeing
that these fugitives are delivered up resides in the power of Congress
and the national judicature, and my friend at the head of the Judiciary
Committee has a bill on the subject now before the Senate, which, with
some amendments to it, I propose to support, with all its provisions,
to the fullest extent. And I desire to call the attention of all sober-
minded men at the North, of all conscientious men, of all men who are
not carried away by some fanatical idea or some false impression, to
their constitutional obligations. I put it to all the sober and sound
minds at the North as a question of morals and a question of conscience.
What right have they, in their legislative capacity or any other capacity,
to endeavor to get round this Constitution, or to embarrass the free
exercise of the rights secured by the Constitution to the persons whose
slaves escape from them? None at all; none at all. Neither in the forum
of conscience, nor before the face of the Constitution, are they, in my
opinion, justified in such an attempt. Of course it is a matter for their
consideration. They probably, in the excitement of the times, have not
stopped to consider of this. They have followed what seemed to be
the current of thought and of motives, as the occasion arose, and they

have neglected to investigate fully the real question, and to consider their constitutional obligations, which, I am sure, if they did consider, they would fulfil with alacrity. I repeat, therefore, Sir, that here is a well-founded ground of complaint against the North, which ought to be removed, which it is now in the power of the different departments of this government to remove; which calls for the enactment of proper laws authorizing the judicature of this government, in the several States, to do all that is necessary for the recapture of fugitive slaves and for their restoration to those who claim them. Wherever I go, and whenever I speak on the subject, and when I speak here I desire to speak to the whole North, I say that the South has been injured in this respect, and has a right to complain; and the North has been too careless of what I think the Constitution peremptorily and emphatically enjoins upon her as a duty.

Complaint has been made against certain resolutions that emanate from legislatures at the North, and are sent here to us, not only on the subject of slavery in the District, but sometimes recommending Congress to consider the means of abolishing slavery in the States. I should be sorry to be called upon to present any resolutions here which could not be referable to any committee or any power in Congress; and therefore I should be unwilling to receive from the legislature of Massachusetts any instructions to present resolutions expressive of any opinion whatever on the subject of slavery, as it exists at the present moment in the States, for two reasons: first, because I do not consider that the legislature of Massachusetts has any thing to do with it; and next, because I do not consider that I, as her representative here, have any thing to do with it. It has become, in my opinion, quite too common; and if the legislatures of the States do not like that opinion, they have a great deal more power to put it down than I have to uphold it; it has become, in my opinion, quite too common a practice for the State legislatures to present resolutions here on all subjects and to instruct us on all subjects. There is no public man that requires instruction more than I do, or who requires information more than I do, or desires it more heartily; but I do not like to have it in too imperative a shape. I took notice, with pleasure, of some remarks made upon this subject, the other day, in the Senate of Massachusetts, by a young man of talent and character, of whom the best hopes may be entertained. I mean Mr. Hillard. He told the Senate of Massachusetts that he would vote for no instructions whatever to be forwarded to members of

Congress, nor for any resolutions to be offered expressive of the sense
of Massachusetts as to what her members of Congress ought to do. He
said that he saw no propriety in one set of public servants giving
instructions and reading lectures to another set of public servants.
To his own master each of them must stand or fall, and that master
is his constituents. I wish these sentiments could become more common.
I have never entered into the question, and never shall, as to the
binding force of instructions. I will, however, simply say this: if there
be any matter pending in this body, while I am a member of it, in which
Massachusetts has an interest of her own not adverse to the general
interests of the country, I shall pursue her instructions with gladness
of heart and with all the efficiency which I can bring to the occasion.
But if the question be one which affects her interest, and at the same
time equally affects the interests of all the other States, I shall no more
regard her particular wishes or instructions than I should regard the
wishes of a man who might appoint me an arbitrator or referee to
decide some question of important private right between him and his
neighbor, and then *instruct* me to decide in his favor. If ever there was
a government upon earth it is this government, if ever there was a body
upon earth it is this body, which should consider itself as composed
by agreement of all, each member appointed by some, but organized
by the general consent of all, sitting here, under the solemn obligations
of oath and conscience, to do that which they think to be best for the
good of the whole.

Then, Sir, there are the Abolition societies, of which I am unwilling
to speak, but in regard to which I have very clear notions and opinions.
I do not think them useful. I think their operations for the last twenty
years have produced nothing good or valuable. At the same time, I
believe thousands of their members to be honest and good men,
perfectly well-meaning men. They have excited feelings; they think
they must do something for the cause of liberty; and, in their sphere
of action, they do not see what else they can do than to contribute to
an Abolition press, or an Abolition society, or to pay an Abolition
lecturer. I do not mean to impute gross motives even to the leaders of
these societies, but I am not blind to the consequences of their proceedings. I cannot but see what mischiefs their interference with the
South has produced. And is it not plain to every man? Let any gentleman who entertains doubts on this point recur to the debates in the
Virginia House of Delegates in 1832, and he will see with what freedom

a proposition made by Mr. Jefferson Randolph for the gradual abolition
of slavery was discussed in that body. Every one spoke of slavery as
he thought; very ignominious and disparaging names and epithets
were applied to it. The debates in the House of Delegates on that
occasion, I believe, were all published. They were read by every colored
man who could read, and to those who could not read, those debates
were read by others. At that time Virginia was not unwilling or afraid
to discuss this question, and to let that part of her population know as
much of the discussion as they could learn. That was in 1832. As has
been said by the honorable member from South Carolina, these
Abolition societies commenced their course of action in 1835. It is
said, I do not know how true it may be, that they sent incendiary
publications into the slave States; at any rate, they attempted to arouse,
and did arouse, a very strong feeling; in other words, they created
great agitation in the North against Southern slavery. Well, what was
the result? The bonds of the slaves were bound more firmly than before,
their rivets were more strongly fastened. Public opinion, which in
Virginia had begun to be exhibited against slavery, and was opening
out for the discussion of the question, drew back and shut itself up in
its castle. I wish to know whether any body in Virginia can now talk
openly as Mr. Randolph, Governor McDowell, and others talked in
1832, and sent their remarks to the press? We all know the fact, and
we all know the cause; and every thing that these agitating people
have done has been, not to enlarge, but to restrain, not to set free, but
to bind faster, the slave population of the South.

Again, Sir, the violence of the Northern press is complained of.
The press violent! Why, Sir, the press is violent everywhere. There
are outrageous reproaches in the North against the South, and there
are reproaches as vehement in the South against the North. Sir, the
extremists of both parts of this country are violent; they mistake loud
and violent talk for eloquence and for reason. They think that he who
talks loudest reasons best. And this we must expect, when the press is
free, as it is here, and I trust always will be; for, with all its licentiousness
and all its evil, the entire and absolute freedom of the press is essential
to the preservation of government on the basis of a free constitution.
Wherever it exists there will be foolish and violent paragraphs in the
newspapers, as there are, I am sorry to say, foolish and violent speeches
in both houses of Congress. In truth, Sir, I must say that, in my opinion,
the vernacular tongue of the country has become greatly vitiated,

depraved, and corrupted by the style of our Congressional debates. And if it were possible for those debates to vitiate the principles of the people as much as they have depraved their tastes, I should cry out, "God save the Republic!"

Well, in all this I see no solid grievance, no grievance presented by the South, within the redress of the government, but the single one to which I have referred; and that is, the want of a proper regard to the injunction of the Constitution for the delivery of fugitive slaves.

There are also complaints of the North against the South. I need not go over them particularly. The first and gravest is, that the North adopted the Constitution, recognizing the existence of slavery in the States, and recognizing the right, to a certain extent, of the representation of slaves in Congress, under a state of sentiment and expectation which does not now exist; and that, by events, by circumstances, by the eagerness of the South to acquire territory and extend her slave population, the North finds itself, in regard to the relative influence of the South and the North, of the free States and the slave States, where it never did expect to find itself when they agreed to the compact of the Constitution. They complain, therefore, that, instead of slavery being regarded as an evil, as it was then, an evil which all hoped would be extinguished gradually, it is now regarded by the South as an institution to be cherished, and preserved, and extended; an institution which the South has already extended to the utmost of her power by the acquisition of new territory.

Well, then, passing from that, every body in the North reads; and every body reads whatsoever the newspapers contain; and the newspapers, some of them, especially those presses to which I have alluded, are careful to spread about among the people every reproachful sentiment uttered by any Southern man bearing at all against the North; every thing that is calculated to exasperate and to alienate; and there are many such things, as every body will admit, from the South, or some portion of it, which are disseminated among the reading people; and they do exasperate, and alienate, and produce a most mischievous effect upon the public mind at the North. Sir, I would not notice things of this sort appearing in obscure quarters; but one thing has occurred in this debate which struck me very forcibly. An honorable member from Louisiana addressed us the other day on this subject. I suppose there is not a more amiable and worthy gentleman in this chamber, nor a gentleman who would be more slow to give offence to any body, and he did not mean in his remarks to give offence. But what did he say? Why, Sir, he took pains to run a contrast between the slaves of the South and the laboring people of the North, giving the preference, in all points of condition, and comfort, and happiness, to the slaves of the South. The honorable member, doubtless, did not suppose that he gave any offence, or did any injustice. He was merely expressing his opinion. But does he know how remarks of that sort will be received by the laboring people of the North? Why, who are the laboring people of the North? They are the whole North. They are the people who till their own farms with their own hands; freeholders, educated men, independent men. Let me say, Sir, that five sixths of the whole property of the North is in the hands of the laborers of the North; they cultivate their farms, they educate their children, they provide the means of independence. If they are not freeholders, they earn wages; these wages accumulate, are turned into capital, into new freeholds, and small capitalists are created. Such is the case, and such the course of things, among the industrious and frugal. And what can these people think when so respectable and worthy a gentleman as the member from Louisiana undertakes to prove that the absolute ignorance and the abject slavery of the South are more in conformity with the high purposes and destiny of immortal, rational human beings, than the educated, the independent free labor of the North?

There is a more tangible and irritating cause of grievance at the North. Free blacks are constantly employed in the vessels of the North, generally as cooks or stewards. When the vessel arrives at a Southern port, these free colored men are taken on shore, by the police or municipal authority, imprisoned, and kept in prison till the vessel is again ready to sail. This is not only irritating, but exceedingly unjustifiable and oppressive. Mr. Hoar's mission, some time ago, to South Carolina, was a well-intended effort to remove this cause of complaint. The North thinks such imprisonments illegal and unconstitutional; and as the cases occur constantly and frequently, they regard it as a great grievance.

Now, Sir, so far as any of these grievances have their foundation in matters of law, they can be redressed, and ought to be redressed; and so far as they have their foundation in matters of opinion, in sentiment, in mutual crimination and recrimination, all that we can do is to endeavor to allay the agitation, and cultivate a better feeling and more fraternal sentiments between the South and the North.

Mr. President, I should much prefer to have heard from every member on this floor declarations of opinion that this Union could never be dissolved, than the declaration of opinion by any body, that, in any case, under the pressure of any circumstances, such a dissolution was possible. I hear with distress and anguish the word "secession," especially when it falls from the lips of those who are patriotic, and known to the country, and known all over the world, for their political services. Secession! Peaceable secession! Sir, your eyes and mine are never destined to see that miracle. The dismemberment of this vast country without convulsion! The breaking up of the fountains of the great deep without ruffling the surface! Who is so foolish, I beg every body's pardon, as to expect to see any such thing? Sir, he who sees these States, now revolving in harmony around a common centre, and expects to see them quit their places and fly off without convulsion, may look the next hour to see the heavenly bodies rush from their spheres, and jostle against each other in the realms of space, without causing the wreck of the universe. There can be no such thing as a peaceable secession. Peaceable secession is an utter impossibility. Is the great Constitution under which we live, covering this whole country, is it to be thawed and melted away by secession, as the snows on the mountain melt under the influence of a vernal sun, disappear almost unobserved, and run off? No, Sir! No, Sir! I will not state what might produce the disruption of the Union; but, Sir, I see as plainly as I see the sun in heaven what that disruption itself must produce; I see that it must produce war, and such a war as I will not describe, *in its twofold character*.

Peaceable secession! Peaceable secession! The concurrent agreement of all the members of this great republic to separate! A voluntary separation, with alimony on one side and on the other. Why, what would be the result? Where is the line to be drawn? What States are to secede? What is to remain American? What am I to be? An American no longer? Am I to become a sectional man, a local man, a separatist, with no country in common with the gentlemen who sit around me here, or who fill the other house of Congress? Heaven forbid! Where is the flag of the republic to remain? Where is the eagle still to tower? or is he to cower, and shrink, and fall to the ground? Why, Sir, our ancestors, our fathers and our grandfathers, those of them that are yet living amongst us with prolonged lives, would rebuke and reproach us; and our children and our grandchildren would cry out shame upon us, if we of this generation should dishonor these ensigns of the power of the government and the harmony of the Union which is every day felt among us with so much joy and gratitude. What is to become of the army? What is to become of the navy? What is to become of the public lands? How is each of the thirty States to defend itself? I know, although the idea has not been stated distinctly, there is to be, or it is supposed possible that there will be, a Southern Confederacy. I do not mean, when I allude to this statement, that any one seriously contemplates such a state of things. I do not mean to say that it is true, but I have heard it suggested elsewhere, that the idea has been entertained, that, after the dissolution of this Union, a Southern Confederacy might be formed. I am sorry, Sir, that it has ever been thought of, talked of or dreamed of, in the wildest flights of human imagination. But the idea, so far as it exists, must be of a separation, assigning the slave States to one side and the free States to the other. Sir, I may express myself too strongly, perhaps, but there are impossibilities in the natural as well as in the physical world, and I hold the idea of a separation of these States, those that are free to form one government, and those that are slave-holding to form another, as such an impossibility. We could not separate the States by any such line, if we were to draw it. We could not sit down here to-day and draw a line of separation that would satisfy any five men in the country. There are natural causes that would keep and tie us together, and there are social and domestic relations which we could not break if we would, and which we should not if we could.

Sir, nobody can look over the face of this country at the present moment, nobody can see where its population is the most dense and growing, without being ready to admit, and compelled to admit, that ere long the strength of America will be in the Valley of the Mississippi. Well, now, Sir, I beg to inquire what the wildest enthusiast has to say on the possibility of cutting that river in two, and leaving free States at its source and on its branches, and slave States down near its mouth, each forming a separate government? Pray, Sir, let me say to the people of this country, that these things are worthy of their pondering and of their consideration. Here, Sir, are five millions of freemen in the free States north of the river Ohio. Can any body suppose that this population can be severed, by a line that divides them from the territory of a foreign and an alien government, down somewhere, the Lord knows where, upon the lower banks of the Mississippi? What would become of Missouri? Will she join the *arrondissement* of the slave States? Shall the man from the Yellow Stone and the Platte be connected, in the new republic, with the man who lives on the southern extremity of the Cape of Florida? Sir, I am ashamed to pursue this line of remark. I dislike it, I have an utter disgust for it. I would rather hear of natural blasts and mildews, war, pestilence, and famine, than to hear gentlemen talk of secession. To break up this great government! to dismember this glorious country! to astonish Europe with an act of folly such as Europe for two centuries has never beheld in any government of any people! No, Sir! no, Sir! There will be no secession! Gentlemen are not serious when they talk of secession.

Sir, I hear there is to be a convention held at Nashville. I am bound to believe that, if worthy gentlemen meet at Nashville in convention, their object will be to adopt conciliatory counsels; to advise the South to forbearance and moderation, and to advise the North to forbearance and moderation; and to inculcate principles of brotherly love and affection, and attachment to the Constitution of the country as it now is. I believe, if the convention meet at all, it will be for this purpose; for certainly, if they meet for any purpose hostile to the Union, they have been singularly inappropriate in their selection of a place. I remember, Sir, that, when the treaty of Amiens was concluded between France and England, a sturdy Englishman and a distinguished orator, who regarded the conditions of the peace as ignominious to England, said in the House of Commons, that, if King William could know the terms of that treaty, he would turn in his coffin! Let me commend this saying of Mr. Windham, in all its emphasis and in all its force, to any persons who shall meet at Nashville for the purpose of concerting measures for the overthrow of this Union over the bones of Andrew Jackson!

Sir, I wish now to make two remarks, and hasten to a conclusion. I wish to say, in regard to Texas, that if it should be hereafter, at any time, the pleasure of the government of Texas to cede to the United States a portion, larger or smaller, of her territory which lies adjacent to New Mexico, and north of 36° 30′ of north latitude, to be formed into free States, for a fair equivalent in money or in the payment of her debt, I think it an object well worthy the consideration of Congress, and I shall be happy to concur in it myself, if I should have a connection with the government at that time.

I have one other remark to make. In my observations upon slavery as it has existed in this country, and as it now exists, I have expressed no opinion of the mode of its extinguishment or melioration. I will say, however, though I have nothing to propose, because I do not deem myself so competent as other gentlemen to take any lead on this subject, that if any gentleman from the South shall propose a scheme, to be carried on by this government upon a large scale, for the transportation of free colored people to any colony or any place in the world, I should be quite disposed to incur almost any degree of expense to accomplish that object. Nay, Sir, following an example set more than twenty years ago by a great man, then a Senator from New York, I would return to Virginia, and through her to the whole South, the money received from the lands and territories ceded by her to this government, for any such purpose as to remove, in whole or in part, or in any way to diminish or deal beneficially with, the free colored population of the Southern States. I have said that I honor Virginia for her cession of this territory. There have been received into the treasury of the United States eighty millions of dollars, the proceeds of the sales of the public lands ceded by her. If the residue should be sold at the same rate, the whole aggregate will exceed two hundred millions of dollars. If Virginia and the South see fit to adopt any proposition to relieve themselves from the free people of color among them, or such as may be made free, they have my full consent that the government shall pay them any sum of money out of the proceeds of that cession which may be adequate to the purpose.

And now, Mr. President, I draw these observations to a close. I have spoken freely, and I meant to do so. I have sought to make no display. I have sought to enliven the occasion by no animated discussion, nor have I attempted any train of elaborate argument. I have wished only to speak my sentiments, fully and at length, being desirous, once and for all, to let the Senate know, and to let the country know, the opinions and sentiments which I entertain on all these subjects. These opinions are not likely to be suddenly changed. If there be any future service that I can render to the country, consistently with these sentiments and opinions, I shall cheerfully render it. If there be not, I shall still be glad to have had an opportunity to disburden myself from the bottom of my heart, and to make known every political sentiment that therein exists.

And now, Mr. President, instead of speaking of the possibility or utility of secession, instead of dwelling in those caverns of darkness, instead of groping with those ideas so full of all that is horrid and horrible, let us come out into the light of day; let us enjoy the fresh air of Liberty and Union; let us cherish those hopes which belong to us; let us devote outselves to those great objects that are fit for our consideration and our action; let us raise our conceptions to the magnitude and the importance of the duties that devolve upon us; let our comprehension be as broad as the country for which we act, our aspirations as high as its certain destiny; let us not be pigmies in a case that calls for men. Never did there devolve on any generation of men higher trusts than now devolve upon us, for the preservation of this Constitution and the harmony and peace of all who are destined to live under it. Let us make our generation one of the strongest and brightest links in that golden chain which is destined, I fondly believe, to grapple the people of all the States to this Constitution for ages to come. We have a great, popular, constitutional government, guarded by law and by judicature, and defended by the affections of the whole people. No monarchial throne presses these States together, no iron chain of military power encircles them; they live and stand under a government popular in its form, representative in its character, founded upon principles of equality, and so constructed, we hope, as to last for ever. In all its history it has been beneficent; it has trodden down no man's liberty; it has crushed no State. Its daily respiration is liberty and patriotism; its yet youthful veins are full of enterprise, courage, and honorable love of glory and renown. Large before, the country has now, by recent events, become vastly larger. This republic now extends, with a vast breadth, across the whole continent. The two great seas of the world wash the one and the other shore. We realize, on a mighty scale, the beautiful description of the ornamental border of the buckler of Achilles:—

> "Now, the broad shield complete, the artist crowned
> With his last hand, and poured the ocean round;
> In living silver seemed the waves to roll,
> And beat the buckler's verge, and bound the whole."

16. EMERSON

"Politics"

Ralph Waldo Emerson (1803–1882) was one of the leading poets and essayists of the nineteenth century. Whatever his philosophic importance may be, his essay "Politics" (1841), presented here in its entirety, is a worthy and valuable contribution in the development of American conservative thought. Emerson accepted the existence of the social differences resulting from wealth and poverty but believed that by self-reliance a man could rise in social standing. He believed in improvement and change in American life but felt, as do many conservatives, that a better society can be obtained not by political or economic legislation but by "the influence of private character." Emerson helped revive some of the Puritan ideas of individualism and work but related them to the needs of a capitalist economic order. He did not have a scholarly contempt for business but felt that individual liberty and equality were best achieved through economic effort by individuals largely unrestrained by government. Like most conservatives, Emerson was suspicious of all political movements and political parties.

> Gold and iron are good
> To buy iron and gold;
> All earth's fleece and food
> For their like are sold.
> Boded Merlin wise,
> Proved Napoleon great,—
> Nor kind nor coinage buys
> Aught above its rate.
> Fear, Craft, and Avarice
> Cannot rear a State.
> Out of dust to build
> What is more than dust,—
> Walls Amphion piled
> Phœbus stablish must.

When the Muses nine
With the Virtues meet,
Find to their design
An Atlantic seat,
By green orchard boughs
Fended from the heat,
Where the statesman ploughs
Furrow for the wheat;
When the Church is social worth,
When the state-house is the hearth,
Then the perfect State is come,
The republican at home.

In dealing with the State, we ought to remember that its institutions are not aboriginal, though they existed before we were born: that they are not superior to the citizen: that every one of them was once the act of a single man: every law and usage was a man's expedient to meet a particular case: that they all are imitable, all alterable; we may make as good; we may make better. Society is an illusion to the young citizen. It lies before him in rigid repose, with certain names, men, and institutions, rooted like oak-trees to the centre, round which all arrange themselves the best they can. But the old statesman knows that society is fluid; there are no such roots and centres; but any particle may suddenly become the centre of the movement, and compel the system to gyrate round it, as every man of strong will, like Pisistratus, or Cromwell, does for a time, and every man of truth, like Plato, or Paul, does forever. But politics rest on necessary foundations, and cannot be treated with levity. Republics abound in young civilians, who believe that the laws make the city, that grave modifications of the policy and modes of living, and employments of the population, that commerce, education, and religion, may be voted in or out; and that any measure, though it were absurd, may be imposed on a people, if only you can get sufficient voices to make it a law. But the wise know that foolish legislation is a rope of sand, which perishes in the twisting; that the State must follow, and not lead the character and progress of the citizen; the strongest usurper is quickly got rid of; and they only who build on Ideas, build for eternity; and that the form of government which prevails, is the expression of what cultivation exists in the population which permits it. The law is only a memorandum. We are superstitious, and esteem the statute somewhat: so much life as it has in the character of living men, is its force. The statute stands there to say, yesterday we agreed so and so, but how feel ye this article to-day? Our statute is a currency, which we stamp with our own portrait: it soon becomes unrecognizable, and in process of time will return to the mint. Nature is not democratic, nor limited-monarchial, but despotic, and will not be fooled or abated of any jot of her authority, by the pertest of her sons: and as fast as the public mind is opened to more intelligence, the code is seen to be brute and stammering. It speaks not articulately, and must be made to. Meantime the education of the general mind never stops. The reveries of the true and simple are prophetic. What the tender poetic youth dreams, and prays, and paints to-day, but shuns the ridicule of saying aloud, shall presently be the resolutions of public bodies, then shall be carried as grievance and bill of rights through conflict and war, and then shall be triumphant law and establishment for a hundred years, until it gives place, in turn, to new prayers and pictures. The history of the State sketches in coarse outline the progress of thought, and follows at a distance the delicacy of culture and of aspiration.

The theory of politics, which has possessed the mind of men, and which they have expressed the best they could in their laws and in their revolutions, considers persons and property as the two objects for whose protection government exists. Of persons, all have equal rights, in virtue of being identical in nature. This interest, of course, with its whole power demands a democracy. Whilst the rights of all as persons are equal, in virtue of their access to reason, their rights in property are very unequal. One man owns his clothes, and another owns a county. This accident, depending primarily on the skill and virtue of the parties, of which there is every degree, and, secondarily, on patrimony, falls unequally, and its rights, of course, are unequal. Personal rights, universally the same, demand a government framed on the ratio of the census: property demands a government framed on the ratio of owners and of owning. Laban, who has flocks and herds, wishes them looked after by an officer on the frontiers, lest the Midianites shall drive them off, and pays a tax to that end. Jacob has no flocks or herds, and no fear of the Midianites, and pays no tax to the officer. It seemed fit that Laban and Jacob should have equal rights to elect the officer, who is to defend their persons, but that Laban, and not Jacob, should elect the officer who is to guard the sheep and cattle. And, if question arise whether additional officers or watchtowers should be provided, must not Laban and Isaac, and those who must sell part of their herds to buy protection for the rest, judge better of this, and with more right, than Jacob, who, because he is a youth and a traveller, eats their bread and not his own?

In the earliest society the proprietors made their own wealth, and so long as it comes to the owners in the direct way, no other opinion would arise in any equitable community, than that property should make the law for property, and persons the law for persons.

But property passes through donation or inheritance to those who do not create it. Gift, in one case, makes it as really the new owner's, as labor made it the first owner's: in the other case, of patrimony, the law makes an ownership, which will be valid in each man's view according to the estimate which he sets on the public tranquillity.

It was not, however, found easy to embody the readily admitted principle, that property should make law for property, and persons for persons: since persons and property mixed themselves in every transaction. At last it seemed settled, that the rightful distinction was, that the proprietors should have more elective franchise than non-proprietors, on the Spartan principle of "calling that which is just, equal; not that which is equal, just."

That principle no longer looks so self-evident as it appeared in former times, partly, because doubts have arisen whether too much weight had not been allowed in the laws, to property, and such a structure given to our usages, as allowed the rich to encroach on the poor, and to keep them poor; but mainly, because there is an instinctive sense, however obscure and yet inarticulate, that the whole constitution of property, on its present tenures, is injurious, and its influence on persons deteriorating and degrading; that truly, the only interest for the consideration of the State, is persons: that property will always follow persons; that the highest end of government is the culture of men: and if men can be educated, the institutions will share their improvement, and the moral sentiment will write the law of the land.

If it be not easy to settle the equity of this question, the peril is less when we take note of our natural defences. We are kept by better guards than the vigilance of such magistrates as we commonly elect. Society always consists, in greatest part, of young and foolish persons. The old, who have seen through the hypocrisy of courts and statesmen, die, and leave no wisdom to their sons. They believe their own newspaper, as their fathers did at their age. With such an ignorant and deceivable majority, States would soon run to ruin, but that there are limitations, beyond which the folly and ambition of governors cannot go. Things have their laws, as well as men; and things refuse to be trifled with. Property will be protected. Corn will not grow, unless it is planted and manured; but the farmer will not plant or hoe it, unless the chances are a hundred to one, that he will cut and harvest it. Under any forms, persons and property must and will have their just sway. They exert their power, as steadily as matter its attraction. Cover up a pound of earth never so cunningly, divide and subdivide it; melt it to liquid, convert it to gas; it will always weigh a pound: it will always attract and resist other matter, by the full virtue of one pound weight;—and the attributes of a person, his wit and his moral energy, will exercise, under any law or extinguishing tyranny, their proper force,—if not overtly, then covertly; if not for the law, then against it; if not wholesomely, then poisonously; with right, or by might.

The boundaries of personal influence it is impossible to fix, as persons are organs of moral or supernatural force. Under the dominion of an idea, which possesses the minds of multitudes, as civil freedom, or the religious sentiment, the powers of persons are no longer subjects of calculation. A nation of men unanimously bent on freedom, or conquest, can easily confound the arithmetic of statists, and achieve extravagant actions, out of all proportion to their means; as the Greeks, the Saracens, the Swiss, the Americans, and the French have done.

In like manner, to every particle of property belongs its own attraction. A cent is the representative of a certain quantity of corn or other commodity. Its value is in the necessities of the animal man. It is so much warmth, so much bread, so much water, so much land. The law may do what it will with the owner of property, its just power will still attach to the cent. The law may in a mad freak say, that all shall have power except the owners of property: they shall have no vote. Nevertheless, by a higher law, the property will, year after year, write every statute that respects property. The non-proprietor will be the scribe of the proprietor. What the owners wish to do, the whole power of property will do, either through the law, or else in defiance of it. Of course, I speak of all the property, not merely of the great estates. When the rich are outvoted, as frequently happens, it is the joint treasury of the poor which exceeds their accumulations. Every man owns something, if it is only a cow, or a wheelbarrow, or his arms, and so has that property to dispose of.

The same necessity which secures the rights of person and property against the malignity of folly of the magistrate, determines the form and methods of governing, which are proper to each nation, and to its habit of thought, and nowise transferable to other states of society. In this country, we are very vain of our political institutions, which are singular in this, that they sprung, within the memory of living men, from the character and condition of the people, which they still express with sufficient fidelity,—and we ostentatiously prefer them to any other in history. They are not better, but only fitter for us. We may be wise in asserting the advantage in modern times of the democratic form, but to other states of society, in which religion consecrated the monarchial, that and not this was expedient. Democracy is better for us, because the religious sentiment of the present time accords better with it. Born democrats, we are nowise qualified to judge of monarchy, which, to our fathers living in the monarchial idea, was also relatively right. But our institutions, though in coincidence with the spirit of the age, have not any exemption from the practical defects which have discredited other forms. Every actual State is corrupt. Good men must not obey the laws too well. What satire on government can equal the severity of censure conveyed in the word *politic*, which now for ages has signified *cunning*, intimating that the State is a trick?

The same benign necessity and the same practical abuse appear in the parties into which each State divides itself, of opponents and defenders of the administration of the government. Parties are also founded on instincts, and have better guides to their own humble aims than the sagacity of their leaders. They have nothing perverse in their origin, but rudely mark some real and lasting relation. We might as wisely reprove the east wind, or the frost, as a political party, whose members, for the most part, could give no account of their position, but stand for the defence of those interests in which they find themselves. Our quarrel with them begins, when they quit this deep natural ground at the bidding of some leader, and, obeying personal considerations, throw themselves into the maintenance and defence of points, nowise belonging to their system. A party is perpetually corrupted by personality. Whilst we absolve the association from dishonesty, we cannot extend the same charity to their leaders. They reap the rewards of the docility and zeal of the masses which they direct. Ordinarily, our parties are parties of circumstance, and not of principle; as, the planting interest in conflict with the commercial; the party of capitalists, and that of operatives; parties which are identical in their moral character, and which can easily change ground with each other, in the support of many of their measures. Parties of principle, as, religious sects, or the party of free-trade, of universal suffrage, of abolition of slavery, of abolition of capital punishment, degenerate into personalities, or would inspire enthusiasm. The vice of our leading parties in this country (which may be cited as a fair specimen of these societies of opinion) is, that they do not plant themselves on the deep and necessary grounds to which they are respectively entitled, but lash themselves to fury in the carrying of some local and momentary measure, nowise useful to the commonwealth. Of the two great parties, which, at this hour, almost share the nation between them, I should say, that, one has the best cause, and the other contains the best men. The philosopher, the poet, or the religious man, will, of course, wish to cast his vote with the democrat, for free-trade, for wide suffrage, for the abolition of legal cruelties in the penal code, and for facilitating in every manner the access of the young and the poor to the sources of wealth and power. But he can rarely accept the persons whom the so-called popular party propose to him as representatives of these liberalities. They have not at heart the ends which give to the name of democracy what hope and virtue are in it. The spirit of our American radicalism is destructive and aimless: it is not loving; it has no ulterior and divine ends; but is destructive only out of hatred and selfishness. On the other side, the conservative party, composed of the most moderate, able, and cultivated part of the population, is timid, and merely defensive of property. It vindicates no right, it aspires to no real good, it brands no crime, it proposes no generous policy, it does not build, nor write, nor cherish the arts, nor foster religion, nor establish schools, nor encourage science, nor emancipate the slave, nor befriend the poor, or the Indian, or the immigrant. From neither party, when in power, has the world any benefit to expect in science, art, or humanity, at all commensurate with the resources of the nation.

I do not for these defects despair of our republic. We are not at the mercy of any waves of chance. In the strife of ferocious parties, human nature always finds itself cherished, as the children of the convicts at Botany Bay are found to have as healthy a moral sentiment as other children. Citizens of feudal states are alarmed at our democratic institutions lapsing into anarchy: and the older and more cautious among ourselves are learning from Europeans to look with some terror at our turbulent freedom. It is said that in our license of construing the Constitution, and in the despotism of public opinion, we have no anchor; and one foreign observer thinks he has found the safeguard in the sanctity of Marriage among us; and another thinks he has found it in our Calvinism. Fisher Ames expressed the popular security more wisely, when he compared a monarchy and a republic, saying, "that a monarchy is a merchantman, which sails well, but will sometimes strike on a rock, and go to the bottom; whilst a republic is a raft, which would never sink, but then your feet are always in water." No forms can have any dangerous importance, whilst we are befriended by the laws of things. It makes no difference how many tons' weight of atmosphere presses on our heads, so long as the same pressure resists it within our lungs. Augment the mass a thousand fold, it cannot begin to crush us, as long as reaction is equal to action. The fact of two poles, of two forces, centripetal, and centrifugal, is universal, and each force by its own activity develops the other. Wild liberty develops iron conscience. Want of liberty, by strengthening law and decorum, stupefies conscience. "Lynch-law" prevails only where there is greater hardihood and self-subsistency in the leaders. A mob cannot be a permanency; everybody's interest requires that it should not exist, and only justice satisfies all.

We must trust infinitely to the beneficent necessity which shines through all laws. Human nature expresses itself in them as characteristically as in statues, or songs, or railroads, and an abstract of the codes of nations would be a transcript of the common conscience. Governments have their origin in the moral identity of men. Reason for one is seen to be reason for another, and for every other. There is a middle measure which satisfies all parties, be they never so many, or so resolute for their own. Every man finds a sanction for his simplest claims and deeds in decisions of his own mind, which he calls Truth and Holiness. In these decisions all the citizens find a perfect agreement, and only in these; not in what is good to eat, good to wear, good use of time, or what amount of land, or of public aid, each is entitled to claim. This truth and justice men presently endeavor to make application of, to the measuring of land, the apportionment of service, the protection of life and property. Their first endeavors, no doubt, are very awkward. Yet absolute right is the first governor; or, every government is an impure theocracy. The idea after which each community is aiming to make and mend its law, is, the will of the wise man. The wise man, it cannot find in nature, and it makes awkward but earnest efforts to secure his government by contrivance; as, by causing the entire people to give their voices on every measure; or, by a double choice to get the representation of the whole; or, by a selection of the best citizens; or, to secure the advantages of efficiency and internal peace, by confiding the government to one, who may himself select his agents. All forms of government symbolize an immortal government, common to all dynasties and independent of numbers, perfect where two men exist, perfect where there is only one man.

Every man's nature is a sufficient advertisement to him of the character of his fellows. My right and my wrong, is their right and their wrong. Whilst I do what is fit for me, and abstain from what is unfit, my neighbor and I shall often agree in our means, and work together for a time to one end. But whenever I find my dominion over myself not sufficient for me, and undertake the direction of him also, I overstep the truth, and come into false relations to him. I may have so much more skill or strength than he, that he cannot express adequately his sense of wrong, but it is a lie, and hurts like a lie both him and me. Love and nature cannot maintain the assumption: it must be executed by a practical lie, namely, by force. This undertaking for another, is the blunder which stands in colossal ugliness in the governments of the world. It is the same thing in numbers, as in a pair, only not quite so intelligible. I can see well enough a great difference between my setting myself down to a self-control, and my going to make somebody else act after my views: but when a quarter of the human race assume to tell me what I must do, I may be too much disturbed by the circumstances to see so clearly the absurdity of their command. Therefore, all public ends look vague and quixotic beside private ones. For, any laws but those which men make for themselves, are laughable. If I put myself in the place of my child, and we stand in one thought, and see that things are thus or thus, that perception is law for him and me. We are both there, both act. But if, without carrying him into the thought, I look over into his plot, and, guessing how it is with him, ordain this or that, he will never obey me. This is the history of governments,—one man does something which is to bind another. A man who cannot be acquainted with me, taxes me; looking from afar at me, ordains that a part of my labor shall go to this or that whimsical end, not as I but as he happens to fancy. Behold the consequence. Of all debts, men are least willing to pay the taxes. What a satire is this on government! Everywhere they think they get their money's worth, except for these.

Hence, the less government we have, the better,—the fewer laws, and the less confided power. The antidote to this abuse of formal Government, is, the influence of private character, the growth of the Individual; the appearance of the principal to supersede the proxy; the appearance of the wise man, of whom the existing government is, it must be owned, but a shabby imitation. That which all things tend to educe, which freedom, cultivation, intercourse, revolutions, go to form and deliver, is character; that is the end of nature, to reach unto this coronation of her king. To educate the wise man, the State exists, and with the appearance of the wise man, the State expires. The appearance of character makes the State unnecessary. The wise man is the State. He needs no army, fort, or navy,—he loves men too well; no bribe, or feast, or palace, to draw friends to him; no vantage ground, no favorable circumstance. He needs no library, for he has not done thinking; no church, for he is a prophet; no statute-book, for he has the lawgiver; no money, for he is value; no road, for he is at home where he is; no experience, for the life of the creator shoots through him, and looks from his eyes. He has no personal friends, for he who has the spell to draw the prayer and piety of all men unto him, needs not husband and educate a few, to share with him a select and poetic life. His relation to men is angelic; his memory is myrrh to them; his presence, frankincense and flowers.

We think our civilization near its meridian, but we are yet only at the cock-crowing and the morning star. In our barbarous society the influence of character is in its infancy. As a political power, as the rightful lord who is to tumble all rulers from their chairs, its presence is hardly yet suspected. Malthus and Ricardo quite omit it; the Annual Register is silent; in the Conversations' Lexicon, it is not set down; the President's Message, the Queen's Speech, have not mentioned it; and yet it is never nothing. Every thought which genius and piety throw into the world, alters the world. The gladiators in the lists of power feel, through all their frocks of force and simulation, the presence of worth. I think the very strife of trade and ambition are confession of this divinity; and successes in those fields are the poor amends, the fig-leaf with which the shamed soul attempts to hide its nakedness. I find the like unwilling homage in all quarters. It is because we know how much is due from us, that we are impatient to show some petty talent as a substitute for worth. We are haunted by a conscience of this right to grandeur of character, and are false to it. But each of us has some talent, can do somewhat useful, or graceful, or formidable, or amusing, or lucrative. That we do, as an apology to others and to ourselves, for not reaching the mark of a good and equal life. But it does not satisfy *us*, while we thrust it on the notice of our companions. It may throw dust in their eyes, but does not smooth our own brow, or give us the tranquillity of the strong when we walk abroad. We do penance as we go. Our talent is a sort of expiation, and we are constrained to reflect on our splendid moment, with a certain humiliation, as somewhat too fine, and not as one act of many acts, a fair expression of our permanent energy. Most persons of ability meet in society with a kind of tacit appeal. Each seems to say, "I am not all here." Senators and presidents have climbed so high with pain enough, not because they think the place specially agreeable, but as an apology for real worth, and to vindicate their manhood in our eyes. This conspicuous chair is their compensation to themselves for being of a poor, cold, hard nature. They must do what they can. Like one class of forest animals, they have nothing but a prehensile tail: climb they must, or crawl. If a man found himself so rich-natured that he could enter into strict relations with the best persons, and make life serene around him by the dignity and sweetness of his behavior, could he afford to circumvent the favor of the caucus and the press, and covet relations so hollow and pompous as those of a politician? Surely nobody would be a charlatan, who could afford to be sincere.

The tendencies of the times favor the idea of self government, and leave the individual, for all code to the rewards and penalties of his own constitution which work with more energy than we believe, whilst we depend on artificial restraints. The movement in this direction has been very marked in modern history. Much has been blind and discreditable, but the nature of the revolution is not affected by the vices of the revolters; for this is a purely moral force. It was never adopted by any party in history, neither can be. It separates the individual from all party, and unites him, at the same time, to the race. It promises a recognition of higher rights than those of personal freedom, or the security of property. A man has a right to be employed, to be trusted, to be loved, to be revered. The power of love, as the basis of a State, has never been tried. We must not imagine that all things are lapsing into confusion, if every tender protestant be not compelled to bear his part in certain social conventions: nor doubt that roads can be built, letters carried, and the fruit of labor secured, when the government of force is at an end. Are our methods now so excellent that all competitition is hopeless? could not a nation of friends even devise better ways? On the other hand, let not the most conservative and timid fear anything from a premature surrender of the bayonet, and the system of force. For, according to the order of nature, which is quite superior to our will, it stands thus; there will always be a government of force, where men are selfish; and when they are pure enough to abjure the code of force, they will be wise enough to see how these public ends of the post-office, of the highway, of commerce, and the exchange of property, of museums and libraries, of institutions of art and science, can be answered.

We live in a very low state of the world, and pay unwilling tribute to governments founded on force. There is not, among the most religious and instructed men of the most religious and civil nations, a reliance on the moral sentiment, and a sufficient belief in the unity of things to persuade them that society can be maintained without artificial restraints, as well as the solar system; or that the private citizen might be reasonable, and a good neighbor, without the hint of a jail or a confiscation. What is strange too, there never was in any man sufficient faith in the power of rectitude, to inspire him with the broad design of renovating the State on the principle of right and love. All those who have pretended this design, have been partial reformers, and have admitted in some manner the supremacy of the bad State. I do not call to mind a single human being who has steadily denied the authority of the laws, on the simple ground of his own moral nature. Such designs, full of genius and full of fate as they are, are not entertained except avowedly as air-pictures. If the individual who exhibits them, dare to think them practicable, he disgusts scholars and churchmen: and men of talent, and women of superior sentiments, cannot hide their contempt. Not the less does nature continue to fill the heart of youth with suggestions of this enthusiasm, and there are now men,—if indeed I can speak in the plural number,—more exactly, I will say, I have just been conversing with one man, to whom no weight of adverse experience will make it for a moment appear impossible, that thousands of human beings might exercise towards each other the grandest and simplest sentiments, as well as a knot of friends or a pair of lovers.

IV

States' Rights and Slavery

Several of the concepts of John Locke's political philosophy seem to leave no room for the social institution of slavery. The equality of men, their natural rights, and the concept of liberty itself were violated by the existence of slavery. An effort was made by Southern intellectual leaders to defend their strange and anachronistic social system, but this could not be done in the vocabulary of John Locke.

As a result of the ferment among Southern intellectuals, a direct challenge to dominant Lockeanism was created, and from this response arose the most unique products of American political thought. John C. Calhoun constructed an elaborate and original revision of the accepted concepts of popular government. John Taylor, James H. Harper, James H. Hammond, and George Fitzhugh also contributed fresh insights into problems which had previously gone undisputed in American democracy.

It is not accurate to call these writings either conservative or liberal, because they fall outside the usual spectrum of American ideas. Some of the racist and class-bound ideas are closer to currents present in European conservatism than to earlier American experience. That the proslavery writers were not modern American conservatives is evident from their attack upon the industrialist capitalist system of the North. These writers derided the Northern factory owners and workers even more than they did their own slaves.

However, the proslavery writers did help introduce several new conservative themes into American political discourse. In place of the classless assumptions of early American democrats, these writers perceived the necessity of the existence of a class structure as an unchangeable social fact. The inequality of man was accepted as an inevitable condition, regardless of the optimistic assumptions of Locke. The social problem, then, was not to build a false equality but to make men aware of their differences, so that they might learn to accept them.

Another theme introduced by proslavery writers was an anti-individualism which accepted the superiority of the society over the claim of any man to his private rights. The movement toward greater personal liberty was seen as a possible threat to society.

To these two negative themes was added a third, which has enjoyed much more popularity among American conservatives—states' rights. States' rights had originally been the rallying ground of the Jeffersonian liberals against a powerful, threatening national government. The defense of local differences and the vitality of local government in democratic life was captured as an idea by American conservatives in the early nineteenth century. It has remained a valuable part of the American conservative armory of ideas, but its expression is clearly separable from the defense of slavery.

The Southern dream of creating a conservative citadel free from the radical forces sweeping the world was doomed, as was the attempt to build an American conservatism upon the ideas of Thomas Hobbes rather than those of John Locke. The Southern desire for stability proved greater than the desire for freedom; the desire for order proved greater than the desire for freedom and individuality. The political theory of the mid-nineteenth-century South demonstrates the futility of abandoning the ideas of Locke for a brand of conservatism foreign to the American experience.

17.   CALHOUN

"A Disquisition on Government"

John C. Calhoun (1782–1850) was the leading theoretician of sectionalism and states' rights in America. A leading statesman and politician, Calhoun was a Senator from South Carolina, Secretary of War, twice Vice President, and on two occasions a candidate for President of the United States. Although known in his own time principally as a defender of slavery, he is better known today as America's most original political theorist because of his views on class conflict and representative government. Calhoun expanded the idea of minority rights to include the new concept of "concurrent majority," which allowed for a sectional check upon the numerical majority. His defense of a regional aristocracy was brilliantly presented in "A Disquisition on Government,"* from which the following selection is taken. The "Disquisition" was published soon after Calhoun's death and is a major contribution to the theory of representative government and an important criticism of democracy.

. . . But, as there can be no constitution without the negative power, and no negative power without the concurrent majority;—it follows, necessarily, that where the numerical majority has the sole control of the government, there can be no constitution; as constitution implies limitation or restriction,—and, of course, is inconsistent with the idea of sole or exclusive power. And hence, the numerical, unmixed with the concurrent majority, necessarily forms, in all cases, absolute government.

It is, indeed, the single, or *one power*, which excludes the negative, and constitutes absolute government; and not the *number* in whom the power is vested. The numerical majority is as truly a *single power*, and

---

* From C. Gordon Post edition (New York: Liberal Arts Press, 1953), pp. 36–91.

excludes the negative as completely as the absolute government of one, or of the few. The former is as much the absolute government of the democratic, or popular form, as the latter of the monarchical or aristocratical. It has, accordingly, in common with them, the same tendency to oppression and abuse of power.

Constitutional governments, of whatever form, are, indeed, much more similar to each other, in their structure and character, than they are, respectively, to the absolute governments, even of their own class. All constitutional governments, of whatever class they may be, take the sense of the community by its parts,—each through its appropriate organ; and regard the sense of all its parts, as the sense of the whole. They all rest on the right of suffrage, and the responsibility of rulers, directly or indirectly. On the contrary, all absolute governments, of whatever form, concentrate power in one uncontrolled and irresponsible individual or body, whose will is regarded as the sense of the community. And, hence, the great and broad distinction between governments is,—not that of the one, the few, or the many,—but of the constitutional and the absolute.

From this there results another distinction, which, although secondary in its character, very strongly marks the difference between these forms of government. I refer to their respective conservative principle;—that is, the principle by which they are upheld and preserved. This principle, in constitutional governments, is *compromise;*—and in absolute governments, is *force;*—as will be next explained.

It has been already shown, that the same constitution of man which leads those who govern to oppress the governed,—if not prevented,— will, with equal force and certainty, lead the latter to resist oppression, when possessed of the means of doing so peaceably and successfully. But absolute governments, of all forms, exclude all other means of resistance to their authority, than that of force; and, of course, leave no other alternative to the governed, but to acquiesce in oppression, however great it may be, or to resort to force to put down the government. But the dread of such a resort must necessarily lead the government to prepare to meet force in order to protect itself; and hence, of necessity, force becomes the conservative principle of all such governments.

On the contrary, the government of the concurrent majority, where the organism is perfect, excludes the possibility of oppression, by giving to each interest, or portion, or order,—where there are established classes,—the means of protecting itself, by its negative, against all measures calculated to advance the peculiar interests of others at its expense. Its effect, then, is, to cause the different interests, portions, or orders,—as the case may be,—to desist from attempting to adopt any measure calculated to promote the prosperity of one, or more, by sacrificing that of others; and thus to force them to unite in such measures only as would promote the prosperity of all, as the only means to prevent the suspension of the action of the government;—and, thereby, to avoid anarchy, the greatest of all evils. It is by means of such authorized and effectual resistance, that oppression is prevented, and the necessity of resorting to force superseded, in governments of the concurrent majority;—and, hence, compromise, instead of force, becomes their conservative principle.

It would, perhaps, be more strictly correct to trace the conservative principle of constitutional governments to the necessity which compels the different interests, or portions, or orders, to compromise,—as the only way to promote their respective prosperity, and to avoid anarchy,—rather than to the compromise itself. No necessity can be more urgent and imperious, than that of avoiding anarchy. It is the same as that which makes government indispensable to preserve society; and is not less imperative than that which compels obedience to superior force. Traced to this source, the voice of a people,—uttered under the necessity of avoiding the greatest of calamities, through the organs of a government so constructed as to suppress the expression of all partial and selfish interests, and to give a full and faithful utterance to the sense of the whole community, in reference to its common welfare,—may, without impiety, be called *the voice of God*. To call any other so, would be impious.

In stating that force is the conservative principle of absolute, and compromise of constitutional governments, I have assumed both to be perfect in their kind; but not without bearing in mind, that few or none, in fact, have ever been so absolute as not to be under some restraint, and none so perfectly organized as to represent fully and perfectly the voice of the whole community. Such being the case, all must, in practice, depart more or less from the principles by which they are respectively upheld and preserved; and depend more or less for support, on force, or compromise, as the absolute or the constitutional form predominates in their respective organizations.

Nor, in stating that absolute governments exclude all other means of resistance to its authority than that of force, have I overlooked the case of governments of the numerical majority, which form, apparently, an exception. It is true that, in such governments, the minor and subject party, for the time, have the right to oppose and resist the major and dominant party, for the time, through the ballot-box; and may turn them out, and take their place, if they can obtain a majority of votes. But, it is no less true, that this would be a mere change in the relations of the two parties. The minor and subject party would become the major and dominant party, with the same absolute authority and tendency to abuse power; and the major and dominant party would become the minor and subject party, with the same right to resist through the ballot-box; and, if successful, again to change relations, with like effect. But such a state of things must necessarily be temporary. The conflict between the two parties must be transferred, sooner or later, from an appeal to the ballot-box to an appeal to force;—as I shall next proceed to explain.

The conflict between the two parties, in the government of the numerical majority, tends necessarily to settle down into a struggle for the honors and emoluments of the government; and each, in order to obtain an object so ardently desired, will, in the process of the struggle, resort to whatever measure may seem best calculated to effect this purpose. The adoption, by the one, of any measure, however objectionable, which might give it an advantage, would compel the other to follow its example. In such case, it would be indispensable to success to avoid division and keep united;—and hence, from a necessity inherent in the nature of such governments, each party must be alternately forced, in order to insure victory, to resort to measures to concentrate the control over its movements in fewer and fewer hands, as the struggle became more and more violent. This, in process of time, must lead to party organization, and party caucuses and discipline; and these, to the conversion of the honors and emoluments of the government into means of rewarding partisan services, in order to secure the fidelity and increase the zeal of the members of the party. The effect of the whole combined, even in the earlier stages of the process, when they exert the least pernicious influence, would be to place the control of the two parties in the hands of their respective majorities; and the government itself, virtually, under the control of the majority of the dominant party, for the time, instead of the majority of the whole community;—where the theory of this form of government vests it. Thus, in the very first stage of the process, the government becomes the government of a minority instead of a majority;—a minority, usually, and under the most favorable circumstances, of not much more than one-fourth of the whole community.

But the process, as regards the concentration of power, would not stop at this stage. The government would gradually pass from the hands of the majority of the party into those of its leaders; as the struggle became more intense, and the honors and emoluments of the government the all-absorbing objects. At this stage, principles and policy would lose all influence in the elections; and cunning, falsehood, deception, slander, fraud, and gross appeals to the appetites of the lowest and most worthless portions of the community, would take the place of sound reason and wise debate. After these have thoroughly debased and corrupted the community, and all the arts and devices of party have been exhausted, the government would vibrate between the two factions (for such will parties have become) at each successive election. Neither would be able to retain power beyond some fixed term; for those seeking office and patronage would become too numerous to be rewarded by the offices and patronage at the disposal of the government; and these being the sole objects of pursuit, the disappointed would, at the next succeeding election, throw their weight into the opposite scale, in the hope of better success at the next turn of the wheel. These vibrations would continue until confusion, corruption, disorder, and anarchy, would lead to an appeal to force;—to be followed by a revolution in the form of the government. Such must be the end of the government of the numerical majority; and such, in brief, the process through which it must pass, in the regular course of events, before it can reach it.

This transition would be more or less rapid, according to circumstances. The more numerous the population, the more extensive the country, the more diversified the climate, productions, pursuits and character of the people, the more wealthy, refined, and artificial their condition,—and the greater the amount of revenues and disbursements,—the more unsuited would the community be to such a government, and the more rapid would be the passage. On the other hand, it might be slow in its progress amongst small communities, during the early stages of their existence, with inconsiderable revenues and disbursements, and a population of simple habits; provided the people are sufficiently intelligent to exercise properly, the right of suffrage, and sufficiently conversant with the rules necessary to govern the deliberations of legislative bodies. It is, perhaps, the only form of popular government suited to a people, while they remain in such a condition. Any other would be not only too complex and cumbersome, but unnecessary to guard against oppression, where the motive to use power for that purpose would be so feeble. And hence, colonies, from countries having constitutional governments, if left to themselves, usually adopt governments based on the numerical majority. But as population increases, wealth accumulates, and, above all, the revenues and expenditures become large,—governments of this form must become less and less suited to the condition of society; until, if not in the mean time changed into governments of the concurrent majority, they must end in an appeal to force, to be followed by a radical change in its structure and character; and, most probably, into monarchy in its absolute form,—as will be next explained.

Such, indeed, is the repugnance between popular governments and force,—or, to be more specific,—military power,—that the almost necessary consequence of a resort to force, by such governments, in order to maintain their authority, is, not only a change of their form, but a change into the most opposite,—that of absolute monarchy. The two are the opposites of each other. From the nature of popular governments, the control of its powers is vested in the many; while military power, to be efficient, must be vested in a single individual. When, then, the two parties, in governments of the numerical majority, resort to force, in their struggle for supremacy, he who commands the successful party will have the control of the government itself. And, hence, in such contests, the party which may prevail, will usually find, in the commander of its forces, a master, under whom the great body of the community will be glad to find protection against the incessant agitation and violent struggles of two corrupt factions,—looking only to power as the means of securing to themselves the honors and emoluments of the government.

From the same cause, there is a like tendency in aristocratical to terminate in absolute governments of the monarchical form; but by no means as strong, because there is less repugnance between military power and aristocratical, than between it and democratical governments.

A broader position may, indeed, be taken; viz. that there is a tendency, in constitutional governments of every form, to degenerate into their respective absolute forms; and, in all absolute governments, into that of the monarchical form. But the tendency is much stronger in constitutional governments of the democratic form to degenerate into their respective absolute forms, than in either of the others; because, among other reasons, the distinction between the constitutional and absolute forms of aristocratical and monarchical governments, is far more strongly marked than in democratic governments. The effect of this is, to make the different orders or classes in an aristocracy, or monarchy, far more jealous and watchful of encroachment on their respective rights; and more resolute and persevering in resisting attempts to concentrate power in any one class or order. On the contrary, the line between the two forms, in popular governments, is so imperfectly understood, that honest and sincere friends of the constitutional form not unfrequently, instead of jealously watching and arresting their tendency to degenerate into their absolute forms, not only regard it with approbation, but employ all their powers to add to its strength and to increase its impetus, in the vain hope of making the government more perfect and popular. The numerical majority, perhaps, should usually be one of the elements of a constitutional democracy; but to make it the sole element, in order to perfect the constitution and make the government more popular, is one of the greatest and most fatal of political errors.

Among the other advantages which governments of the concurrent have over those of the numerical majority,—and which strongly illustrates their more popular character, is,—that they admit, with safety, a much greater extension of the right of suffrage. It may be safely extended in such governments to universal suffrage: that is,—to every male citizen of mature age, with few ordinary exceptions; but it cannot be so far extended in those of the numerical majority, without placing them ultimately under the control of the more ignorant and dependent portions of the community. For, as the community becomes populous, wealthy, refined, and highly civilized, the difference between the rich and the poor will become more strongly marked; and the number of the ignorant and dependent greater in proportion to the rest of the community. With the increase of this difference, the tendency to conflict between them will become stronger; and, as the poor and dependent become more numerous in proportion, there will be, in governments of the numerical majority, no want of leaders among the wealthy and ambitious, to excite and direct them in their efforts to obtain the control.

The case is different in governments of the concurrent majority. There, mere numbers have not the absolute control; and the wealthy and intelligent being identified in interest with the poor and ignorant of their respective portions or interests of the community, become their leaders and protectors. And hence, as the latter would have neither hope nor inducement to rally the former in order to obtain the control, the right of suffrage, under such a government, may be safely enlarged to the extent stated, without incurring the hazard to which such enlargement would expose governments of the numerical majority.

In another particular, governments of the concurrent majority have greatly the advantage. I allude to the difference in their respective tendency, in reference to dividing or uniting the community. That of the concurrent, as has been shown, is to unite the community, let its interests be ever so diversified or opposed; while that of the numerical is to divide it into two conflicting portions, let its interests be, naturally, ever so united and identified.

That the numerical majority will divide the community, let it be ever so homogeneous, into two great parties, which will be engaged in perpetual struggles to obtain the control of the government, has already been established. The great importance of the object at stake, must necessarily form strong party attachments and party antipathies;— attachments on the part of the members of each to their respective parties, through whose efforts they hope to accomplish an object dear to all; and antipathies to the opposite party, as presenting the only obstacle to success.

In order to have a just conception of their force, it must be taken into consideration, that the object to be won or lost appeals to the strongest passions of the human heart,—avarice, ambition, and rivalry. It is not then wonderful, that a form of government, which periodically stakes all its honors and emoluments, as prizes to be contended for, should divide the community into two great hostile parties; or that party attachments, in the progress of the strife, should become so strong among the members of each respectively, as to absorb almost every feeling of our nature, both social and individual; or that their mutual antipathies should be carried to such an excess as to destroy, almost entirely, all sympathy between them, and to substitute in its place strongest the aversion. Nor is it surprising, that under their joint influence, the community should cease to be the common centre of attachment, or that each party should find that centre only in itself. It is thus, that, in such governments, devotion to party becomes stronger than devotion to country;—the promotion of the interests of party more important than the promotion of the common good of the whole, and its triumph and ascendancy, objects of far greater solicitude, than the safety and prosperity of the community. It is thus, also, that the numerical majority, by regarding the community as a unit, and having, as such, the same interests throughout all its parts, must, by its necessary operation, divide it into two hostile parts, waging, under the forms of law, incessant hostilities against each other.

The concurrent majority, on the other hand, tends to unite the most opposite and conflicting interests, and to blend the whole in one common attachment to the country. By giving to each interest, or portion, the power of self-protection, all strife and struggle between them for ascendancy, is prevented; and, thereby, not only every feeling calculated to weaken the attachment to the whole is suppressed, but the individual and the social feelings are made to unite in one common devotion to country. Each sees and feels that it can best promote its own prosperity by conciliating the goodwill, and promoting the prosperity of the others. And hence, there will be diffused throughout the whole community kind feelings between its different portions; and, instead of antipathy, a rivalry amongst them to promote the interests of each other, as far as this can be done consistently with the interest of all. Under the combined influence of these causes, the interests of each would be merged in the common interests of the whole; and thus, the community would become a unit, by becoming the common centre of attachment of all its parts. And hence, instead of faction, strife, and struggle for party ascendancy, there would be patriotism, nationality, harmony, and a struggle only for supremacy in promoting the common good of the whole.

But the difference in their operation, in this respect, would not end here. Its effects would be as great in a moral, as I have attempted to show they would be in a political point of view. Indeed, public and private morals are so nearly allied, that it would be difficult for it to be otherwise. That which corrupts and debases the community, politically, must also corrupt and debase it morally. The same cause, which, in governments of the numerical majority, gives to party attachments and antipathies such force, as to place party triumph and ascendancy above the safety and prosperity of the community, will just as certainly give them sufficient force to overpower all regard for truth, justice, sincerity, and moral obligations of every description. It is, accordingly, found that, in the violent strifes between parties for the high and glittering prize of governmental honors and emoluments,—falsehood, injustice, fraud, artifice, slander, and breach of faith, are freely resorted to, as legitimate weapons;—followed by all their corrupting and debasing influences.

In the government of the concurrent majority, on the contrary, the same cause which prevents such strife, as the means of obtaining power, and which makes it the interest of each portion to conciliate and promote the interests of the others, would exert a powerful influence towards purifying and elevating the character of the government and the people, morally, as well as politically. The means of acquiring power,—or, more correctly, influence,—in such governments, would be the reverse. Instead of the vices, by which it is acquired in that of the numerical majority, the opposite virtues—truth, justice, integrity, fidelity, and all others, by which respect and confidence are inspired, would be the most certain and effectual means of acquiring it.

Nor would the good effects resulting thence be confined to those who take an active part in political affairs. They would extend to the whole community. For of all the causes which contribute to form the character of a people, those by which power, influence, and standing in the government are most certainly and readily obtained, are, by far, the most powerful. These are the objects most eagerly sought of all others by the talented and aspiring; and the possession of which commands the greatest respect and admiration. But, just in proportion to this respect and admiration will be their appreciation by those, whose energy, intellect, and position in society, are calculated to exert the greatest influence in forming the character of a people. If knowledge, wisdom, patriotism, and virtue, be the most certain means of acquiring them, they will be most highly appreciated and assiduously cultivated; and this would cause them to become prominent traits in the character of the people. But if, on the contrary, cunning, fraud, treachery, and party devotion be the most certain, they will be the most highly prized, and become marked features in their character. So powerful, indeed, is the operation of the concurrent majority, in this respect, that, if it were possible for a corrupt and degenerate community to establish and maintain a well-organized government of the kind, it would of itself purify and regenerate them; while, on the other hand, a government based wholly on the numerical majority, would just as certainly corrupt and debase the most patriotic and virtuous people. So great is their difference in this respect, that, just as the one or the other element predominates in the construction of any government, in the same proportion will the character of the government and the people rise or sink in the scale of patriotism and virtue. Neither religion nor education can counteract the strong tendency of the numerical majority to corrupt and debase the people.

If the two be compared, in reference to the ends for which government is ordained, the superiority of the government of the concurrent majority will not be less striking. These, as has been stated, are twofold; to protect, and to perfect society. But to preserve society, it is necessary to guard the community against injustice, violence, and anarchy within, and against attacks from without. If it fail in either, it would fail in the primary end of government, and would not deserve the name.

To perfect society, it is necessary to develope the faculties, intellectual and moral, with which man is endowed. But the main spring to their development, and, through this, to progress, improvement and civilization, with all their blessings, is the desire of individuals to better their condition. For, this purpose, liberty and security are indispensable. Liberty leaves each free to pursue the course he may deem best to promote his interest and happiness, as far as it may be compatible with the primary end for which government is ordained;— while security gives assurance to each, that he shall not be deprived of the fruits of his exertions to better his condition. These combined, give to this desire the strongest impulse of which it is susceptible. For, to extend liberty beyond the limits assigned, would be to weaken the government and to render it incompetent to fulfil its primary end,—the protection of society against dangers, internal and external. The effect of this would be, insecurity; and, of insecurity,—to weaken the impulse of individuals to better their condition, and thereby retard progress and improvement. On the other hand, to extend the powers of the government, so as to contract the sphere assigned to liberty, would have the same effect, by disabling individuals in their efforts to better their condition.

Herein is to be found the principle which assigns to power and liberty, their proper spheres, and reconciles each to the other under all circumstances. For, if power be necessary to secure to liberty the fruits of its exertions, liberty, in turn, repays power with interest, by increased population, wealth, and other advantages, which progress and improvement bestow on the community. By thus assigning to each its appropriate sphere, all conflicts between them cease; and each is made to co-operate with and assist the other, in fulfilling the great ends for which government is ordained.

But the principle, applied to different communities, will assign to them different limits. It will assign a larger sphere to power and a more contracted one to liberty, or the reverse, according to circumstances. To the former, there must ever be allotted, under all circumstances, a sphere sufficiently large to protect the community against danger from without and violence and anarchy within. The residuum belongs to liberty. More cannot be safely or rightly allotted to it.

But some communities require a far greater amount of power than others to protect them against anarchy and external dangers; and, of course, the sphere of liberty in such, must be proportionally contracted. The causes calculated to enlarge the one and contract the other, are numerous and various. Some are physical;—such as open and exposed frontiers, surrounded by powerful and hostile neighbors. Others are moral;—such as the different degrees of intelligence, patriotism, and virtue among the mass of the community, and their experience and proficiency in the art of self-government. Of these, the moral are, by far, the most influential. A community may possess all the necessary moral qualifications, in so high a degree, as to be capable of self-government under the most adverse circumstances; while, on the other hand, another may be so sunk in ignorance and vice, as to be incapable of forming a conception of liberty, or of living, even when most favored by circumstances, under any other than an absolute and despotic government.

The principle, in all communities, according to these numerous and various causes, assigns to power and liberty their proper spheres. To allow to liberty, in any case, a sphere of action more extended than this assigns, would lead to anarchy; and this, probably, in the end, to a contraction instead of an enlargement of its sphere. Liberty, then, when forced on a people unfit for it, would, instead of a blessing, be a curse; as it would, in its reaction, lead directly to anarchy,—the greatest of all curses. No people, indeed, can long enjoy more liberty than that to which their situation and advanced intelligence and morals fairly entitle them. If more than this be allowed, they must soon fall into confusion and disorder,—to be followed, if not by anarchy and despotism, by a change to a form of government more simple and absolute; and, therefore, better suited to their condition. And hence, although it may be true, that a people may not have as much liberty as they are fairly entitled to, and are capable of enjoying,—yet the reverse is unquestionably true,—that no people can long possess more than they are fairly entitled to.

Liberty, indeed, though among the greatest of blessings, is not so great as that of protection; inasmuch, as the end of the former is the progress and improvement of the race,—while that of the latter is its preservation and perpetuation. And hence, when the two come into conflict, liberty must, and ever ought, to yield to protection; as the existence of the race is of greater moment than its improvement.

It follows, from what has been stated, that it is a great and dangerous error to suppose that all people are equally entitled to liberty. It is a reward to be earned, not a blessing to be gratuitously lavished on all alike;—a reward reserved for the intelligent, the patriotic, the virtuous and deserving;—and not a boon to be bestowed on a people too ignorant, degraded and vicious, to be capable either of appreciating or of enjoying it. Nor is it any disparagement to liberty, that such is, and ought to be the case. On the contrary, its greatest praise,—its proudest distinction is, that an all-wise Providence has reserved it, as the noblest and highest reward for the development of our faculties, moral and intellectual. A reward more appropriate than liberty could not be conferred on the deserving;—nor a punishment inflicted on the undeserving more just, than to be subject to lawless and despotic rule. This dispensation seems to be the result of some fixed law;—and every effort to disturb or defeat it, by attempting to elevate a people in the scale of liberty, above the point to which they are entitled to rise, must ever prove abortive, and end in disappointment. The progress of a people rising from a lower to a higher point in the scale of liberty, is necessarily slow;—and by attempting to precipitate, we either retard, or permanently defeat it.

There is another error, not less great and dangerous, usually associated with the one which has just been considered. I refer to the opinion, that liberty and equality are so intimately united, that liberty cannot be perfect without perfect equality.

That they are united to a certain extent,—and that equality of citizens, in the eyes of the law, is essential to liberty in a popular government, is conceded. But to go further, and make equality of *condition* essential to liberty, would be to destroy both liberty and progress. The reason is, that inequality of condition, while it is a necessary consequence of liberty, is, at the same time, indispensable to progress. In order to understand why this is so, it is necessary to bear in mind, that the main spring to progress is, the desire of individuals to better their condition; and that the strongest impulse which can be given to it is, to leave individuals free to exert themselves in the manner they may deem best for that purpose, as far at least as it can be done consistently with the ends for which government is ordained,—and to secure to all the fruits of their exertions. Now, as individuals differ greatly from each other, in intelligence, sagacity, energy, perseverance, skill, habits of industry and economy, physical power, position and opportunity,—the necessary effect of leaving all free to exert themselves to better their condition, must be a corresponding inequality between those who may possess these qualities and advantages in a high degree, and those who may be deficient in them. The only means by which this result can be prevented are, either to impose such restrictions on the exertions of those who may possess them in a high degree, as will place them on a level with those who do not; or to deprive them of the fruits of their exertions. But to impose such restrictions on them would be destructive of liberty,—while, to deprive them of the fruits of their exertions, would be to destroy the desire of bettering their condition. It is, indeed, this inequality of condition between the front and rear ranks, in the march of progress, which gives so strong an impulse to the former to maintain their position, and to the latter to press forward into their files. This gives to progress its greatest impulse. To force the front rank back to the rear, or attempt to push forward the rear into line with the front, by the interposition of the government, would put an end to the impulse, and effectually arrest the march of progress.

These great and dangerous errors have their origin in the prevalent opinion that all men are born free and equal;—than which nothing can be more unfounded and false. It rests upon the assumption of a fact, which is contrary to universal observation, in whatever light it may be regarded. It is, indeed, difficult to explain how an opinion so destitute of all sound reason, ever could have been so extensively entertained, unless we regard it as being confounded with another, which has some semblance of truth;—but which, when properly understood, is not less false and dangerous. I refer to the assertion, that all men are equal in the state of nature; meaning, by a state of nature, a state of individuality, supposed to have existed prior to the social and political state; and in which men lived apart and independent of each other. If such a state ever did exist, all men would have been, indeed, free and equal in it; that is, free to do as they pleased, and exempt from the authority or control of others—as, by supposition, it existed anterior to society and government. But such a state is purely hypothetical. It never did, nor can exist; as it is inconsistent with the preservation and perpetuation of the race. It is, therefore, a great misnomer to call it *the state of nature*. Instead of being the natural state of man, it is, of all conceivable states, the most opposed to his nature—most repugnant to his feelings, and most incompatible with his wants. His natural state is, the social and political—the one for which his Creator made him, and the only one in which he can preserve and perfect his race. As, then, there never was such a state as the, so called, state of nature, and never can be, it follows, that men, instead of being born in it, are born in the social and political state; and of course, instead of being born free and equal, are born subject, not only to parental authority, but to the laws and institutions of the country where born, and under whose protection they draw their first breath. With these remarks, I return from this digression, to resume the thread of the discourse.

It follows, from all that has been said, that the more perfectly a government combines power and liberty,—that is, the greater its power and the more enlarged and secure the liberty of individuals, the more perfectly it fulfils the ends for which government is ordained. To show, then, that the government of the concurrent majority is better calculated to fulfil them than that of the numerical, it is only necessary to explain why the former is better suited to combine a higher degree of power and a wider scope of liberty than the latter. I shall begin with the former.

The concurrent majority, then, is better suited to enlarge and secure the bounds of liberty, because it is better suited to prevent government from passing beyond its proper limits, and to restrict it to its primary end,—the protection of the community. But in doing this, it leaves, necessarily, all beyond it open and free to individual exertions; and thus enlarges and secures the sphere of liberty to the greatest extent which the condition of the community will admit, as has been explained. The tendency of government to pass beyond its proper limits is what exposes liberty to danger, and renders it insecure; and it is the strong counteraction of governments of the concurrent majority to this tendency which makes them so favorable to liberty. On the contrary, those of the numerical, instead of opposing and counteracting this tendency, add to it increased strength, in consequence of the violent party struggles incident to them, as has been fully explained. And hence their encroachments on liberty, and the danger to which it is exposed under such governments.

So great, indeed, is the difference between the two in this respect, that liberty is little more than a name under all governments of the absolute form, including that of the numerical majority; and can only have a secure and durable existence under those of the concurrent or constitutional form. The latter, by giving to each portion of the community which may be unequally affected by its action, a negative on the others, prevents all partial or local legislation, and restricts its action to such measures as are designed for the protection and the good of the whole. In doing this, it secures, at the same time, the rights and liberty of the people, regarded individually; as each portion consists of those who, whatever may be the diversity of interests among themselves, have the same interest in reference to the action of the government.

Such being the case, the interest of each individual may be safely confided to the majority, or voice of his portion, against that of all others, and, of course, the government itself. It is only through an organism which vests each with a negative, in some one form or another, that those who have like interests in preventing the government from passing beyond its proper sphere, and encroaching on the rights and liberty of individuals, can co-operate peaceably and effectually in resisting the encroachments of power, and thereby preserve their rights and liberty. Individual resistance is too feeble, and the difficulty of concert and co-operation too great, unaided by such an organism, to oppose, successfully, the organized power of government, with all the means of the community at its disposal; especially in populous countries of great extent, where concert and co-operation are almost impossible. Even when the oppression of the government comes to be too great to be borne, and force is resorted to in order to overthrow it, the result is rarely ever followed by the establishment of liberty. The force sufficient to overthrow an oppressive government is usually sufficient to establish one equally, or more, oppressive in its place. And hence, in no governments, except those that rest on the principle of the concurrent or constitutional majority, can the people guard their liberty against power; and hence, also, when lost, the great difficulty and uncertainty of regaining it by force.

It may be further affirmed, that, being more favorable to the enlargement and security of liberty, governments of the concurrent, must necessarily be more favorable to progress, development, improvement, and civilization,—and, of course, to the increase of power which results from, and depends on these, than those of the numerical majority. That it is liberty which gives to them their greatest impulse, has already been shown; and it now remains to show, that these, in turn, contribute greatly to the increase of power.

In the earlier stages of society, numbers and individual prowess constituted the principal elements of power. In a more advanced stage, when communities had passed from the barbarous to the civilized state, discipline, strategy, weapons of increased power, and money,—as the means of meeting increased expense,—became additional and important elements. In this stage, the effects of progress and improvement on the increase of power, began to be disclosed; but still numbers and personal prowess were sufficient, for a long period, to enable barbarous nations to contend successfully with the civilized,—and, in the end, to overpower them,—as the pages of history abundantly testify. But a more advanced progress, with its numerous inventions and improvements, has furnished new and far more powerful and destructive implements of offence and defence, and greatly increased the intelligence and wealth, necessary to engage the skill and meet the increased expense required for their construction and application to purposes of war. The discovery of gunpowder, and the use of steam as an impelling force, and their application to military purposes, have for ever settled the question of ascendency between civilized and barbarous communities, in favor of the former. Indeed, these, with other improvements, belonging to the present state of progress, have given to communities the most advanced, a superiority over those the least so, almost as great as that of the latter over the brute creation. And among the civilized, the same causes have decided the question of superiority, where other circumstances are nearly equal, in favor of those whose governments have given the greatest impulse to development, progress, and improvement; that is, to those whose liberty is the largest and best secured. Among these, England and the United States afford striking examples, not only of the effects of liberty in increasing power, but of the more perfect adaptation of governments founded on the principle of the concurrent, or constitutional majority, to enlarge and secure liberty. They are both governments of this description, as will be shown hereafter.

But in estimating the power of a community, moral, as well as physical causes, must be taken into the calculation; and in estimating the effects of liberty on power, it must not be overlooked, that it is, in itself, an important agent in augmenting the force of moral, as well as of physical power. It bestows on a people elevation, self-reliance, energy, and enthusiasm; and these combined, give to physical power a vastly augmented and almost irresistible impetus.

These, however, are not the only elements of moral power. There are others, and among them harmony, unanimity, devotion to country, and a disposition to elevate to places of trust and power, those who are distinguished for wisdom and experience. These, when the occasion requires it, will, without compulsion, and from their very nature, unite and put forth the entire force of the community in the most efficient manner, without hazard to its institutions or its liberty.

All these causes combined, give to a community its maximum of power. Either of them, without the other, would leave it comparatively feeble. But it cannot be necessary, after what has been stated, to enter into any further explanation or argument in order to establish the superiority of governments of the concurrent majority over the numerical, in developing the great elements of moral power. So vast is this superiority, that the one, by its operation, necessarily leads to their development, while the other as necessarily prevents it,—as has been fully shown.

Such are the many and striking advantages of the concurrent over the numerical majority. Against the former but two objections can be made. The one is, that it is difficult of construction, which has already been sufficiently noticed; and the other, that it would be impracticable to obtain the concurrence of conflicting interests, where they were numerous and diversified; or, if not, that the process for this purpose, would be too tardy to meet, with sufficient promptness, the many and dangerous emergencies, to which all communities are exposed. This objection is plausible; and deserves a fuller notice than it has yet received.

The diversity of opinion is usually so great, on almost all questions of policy, that it is not surprising, on a slight view of the subject, it should be thought impracticable to bring the various conflicting interests of a community to unite on any one line of policy;—or, that a government, founded on such a principle, would be too slow in its movements and too weak in its foundation to succeed in practice. But, plausible as it may seem at the first glance, a more deliberate view will show, that this opinion is erroneous. It is true, that, when there is no urgent necessity, it is difficult to bring those who differ, to agree on any one line of action. Each will naturally insist on taking the course he may think best;—and, from pride of opinion, will be unwilling to yield to others. But the case is different when there is an urgent necessity to unite on some common course of action; as reason and experience both prove. When something *must* be done,—and when it can be done only by the united consent of all,—the necessity of the case will force to a compromise;—be the cause of that necessity what it may. On all questions of acting, necessity, where it exists, is the overruling motive; and where, in such cases, compromise among the parties is an indispensable condition to acting, it exerts an overruling influence in predisposing them to acquiesce in some one opinion or course of action. Experience furnishes many examples in confirmation of this important truth. Among these, the trial by jury is the most familiar, and on that account, will be selected for illustration.

In these, twelve individuals, selected without discrimination, must unanimously concur in opinion,—under the obligations of an oath to find a true verdict, according to law and evidence; and this, too, not unfrequently under such great difficulty and doubt, that the ablest and most experienced judges and advocates differ in opinion, after careful examination. And yet, as impracticable as this mode of trial would seem to a superficial observer, it is found, in practice, not only to succeed, but to be the safest, the wisest and the best that human ingenuity has ever devised. When closely investigated, the cause will be found in the necessity, under which the jury is placed, to agree unanimously, in order to find a verdict. This necessity acts as the predisposing cause of concurrence in some common opinion; and with such efficacy, that a jury rarely fails to find a verdict.

Under its potent influence, the jurors take their seats with the disposition to give a fair and impartial hearing to the arguments on both sides,—meet together in the jury-room,—not as disputants, but calmly to hear the opinions of each other, and to compare and weigh the arguments on which they are founded;—and, finally, to adopt that which, on the whole, is thought to be true. Under the influence of this *disposition* to *harmonize*, one after another falls into the same opinion, until unanimity is obtained. Hence its practicability;—and hence, also, its peculiar excellence. Nothing, indeed, can be more favorable to the success of truth and justice, than this predisposing influence caused by the necessity of being unanimous. It is so much so, as to compensate for the defect of legal knowledge, and a high degree of intelligence on the part of those who usually compose juries. If the necessity of unanimity were dispensed with, and the finding of a jury made to depend on a bare majority, jury-trial, instead of being one of the greatest improvements in the judicial department of government, would be one of the greatest evils that could be inflicted on the community. It would be, in such case, the conduit through which all the factious feelings of the day would enter and contaminate justice at its source.

But the same cause would act with still greater force in predisposing the various interests of the community to agree in a well organized government, founded on the concurrent majority. The necessity for unanimity, in order to keep the government in motion, would be far more urgent, and would act under circumstances still more favorable to secure it. It would be superfluous, after what has been stated, to add other reasons in order to show that no necessity, physical or moral, can be more imperious than that of government. It is so much so that, to suspend its action altogether, even for an inconsiderable period, would subject the community to convulsions and anarchy. But in governments of the concurrent majority such fatal consequences can only be avoided by the unanimous concurrence or acquiescence of the various portions of the community. Such is the imperious character of the necessity which impels to compromise under governments of this description.

But to have a just conception of the overpowering influence it would exert, the circumstances under which it would act must be taken into consideration. These will be found, on comparison, much more favorable than those under which juries act. In the latter case there is nothing besides the necessity of unanimity in finding a verdict, and the inconvenience to which they might be subjected in the event of division, to induce juries to agree, except the love of truth and justice, which, when not counteracted by some improper motive or bias, more or less influences all, not excepting the most depraved. In the case of governments of the concurrent majority, there is, besides these, the love of country, than which, if not counteracted by the unequal and oppressive action of government, or other causes, few motives exert a greater sway. It comprehends, indeed, within itself, a large portion both of our individual and social feelings; and, hence, its almost boundless control when left free to act. But the government of the concurrent majority leaves it free, by preventing abuse and oppression, and, with them, the whole train of feelings and passions which lead to discord and conflict between different portions of the community. Impelled by the imperious necessity of preventing the suspension of the action of government, with the fatal consequences to which it would lead, and by the strong additional impulse derived from an ardent love of country, each portion would regard the sacrifice it might have to make by yielding its peculiar interest to secure the common interest and safety of all, including its own, as nothing compared to the evils that would be inflicted on all, including its own, by pertinaciously adhering to a different line of action. So powerful, indeed, would be the motives for concurring, and under such circumstances, so weak would be those opposed to it, the wonder would be, not that there should, but that there should not be a compromise.

But to form a juster estimate of the full force of this impulse to compromise, there must be added that, in governments of the concurrent majority, each portion, in order to advance its own peculiar interests, would have to conciliate all others, by showing a disposition to advance theirs; and, for this purpose, each would select those to represent it, whose wisdom, patriotism, and weight of character, would command the confidence of the others. Under its influence,—and with representatives so well qualified to accomplish the object for which they were selected,—the prevailing desire would be, to promote the common interests of the whole; and, hence, the competition would be, not which should yield the least to promote the common good, but which should yield the most. It is thus, that concession would cease to be considered a sacrifice,—would become a free-will offering on the altar of the country, and lose the name of compromise. And herein is to be found the feature, which distinguishes governments of the concurrent majority so strikingly from those of the numerical. In the latter, each faction, in the struggle to obtain the control of the government, elevates to power the designing, the artful, and unscrupulous, who, in their devotion to party,—instead of aiming at the good of the whole,—aim exclusively at securing the ascendency of party.

When traced to its source, this difference will be found to originate in the fact, that, in governments of the concurrent majority, individual feelings are, from its organism, necessarily enlisted on the side of the social, and made to unite with them in promoting the interests of the whole, as the best way of promoting the separate interests of each; while, in those of the numerical majority, the social are necessarily enlisted on the side of the individual, and made to contribute to the interest of parties, regardless of that of the whole. To effect the former,— to enlist the individual on the side of the social feelings to promote the good of the whole, is the greatest possible achievement of the science of government; while, to enlist the social on the side of the individual to promote the interest of parties at the expense of the good of the whole, is the greatest blunder which ignorance can possibly commit.

To this, also, may be referred the greater solidity of foundation on which governments of the concurrent majority repose. Both, ultimately, rest on necessity; for force, by which those of the numerical majority are upheld, is only acquiesced in from necessity; a necessity not more imperious, however, than that which compels the different portions, in governments of the concurrent majority, to acquiesce in compromise. There is, however, a great difference in the motive, the feeling, the aim, which characterize the act in the two cases. In the one, it is done with that reluctance and hostility ever incident to enforced submission to what is regarded as injustice and oppression; accompanied by the desire and purpose to seize on the first favorable opportunity for resistance:—but in the other, willingly and cheerfully, under the impulse of an exalted patriotism, impelling all to acquiesce in whatever the common good requires.

It is, then, a great error to suppose that the government of the concurrent majority is impracticable;—or that it rests on a feeble foundation. History furnishes many examples of such governments;— and among them, one, in which the principle was carried to an extreme that would be thought impracticable, had it never existed. I refer to that of Poland. In this it was carried to such an extreme that, in the election of her kings, the concurrence or acquiescence of every individual of the nobles and gentry present, in an assembly numbering usually from one hundred and fifty to two hundred thousand, was required to make a choice; thus giving to each individual a veto on his election. So, likewise, every member of her Diet, (the supreme legislative body,) consisting of the king, the senate, bishops and deputies of the nobility and gentry of the palatinates, possessed a veto on all its proceedings;—

thus making an unanimous vote necessary to enact a law, or to adopt any measure whatever. And, as if to carry the principle to the utmost extent, the veto of a single member not only defeated the particular bill or measure in question, but prevented all others, passed during the session, from taking effect. Further, the principle could not be carried. It, in fact, made every individual of the nobility and gentry, a distinct element in the organism;—or, to vary the expression, made him an *Estate of the kingdom*. And yet this government lasted, in this form, more than two centuries; embracing the period of Poland's greatest power and renown. Twice, during its existence, she protected Christendom, when in great danger, by defeating the Turks under the walls of Vienna, and permanently arresting thereby the ride of their conquests westward.

It is true her government was finally subverted, and the people subjugated, in consequence of the extreme to which the principle was carried; not, however, because of its tendency to dissolution *from weakness*, but from the facility it afforded to powerful and unscrupulous neighbors to control, by their intrigues, the election of her kings. But the fact, that a government, in which the principle was carried to the utmost extreme, not only existed, but existed for so long a period, in great power and splendor, is proof conclusive both of its practicability and its compatibility with the power and permanency of government.

Another example, not so striking indeed, but yet deserving notice, is furnished by the government of a portion of the aborigines of our own country. I refer to the Confederacy of the Six Nations, who inhabited what now is called the western portion of the State of New-York. One chief delegate, chosen by each nation,—associated with six others of his own selection,—and making, in all, forty-two members, —constituted their federal, or general government. When met, they formed the council of the union,—and discussed and decided all questions relating to the common welfare. As in the Polish Diet, each member possessed a veto on its decision; so that nothing could be done without the united consent of all. But this, instead of making the Confederacy weak, or impracticable, had the opposite effect. It secured harmony in council and action, and with them a great increase of power. The Six Nations, in consequence, became the most powerful of all the Indian tribes within the limits of our country. They carried their conquest and authority far beyond the country they originally occupied.

I pass by, for the present, the most distinguished of all these examples;
—the Roman Republic;—where the veto, or negative power, was carried,
not indeed to the same extreme as in the Polish government, but very
far, and with great increase of power and stability;—as I shall show
more at large hereafter.

It may be thought,—and doubtless many have supposed, that the
defects inherent in the government of the numerical majority may be
remedied by a free press, as the organ of public opinion,—especially
in the more advanced stage of society,—so as to supersede the necessity
of the concurrent majority to counteract its tendency to oppression and
abuse of power. It is not my aim to detract from the importance of the
press, nor to underestimate the great power and influence which it
has given to public opinion. On the contrary, I admit these are so great,
as to entitle it to be considered a new and important political element.
Its influence is, at the present day, on the increase; and it is highly
probable that it may, in combination with the causes which have contributed to raise it to its present importance, effect, in time, great changes,
—social and political. But, however important its present influence
may be, or may hereafter become,—or, however great and beneficial
the changes to which it may ultimately lead, it can never counteract
the tendency of the numerical majority to the abuse of power,—nor
supersede the necessity of the concurrent, as an essential element in
the formation of constitutional governments. These it cannot effect for
two reasons, either of which is conclusive.

The one is, that it cannot change that principle of our nature, which
makes constitutions necessary to prevent government from abusing its
powers,—and government necessary to protect and perfect society.

Constituting, as this principle does, an essential part of our nature,—
no increase of knowledge and intelligence, no enlargement of our
sympathetic feelings, no influence of education, or modification of the
condition of society can change it. But so long as it shall continue to be
an essential part of our nature, so long will government be necessary;
and so long as this continues to be necessary, so long will constitutions,
also, be necessary to counteract its tendency to the abuse of power,—
and so long must the concurrent majority remain an essential element
in the formation of constitutions. The press may do much,—by giving
impulse to the progress of knowledge and intelligence, to aid the cause
of education, and to bring about salutary changes in the condition of
society. These, in turn, may do much to explode political errors,—to

teach how governments should be constructed in order to fulfil their ends; and by what means they can be best preserved, when so constructed. They may, also, do much to enlarge the social, and to restrain the individual feelings;—and thereby to bring about a state of things, when far less power will be required by governments to guard against internal disorder and violence, and external danger; and when, of course, the sphere of power may be greatly contracted and that of liberty proportionally enlarged. But all this would not change the nature of man; nor supersede the necessity of government. For so long as government exists, the possession of its control, as the means of directing its action and dispensing its honors and emoluments, will be an object of desire. While this continues to be the case, it must, in governments of the numerical majority, lead to party struggles; and, as has been shown, to all the consequences, which necessarily follow in their train, and, against which, the only remedy is the concurrent majority.

The other reason is to be found in the nature of the influence, which the press politically exercises.

It is similar, in most respects, to that of suffrage. They are, indeed, both organs of public opinion. The principal difference is, that the one has much more agency in forming public opinion, while the other gives a more authentic and authoritative expression to it. Regarded in either light, the press cannot, of itself, guard any more against the abuse of power, than suffrage; and for the same reason.

If what is called public opinion were always the opinion of the whole community, the press would, as its organ, be an effective guard against the abuse of power, and supersede the necessity of the concurrent majority; just as the right of suffrage would do, where the community, in reference to the action of government, had but one interest. But such is not the case. On the contrary, what is called public opinion, instead of being the united opinion of the whole community, is, usually, nothing more than the opinion or voice of the strongest interest, or combination of interests; and, not unfrequently, of a small, but energetic and active portion of the whole. Public opinion, in relation to government and its policy, is as much divided and diversified, as are the interests of the community; and the press, instead of being the organ of the whole, is usually but the organ of these various and diversified interests respectively; or, rather, of the parties growing out of them. It is used by them as the means of controlling public opinion, and of so moulding it, as to promote their peculiar interests, and to aid in carrying on the warfare of party. But as the organ and instrument of parties, in governments of the numerical majority, it is as incompetent as suffrage itself, to counteract the tendency to oppression, and abuse of power;—and can, no more than that, supersede the necessity of the concurrent majority. On the contrary, as the instrument of party warfare, it contributes greatly to increase party excitement, and the violence and virulence of party struggles; and, in the same degree, the tendency to oppression and abuse of power. Instead, then, of superseding the necessity of the concurrent majority, it increases it, by increasing the violence and force of party feelings,—in like manner as party caucuses and party machinery; of the latter of which, indeed, it forms an important part.

In one respect, and only one, the government of the numerical majority has the advantage over that of the concurrent, if, indeed, it can be called an advantage. I refer to its simplicity and facility of construction. It is simple indeed, wielded, as it is, by a single power— the will of the greater number—and very easy of construction. For this purpose, nothing more is necessary than universal suffrage, and the regulation of the manner of voting, so as to give to the greater number the supreme control over every department of government.

But, whatever advantages simplicity and facility of construction may give it, the other forms of absolute government possess them in a still higher degree. The construction of the government of the numerical majority, simple as it is, requires some preliminary measures and arrangements; while the others, especially the monarchical, will, in its absence, or where it proves incompetent, force themselves on the community. And hence, among other reasons, the tendency of all governments is, from the more complex and difficult of construction, to the more simple and easily constructed; and, finally, to absolute monarchy, as the most simple of all. Complexity and difficulty of construction, as far as they form objections, apply, not only to governments of the concurrent majority of the popular form, but to constitutional governments of every form. The least complex, and the most easily constructed of them, are much more complex and difficult of construction than any one of the absolute forms. Indeed, so great has been this difficulty, that their construction has been the result, not so much of wisdom and patriotism, as of favorable combinations of circumstances. They have, for the most part, grown out of the struggles between conflicting interests, which, from some fortunate turn, have ended in a compromise, by which both parties have been admitted, in some one way or another, to have a separate and distinct voice in the government. Where this has not been the case, they have been the product of fortunate circumstances, acting in conjunction with some pressing danger, which forced their adoption, as the only means by which it could be avoided. It would seem that it has exceeded human sagacity deliberately to plan and construct constitutional governments, with a full knowledge of the principles on which they were formed; or to reduce them to practice without the pressure of some immediate and urgent necessity. Nor is it surprising that such should be the case; for it would seem almost impossible for any man, or body of men, to be so profoundly and thoroughly acquainted with the people of any community which has made any considerable progress in civilization and wealth, with all the diversified interests ever accompanying them, as to be able to organize constitutional governments suited to their condition. But, even were this possible, it would be difficult to find any community sufficiently enlightened and patriotic to adopt such a government, without the compulsion of some pressing necessity. A constitution, to succeed, must spring from the bosom of the community, and be adapted to the intelligence and character of the people, and all the multifarious relations, internal and external, which distinguish one people from another. If it does not, it will prove, in practice, to be, not a constitution, but a cumbrous and useless machine, which must be speedily superseded and laid aside, for some other more simple, and better suited to their condition.

It would thus seem almost necessary that governments should commence in some one of the simple and absolute forms, which, however well suited to the community in its earlier stages, must, in its progress, lead to oppression and abuse of power, and, finally, to an appeal to force,—to be succeeded by a military despotism,—unless the conflicts to which it leads should be fortunately adjusted by a compromise, which will give to the respective parties a participation in the control of the government; and thereby lay the foundation of a constitutional government, to be afterwards matured and perfected. Such governments have been, emphatically, the product of circumstances. And hence, the difficulty of one people imitating the government of another. And hence, also, the importance of terminating all civil conflicts by a compromise, which shall prevent either party from obtaining complete control, and thus subjecting the other.

Of the different forms of constitutional governments, the popular is the most complex and difficult of construction. It is, indeed, so difficult, that ours, it is believed, may with truth be said to be the only one of a purely popular character, of any considerable importance, that ever existed. The cause is to be found in the fact, that, in the other two forms, society is arranged in artificial orders or classes. Where these exist, the line of distinction between them is so strongly marked as to throw into shade, or, otherwise, to absorb all interests which are foreign to them respectively. Hence, in an aristocracy, all interests are, politically, reduced to two,—the nobles and the people; and in a monarchy, with a nobility, into three,—the monarch, the nobles, and the people. In either case, they are so few that the sense of each may be taken separately, through its appropriate organ, so as to give to each a concurrent voice, and a negative on the other, through the usual departments of the government, without making it too complex, or too tardy in its movements to perform, with promptness and energy, all the necessary functions of government.

The case is different in constitutional governments of the popular form. In consequence of the absence of these artificial distinctions, the various natural interests, resulting from diversity of pursuits, condition, situation and character of different portions of the people,—and from the action of the government itself,—rise into prominence, and struggle to obtain the ascendency. They will, it is true, in governments of the numerical majority, ultimately coalesce, and form two great parties; but not so closely as to lose entirely their separate character and existence. These they will ever be ready to re-assume, when the objects for which they coalesced are accomplished. To overcome the difficulties occasioned by so great a diversity of interests, an organism far more complex is necessary.

Another obstacle, difficult to be overcome, opposes the formation of popular constitutional governments. It is much more difficult to terminate the struggles between conflicting interests, by compromise, in absolute popular governments, than in an aristocracy or monarchy.

In an aristocracy, the object of the people, in the ordinary struggle between them and the nobles, is not, at least in its early stages, to overthrow the nobility and revolutionize the government,—but to participate in its powers. Notwithstanding the oppression to which they may be subjected, under this form of government, the people commonly feel no small degree of respect for the descendants of a long line of distinguished ancestors; and do not usually aspire to more,—in opposing the authority of the nobles,—than to obtain such a participation in the powers of the government, as will enable them to correct its abuses and to lighten their burdens. Among the nobility, on the other hand, it sometimes happens that there are individuals of great influence with both sides, who have the good sense and patriotism to interpose, in order to effect a compromise by yielding to the reasonable demands of the people; and, thereby, to avoid the hazard of a final and decisive appeal to force. It is thus, by a judicious and timely compromise, the people, in such governments, may be raised to a participation in the administration sufficient for their protection, without the loss of authority on the part of the nobles.

In the case of a monarchy, the process is somewhat different. Where it is a military despotism, the people rarely have the spirit or intelligence to attempt resistance; or, if otherwise, their resistance must almost necessarily terminate in defeat, or in a mere change of dynasty,—by the elevation of their leader to the throne. It is different, where the monarch is surrounded by an hereditary nobility. In a struggle between him and them, both (but especially the monarch) are usually disposed to court the people, in order to enlist them on their respective sides,—a state of things highly favorable to their elevation. In this case, the struggle, if it should be long continued without decisive results, would almost necessarily raise them to political importance, and to a participation in the powers of the government.

The case is different in an absolute Democracy. Party conflicts between the majority and minority, in such governments, can hardly ever terminate in compromise.—The object of the opposing minority is to expel the majority from power; and of the majority to maintain their hold upon it. It is, on both sides, a struggle for the whole,—a struggle that must determine which shall be the governing, and which the subject party;—and, in character, object and result, not unlike that between competitors for the sceptre in absolute monarchies. Its regular course, as has been shown, is, excessive violence,—an appeal to force,—followed by revolution,—and terminating at last, in the elevation to supreme power of the general of the successful party. And hence, among other reasons, aristocracies and monarchies more readily assume the constitutional form than absolute popular governments.

Of the three different forms, the monarchical has heretofore been much the most prevalent, and, generally, the most powerful and durable. This result is doubtless to be attributed principally to the fact that, in its absolute form, it is the most simple and easily constructed. And hence, as government is indispensable, communities having too little intelligence to form or preserve the others, naturally fall into this. It may also, in part, be attributed to another cause, already alluded to; that, in its organism and character, it is much more closely assimilated than either of the other two, to military power; on which all absolute governments depend for support. And hence, also, the tendency of the others, and of constitutional governments which have been so badly constructed or become so disorganized as to require force to support them,—to pass into military despotism,—that is, into monarchy in its most absolute and simple form. And hence, again, the fact, that revolutions in absolute monarchies, end, almost invariably, in a change of dynasty,—and not of the forms of the government; as is almost universally the case in the other systems.

But there are, besides these, other causes of a higher character, which contribute much to make monarchies the most prevalent, and, usually, the most durable governments. Among them, the leading one is, they are the most susceptible of improvement;—that is, they can be more easily and readily modified, so as to prevent, to a limited extent, oppression and abuse of power, without assuming the constitutional form, in its strict sense. It slides, almost naturally, into one of the most important modifications. I refer to hereditary descent. When this becomes well defined and firmly established, the community or kingdom, comes to be regarded by the sovereign as the hereditary possession of his family,—a circumstance which tends strongly to identify his interests with those of his subjects, and thereby, to mitigate the rigor of the government. It gives, besides, great additional security to his person; and prevents, in the same degree, not only the suspicion and hostile feelings incident to insecurity,—but invites all those kindly feelings which naturally spring up on both sides, between those whose interests are identified,—when there is nothing to prevent it. And hence the strong feelings of paternity on the side of the sovereign,—and of loyalty on that of his subjects, which are often exhibited in such governments.

There is another improvement of which it is readily susceptible, nearly allied to the preceding. The hereditary principle not unfrequently extends to other families,—especially to those of the distinguished chieftains, by whose aid the monarchy was established, when it originates in conquest. When this is the case,—and a powerful body of hereditary nobles surround the sovereign, they oppose a strong resistance to his authority, and he to theirs,—tending to the advantage and security of the people. Even when they do not succeed in obtaining a participation in the powers of the government, they usually acquire sufficient weight to be felt and respected. From this state of things, such governments usually, in time, settle down on some fixed rules of action, which the sovereign is compelled to respect, and by which increased protection and security are acquired by all. It was thus the enlightened monarchies of Europe were formed, under which the people of that portion of the globe have made such great advances in power, intelligence, and civilization.

To these may be added the greater capacity, which governments of the monarchical form have exhibited, to hold under subjection a large extent of territory, and a numerous population; and which has made them more powerful than others of a different form, to the extent, that these constitute an element of power. All these causes combined, have given such great and decisive advantages, as to enable them, heretofore, to absorb, in the progress of events, the few governments which have, from time to time, assumed different forms;—not excepting even the mighty Roman Republic, which, after attaining the highest point of power, passed, seemingly under the operation of irresistible causes, into a military despotism. I say, heretofore,—for it remains to be seen whether they will continue to retain their advantages, in these respects, over the others, under the great and growing influence of public opinion, and the new and imposing form which popular government has assumed with us.

These have already effected great changes, and will probably effect still greater,—adverse to the monarchical form; but, as yet, these changes have tended rather to the absolute, than to the constitutional form of popular government,—for reasons which have been explained. If this tendency should continue permanently in the same direction, the monarchical form must still retain its advantages, and continue to be the most prevalent. Should this be the case, the alternative will be between monarchy and popular government, in the form of the numerical majority,—or absolute democracy; which, as has been shown, is not only the most fugitive of all the forms, but has the strongest tendency of all others to the monarchical. If, on the contrary, this tendency, or the changes referred to, should incline to the constitutional form of popular government,—and a proper organism come to be regarded as not less indispensable than the right of suffrage to the establishment of such governments,—in such case, it is not improbable that, in the progress of events, the monarchical will cease to be the prevalent form of government. Whether they will take this direction, at least for a long time, will depend on the success of our government,—and a correct understanding of the principles on which it is constructed.

To comprehend more fully the force and bearing of public opinion, and to form a just estimate of the changes to which, aided by the press, it will probably lead, politically and socially,—it will be necessary to consider it in connection with the causes that have given it an influence so great, as to entitle it to be regarded as a new political element. They will, upon investigation, be found in the many discoveries and inventions made in the last few centuries.

Among the more prominent of those of an earlier date, stand the practical application of the magnetic power to the purposes of navigation, by the invention of the mariner's compass; the discovery of the mode of making gunpowder, and its application to the art of war; and the invention of the art of printing. Among the more recent are, the numerous chemical and mechanical discoveries and inventions, and their application to the various arts of production; the application of steam to machinery of almost every description, especially to such as is designed to facilitate transportation and travel by land and water; and, finally, the invention of the magnetic telegraph.

All these have led to important results. Through the invention of the mariner's compass, the globe has been circumnavigated and explored, and all who inhabit it, with but few exceptions, brought within the sphere of an all-pervading commerce, which is daily diffusing over its surface the light and blessings of civilization. Through that of the art of printing, the fruits of observation and reflection, of discoveries and inventions, with all the accumulated stores of previously acquired knowledge, are preserved and widely diffused. The application of gunpowder to the art of war, has for ever settled the long conflict for ascendency between civilization and barbarism, in favor of the former, and thereby guarantied that, whatever knowledge is now accumulated, or may hereafter be added, shall never again be lost. The numerous discoveries and inventions, chemical and mechanical, and the application of steam to machinery, have increased, many-fold, the productive

powers of labor and capital; and have, thereby, greatly increased the
number, who may devote themselves to study and improvement,—
and the amount of means necessary for commercial exchanges,—
especially between the more and the less advanced and civilized portions
of the globe,—to the great advantage of both, but particularly of the
latter. The application of steam to the purposes of travel and transportation, by land and water, has vastly increased the facility, cheapness
and rapidity of both;—diffusing, with them, information and intelligence almost as quickly and as freely as if borne by the winds; while
the electrical wires outstrip them, in velocity—rivalling, in rapidity, even
thought itself.

The joint effect of all has been, a great increase and diffusion of
knowledge; and, with this, an impulse to progress and civilization
heretofore unexampled in the history of the world,—accompanied by
a mental energy and activity unprecedented.

To all these causes, public opinion, and its organ, the press, owe
their origin and great influence. Already they have attained a force
in the more civilized portions of the globe sufficient to be felt by all
governments, even the most absolute and despotic. But, as great as
they now are, they have as yet attained nothing like their maximum
force. It is probable, that not one of the causes, which have contributed
to their formation and influence, has yet produced its full effect; while
several of the most powerful have just begun to operate; and many
others, probably of equal or even greater force, yet remain to be brought
to light.

When the causes now in operation have produced their full effect,
and inventions and discoveries shall have been exhausted,—if that
may ever be,—they will give a force to public opinion, and cause
changes, political and social, difficult to be anticipated. What will be
their final bearing, time only can decide with any certainty. That they
will, however, greatly improve the condition of man ultimately,—it
would be impious to doubt. It would be to suppose, that the all-wise
and beneficent Being,—the Creator of all,—had so constituted man,
as that the employment of the high intellectual faculties, with which
He has been pleased to endow him, in order that he might develop the
laws that control the great agents of the material world, and make
them subservient to his use,—would prove to him the cause of permanent evil,—and not of permanent good. If, then, such a supposition
be inadmissible, they must, in their orderly and full development, end

in his permanent good. But this cannot be, unless the ultimate effect of their action, politically, shall be, to give ascendency to that form of government best calculated to fulfil the ends for which government is ordained. For, so completely does the well-being of our race depend on good government, that it is hardly possible any change, the ultimate effect of which should be otherwise, could prove to be a permanent good.

It is, however, not improbable, that many and great, but temporary evils, will follow the changes they have effected, and are destined to effect. It seems to be a law in the political, as well as in the material world, that great changes cannot be made, except very gradually, without convulsions and revolutions; to be followed by calamities, in the beginning, however beneficial they may prove to be in the end. The first effect of such changes, on long established governments, will be, to unsettle the opinions and principles in which they originated,— and which have guided their policy,—before those, which the changes are calculated to form and establish, are fairly developed and understood. The interval between the decay of the old and the formation and establishment of the new, constitutes a period of transition, which must always necessarily be one of uncertainty, confusion, error, and wild and fierce fanaticism.

The governments of the more advanced and civilized portions of the world are now in the midst of this period. It has proved, and will continue to prove a severe trial to existing political institutions of every form. Those governments which have not the sagacity to perceive what is truly public opinion,—to distinguish between it and the mere clamor of faction, or shouts of fanaticism,—and the good sense and firmness to yield, timely and cautiously, to the claims of the one,—and to resist, promptly and decidedly, the demands of the other,—are doomed to fall. Few will be able successfully to pass through this period of transition; and these, not without shocks and modifications, more or less considerable. It will endure until the governing and the governed shall better understand the ends for which government is ordained, and the form best adapted to accomplish them, under all the circumstances in which communities may be respectively placed. . . .

18.   FITZHUGH
Defense of Slavery

George Fitzhugh (1806–1881) was a Virginia lawyer and publicist of the proslavery cause. During the 1850's the North was undergoing a period of growing radicalism, including abolitionism, Utopian socialism, and the women's rights movements. It was against these movements, and especially against abolition, that Fitzhugh directed his intellectual energies.

In *Sociology for the South* (1854), from which this selection* is taken, Fitzhugh openly rejected the assumptions of John Locke, replacing Locke's emphasis on individualism with a stress on the organic nature of society which he derived from Aristotle. Fitzhugh attacked, in turn, the doctrines of equality, national rights, and laissez-faire. His view of society was hierarchical, paternalistic, and traditional. Fitzhugh felt that liberalism and individualism would destroy the values of the community and the family—beliefs which are still accepted today by many American conservatives.

Liberty and equality are new things under the sun. The free states of antiquity abounded with slaves. The feudal system that supplanted Roman institutions changed the form of slavery, but brought with it neither liberty nor equality. France and the Northern States of our Union have alone fully and fairly tried the experiment of a social organization founded upon universal liberty and equality of rights. England has only approximated to this condition in her commercial and manufacturing cities. The examples of small communities in Europe are not fit exponents of the working of the system. In France and in our Northern States the experiment has already failed, if we are to form our opinions from the discontent of the masses, or to believe the evidence of the Socialists, Communists, Anti-Renters, and a thousand other agrarian sects that have arisen in these countries, and threaten

* From the Appendix chapter, "Slavery Justified: Liberty and Equality—Socialism—Young England—Domestic Slavery," in *Sociology for the South* (Richmond, Va.: A. Morris, 1854), pp. 226–33, 235–36, 241–49.

to subvert the whole social fabric. The leaders of these sects, at least in France, comprise within their ranks the greater number of the most cultivated and profound minds in the nation, who have made government their study. Add to the evidence of these social philosophers, who, watching closely the working of the system, have proclaimed to the world its total failure, the condition of the working classes, and we have conclusive proof that liberty and equality have not conduced to enhance the comfort or the happiness of the people. Crime and pauperism have increased. Riots, trades unions, strikes for higher wages, discontent breaking out into revolution, are things of daily occurrence, and show that the poor see and feel quite as clearly as the philosophers, that their condition is far worse under the new than under the old order of things. Radicalism and Chartism in England owe their birth to the free and equal institutions of her commercial and manufacturing districts, and are little heard of in the quiet farming districts, where remnants of feudalism still exist in the relation of landlord and tenant, and in the laws of entail and primogeniture.

So much for experiment. We will now endeavor to treat the subject theoretically, and to show that the system is on its face self-destructive and impracticable. When we look to the vegetable, animal and human kingdoms, we discover in them all a constant conflict, war, or race of competition, the result of which is, that the weaker or less healthy genera, species and individuals are continually displaced and exterminated by the stronger and more hardy. It is a means by which some contend Nature is perfecting her own work. We, however, witness the war, but do not see the improvement. Although from the earliest date of recorded history, one race of plants has been eating out and taking the place of another, the stronger or more cunning animals been destroying the feebler, and man exterminating and supplanting his fellow, still the plants, the animals and the men of to-day seem not at all superior, even in those qualities of strength and hardihood to which they owe their continued existence, to those of thousands of years ago. To this propensity of the strong to oppress and destroy the weak, government owes it existence. So strong is this propensity, and so destructive to human existence, that man has never yet been found so savage as to be without government. Forgetful of this important fact, which is the origin of all governments, the political economists and the advocates of liberty and equality propose to enhance the well being of man by trammeling his conduct as little as possible, and encouraging what they call FREE COMPETITION. Now, free competition is but another name for liberty and equality, and we must acquire precise and accurate notions about it in order to ascertain how free institutions will work. It is, then, that war or conflict to which Nature impels her creatures, and which government was intended to restrict. It is true, it is that war somewhat modified and restricted, for the warmest friends of freedom would have some government. The question is, whether the proposed restrictions are sufficient to neutralize the self-destructive tendencies which nature impresses on society. We proceed to show that the war of the wits, of mind with mind, which free competition or liberty and equality beget and encourage, is quite as oppressive, cruel and exterminating, as the war of the sword, of theft, robbery, and murder, which it forbids. It is only substituting strength of mind for strength of body. Men are told it is their duty to compete, to endeavor to get ahead of and supplant their fellow men, by the exercise of all the intellectual and moral strength with which nature and education have endowed them. "Might makes right," is the order of creation, and this law of nature, so far as mental might is concerned, is restored by liberty to man. The struggle to better one's condition, to pull others down or supplant them, is the great organic law of free society. All men being equal, all aspire to the highest honors and the largest possessions. Good men and bad men teach their children one and the same lesson—-"Go ahead, push your way in the world." In such society, virtue, if virtue there be, loses all her loveliness because of her selfish aims. None but the selfish virtues are encouraged, because none other aid a man in the race of free competition. Good men and bad men have the same end in view, are in pursuit of the same object— self-promotion, self-elevation. The good man is prudent, cautious, and cunning of fence; he knows well the arts (the virtues, if you please,) which will advance his fortunes and enable him to depress and supplant others; he bides his time, takes advantage of the follies, the improvidence, and vices of others, and makes his fortune out of the misfortunes of his fellow men. The bad man is rash, hasty, and unskillful. He is equally selfish, but not half so cunning. Selfishness is almost the only motive of human conduct with good and bad in free society, where every man is taught that he may change and better his condition. A vulgar adage, "Every man for himself, and devil take the hindmost," is the moral which liberty and free competition inculcate. Now, there are no more honors and wealth in proportion to numbers, in this generation, than in the one which preceded it, population fully keeps pace with the means of subsistence; hence, these who better their condition or rise to higher places in society, do so generally by pulling down others or pushing them from their places. Where men of strong minds, of strong wills, and of great self-control, come into free competition with the weak and improvident, the latter soon become the inmates of jails and penitentiaries.

The statistics of France, England and America show that pauperism and crime advance *pari passu* with liberty and equality. How can it be otherwise, when all society is combined to oppress the poor and weak minded? The rich man, however good he may be, employs the laborer who will work for the least wages. If he be a good man, his punctuality enables him to cheapen the wages of the poor man. The poor war with one another in the race of competition, in order to get employment, by underbidding; for laborers are more abundant than employers. Population increases faster than capital. Look to the situation of woman when she is thrown into this war of competition, and has to support herself by her daily wages. For the same or equally valuable services she gets not half the pay that man does, simply because the modesty of her sex prevents her from resorting to all the arts and means of competition which men employ. He who would emancipate woman, unless he could make her as coarse and strong in mind and body as man, would be her worst enemy; her subservience to and dependence on man, is necessary to her very existence. She is not a soldier fitted to enlist in the war of free competition. We do not set children and women free because they are not capable of taking care of themselves, not equal to the constant struggle of society. To set them free would be to give the lamb to the wolf to take care of. Society would quickly devour them. If the children of ten years of age were remitted to all the rights of person and property which men enjoy, all can perceive how soon ruin and penury would overtake them. But half of mankind are but grown-up children, and liberty is as fatal to them as it would be to children.

We will cite another familiar instance to prove and illustrate the destructive effects of liberty or free competition. It is that where two races of men of different capacity are brought into juxtaposition. It is the boast of the Anglo-Saxon, that by the arts of peace, under the influence of free trade he can march to universal conquest. However true this may be, all know that if Englishmen or Americans settle among inferior races, they soon become the owners of the soil, and gradually extirpate or reduce to poverty the original owners. They are the wiregrass of nations. The same law of nature which enables and impels the stronger race to oppress and exterminate the weaker, is constantly at work in the bosom of every society, between its stronger and weaker members. Liberty and equality rather encourage than restrict this law in its deadly operation. A Northern gentleman, who was both statesman and philosopher, once told us, that his only objection to domestic slavery was, that it would perpetuate an inferior race, who, under the influence of free trade and free competition, would otherwise disappear from the earth. China and Japan acted wisely to anticipate this new philosophy and exclude Europeans.

One step more, and that the most difficult in this process of reasoning and illustration, and we have done with this part of our subject. Liberty and equality throw the whole weight of society on its weakest members; they combine all men in oppressing precisely that part of mankind who most need sympathy, aid and protection. The very astute and avaricious man, when left free to exercise his faculties, is injured by no one in the field of competition, but levies a tax on all with whom he deals. The sensible and prudent, but less astute man, is seldom worsted in competing with his fellow men, and generally benefited. The very simple and improvident man is the prey of every body. The simple man represents a class, the common day laborers. The employer cheapens their wages, and the retail dealer takes advantage of their ignorance, their inability to visit other markets, and their want of credit, to charge them enormous profits. They bear the whole weight of society on their shoulders; they are the producers and artificers of all the necessaries, the comforts, the luxuries, the pomp and splendor of the world; they create it all, and enjoy none of it; they are the muzzled ox that treadeth out the straw; they are at constant war with those above them, asking higher wages but getting lower; for they are also at war with each other, underbidding to get employment. This process of underbidding never ceases so long as employers want profits or laborers want employment. It ends when wages are reduced too low to afford subsistence, in filling poor-houses, and jails, and graves. It has reached that point already in France, England and Ireland. A half million died of hunger in one year in Ireland—they died because in the eye of the law they were the equals, and liberty had made them the enemies, of their landlords and employers. Had they been vassals or serfs, they would have been beloved, cherished and taken care of by those same landlords and employers. Slaves never die of hunger, scarcely ever feel want.

The bestowing upon men equality of rights, is but giving license to the strong to oppress the weak. It begets the grossest inequalities of condition. Menials and day laborers are and must be as numerous as in a land of slavery. And these menials and laborers are only taken care of while young, strong and healthy. If the laborer gets sick, his wages cease just as his demands are greatest. If two of the poor get married, who being young and healthy, are getting good wages, in a few years they may have four children. Their wants have increased, but the mother has enough to do to nurse the four children, and the wages of the husband must support six. There is no equality, except in theory, in such society, and there is no liberty. The men of property, those who own lands and money, are masters of the poor; masters, with none of the feelings, interests or sympathies of masters; they employ them when they please, and for what they please, and may leave them to die in the highway, for it is the only home to which the poor in free countries are entitled. . . .

The moral effect of free society is to banish Christian virtue, that virtue which bids us love our neighbor as ourself, and to substitute the very equivocal virtues proceeding from mere selfishness. The intense struggle to better each one's pecuniary condition, the rivalries, the jealousies, the hostilities which it begets, leave neither time nor inclination to cultivate the heart or the head. Every finer feeling of our nature is chilled and benumbed by its selfish atmosphere; affection is under the ban, because affection makes us less regretful of mere self; hospitality is considered criminal waste, chivalry a stumbling-block, and the code of honor foolishness; taste, sentiment, imagination, are forbidden ground, because no money is to be made by them. Gorgeous pageantry and sensual luxury are the only pleasures indulged in, because they alone are understood and appreciated, and they are appreciated just for what they cost in dollars and cents. What makes money, and what costs money, are alone desired. Temperance, frugality, thrift, attention to business, industry, and skill in making bargains are virtues in high repute, because they enable us to supplant others and increase our own wealth. The character of our Northern brethren, and of the Dutch, is proof enough of the justice of these reflections. The Puritan fathers had lived in Holland, and probably imported Norway rats and Dutch morality in the Mayflower.

Liberty and equality are not only destructive to the morals, but to the happiness of society. Foreigners have all remarked on the care-worn thoughtful, unhappy countenances of our people, and the remark only applies to the North, for travellers see little of us at the South, who live far from highways and cities, in contentment on our farms. . . .

Self-interest makes the employer and free laborer enemies. The one prefers to pay low wages, the other needs high wages. War, constant war, is the result, in which the operative perishes, but is not vanquished; he is hydra-headed, and when he dies two take his place. But numbers diminish his strength. The competition among laborers to get employment begets an intestine war, more destructive than the war from above. There is but one remedy for this evil, so inherent in free society, and that is, to identify the interests of the weak and the strong, the poor and the rich. Domestic Slavery does this far better than any other institution. Feudalism only answered the purpose in so far as Feudalism retained the features of slavery. To it (slavery) Greece and Rome, Egypt and Judea, and all the other distinguished States of antiquity, were indebted for their great prosperity and high civilization; a prosperity and a civilization which appear almost miraculous, when we look to their ignorance of the physical sciences. In the moral sciences they were our equals, in the fine arts vastly our superiors. Their poetry, their painting, their sculpture, their drama, their elocution, and their architecture, are models which we imitate, but never equal. In the science of government and of morals, in pure metaphysics, and in all the walks of intellectual philosophy, we have been beating the air with our wings or revolving in circles, but have not advanced an inch. Kant is not ahead of Aristotle—and Juvenal has expressed in little more than a line the modern utilitarian morality—

> Quis enim virtutem amplectitur ipsam
> Prooemia si tollas?*

Terence, himself a slave, with a heart no doubt filled with the kindly affections which the relation of master and slave begets, uttered the loftiest sentiment that ever emanated from uninspired man:

> Homo sum; humani nihil a me alienum puto.†

* "Who indeed embraces virtue itself if you remove the rewards?"
† "I am a man; nothing human is alien to me."

But this high civilization and domestic slavery did not merely co-exist, they were cause and effect. Every scholar whose mind is at all imbued with ancient history and literature, sees that Greece and Rome were indebted to this institution alone for the taste, the leisure and the means to cultivate their heads and their hearts; had they been tied down to Yankee notions of thrift, they might have produced a Franklin, with his "penny saved is a penny gained;" they might have had utilitarian philosophers and invented the spinning jenny, but they never would have produced a poet, an orator, a sculptor or an architect; they would never have uttered a lofty sentiment, achieved a glorious feat in war, or created a single work of art.

A modern Yankee, or a Dutchman, is the fair result of liberty and equality. French character has not yet been subdued and tamed into insignificance by their new institutions; and besides, the pursuit of arms elevates and purifies the sentiments of Frenchmen. In what is the Yankee or Dutchman comparable to the Roman, Athenian or Spartan? In nothing save his care of his self and his skill in driving a bargain. The ruins of Thebes, of Nineveh, and of Balbec, the obelisks and pyramids of Egypt, the lovely and time-defying relics of Roman and Grecian art, the Doric column and the Gothic spire, alike attest the taste, the genius and the energy of society where slavery existed.

Quis locus,
*Quoc regio in terris non nostri glena laboris?**

And now Equality, where then are thy monuments? And Echo answers where! Echo deep, deep, from the bowels of the earth, where women and children drag out their lives in darkness, harnessed like horses to heavy cars loaded with ore. Or, perhaps, it is an echo from some grand, gloomy and monotonous factory, where pallid children work fourteen hours a day, and go home at night to sleep in damp cellars. It may be too, this cellar contains aged parents too old to work, and cast off by their employer to die. Great railroads and mighty steamships too, thou mayest boast, but still the operatives who construct them are being destined to poverty and neglect. Not a vestige of art canst thou boast; not a ray of genius illumes thy handiwork. The sordid spirit of mammon presides o'er all, and from all proceed the sighs and groans of the oppressed.

* "What place, what region on the earth, is not full of our labor?"—Horace.

Domestic slavery in the Southern States has produced the same results in elevating the character of the master that it did in Greece and Rome. He is lofty and independent in his sentiments, generous, affectionate, brave and eloquent; he is superior to the Northerner in every thing but the arts of thrift. History proves this. A Yankee sometimes gets hold of the reins of State, attempts Apollo, but acts Phæton. Scipio and Aristides, Calhoun and Washington, are the noble results of domestic slavery. Like Egyptian obelisks 'mid the waste of time—simple, severe, sublime,—they point ever heavenward, and lift the soul by their examples. Adams and Van Buren, cunning, complex and tortuous, are fit exponents of the selfish system of universal liberty.* Coriolanus, marching to the gates of Rome with dire hate and deadly indignation, is grand and noble in his revenge. Adams and Van Buren, insidiously striking with reptile fangs at the South, excite in all bosoms hatred and contempt; but we will not indulge in sweeping denunciation. In public and in private life, the North has many noble and generous souls. Men who, like Webster and Cass, Dickinson and Winthrop, can soar in lofty eloquence beyond the narrow prejudices of time and place, see man in all his relations, and contemn the narrow morality which makes the performance of one duty the excuse for a thousand crimes. We speak only of the usual and common effects of slavery and of equality. The Turk, half civilized as he is, exhibits the manly, noble and generous traits of character peculiar to the slave owner; he is hospitable, generous, truthful, brave, and strictly honest. In many respects, he is the finest specimen of humanity to be found in the world.

But the chief and far most important enquiry is, how does slavery affect the condition of the slave? One of the wildest sects of Communists in France proposes not only to hold all property in common, but to divide the profits, not according to each man's in-put and labor, but according to each man's wants. Now this is precisely the system of domestic slavery with us. We provide for each slave, in old age and in infancy, in sickness and in health, not according to his labor, but according to his wants. The master's wants are more costly and refined, and he therefore gets a larger share of the profits. A Southern farm is the beau ideal of Communism; it is a joint concern, in which the slave

---

* The North was pushing the Wilmot Proviso when this was written. We wrote under angry excitement. We did Mr. Van Buren injustice and the North injustice. We believe Mr. Van Buren thoroughly patriotic, though wrong on the Proviso; and we think Northerners more fanatical than selfish.

consumes more than the master, of the coarse products, and is far happier, because although the concern may fail, he is always sure of a support; he is only transferred to another master to participate in the profits of another concern; he marries when he pleases, because he knows he will have to work no more with a family than without one, and whether he live or die, that family will be taken care of; he exhibits all the pride of ownership, despises a partner in a smaller concern, "a poor man's negro," boasts of "our crops, horses, fields and cattle;" and is as happy as a human being can be. And why should he not?— he enjoys as much of the fruits of the farm as he is capable of doing, and the wealthiest can do no more. Great wealth brings many additional cares, but few additional enjoyments. Our stomachs do not increase in capacity with our fortunes. We want no more clothing to keep us warm. We may create new wants, but we cannot create new pleasures. The intellectual enjoyments which wealth affords are probably balanced by the new cares it brings along with it.

There is no rivalry, no competition to get employment among slaves, as among free laborers. Nor is there a war between master and slave. The master's interest prevents his reducing the slave's allowance or wages in infancy or sickness, for he might lose the slave by so doing. His feeling for his slave never permits him to stint him in old age. The slaves are all well fed, well clad, have plenty of fuel, and are happy. They have no dread of the future—no fear of want. A state of dependence is the only condition in which reciprocal affection can exist among human beings—the only situation in which the war of competition ceases, and peace, amity and good will arise. A state of independence always begets more or less of jealous rivalry and hostility. A man loves his children because they are weak, helpless and dependent, he loves his wife for similar reasons. When his children grow up and assert their independence, he is apt to transfer his affection to his grand-children. He ceases to love his wife when she becomes masculine or rebellious; but slaves are always dependent, never the rivals of their master. Hence, though men are often found at variance with wife or children, we never saw one who did not like his slaves, and rarely a slave who was not devoted to his master. "I am thy servant!" disarms me of the power of master. Every man feels the beauty, force and truth of this sentiment of Sterne. But he who acknowledges its truth, tacitly admits that dependence is a tie of affection, that the relation of master and slave is one of mutual good will. Volumes written on the subject would not prove as much as this single sentiment. It has found its way to the heart of every reader, and carried conviction along with it. The slave-holder is like other men, he will not tread on the worm nor break the bruised seed. The ready submission of the slave, nine times out of ten, disarms his wrath even when the slave has offended. The habit of command may make him imperious and fit him for rule; but he is only imperious when thwarted or crossed by his equals; he would scorn to put on airs of command among blacks, whether slaves or free; he always speaks to them in a kind and subdued tone. We go farther, and say the slave-holder is better than others—because he has greater occasion for the exercise of the affections. His whole life is spent in providing for the minutest wants of others, in taking care of them in sickness and in health. Hence he is the least selfish of men. Is not the old bachelor who retires to seclusion, always selfish? Is not the head of a large family almost always kind and benevolent? And is not the slave-holder the head of the largest family? Nature compels master and slave to be friends; nature makes employers and free laborers enemies.

The institution of slavery gives full development and full play to the affections. Free society chills, stints and eradicates them. In a homely way the farm will support all, and we are not in a hurry to send our children into the world, to push their way and make their fortunes, with a capital of knavish maxims. We are better husbands, better fathers, better friends, and better neighbors than our Northern brethren. The tie of kindred to the fifth degree is often a tie of affection with us. First cousins are scarcely acknowledged at the North, and even children are prematurely pushed off into the world. Love for others is the organic law of our society, as self-love is of theirs.

Every social structure must have its substratum. In free society this substratum, the weak, poor and ignorant, is borne down upon and oppressed with continually increasing weight by all above. We have solved the problem of relieving this substratum from the pressure from above. The slaves are the substratum, and the master's feelings and interests alike prevent him from bearing down upon and oppressing them. With us the pressure on society is like that of air or water, so equally diffused as not any where to be felt. With them it is the pressure of the enormous screw, never yielding, continually increasing. Free laborers are little better than trespassers on this earth given by God to all mankind. The birds of the air have nests, and the foxes have holes, but they have not where to lay their heads. They are driven to cities to dwell in damp and crowded cellars, and thousands are even forced to lie in the open air. This accounts for the rapid growth of Northern cities. The feudal Barons were more generous and hospitable and less tyrannical than the petty land-holders of modern times. Besides, each inhabitant of the barony was considered as having some right of residence, some claim to protection from the Lord of the Manor. A few of them escaped to the municipalities for purposes of trade, and to enjoy a larger liberty. Now penury and the want of a home drive thousands to towns. The slave always has a home, always an interest in the proceeds of the soil. . . .

V

Social Darwinism

In the closing decades of the nineteenth century American conservatism expanded its traditional commitment to individual liberty to include also the idea of laissez-faire. The belief that government should play a limited role in the economy was not a common conservative principle in the beginnings of the nation's history; on the contrary, it was an important doctrine of Jeffersonian liberalism. So popular did the idea of laissez-faire become with conservatives that many came to believe that a threat to business in the form of government intervention was equivalent to a threat to individual freedom. That a relationship between liberty and capitalism existed was taken for granted, but beyond this, some conservatives asserted that all restraints on capitalism injured liberty.

What, then, were the origins of the laissez-faire policy adopted by American conservatives following the Civil War? The idea that government is inherently inefficient and that individual action is preferable to collective action was a possible interpretation of John Locke's philosophy. Government might be limited to the critical functions of providing peace and order while guaranteeing individual rights. The consent theory of Locke's social contract could be taken to signify the superiority of the individual to the state in a moral, political, and economic way. Government must stand aside and give the individual free reign. It was from Locke that Jefferson derived his belief in laissez-faire, but by the late nineteenth century the doctrine was more suitable for the growing, ambitious class of new industrialists than it had been for self-reliant farmers, because the businessmen needed passive government if they were to expand their activities.

In the middle of the nineteenth century the laissez-faire ideas of English economists and philosophers such as Jeremy Bentham (1748–1832), David Ricardo (1772–1823), and James Mill (1773–1836) began to be taught in American colleges and universities. Intellectual journals such as the *Nation* became champions of the new version of liberty.

Another Englishman, Herbert Spencer (1820–1903), helped add the prestige of modern science to the doctrine of laissez-faire by grafting upon it the idea of social competition in the name of "survival of the fittest." The literal application of Darwin's theories to society which is found in social Darwinism was never intended by Darwin himself. But it seemed to many theorists a logical extension of the biological struggle that motivated the evolutionary process. Spencer maintained that in the social and economic spheres competition among individuals and groups was a natural phenomenon; if not artificially interrupted by outside forces—meaning the government—men would produce a progressively better society. The poor might suffer and the rich prosper, but this process was for the long-term good of all mankind.

In the period following the Civil War, America began to change from an agrarian to an industrial society. The aristocratic agrarian conservatism of Calhoun did not appeal to the Northern tradesmen and businessmen who were emerging from obscure positions to dominance in American life. Great fortunes were amassed by some industrial leaders, and vast new economic opportunities were opened to many Americans. A conservative doctrine which justified and glorified these new changes was bound to appeal to many Americans—those who had gained riches and those who hadn't yet done so. Horatio Alger was a folk hero and Andrew Carnegie a real hero.

These doctrines of laissez-faire and survival of the fittest were accepted by only a few in their extreme forms. More popular were the thoughts of men such as the Reverend Russell H. Conwell, who proclaimed that every man could be rich "and it is your duty to get rich." Poverty was not equivalent to piety, and riches were a positive good. Hard work could bring success, and success was defined as material prosperity. Although the emphasis upon economic liberty was frequently stated in an exaggerated form in the decades prior to World War I, the doctrine became, nonetheless, an important aspect of twentieth-century conservatism.

19. SUMNER

The Law of Competition

William Graham Sumner (1840–1910), a Yale sociologist and economist, was considered America's leading spokesman for the theory of economic individualism, most commonly known as social Darwinism. Sumner borrowed heavily from the evolutionary theories of Herbert Spencer, whose *Social Statics* (1850) appeared nine years before Charles Darwin's famous *Origin of Species* (1859).

Sumner stated the case for laissez-faire individualism in its most extreme form. He believed that each man should be free to compete for survival with his fellowman. The fit would survive, under this system, and the weak perish. The end result of this ruthless competition, Sumner held, would be the betterment of all mankind, through the survival of superior individuals. Aid to the poor, the weak, and the deformed was opposed by him as inconsistent with the progressive laws of social and economic evolution. This drastic anti-government philosophy was best stated by Sumner in his 1883 study, *What Social Classes Owe to Each Other*. The following selection* constitutes the first two chapters of the book.

On a New Philosophy: That Poverty Is the Best Policy

It is commonly asserted that there are in the United States no classes, and any allusion to classes is resented. On the other hand, we constantly read and hear discussions of social topics in which the existence of social classes is assumed as a simple fact. "The poor," "the weak," "the laborers," are expressions which are used as if they had exact and well-understood definition. Discussions are made to bear upon the assumed rights, wrongs, and misfortunes of certain social classes; and

* (New York: Harper and Bros., 1883), pp. 13–37.

all public speaking and writing consists, in a large measure, of the discussion of general plans for meeting the wishes of classes of people who have not been able to satisfy their own desires. These classes are sometimes discontented, and sometimes not. Sometimes they do not know that anything is amiss with them until the "friends of humanity" come to them with offers of aid. Sometimes they are discontented and envious. They do not take their achievements as a fair measure of their rights. They do not blame themselves or their parents for their lot, as compared with that of other people. Sometimes they claim that they have a right to everything of which they feel the need for their happiness on earth. To make such a claim against God and Nature would of course, be only to say that we claim a right to live on earth if we can. But God and Nature have ordained the chances and conditions of life on earth once for all. The case cannot be reopened. We cannot get a revision of the laws of human life. We are absolutely shut up to the need and duty, if we would learn how to live happily, of investigating the laws of Nature, and deducing the rules of right living in the world as it is. These are very wearisome and commonplace tasks. They consist in labor and self-denial repeated over and over again in learning and doing. When the people whose claims we are considering are told to apply themselves to these tasks they become irritated and feel almost insulted. They formulate their claims as rights against society—that is, against some other men. In their view they have a right, not only to *pursue* happiness, but to *get* it; and if they fail to get it, they think they have a claim to the aid of other men—that is, to the labor and self-denial of other men—to get it for them. They find orators and poets who tell them that they have grievances, so long as they have unsatisfied desires.

Now, if there are groups of people who have a claim to other people's labor and self-denial, and if there are other people whose labor and self-denial are liable to be claimed by the first groups, then there certainly are "classes," and classes of the oldest and most vicious type. For a man who can command another man's labor and self-denial for the support of his own existence is a privileged person of the highest species conceivable on earth. Princes and paupers meet on this plane, and no other men are on it all. On the other hand, a man whose labor and self-denial may be diverted from his maintenance to that of some other man is not a free man, and approaches more or less toward the position of a slave. Therefore we shall find that, in all the notions which we are to discuss, this elementary contradiction, that there are classes and that there are not classes, will produce repeated confusion and absurdity. We shall find that, in our efforts to eliminate the old vices of class government, we are impeded and defeated by new products of the worst class theory. We shall find that all the schemes for producing equality and obliterating the organization of society produce a new differentiation based on the worst possible distinction—the right to claim and the duty to give one man's effort for another man's satisfaction. We shall find that every effort to realize equality necessitates a sacrifice of liberty.

It is very popular to pose as a "friend of humanity," or a "friend of the working classes." The character, however, is quite exotic in the United States. It is borrowed from England, where some men, otherwise of small account, have assumed it with great success and advantage. Anything which has a charitable sound and a kind-hearted tone generally passes without investigation, because it is disagreeable to assail it. Sermons, essays, and orations assume a conventional standpoint with regard to the poor, the weak, etc.; and it is allowed to pass as an unquestioned doctrine in regard to social classes that "the rich" ought to "care for the poor"; that Churches especially ought to collect capital from the rich and spend it for the poor; that parishes ought to be clusters of institutions by means of which one social class should perform its duties to another; and that clergymen, economists, and social philosophers have a technical and professional duty to devise schemes for "helping the poor." The preaching in England used all to be done to the poor—that they ought to be contented with their lot and respectful to their betters. Now, the greatest part of the preaching in America consists in injunctions to those who have taken care of themselves to perform their assumed duty to take care of others. Whatever may be one's private sentiments, the fear of appearing cold and hard-hearted causes these conventional theories of social duty and these assumptions of social fact to pass unchallenged.

Let us notice some distinctions which are of prime importance to a correct consideration of the subject which we intend to treat.

Certain ills belong to the hardships of human life. They are natural. They are part of the struggle with Nature for existence. We cannot blame our fellow-men for our share of these. My neighbor and I are both struggling to free ourselves from these ills. The fact that my neighbor has succeeded in this struggle better than I constitutes no grievance for me. Certain other ills are due to the malice of men, and to the imperfections or errors of civil institutions. These ills are an object of agitation, and a subject of discussion. The former class of ills is to be met only by manly effort and energy; the latter may be corrected by associated effort. The former class of ills is constantly grouped and generalized, and made the object of social schemes. We shall see, as we go on, what that means. The second class of ills may fall on certain social classes, and reform will take the form of interference by other classes in favor of that one. The last fact is, no doubt, the reason why people have been led, not noticing distinctions, to believe that the same method was applicable to the other class of ills. The distinction here made between the ills which belong to the struggle for existence and those which are due to the faults of human institutions is of prime importance.

It will also be important, in order to clear up our ideas about the notions which are in fashion, to note the relation of the economic to the political significance of assumed duties of one class to another. That is to say, we may discuss the question whether one class owes duties to another by reference to the economic effects which will be produced on the classes and society; or we may discuss the political expediency of formulating and enforcing rights and duties respectively between the parties. In the former case we might assume that the givers of aid were willing to give it, and we might discuss the benefit or mischief of their activity. In the other case we must assume that some at least of those who were forced to give aid did so unwillingly. Here, then, there would be a question of rights. The question whether voluntary charity is mischievous or not is one thing; the question whether legislation which forces one man to aid another is right and wise, as well as economically beneficial, is quite another question. Great confusion and consequent error is produced by allowing these two questions to become entangled in the discussion. Especially we shall need to notice the attempts to apply legislative methods of reform to the ills which belong to the order of Nature.

There is no possible definition of "a poor man." A pauper is a person who cannot earn his living; whose producing powers have fallen positively below his necessary consumption; who cannot, therefore, pay his way. A human society needs the active co-operation and productive energy of every person in it. A man who is present as a consumer, yet who does not contribute either by land, labor, or capital to the work of society, is a burden. On no sound political theory ought such a person to share in the political power of the State. He drops out of the ranks of workers and producers. Society must support him. It accepts the burden, but he must be cancelled from the ranks of the rulers likewise. So much for the pauper. About him no more need be said. But he is not the "poor man." The "poor man" is an elastic term, under which any number of social fallacies may be hidden.

Neither is there any possible definition of "the weak." Some are weak in one way, and some in another; and those who are weak in one sense are strong in another. In general, however, it may be said that those whom humanitarians and philanthropists call the weak are the ones through whom the productive and conservative forces of society are wasted. They constantly neutralize and destroy the finest efforts of the wise and industrious, and are a dead-weight on the society in all its struggles to realize any better things. Whether the people who mean no harm, but are weak in the essential powers necessary to the performance of one's duties in life, or those who are malicious and vicious, do the more mischief, is a question not easy to answer.

Under the names of the poor and the weak, the negligent, shiftless, inefficient, silly, and imprudent are fastened upon the industrious and prudent as a responsibility and a duty. On the one side, the terms are extended to cover the idle, intemperate, and vicious, who, by the combination, gain credit which they do not deserve, and which they could not get if they stood alone. On the other hand, the terms are extended to include wage-receivers of the humblest rank, who are degraded by the combination. The reader who desires to guard himself against fallacies should always scrutinize the terms "poor" and "weak" as used, so as to see which or how many of these classes they are made to cover.

The humanitarians, philanthropists, and reformers, looking at the facts of life as they present themselves, find enough which is sad and unpromising in the condition of many members of society. They see wealth and poverty side by side. They note great inequality of social position and social chances. They eagerly set about the attempt to account for what they see, and to devise schemes for remedying what they do not like. In their eagerness to recommend the less fortunate classes to pity and consideration they forget all about the rights of other classes; they gloss over all the faults of the classes in question, and they exaggerate their misfortunes and their virtues. They invent new theories of property, distorting rights and perpetuating injustice, as anyone is sure to do who sets about the readjustment of social relations with the interests of one group distinctly before his mind, and the interests of all other groups thrown into the background. When I have read certain of these discussions I have thought that it must be quite disreputable to be respectable, quite dishonest to own property, quite unjust to go one's own way and earn one's own living, and that the only really admirable person was the good-for-nothing. The man who by his own effort raises himself above poverty appears, in these discussions, to be of no account. The man who has done nothing to raise himself above poverty finds that the social doctors flock about him, bringing the capital which they have collected from the other class, and promising him the aid of the State to give him what the other had to work for. In all these schemes and projects the organized intervention of society through the State is either planned or hoped for, and the State is thus made to become the protector and guardian of certain classes. The agents who are to direct the State action are, of course, the reformers and philanthropists. Their schemes, therefore, may always be reduced to this type—that A and B decide what C shall do for D. It will be interesting to inquire, at a later period of our discussion, who C is, and what the effect is upon him of all these arrangements. In all the discussions attention is concentrated on A and B, the noble social reformers, and on D, the "poor man." I call C the Forgotten Man, because I have never seen that any notice was taken of him in any of the discussions. When we have disposed of A, B, and D we can better appreciate the case of C, and I think that we shall find that he deserves our attention, for the worth of his character and the magnitude of his unmerited burdens. Here it may suffice to observe that, on the theories of the social philosophers to whom I have referred, we should get a new maxim of judicious living: Poverty is the best policy. If you get wealth, you will have to support other people; if you do not get wealth, it will be the duty of other people to support you.

No doubt one chief reason for the unclear and contradictory theories of class relations lies in the fact that our society, largely controlled in all its organization by one set of doctrines, still contains survivals of old social theories which are totally inconsistent with the former. In the Middle Ages men were united by custom and prescription into associations, ranks, guilds, and communities of various kinds. These ties endured as long as life lasted. Consequently society was dependent, throughout all its details, on status, and the tie, or bond, was sentimental. In our modern state, and in the United States more than anywhere else, the social structure is based on contract, and status is of the least importance. Contract, however, is rational—even rationalistic. It is also realistic, cold, and matter-of-fact. A contract relation is based on a sufficient reason, not on custom or prescription. It is not permanent. It endures only so long as the reason for it endures. In a state based on contract sentiment is out of place in any public or common affairs. It is relegated to the sphere of private and personal relations, where it depends not at all on class types, but on personal acquaintance and personal estimates. The sentimentalists among us always seize upon the survivals of the old order. They want to save them and restore them. Much of the loose thinking also which troubles us in our social discussions arises from the fact that men do not distinguish the elements of status and of contract which may be found in our society.

Whether social philosophers think it desirable or not, it is out of the question to go back to status or to the sentimental relations which once united baron and retainer, master and servant, teacher and pupil, comrade and comrade. That we have lost some grace and elegance is undeniable. That life once held more poetry and romance is true enough. But it seems impossible that any one who has studied the matter should doubt that we have gained immeasurably, and that our farther gains lie in going forward, not in going backward. The feudal ties can never be restored. If they could be restored they would bring back personal caprice, favoritism, sycophancy, and intrigue. A society based on contract is a society of free and independent men, who form ties without favor or obligation, and co-operate without cringing or intrigue. A society based on contract, therefore, gives the utmost room and chance for individual development, and for all the self-reliance and dignity of a free man. That a society of free men, co-operating under contract, is by far the strongest society which has ever yet existed; that no such society has ever yet developed the full measure of strength of which it is capable; and that the only social improvements which are now conceivable lie in the direction of more complete realization of a society of free men united by contract, are points which cannot be controverted. It follows, however, that one man, in a free state, cannot claim help from, and cannot be charged to give help to, another.

To understand the full meaning of this assertion it will be worth while to see what a free democracy is.

That a Free Man Is a Sovereign, but That a Sovereign Cannot Take "Tips"

A free man, a free country, liberty, and equality are terms of constant use among us. They are employed as watchwords as soon as any social questions come into discussion. It is right that they should be so used. They ought to contain the broadest convictions and most positive faiths of the nation, and so they ought to be available for the decision of questions of detail.

In order, however, that they may be so employed successfully and correctly it is essential that the terms should be correctly defined, and that their popular use should conform to correct definitions. No doubt it is generally believed that the terms are easily understood, and present no difficulty. Probably the popular notion is, that liberty means doing as one has a mind to, and that it is a metaphysical or sentimental good. A little observation shows that there is no such thing in the world as doing as one has a mind to. There is no man, from the tramp up to the President, the Pope, or the Czar, who can do as he has a mind to. There never has been any man, from the primitive barbarian up to a Humboldt or a Darwin, who could do as he had a mind to. The "Bohemian" who determines to realize some sort of liberty of this kind accomplishes his purpose only by sacrificing most of the rights and turning his back on most of the duties of a civilized man, while filching as much as he can of the advantages of living in a civilized state. Moreover, liberty is not a metaphysical or sentimental thing at all. It is positive, practical, and actual. It is produced and maintained by law and institutions, and is, therefore, concrete and historical. Sometimes we speak distinctively of civil liberty; but if there be any liberty other than civil liberty—that is, liberty under law—it is a mere fiction of the schoolmen, which they may be left to discuss.

Even as I write, however, I find in a leading review the following definition of liberty: Civil liberty is "the result of the restraint exercised by the sovereign people on the more powerful individuals and classes of the community, preventing them from availing themselves of the excess of their power to the detriment of the other classes." This definition lays the foundation for the result which it is apparently desired to reach, that "a government by the people can in no case become a paternal government, since its law-makers are its mandatories and servants carrying out its will, and not its fathers or its masters." Here we have the most mischievous fallacy under the general topic which I am discussing distinctly formulated. In the definition of liberty it will be noticed that liberty is construed as the act of the sovereign people against somebody who must, of course, be differentiated from the sovereign people. Whenever "people" is used in this sense for anything less than the total population, man, woman, child, and baby, and whenever the great dogmas which contain the word "people" are construed under the limited definition of "people," there is always fallacy.

History is only a tiresome repetition of one story. Persons and classes have sought to win possession of the power of the State in order to live luxuriously out of the earnings of others. Autocracies, aristocracies, theocracies, and all other organizations for holding political power, have exhibited only the same line of action. It is the extreme of political error to say that if political power is only taken away from generals, nobles, priests, millionnaires, and scholars, and given to artisans and peasants, these latter may be trusted to do only right and justice, and never to abuse the power; that they will repress all excess in others, and commit none themselves. They will commit abuse, if they can and dare, just as others have done. The reason for the excesses of the old governing classes lies in the vices and passions of human nature—cupidity, lust, vindictiveness, ambition, and vanity. These vices are confined to no nation, class, or age. They appear in the church, the academy, the workshop, and the hovel, as well as in the army or the palace. They have appeared in autocracies, aristocracies, theocracies, democracies, and ochlocracies, all alike. The only thing which has ever restrained these vices of human nature in those who had political power is law sustained by impersonal institutions. If political power be given to the masses who have not hitherto had it, nothing will stop them from abusing it but laws and institutions. To say that a popular government cannot be paternal is to give it a charter that it can do no wrong. The trouble is that a democratic government is in greater danger than any other of becoming paternal, for it is sure of itself, and ready to undertake anything, and its power is excessive and pitiless against dissentients.

What history shows is, that rights are safe only when guaranteed against all arbitrary power, and all class and personal interest. Around an autocrat there has grown up an oligarchy of priests and soldiers. In time a class of nobles has been developed, who have broken into the oligarchy and made an aristocracy. Later the *demos*, rising into an independent development, has assumed power and made a democracy. Then the mob of a capital city has overwhelmed the democracy in an ochlocracy. Then the "idol of the people," or the military "savior of society," or both in one, has made himself autocrat, and the same old vicious round has recommenced. Where in all this is liberty? There has been no liberty at all, save where a state has known how to break out, once for all, from this delusive round; to set barriers to selfishness, cupidity, envy, and lust, in *all* classes, from highest to lowest, by laws and institutions; and to create great organs of civil life which can eliminate, as far as possible, arbitrary and personal elements from the adjustment of interests and the definition of rights. Liberty is an affair of laws and institutions which bring rights and duties into equilibrium. It is not at all an affair of selecting the proper class to rule.

The notion of a free state is entirely modern. It has been developed with the development of the middle class, and with the growth of a commercial and industrial civilization. Horror at human slavery is not a century old as a common sentiment in a civilized state. The idea of the "free man," as we understand it, is the product of a revolt against mediaeval and feudal ideas; and our notion of equality, when it is true and practical, can be explained only by that revolt. It was in England that the modern idea found birth. It has been strengthened by the industrial and commercial development of that country. It has been inherited by all the English-speaking nations, who have made liberty real because they have inherited it, not as a notion, but as a body of institutions. It has been borrowed and imitated by the military and police states of the European continent so fast as they have felt the influence of the expanding industrial civilization; but they have realized it only imperfectly, because they have no body of local institutions or traditions, and it remains for them as yet too much a matter of "declarations" and pronunciamentos.

The notion of civil liberty which we have inherited is that of *a status created for the individual by laws and institutions, the effect of which is that each man is guaranteed the use of all his own powers exclusively for his own welfare.* It is not at all a matter of elections, or universal

suffrage, or democracy. All institutions are to be tested by the degree
to which they guarantee liberty. It is not to be admitted for a moment
that liberty is a means to social ends, and that it may be impaired for
major considerations. Any one who so argues has lost the bearing and
relation of all the facts and factors in a free state. A human being has
a life to live, a career to run. He is a centre of powers to work, and of
capacities to suffer. What his powers may be—whether they can carry
him far or not; what his chances may be, whether wide or restricted;
what his fortune may be whether to suffer much or little—are questions
of his personal destiny which he must work out and endure as he
can; but for all that concerns the bearing of the society and its institutions upon that man, and upon the sum of happiness to which he
can attain during his life on earth, the product of all history and all
philosophy up to this time is summed up in the doctrine, that he
should be left free to do the most for himself that he can, and should
be guaranteed the exclusive enjoyment of all that he does. If the
society—that is to say, in plain terms, if his fellow-men, either individually, by groups, or in a mass—impinge upon him otherwise than to
surround him with neutral conditions of security, they must do so
under the strictest responsibility to justify themselves. Jealousy and
prejudice against all such interferences are high political virtues in a
free man. It is not at all the function of the State to make men happy.
They must make themselves happy in their own way, and at their own
risk. The functions of the State lie entirely in the conditions or chances
under which the pursuit of happiness is carried on, so far as those
conditions or chances can be affected by civil organization. Hence,
liberty for labor and security for earnings are the ends for which civil
institutions exist, not means which may be employed for ulterior ends.

Now, the cardinal doctrine of any sound political system is, that
rights and duties should be in equilibrium. A monarchical or aristocratic system is not immoral, if the rights and duties of persons and
classes are in equilibrium, although the rights and duties of different
persons and classes are unequal. An immoral political system is created
whenever there are privileged classes—that is, classes who have arro-
gated to themselves rights while throwing the duties upon others.
In a democracy all have equal political rights. That is the fundamental
political principle. A democracy, then, becomes immoral, if all have
not equal political duties. This is unquestionably the doctrine which
needs to be reiterated and inculcated beyond all others, if the democracy

is to be made sound and permanent. Our orators and writers never speak of it, and do not seem often to know anything about it; but the real danger of democracy is, that the classes which have the power under it will assume all the rights and reject all the duties—that is, that they will use the political power to plunder those-who-have. Democracy, in order to be true to itself, and to develop into a sound working system, must oppose the same cold resistance to any claims for favor on the ground of poverty, as on the ground of birth and rank. It can no more admit to public discussion, as within the range of possible action, any schemes for coddling and helping wage-receivers than it could entertain schemes for restricting political power to wage-payers. It must put down schemes for making "the rich" pay for whatever "the poor" want, just as it tramples on the old theories that only the rich are fit to regulate society. One needs but to watch our periodical literature to see the danger that democracy will be construed as a system of favoring a new privileged class of the many and the poor.

Holding in mind, now, the notions of liberty and democracy as we have defined them, we see that it is not altogether a matter of fanfaronade when the American citizen calls himself a "sovereign." A member of a free democracy is, in a sense, a sovereign. He has no superior. He has reached his sovereignty, however, by a process of reduction and division of power which leaves him no inferior. It is very grand to call one's self a sovereign, but it is greatly to the purpose to notice that the political responsibilities of the free man have been intensified and aggregated just in proportion as political rights have been reduced and divided. Many monarchs have been incapable of sovereignty and unfit for it. Placed in exalted situations, and inheritors of grand opportunities they have exhibited only their own imbecility and vice. The reason was, because they thought only of the gratification of their own vanity, and not at all of their duty. The free man who steps forward to claim his inheritance and endowment as a free and equal member of a great civil body must understand that his duties and responsibilities are measured to him by the same scale as his rights and his powers. He wants to be subject to no man. He wants to be equal to his fellows, as all sovereigns are equal. So be it; but he cannot escape the deduction that he can call no man to his aid. The other sovereigns will not respect his independence if he becomes dependent, and they cannot respect his equality if he sues for favors.

The free man in a free democracy, when he cut off all the ties which might pull him down, severed also all the ties by which he might have made others pull him up. He must take all the consequences of his new status. He is, in a certain sense, an isolated man. The family tie does not bring to him disgrace for the misdeeds of his relatives, as it once would have done, but neither does it furnish him with the support which it once would have given. The relations of men are open and free, but they are also loose. A free man in a free democracy derogates from his rank if he takes a favor for which he does not render an equivalent.

A free man in a free democracy has no duty whatever toward other men of the same rank and standing, except respect, courtesy, and good-will. We cannot say that there are no classes, when we are speaking politically, and then say that there are classes, when we are telling A what it is his duty to do for B. In a free state every man is held and expected to take care of himself and his family, to make no trouble for his neighbor, and to contribute his full share to public interests and common necessities. If he fails in this he throws burdens on others. He does not thereby acquire rights against the others. On the contrary, he only accumulates obligations toward them; and if he is allowed to make his deficiencies a ground of new claims, he passes over into the position of a privileged or petted person—emancipated from duties, endowed with claims. This is the inevitable result of combining democratic political theories with humanitarian social theories. It would be aside from my present purpose to show, but it is worth noticing in passing, that one result of such inconsistency must surely be to undermine democracy, to increase the power of wealth in the democracy, and to hasten the subjection of democracy to plutocracy; for a man who accepts any share which he has not earned in another man's capital cannot be an independent citizen.

It is often affirmed that the educated and wealthy have an obligation to those who have less education and property, just because the latter have political equality with the former, and oracles and warnings are uttered about what will happen if the uneducated classes who have the suffrage are not instructed at the care and expense of the other classes. In this view of the matter universal suffrage is not a measure for *strengthening* the State by bringing to its support the aid and affection of all classes, but it is a new burden, and, in fact, a peril. Those who favor it represent it as a peril. This doctrine is politically immoral and vicious. When a community establishes universal suffrage, it is as if it said to each new-comer, or to each young man: "We give you every chance that any one else has. Now come along with us; take care of yourself, and contribute your share to the burdens which we all have to bear in order to support social institutions." Certainly, liberty, and universal suffrage, and democracy are not pledges of care and protection, but they carry with them the exaction of individual responsibility. The State gives equal rights and equal chances just because it does not mean to give anything else. It sets each man on his feet, and gives him leave to run, just because it does not mean to carry him. Having obtained his chances, he must take upon himself the responsibility for his own success or failure. It is a pure misfortune to the community, and one which will redound to its injury, if any man has been endowed with political power who is a heavier burden then than he was before; but it cannot be said that there is any new *duty* created for the good citizens toward the bad by the fact that the bad citizens are a harm to the State.

20.   STRONG

America's Destiny

Josiah Strong (1847–1916) was a gifted Congregationalist minister and an active social reformer. Like many conservatives of the day, he opposed immigration, Roman Catholicism, Mormonism, intemperance, and socialism. Strong's major book, *Our Country* (1885), asserted the simple thesis that America had a mission to save the world for Christianity and that the American Anglo-Saxon held the destiny of his race in his hands. Applying evolutionary thought to international politics, Strong foresaw an eventual American domination over the inferior races of the world. Expansion, he argued, was America's destiny and moral duty. This selection is the fourteenth chapter of *Our Country*,* entitled "The Anglo-Saxon and the World's Future." To it Strong added the following note: "It is only just to say that the substance of this chapter was given to the public as a lecture some three years before the appearance of Prof. John Fiske's "Manifest Destiny" in *Harper's Magazine* . . . which contains some of the same ideas."

Every race which has deeply impressed itself on the human family has been the representative of some great idea—one or more—which has given direction to the nation's life and form to its civilization. Among the Egyptians this seminal idea was life, among the Persians it was light, among the Hebrews it was purity, among the Greeks it was beauty, among the Romans it was law. The Anglo-Saxon is the representative of two great ideas, which are closely related. One of them is that of civil liberty. Nearly all of the civil liberty of the world is enjoyed by Anglo-Saxons: the English, the British colonists, and the people of the United States. To some, like the Swiss, it is permitted by the sufferance of their neighbors; others, like the French, have experimented with it; but, in modern times, the peoples whose love of liberty has won it, and whose genius for self-government has preserved it,

* (New York: The Baker and Taylor Company, 1885), pp. 159–80.

have been Anglo-Saxons. The noblest races have always been lovers of liberty. The love ran strong in early German blood, and has profoundly influenced the institutions of all the branches of the great German family; but it was left for the Anglo-Saxon branch fully to recognize the right of the individual to himself, and formally to declare it the foundation stone of government.

The other great idea of which the Anglo-Saxon is the exponent is that of a pure *spiritual* Christianity. It was no accident that the great reformation of the sixteenth century originated among a Teutonic, rather than a Latin people. It was the fire of liberty burning in the Saxon heart that flamed up against the absolutism of the Pope. Speaking roughly, the peoples of Europe which are Celtic are Roman Catholic, and those which are Teutonic are Protestant; and where the Teutonic race was purest, there Protestantism spread with the greatest rapidity. But, with beautiful exceptions, Protestantism on the continent has degenerated into mere formalism. By confirmation at a certain age, the state churches are filled with members who generally know nothing of a personal spiritual experience. In obedience to a military order, a regiment of German soldiers files into church and partakes of the sacrament, just as it would shoulder arms or obey any other word of command. It is said that, in Berlin and Leipsic, only a little over one per cent of the Protestant population are found in church. Protestantism on the continent seems to be about as poor in spiritual life and power as Romanism. That means that most of the spiritual Christianity in the world is found among Anglo-Saxons and their converts; for this is the great missionary race. If we take all of the German missionary societies together, we find that, in the number of workers and amount of contributions, they do not equal the smallest of the three great English missionary societies. The year that the Congregationalists in the United States gave one dollar and thirty-seven cents per caput to foreign missions, the members of the great German State Church gave only three-quarters of a cent per caput to the same cause. Evidently it is chiefly to the English and American peoples that we must look for the evangelization of the world.

It is not necessary to argue to those for whom I write that the two great needs of mankind, that all men may be lifted up into the light of the highest Christian civilization, are, first, a pure, spiritual Christianity, and second, civil liberty. Without controversy, these are the forces which, in the past, have contributed most to the elevation of the human race, and they must continue to be, in the future, the most efficient ministers to its progress. It follows, then, that the Anglo-Saxon, as the great representative of these two ideas, the depositary of these two greatest blessings, sustains peculiar relations to the world's future, is divinely commissioned to be, in a peculiar sense, his brother's keeper. Add to this the fact of his rapidly increasing strength in modern times, and we have well-nigh a demonstration of his destiny. In 1700 this race numbered less than 6,000,000 souls. In 1800, Anglo-Saxons (I use the term somewhat broadly to include all English-speaking peoples) had increased to about 20,500,000, and now, in 1890, they number more than 120,000,000, having multiplied almost six-fold in ninety years. At the end of the reign of Charles II. the English colonists in American numbered 200,000. During these two hundred years, our population has increased two hundred and fifty-fold. And the expansion of this race has been no less remarkable than its multiplication. In one century the United States has increased its territory ten-fold, while the enormous acquisition of foreign territory by Great Britain—and chiefly within the last hundred years—is wholly unparalleled in history. This mighty Anglo-Saxon race, though comprising only one-thirteenth part of mankind, now rules more than one-third of the earth's surface, and more than one-fourth of its people. And if this race, while growing from 6,000,000 to 120,000,000, thus gained possession of a third portion of the earth, is it to be supposed that when it numbers 1,000,000,000, it will lose the disposition, or lack the power to extend its sway?

This race is multiplying not only more rapidly than any other European race, but more rapidly than *all* the races of continental Europe taken together. There is no exact knowledge of the population of Europe early in the century. We know, however, that the increase on the continent during the ten years from 1870 to 1880 was 6.89 per cent. If this rate of increase is sustained for a century, the population on the continent in 1980 will be 534,000,000; while the one Anglo-Saxon race, if it should multiply for a hundred years as fast as from 1870 to 1880, would in 1980 number 1,111,000,000 souls, an incredible increase, of course.

What then will be the probable numbers of this race a hundred years hence? It is hazardous to venture a prophecy, but we may weigh probabilities. In studying this subject several things must be borne in mind. Heretofore, the great causes which have operated to check the growth of population in the world have been war, famine, and pestilence;

but, among civilized peoples, these causes are becoming constantly less operative. Paradoxical as it seems, the invention of more destructive weapons of war renders war less destructive; commerce and wealth have removed the fear of famine, and pestilence is being brought more and more under control by medical skill and sanitary science. Moreover, Anglo-Saxons, with the exception of the people of Great Britain, who now compose less than one-third of this race, are much less exposed to these checks upon growth than the races of Europe. Again, Europe is crowded, and is constantly becoming more so, which will tend to reduce continually the ratio of increase; while over two-thirds of the Anglo-Saxons occupy lands which invite almost unlimited expansion— the United States, Canada, Australia, and South Africa. Again, emigration from Europe, which will probably increase, is very largely into Anglo-Saxon countries; and, though these foreign elements exert a modifying influence on the Anglo-Saxon stock, their descendants are certain to be Anglo-Saxonized. From 1870 to 1880, Germany lost 987,000 inhabitants by emigration, most of whom came to the United States. In one generation, their children will be counted Anglo-Saxons. This race has been undergoing an unparalleled expansion during the eighteenth and nineteenth centuries, and the conditions for its continued growth are singularly favorable.

We are now prepared to ask what light statistics cast on the future. In Great Britain, from 1840 to 1850 the ratio of increase of the population was 2.49 per cent; during the next ten years it was 5.44 per cent; the next ten years, it was 8.60; from 1870 to 1880, it was 10.57; and from 1880 to 1889 it was 10.08 per cent. That is, for fifty years the ratio of increase has been rapidly rising.

It is not unlikely to continue rising for some time to come; but, remembering that the population is dense, in making our estimate for the next hundred years, we will suppose the ratio of increase to be only one-half as large as that from 1870 to 1880, which would make the population in 1980, 57,000,000. All the great colonies of Britain, except Canada, which has a great future, show a very high ratio of increase in population; that of Australia, from 1870 to 1880, was 56.50 per cent; that of South Africa was 73.28. It is quite reasonable to suppose that the colonies, taken together, will double their population once in twenty-five years for the next century. In the United States, population has, on the average, doubled once in twenty-five years since 1685. Adopting this ratio, then, for the English colonies, their 11,000,000 in 1880 will be 176,000,000 in 1980, and about 234,000,000 in 1990. Turning now to our own country, we find in the following table the ratio of increase of population for each decade of years since 1800:

From 1800 to 1810	36.38 per cent.
„ 1810 „ 1820	34.80 „ „
„ 1820 „ 1830	33.11 „ „
„ 1830 „ 1840	32.66 „ „
„ 1840 „ 1850	35.87 „ „
„ 1850 „ 1860	35.58 „ „
„ 1860 „ 1870	22.59 „ „
„ 1870 „ 1880	30.06 „ „
„ 1880 „ 1890	24.57 „ „

Here we see a falling ratio of increase of about one per cent every ten years from 1800 to 1840—a period when immigration was inconsiderable. During the next twenty years the ratio was decidedly higher, because of a large immigration. It fell off during the war, and again arose from 1870 to 1880, while it seems to have fallen from 1880 to 1890.

If the rate of increase for the next century is as great with immigration as it was from 1800 to 1840 without immigration, we shall have a falling ratio of increase of about one per cent every ten years. Beginning, then, with an increase of twenty-four per cent from 1890 to 1900, our population in 1990 would be 373,000,000, making the total Anglo-Saxon population of the world, at that time, 667,000,000, as compared with 570,000,000 inhabitants of continental Europe. When we consider how much more favorable are the conditions for the increase of population in Anglo-Saxon countries than in continental Europe, and remember that we have reckoned the growth of European population at its rate of increase from 1870 to 1880, while we have reckoned Anglo-Saxon growth at much less than its rate of increase during the same ten years, we may be reasonably confident that a hundred years hence this one race will outnumber all the peoples of continental Europe. And it is possible that, by the close of the next century, the Anglo-Saxons will outnumber all the other civilized races of the world. Does it not look as if God were not only preparing in our Anglo-Saxon civilization the die with which to stamp the peoples of the earth, but as if he were also massing behind that die the mighty power with which to press it?

My confidence that this race is eventually to give its civilization to mankind is not based on mere numbers—China forbid! I look forward to what the world has never yet seen united in the same race; viz., the greatest numbers, *and* the highest civilization.

There can be no reasonable doubt that North America is to be the great home of the Anglo-Saxon, the principal seat of his power, the centre of his life and influence. Not only does it constitute seven-elevenths of his possessions, but here his empire is unsevered, while the remaining four-elevenths are fragmentary and scattered over the earth. Australia will have a great population; but its disadvantages, as compared with North America, are too manifest to need mention. Our continent has room and resources and climate, it lies in the pathway of the nations, it belongs to the zone of power, and already, among Anglo-Saxons, do we lead in population and wealth. Of England, Franklin once wrote: "That pretty island which, compared to America, is but a stepping-stone in a brook, scarce enough of it above water to keep one's shoes dry." England can hardly hope to maintain her relative importance among Anglo-Saxon peoples when her "pretty island" is the home of only one-twentieth part of that race. With the wider distribution of wealth, and increasing facilities of intercourse, intelligence and influence are less centralized, and peoples become more homogeneous; and the more nearly homogeneous peoples are, the more do *numbers* tell.

America is to have the great preponderance of numbers and of wealth, and by the logic of events will follow the scepter of controlling influence. This will be but the consummation of a movement as old as civilization—a result to which men have looked forward for centuries. John Adams records that nothing was "more ancient in his memory than the observation that arts, sciences and empire had traveled westward; and in conversation it was always added that their next leap would be over the Atlantic into America." He recalled a couplet that had been inscribed or rather drilled, into a rock on the shore of Monument Bay in our old colony of Plymouth:

> " 'The Eastern nations sink, their glory ends,
> And empire rises where the sun descends.' "

The brilliant Galiani, who foresaw a future in which Europe should be ruled by America, wrote, during the Revolutionary War: "I will wager in favor of America, for the reason merely physical, that for

5,000 years genius has turned opposite to the diurnal motion, and traveled from the East to the West." Count d'Aranda, after signing the Treaty of Paris in 1773, as representative of Spain, wrote his king: "This Federal Republic is born a pigmy. . . . a day will come when it will be a giant, even a colossus formidable in these countries."

Adam Smith, in his *Wealth of Nations,* predicts the transfer of empire from Europe to America. The traveler, Burnaby, found, in the middle of the last century, that an idea had "entered into the minds of the generality of mankind, that empire is traveling westward; and every one is looking forward with eager and impatient expectation to that destined moment when America is to give the law to the rest of the world." Charles Sumner wrote of the "coming time when the whole continent, with all its various states, shall be a Plural Unit, with one Constitution, one Liberty, and one Destiny," and when "the national example will be more puissant than army or navy for the conquest of the world." It surely needs no prophet's eye to see that the civilization of the *United States* is to be the civilization of America, and that the future of the continent is ours. In 1880, the United States had already become the home of more than one-half of the Anglo-Saxon race; and, if the computations already given are correct, a much larger proportion will be here a hundred years hence. It has been shown that we have room for at least a thousand millions. According to the latest figures, there is in France (1886), a population of 187 to the square mile; in Germany (1885), 221.8; in England and Wales (1889), 498; in Belgium (1888), 530; in the United States (1890)—not including Alaska—21. If our population were as dense as that of France, we should have, this side of Alaska, 555,000,000; if as dense as that of Germany, 658,000,000; if as dense as that of England and Wales, 1,452,000,000; if as dense as that of Belgium 1,574,000,000, or more than the present estimated population of the globe.

And we are to have not only the larger portion of the Anglo-Saxon race, but we may reasonably expect to develop the highest type of Anglo-Saxon civilization. If human progress follows a law of development, if

     "Time's noblest offspring is the last,"

our civilization should be the noblest; for we are

     "The heirs of all the ages in the foremost files of time,"

and not only do we occupy the latitude of power, but *our land is the last to be occupied in that latitude.* There is no other virgin soil in the North Temperate Zone. If the consummation of human progress is not to be looked for here, if there is yet to flower a higher civilization, where is the soil that is to produce it? Whipple says: "There has never been a great migration that did not result in a new form of national genius." Our national genius is Anglo-Saxon, but not English, its distinctive type is the result of a finer nervous organization, which is certainly being developed in this country. "The history of the world's progress from savagery to barbarism, from barbarism to civilization, and, in civilization, from the lower degrees toward the higher, is the history of increase in average longevity, corresponding to, and accompanied by, increase of nervousness. Mankind has grown to be at once more delicate and more enduring, more sensitive to weariness and yet more patient of toil, impressible, but capable of bearing powerful irritation; we are woven of finer fiber, which, though apparently frail, yet outlasts the coarser, as rich and costly garments often times wear better than those of rougher workmanship." The roots of civilization are the nerves; and other things being equal the finest nervous organization will produce the highest civilization. Heretofore, war has been almost the chief occupation of strong races. The mission of the Anglo-Saxon has been largely that of the soldier; but the world is making progress, we are leaving behind the barbarism of war; as civilization advances, it will learn less of war, and concern itself more with the arts of peace, and for these the massive battle-ax must be wrought into tools of finer temper. The physical changes accompanied by mental, which are taking place in the people of the United States are apparently to adapt men to the demands of a higher civilization. But the objection is here interposed that the "physical degeneracy of America" is inconsistent with the supposition of our advancing to a higher civilization. Professor Huxley, when at Buffalo he addressed the American Association of the Advancement of Science, said he had heard of the degeneration of the original American stock, but during his visit to the states he had failed to perceive it. We are not, however, in this matter, dependent on the opinion of even the best observers. During the War of the Confederacy, the Medical Department of the Provost Marshal General's Bureau gathered statistics from the examination of over half a million of men, native and foreign, young and old, sick and sound, drawn from every rank and condition of life, and, hence, fairly representing the whole people. Dr. Baxter's Official Report shows that our native whites were over an inch taller than the English, and nearly two-thirds of an inch taller than the Scotch, who, in height, were superior to all other foreigners. At the age of completed growth, the Irish, who were the stoutest of the foreigners, surpassed the native whites, in girth of chest, less than a quarter of an inch. Statistics as to weight are meager, but Dr. Baxter remarks that it is perhaps not too much to say that the war statistics show "that the mean weight of the white native of the United States is not disproportionate to his stature." Americans were found to be superior to Englishmen not only in height, but also in chest measurement and weight. "Dealers in ready-made clothing in the United States assert that they have been obliged to adopt a larger scale of sizes, in width as well as length, to meet the demands of the average American man, than were required ten years ago." Such facts afford more than a hint that the higher civilization of the future will not lack an adequate physical basis in the people of the United States.

Mr. Darwin is not only disposed to see, in the superior vigor of our people, an illustration of his favorite theory of natural selection, but even intimates that the world's history thus far has been simply preparatory for our future, and tributary to it. He says: "There is apparently much truth in the belief that the wonderful progress of the United States, as well as the character of the people, are the results of natural selection; for the more energetic, restless, and courageous men from all parts of Europe have emigrated during the last ten or twelve generations to that great country, and have there succeeded best. Looking at the distant future, I do not think that the Rev. Mr. Zincke takes an exaggerated view when he says: 'All other series of events— as that which resulted in the culture of mind in Greece, and that which resulted in the Empire of Rome—only appear to have purpose and value when viewed in connection with, or rather as subsidiary to, the great stream of Anglo-Saxon emigration to the West'."

There is abundant reason to believe that the Anglo-Saxon race is to be, is, indeed, already becoming, more effective here than in the mother country. The marked superiority of this race is due, in large measure, to its highly mixed origin. Says Rawlinson: "It is a general rule, now almost universally admitted by ethnologists, that the mixed races of mankind are superior to the pure ones"; and adds: "Even the Jews, who are so often cited as an example of a race at once pure and strong, may, with more reason, be adduced on the opposite side of the argument." The ancient Egyptians, the Greeks, and the Romans, were all mixed races. Among modern races, the most conspicuous example is afforded by the Anglo-Saxons. Mr. Green's studies show that Mr. Tennyson's poetic line,

"Saxon and Norman and Dane are we,"

must be supplemented with Celt and Gaul, Welshman and Irishman, Frisian and Flamand, French Huguenot and German Palatine. What took place a thousand years ago and more in England again transpires to-day in the United States. "History repeats itself"; but, as the wheels of history are the chariot wheels of the Almighty, there is, with every revolution, an onward movement toward the goal of His eternal purposes. There is here a new commingling of races; and, while the largest injections of foreign blood are substantially the same elements that constituted the original Anglo-Saxon admixture, so that we may infer the general type will be preserved, there are strains of other bloods being added, which, if Mr. Emerson's remark is true, that "the best nations are those most widely related," may be expected to improve the stock, and aid it to a higher destiny. If the dangers of immigration, which have been pointed out, can be successfully met for the next few years, until it has passed its climax, it may be expected to add value to the amalgam which will constitute the new Anglo-Saxon race of the New World. Concerning our future, Herbert Spencer says: "One great result is, I think, tolerably clear. From biological truths it is to be inferred that the eventual mixture of the allied varieties of the Aryan race, forming the population, will produce a more powerful type of man than has hitherto existed, and a type of man more plastic, more adaptable, more capable of undergoing the modifications needful for complete social life, I think, whatever difficulties they may have to surmount, and whatever tribulations they may have to pass through, the Americans may reasonably look forward to a time when they will have produced a civilization grander than any the world has known."

It may be easily shown, and is of no small significance, that the two great ideas of which the Anglo-Saxon is the exponent are having a fuller development in the United States than in Great Britain. There the union of Church and State tends strongly to paralyze some of the members of the body of Christ. Here there is no such influence to destroy spiritual life and power. Here, also, has been evolved the form of government consistent with the largest possible civil liberty. Furthermore, it is significant that the marked characteristics of this race are being here emphasized most. Among the most striking features of the Anglo-Saxon is his money-making power—a power of increasing importance in the widening commerce of the world's future. We have seen, in a preceding chapter, that, although England is by far the richest nation of Europe, we have already outstripped her in the race after wealth, and we have only begun the development of our vast resources.

Again, another marked characteristic of the Anglo-Saxon is what may be called an instinct or genius for colonizing. His unequaled energy, his indomitable perseverance, and his personal independence, made him a pioneer. He excels all others in pushing his way into new countries. It was those in whom this tendency was strongest that came to America, and this inherited tendency has been further developed by the westward sweep of successive generations across the continent. So noticeable has this characteristic become that English visitors remark it. Charles Dickens once said that the typical American would hesitate to enter heaven unless assured that he could go farther west.

Again, nothing more manifestly distinguishes the Anglo-Saxon than his intense and persistent energy, and he is developing in the United States an energy which, in eager activity and effectiveness, is peculiarly American.

This is due partly to the fact that Americans are much better fed than Europeans, and partly to the undeveloped resources of a new country, but more largely to our climate, which acts as a constant stimulus. Ten years after the landing of the Pilgrims, the Rev. Francis Higginson, a good observer, wrote: "A sup of New England air is better than a whole flagon of English ale." Thus early had the stimulating effect of our climate been noted. Moreover, our social institutions are stimulating. In Europe the various ranks of society are, like the strata of the earth, fixed and fossilized. There can be no great change without a terrible upheaval, a social earthquake. Here society is like the waters of the sea, mobile; as General Garfield said, and so signally illustrated in his own experience, that which is at the bottom to-day may one day flash on the crest of the highest wave. Every one is free to become whatever he can make of himself; free to transform himself from a rail-splitter or a tanner or a canal-boy, into the nation's President. Our aristocracy, unlike that of Europe, is open to all comers. Wealth, position, influence, are prizes offered for energy; and every farmer's boy, every apprentice and clerk, every friendless and penniless immigrant, is free to enter the lists. Thus many causes co-operate to produce here the most forceful and tremendous energy in the world.

What is the significance of such facts? These tendencies infold the future; they are the mighty alphabet with which God writes his prophecies. May we not, by a careful laying together of the letters, spell out something of his meaning? It seems to me that God, with infinite wisdom and skill, is training the Anglo-Saxon race for an hour sure to come in the world's future. Heretofore there has always been in the history of the world a comparatively unoccupied land westward, into which the crowded countries of the East have poured their surplus populations. But the widening waves of migration, which millenniums ago rolled east and west from the valley of the Euphrates, meet to-day on our Pacific coast. There are no more new worlds. The unoccupied arable lands of the earth are limited, and will soon be taken. The time is coming when the pressure of population on the means of subsistence will be felt here as it is now felt in Europe and Asia. Then will the world enter upon a new stage of its history—*the final competition of races, for which the Anglo-Saxon is being schooled.* Long before the thousand millions are here, the mighty *centrifugal* tendency, inherent in this stock and strengthened in the United States, will assert itself. Then this race of unequaled energy, with all the majesty of numbers and the might of wealth behind it—the representative, let us hope, of the largest liberty, the purest Christianity, the highest civilization— having developed peculiarly aggressive traits calculated to impress its institutions upon mankind, will spread itself over the earth. If I read not amiss, this powerful race will move down upon Mexico, down upon Central and South America, out upon the islands of the sea, over upon Africa and beyond. And can any one doubt that the result of this competition of races will be the "survival of the fittest"? "Any people," says Dr. Bushnell, "that is physiologically advanced in culture, though it be only in a degree beyond another which is mingled with it on strictly equal terms, is sure to live down and finally live out its inferior. Nothing can save the inferior race but a ready and pliant assimilation. Whether the feebler and more abject races are going to be regenerated and raised up, is already very much of a question. What if it should be God's plan to people the world with better and finer material?

"Certain it is, whatever expectations we may indulge, that there is a tremendous overbearing surge of power in the Christian nations, which, if the others are not speedily raised to some vastly higher capacity, will inevitably submerge and bury them forever. These great populations of Christendom—what are they doing, but throwing out their colonies on every side, and populating themselves, if I may so speak, into the possession of all countries and climes?" To this result no war of extermination is needful; the contest is not one of arms, but of vitality and of civilization. "At the present day," says Mr. Darwin, "civilized nations are everywhere supplanting barbarous nations, excepting where the climate opposes a deadly barrier; and they succeed mainly, though not exclusively, through their arts, which are the products of the intellect." Thus the Finns were supplanted by the Aryan races in Europe and Asia, the Tartars by the Russians, and thus the aborigines of North America, Australia and New Zealand are now disappearing before the all-conquering Anglo-Saxons. It seems as if these inferior tribes were only precursors of a superior race, voices in the wilderness crying: "Prepare ye the way of the Lord!" The savage is a hunter; by the incoming of civilization the game is driven away and disappears before the hunter becomes a herder or an agriculturist. The savage is ignorant of many diseases of civilization which, when he is exposed to them, attack him before he learns how to treat them. Civilization also has its vices, of which the uninitiated savage is innocent. He proves an apt learner of vice, but dull enough in the school of morals.

Every civilization has its destructive and preservative elements. The Anglo-Saxon race would speedily decay but for the salt of Christianity. Bring savages into contact with our civilization, and its destructive forces become operative at once, while years are necessary to render effective the saving influences of Christian instruction. Moreover, the pioneer wave of our civilization carries with it more scum than salt. Where there is one missionary, there are hundreds of miners or traders or adventurers ready to debauch the native.

Whether the extinction of inferior races before the advancing Anglo-Saxon seems to the reader sad or otherwise, it certainly appears probable. I know of nothing except climatic conditions to prevent this race from populating Africa as it has peopled North America. And those portions of Africa which are unfavorable to Anglo-Saxon life are less extensive than was once supposed. The Dutch Boers, after two centuries of life there, are as hardy as any race on earth. The Anglo-Saxon has established himself in climates totally diverse—Canada, South Africa, and India—and, through several generations, has preserved his essential race characteristics. He is not, of course, superior to climatic influences; but even in warm climates, he is likely to retain his aggressive vigor long enough to supplant races already enfeebled. Thus, in what Dr. Bushnell calls "the out-populating power of the Christian stock," may be found God's final and complete solution of the dark problem of heathenism among many inferior peoples.

Some of the stronger races, doubtless, may be able to preserve their integrity; but, in order to compete with the Anglo-Saxon, they will probably be forced to adopt his methods and instruments, his civilization and his religion. Significant movements are now in progress among them. While the Christian religion was never more vital, or its hold upon the Anglo-Saxon mind stronger, there is taking place among the nations a widespread intellectual revolt against traditional beliefs. "In every corner of the world," says Mr. Froude, "there is the same phenomenon of the decay of established religions. . . . Among the Mohammedans, Jews, Buddhists, Brahmins, traditionary creeds are losing their hold. An intellectual revolution is sweeping over the world, breaking down established opinions, dissolving foundations on which historical faiths have been built up." The contact of Christian with heathen nations is awakening the latter to new life. Old superstitions are loosening their grasp. The dead crust of fossil faiths is being shattered by the movements of life underneath. In Catholic countries, Catholicism is losing its influence over educated minds, and in some cases the masses have already lost all faith in it. Thus, while on this continent God is training the Anglo-Saxon race for its mission, a complemental work has been in progress in the great world beyond. God has two hands. Not only is he preparing in our civilization the die with which to stamp the nations, but, by what Southey called the "timing of Providence," he is preparing mankind to receive our impress.

Is there room for reasonable doubt that this race, unless devitalized by alcohol and tobacco, is destined to dispossess many weaker races, assimilate others, and mold the remainder, until, in a very true and important sense, it has Anglo-Saxonized mankind? Already "the English language, saturated with Christian ideas, gathering up into itself the best thought of all the ages, is the great agent of Christian civilization throughout the world; at this moment affecting the destinies and molding the character of half the human race." Jacob Grimm, the German philologist, said of this language: "It seems chosen, like its people, to rule in future times in a still greater degree in all the corners of the earth." He predicted, indeed, that the language of Shakespeare would eventually become the language of mankind. Is not Tennyson's noble prophecy to find its fulfillment in Anglo-Saxondom's extending its dominion and influence—

> "Till the war-drum throbs no longer, and the battle-flags are furl'd
> In the Parliament of man, the Federation of the world."

In my own mind, there is no doubt that the Anglo-Saxon is to exercise the commanding influence in the world's future; but the exact nature of that influence is, as yet, undetermined. How far his civilization will be materialistic and atheistic, and how long it will take thoroughly to Christianize and sweeten it, how rapidly he will hasten the coming of the kingdom wherein dwelleth righteousness, or how many ages he may retard it, is still uncertain; but *is now being swiftly determined*. Let us weld together in a chain the various links of our logic which we have endeavored to forge. Is it manifest that the Anglo-Saxon holds in his hands the destinies of mankind for ages to come? Is it evident that the United States is to be the home of this race, the principal seat of his power, the great center of his influence? Is it true . . . that the great West is to dominate the nation's future? Has it been shown . . . that this generation is to determine the character, and hence the destiny of the West? Then may God open the eyes of this generation! When Napoleon drew up his troops before the Mamelukes, under the shadow of the Pyramids, pointing to the latter, he said to his soldiers: "Remember that from yonder heights forty centuries look down on you." Men of this generation, from the pyramid top of opportunity on which God has set us, *we look down on forty centuries!* We stretch our hand into the future with power to mold the destinies of unborn millions.

> "We are living, we are dwelling,
>   In a grand and awful time,
>   In an age on ages telling—
>   To be living is sublime!"

Notwithstanding the great perils which threaten it, I cannot think our civilization will perish; but I believe it is fully in the hands of the Christians of the United States, during the next ten or fifteen years, to hasten or retard the coming of Christ's kingdom in the world by hundreds, and perhaps thousands, of years. We of this generation and nation occupy the Gibraltar of the ages which commands the world's future.

21.   ADAMS
The Decay of Civilization

Brooks Adams (1848–1927) was the brother of the well-known author Henry Adams and shared his pessimism concerning the future of democracy. The brothers were grandsons of John Quincy Adams and were deeply influenced by the conservative heritage drawn from their ancestors. Brooks Adams believed that the outlook for capitalist democracy was not bright because the leaders of American capitalism were too lawless and unsophisticated to provide enlightened direction. Unrestricted economic competition would lead to a disintegration of capital and consequent injury to American civilization. The following selection is the preface of Adams' book *The Law of Civilization and Decay*.*

In offering to the public a second edition of *The Law of Civilization and Decay* I take the opportunity to say emphatically that such value as the essay may have lies in its freedom from any preconceived bias. All theories contained in the book, whether religious or economic, are the effect, and not the cause, of the way in which the facts unfolded themselves. I have been passive.

The value of history lies not in the multitude of facts collected, but in their relation to each other, and in this respect an author can have no larger responsibility than any other scientific observer. If the sequence of events seems to indicate the existence of a law governing social development, such a law may be suggested, but to approve or disapprove of it would be as futile as to discuss the moral bearings of gravitation.

Some years ago, when writing a sketch of the history of the colony of Massachusetts Bay, I became deeply interested in certain religious aspects of the Reformation, which seemed hardly reconcilable with the theories usually advanced to explain them. After the book had been

* (New York: The Macmillan Company, 1897), pp. 57–61.

published, I continued reading theology, and, step by step, was led back, through the schoolmen and the crusades, to the revival of the pilgrimage to Palestine, which followed upon the conversion of the Huns. As ferocious pagans, the Huns had long closed the road to Constantinople; but the change which swept over Europe after the year 1000, when Saint Stephen was crowned, was unmistakable; the West received an impulsion from the East. I thus became convinced that religious enthusiasm, which, by stimulating the pilgrimage, restored communication between the Bosphorus and the Rhine, was the power which produced the accelerated movement culminating in modern centralization.

Meanwhile I thought I had discovered not only that faith, during the eleventh, twelfth, and early thirteenth centuries, spoke by preference through architecture, but also that in France and Syria, at least, a precise relation existed between the ecclesiastical and military systems of building, and that the one could not be understood without the other. In the commercial cities of the same epoch, on the contrary, the religious idea assumed no definite form of artistic expression, for the Gothic never flourished in Venice, Genoa, Pisa, or Florence, nor did any pure school of architecture thrive in the mercantile atmosphere. Furthermore, commerce from the outset seemed antagonistic to the imagination, for a universal decay of architecture set in throughout Europe after the great commercial expansion of the thirteenth century; and the inference I drew from these facts was, that the economic instinct must have chosen some other medium by which to express itself. My observations led me to suppose that the coinage might be such a medium, and I ultimately concluded that, if the development of a mercantile community is to be understood, it must be approached through its money.

Another conviction forced upon my mind, by the examination of long periods of history, was the exceedingly small part played by conscious thought in moulding the fate of men. At the moment of action the human being almost invariably obeys an instinct, like an animal; only after action has ceased does he reflect.

These controlling instincts are involuntary, and divide men into species distinct enough to cause opposite effects under identical conditions. For instance, impelled by fear, one type will rush upon an enemy, and another will run away; while the love of women or of money has stamped certain races as sharply as ferocity or cunning has stamped the lion or the fox.

Like other personal characteristics, the peculiarities of the mind are apparently strongly hereditary, and, if these instincts be transmitted from generation to generation, it is plain that, as the external world changes, those who receive this heritage must rise or fall in the social scale, according as their nervous system is well or ill adapted to the conditions to which they are born. Nothing is commoner, for example, than to find families who have been famous in one century sinking into obscurity in the next, not because the children have degenerated, but because a certain field of activity which afforded the ancestor full scope, has been closed against his offspring. Particularly has this been true in revolutionary epochs such as the Reformation; and families so situated have very generally become extinct.

When this stage had been reached, the Reformation began to wear a new aspect, but several years elapsed before I saw whither my studies led. Only very slowly did a sequence of cause and effect take shape in my mind, a sequence wholly unexpected in character, whose growth resembled the arrangement of the fragments of an inscription, which cannot be read until the stones have been set in a determined order. Finally, as the historical work neared an end, I perceived that the intellectual phenomena under examination fell into a series which seemed to correspond, somewhat closely, with the laws which are supposed to regulate the movements of the material universe.

Theories can be tested only by applying them to facts, and the facts relating to successive phases of human thought, whether conscious or unconscious, constitute history; therefore, if intellectual phenomena are evolved in a regular sequence, history, like matter, must be governed by law. In support of such a conjecture, I venture to offer an hypothesis by which to classify a few of the more interesting intellectual phases through which human society must, apparently, pass, in its oscillations between barbarism and civilization, or, what amounts to the same thing, in its movement from a condition of physical dispersion to one of concentration. The accompanying volume contains the evidence which suggested the hypothesis, although, it seems hardly necessary to add, an essay of this size on so vast a subject can only be regarded as a suggestion.

The theory proposed is based upon the accepted scientific principle that the law of force and energy is of universal application in nature, and that animal life is one of the outlets through which solar energy is dissipated.

Starting from this fundamental proposition, the first deduction is, that, as human societies are forms of animal life, these societies must differ among themselves in energy, in proportion as nature has endowed them, more or less abundantly, with energetic material.

Thought is one of the manifestations of human energy, and among the earlier and simpler phases of thought, two stand conspicuous—Fear and Greed. Fear, which, by stimulating the imagination, creates a belief in an invisible world, and ultimately develops a priesthood; and Greed, which dissipates energy in war and trade.

Probably the velocity of the social movement of any community is proportionate to its energy and mass, and its centralization is proportionate to its velocity; therefore, as human movement is accelerated, societies centralize. In the earlier stages of concentration, fear appears to be the channel through which energy finds the readiest outlet; accordingly, in primitive and scattered communities, the imagination is vivid, and the mental types produced are religious, military, artistic. As consolidation advances, fear yields to greed, and the economic organism tends to supersede the emotional and martial.

Whenever a race is so richly endowed with the energetic material that it does not expend all its energy in the daily struggle for life, the surplus may be stored in the shape of wealth; and this stock of stored energy may be transferred from community to community, either by conquest, or by superiority in economic competition.

However large may be the store of energy accumulated by conquest, a race must, sooner or later, reach the limit of its martial energy, when it must enter on the phase of economic competition. But, as the economic organism radically differs from the emotional and martial, the effect of economic competition has been, perhaps invariably, to dissipate the energy amassed by war.

When surplus energy has accumulated in such bulk as to preponderate over productive energy, it becomes the controlling social force. Thenceforward, capital is autocratic, and energy vents itself through those organisms best fitted to give expression to the power of capital. In this last stage of consolidation, the economic, and, perhaps, the scientific intellect is propagated, while the imagination fades, and the emotional, the martial, and the artistic types of manhood decay. When a social velocity has been attained at which the waste of energetic material is so great that the martial and imaginative stocks fail to reproduce themselves, intensifying competition appears to generate two extreme economic types,—the usurer in his most formidable aspect, and the peasant whose nervous system is best adapted to thrive on scanty nutriment. At length a point must be reached when pressure can go no further, and then, perhaps, one of two results may follow: A stationary period may supervene, which may last until ended by war, by exhaustion, or by both combined, as seems to have been the case with the Eastern Empire; or, as in the Western, disintegration may set in, the civilized population may perish, and a reversion may take place to a primitive form of organism.

The evidence, however, seems to point to the conclusion that, when a highly centralized society disintegrates, under the pressure of economic competition, it is because the energy of the race has been exhausted. Consequently, the survivors of such a community lack the power necessary for renewed concentration, and must probably remain inert until supplied with fresh energetic material by the infusion of barbarian blood.

VI

The Bulwark
of the Courts

In 1895 Justice Stephen J. Field joined with a Supreme Court majority to strike down an income tax which Congress had written into the Wilson–Gorman tariff of 1894. Field considered the act in question to be a clear attempt to evade the literal text of the Constitution, and it seemed to him an assault upon the wealthy classes which would lead eventually to a "war against the rich; a war constantly growing in intensity and bitterness." The Democrats and Populists had succeeded in creating America's first peacetime income tax, but the Supreme Court agreed with Joseph H. Choate, legal counsel for many large business concerns, who claimed that with the enactment of the income tax the march of Communism against the constitutional rights of property had begun.

The income tax decision is representative of the conservative, property-oriented nature of the Supreme Court at the end of the nineteenth century. A conservative tide was moving in the United States, and it had been partly created by the Supreme Court. This tide carried the tribunal for several decades, making it the main bulwark of conservatism in America. Against the liberal forces let loose in the early twentieth century the Court stood firm. It ceased to resist only in the mid-1930's, when the unpopularity of its anachronistic opinions became evident. For almost forty years it gave voice to the conservative sentiments of those who sought to restrain the social and economic experiments of leaders in other political branches of government. Although the least democratic part of American government, the Supreme Court claimed to protect the majority against government's most destructive tendencies.

The chief instrument used by the Court in its defense of property rights was the Fourteenth Amendment to the Constitution. It was generally agreed, when the Amendment was adopted after the Civil War, that its main purpose was to protect the newly freed Negro. The Amendment, among other things, declared that no state shall "deprive any person of life, liberty, or property, without due process of law." The same Lockean language appears in the Fifth Amendment as a barrier to national legislation. But not long after the adoption of the Amendment, the conservative members of the Supreme Court began to read the word "person" to include business corporations, which are fictional persons at law. In this way the freedom of individuals to use their property was extended to businesses, rendering them immune from injury by government. This "substantive due process" argument was a most effective judicial weapon against the experimental social legislation attempted by state and national governments in the years between 1890 and 1937.

In order to strike down state or federal legislation on either Fifth or Fourteenth Amendment grounds, it was necessary for the Supreme Court to substitute its views of the desirability of public policies in place of those of Congress and the state legislatures. Consciously or not, the personal preferences of the justices of the Court became embodied in their legal opinions. What were the objective standards used to define "due process of law"? Only the judges knew, and they, in effect, became the censors of popular majorities.

These individualistic and conservative justices of the Supreme Court acted within the dominant traditions of that tribunal. John Marshall had not favored laissez-faire, but he had defended the obligation of contract against state legislation. Constitutional scholars such as Thomas M. Cooley had espoused conservative doctrines in the 1850's and 1860's. Judicial review itself was essentially a conservative instrument against the force of numbers. Since the Constitution was written primarily as a conservative document, it is not surprising that the Court once played this active role on behalf of American conservatism, a role it has largely ceased to play in the years since the New Deal of the 1930's.

22. FIELD

Priority of Property Rights

Stephen J. Field (1816–1899), lawyer, California state judge, and associate justice of the Supreme Court, was appointed to the Court by Abraham Lincoln. He served on the Court during the period of Congressional domination which humbled President Andrew Johnson, and, consequently, he learned to fear the potential power of uncontrolled legislative majorities. Field believed in the existence of changeless and eternal legal principles found in the Constitution. Upon these principles men rest their property, their contracts, and their rights. In his powerful dissent in the Slaughter-House Cases (1873), from which this selection* is taken, he claimed that the natural rights of men to life, liberty, and property were made secure against governmental interference by the adoption in 1868 of the Fourteenth Amendment to the Constitution. This Amendment contains the statement: "nor shall any State deprive any person of life, liberty, or property, without due process of law." The meaning of this clause was first tested in 1873, in the Slaughter-House Cases, involving Louisiana legislation which had conferred upon one firm a virtual monopoly of the slaughterhouse business in New Orleans. Some of the affected businesses brought suit, claiming a violation of the Fourteenth Amendment. The majority of the Supreme Court rejected the appeal of the competing businessmen on the ground that no portion of the Fourteenth Amendment had been violated by the state legislation. Four justices dissented, but only Stephen J. Field contended that the vested rights of men to conduct business had been violated.

I am unable to agree with the majority of the court in these cases, and will proceed to state the reasons of my dissent from their judgment.

The cases grow out of the act of the legislature of the State of Louisiana, entitled "An act to protect the health of the city of New

* 16 Wallace 36, 89, 93–95, 109–11.

Orleans, to locate the stock-landings and slaughter-houses, and to incorporate 'The Crescent City Live-Stock Landing and Slaughter-House Company,' " which was approved on the eighth of March, 1869, and went into operation on the first of June following. The act creates the corporation mentioned in its title, which is composed of seventeen persons designated by name, and invests them and their successors with the powers usually conferred upon corporations in addition to their special and exclusive privileges. It first declares that it shall not be lawful, after the first day of June, 1869, to "land, keep, or slaughter any cattle, beeves, calves, sheep, swine, or other animals, or to have, keep, or establish any stock-landing, yards, slaughter-houses, or abattoirs within the city of New Orleans or the parishes of Orleans, Jefferson, and St. Bernard," except as provided in the act; and imposes a penalty of two hundred and fifty dollars for each violation of its provisions. It then authorizes the corporation mentioned to establish and erect within the parish of St. Bernard and the corporate limits of New Orleans, below the United States barracks, on the east side of the Mississippi, or at any point below a designated railroad depot on the west side of the river, "wharves, stables, sheds, yards, and buildings, necessary to land, stable, shelter, protect, and preserve all kinds of horses, mules, cattle, and other animals," and provides that cattle and other animals, destined for sale or slaughter in the city of New Orleans or its environs, shall be landed at the landings and yards of the company, and be there yarded, sheltered, and protected, if necessary; and that the company shall be entitled to certain prescribed fees for the use of its wharves, and for each animal landed, and be authorized to detain the animals until the fees are paid, and if not paid within fifteen days to take proceedings for their sale. Every person violating any of these provisions, or landing, yarding, or keeping animals elsewhere, is subjected to a fine of two hundred and fifty dollars.

The act then requires the corporation to erect a grand slaughter-house of sufficient dimensions to accommodate all butchers, and in which five hundred animals may be slaughtered a day, with a sufficient number of sheds and stables for the stock received at the port of New Orleans, at the same time authorizing the company to erect other landing-places and other slaughter-houses at any points consistent with the provisions of the act.

The act then provides that when the slaughter-houses and accessory buildings have been completed and thrown open for use, public notice thereof shall be given for thirty days, and within that time "all other stock-landings and slaughter-houses within the parishes of Orleans, Jefferson, and St. Bernard shall be closed, and it shall no longer be lawful to slaughter cattle, hogs, calves, sheep, or goats, the meat of which is determined [destined] for sale within the parishes aforesaid, under a penalty of one hundred dollars for each and every offence."

The act then provides that the company shall receive for every animal slaughtered in its buildings certain prescribed fees, besides the head, feet, gore, and entrails of all animals except of swine.

Other provisions of the act require the inspection of the animals before they are slaughtered, and allow the construction of railways to facilitate communication with the buildings of the company and the city of New Orleans.

But it is only the special and exclusive privileges conferred by the act that this court has to consider in the cases before it. These privileges are granted for the period of twenty-five years. Their exclusive character not only follows from the provisions I have cited, but it is declared in express terms of the act. In the third section the language is that the corporation "shall have the *sole and exclusive privilege* of conducting and carrying on the live-stock, landing, and slaughter-house business within the limits and privileges granted by the provisions of the act." And in the fourth section the language is, that after the first of June, 1869, the company shall have "the exclusive privilege of having landed at their landing-places all animals intended for sale or slaughter in the parishes of Orleans and Jefferson," and "the exclusive privilege of having slaughtered" in its slaughter-houses all animals, the meat of which is intended for sale in these parishes.

In order to understand the real character of these special privileges, it is necessary to know the extent of country and of population which they affect. The parish of Orleans contains an area of country of 150 square miles; the parish of Jefferson, 384 square miles; and the parish of St. Bernard, 620 square miles. The three parishes together contain an area of 1154 square miles, and they have a population of between two and three hundred thousand people.

The plaintiffs in error deny the validity of the act in question, so far as it confers the special and exclusive privileges mentioned. The first case before us was brought by an association of butchers in the three parishes against the corporation, to prevent the assertion and enforcement of these privileges. The second case was instituted by the

attorney-general of the State, in the name of the State, to protect the
corporation in the enjoyment of these privileges, and to prevent an
association of stock-dealers and butchers from acquiring a tract of land
in the same district with the corporation, upon which to erect suitable
buildings for receiving, keeping, and slaughtering cattle, and preparing
animal food for market. The third case was commenced by the corporation itself, to restrain the defendants from carrying on a business
similar to its own, in violation of its alleged exclusive privileges.

The substance of the averments of the plaintiffs in error is this:
That prior to the passage of the act in question they were engaged in
the lawful and necessary business of procuring and bringing to the
parishes of Orleans, Jefferson, and St. Bernard, animals suitable for
human food, and in preparing such food for market; that in the prosecution of this business they had provided in these parishes suitable
establishments for landing, sheltering, keeping, and slaughtering cattle
and the sale of meat; that with their association about four hundred
persons were connected, and that in the parishes named about a
thousand persons were thus engaged in procuring, preparing, and
selling animal food. And they complain that the business of landing,
yarding, and keeping, within the parishes named, cattle intended for
sale or slaughter, which was lawful for them to pursue before the first
day of June, 1869, is made by that act unlawful for any one except the
corporation named; and that the business of slaughtering cattle and
preparing animal food for market, which it was lawful for them to
pursue in those parishes before that day, is made by that act unlawful
for them to pursue afterwards, except in the buildings of the company,
and upon payment of certain prescribed fees, and a surrender of a
valuable portion of each animal slaughtered. And they contend that
the lawful business of landing, yarding, sheltering, and keeping cattle
intended for sale or slaughter, which they in common with every individual in the community of the three parishes had a right to follow,
cannot be thus taken from them and given over for a period of twenty-
five years to the sole and exclusive enjoyment of a corporation of
seventeen persons or of anybody else. And they also contend that the
lawful and necessary business of slaughtering cattle and preparing
animal food for market, which they and all other individuals had a
right to follow, cannot be thus restricted within this territory of 1154
square miles to the buildings of this corporation, or be subjected to
tribute for the emolument of that body.

No one will deny the abstract justice which lies in the position of the plaintiffs in error; and I shall endeavor to show that the position has some support in the fundamental law of the country.

It is contended in justification for the act in question that it was adopted in the interest of the city, to promote its cleanliness and protect its health, and was the legitimate exercise of what is termed the police power of the State. That power undoubtedly extends to all regulations affecting the health, good order, morals, peace, and safety of society, and is exercised on a great variety of subjects, and in almost numberless ways. All sorts of restrictions and burdens are imposed under it, and when these are not in conflict with any constitutional prohibitions, or fundamental principles, they cannot be successfully assailed in a judicial tribunal. With this power of the State and its legitimate exercise I shall not differ from the majority of the court. But under the pretence of prescribing a police regulation the State cannot be permitted to encroach upon any of the just rights of the citizen, which the Constitution intended to secure against abridgment.

In the law in question there are only two provisions which can properly be called police regulations—the one which requires the landing and slaughtering of animals below the city of New Orleans, and the other which requires the inspection of the animals before they are slaughtered. When these requirements are complied with, the sanitary purposes of the act are accomplished. In all other particulars the act is a mere grant to a corporation created by it of special and exclusive privileges by which the health of the city is in no way promoted. It is plain that if the corporation can, without endangering the health of the public, carry on the business of landing, keeping, and slaughtering cattle within a district below the city embracing an area of over a thousand square miles, it would not endanger the public health if other persons were also permitted to carry on the same business within the same district under similar conditions as to the inspection of the animals. The health of the city might require the removal from its limits and suburbs of all buildings for keeping and slaughtering cattle, but no such object could possibly justify legislation removing such buildings from a large part of the State for the benefit of a single corporation. The pretence of sanitary regulations for the grant of the exclusive privileges is a shallow one, which merits only this passing notice.

It is also sought to justify the act in question on the same principle that exclusive grants for ferries, bridges, and turnpikes are sanctioned. But it can find no support there. Those grants are of franchises of a public character appertaining to the government. Their use usually requires the exercise of the sovereign right of eminent domain. It is for the government to determine when one of them shall be granted, and the conditions upon which it shall be enjoyed. It is the duty of the government to provide suitable roads, bridges, and ferries for the convenience of the public, and if it chooses to devolve this duty to any extent, or in any locality, upon particular individuals or corporations, it may of course stipulate for such exclusive privileges connected with the franchise as it may deem proper, without encroaching upon the freedom or the just rights of others. The grant, with exclusive privileges, of a right thus appertaining to the government, is a very different thing from a grant, with exclusive privileges, of a right to pursue one of the ordinary trades or callings of life, which is a right appertaining solely to the individual.

Nor is there any analogy between this act of Louisiana and the legislation which confers upon the inventor of a new and useful improvement an exclusive right to make and sell to others his invention. The government in this way only secures to the inventor the temporary enjoyment of that which, without him, would not have existed. It thus only recognizes in the inventor a temporary property in the product of his own brain.

The act of Louisiana presents the naked case, unaccompanied by any public considerations, where a right to pursue a lawful and necessary calling, previously enjoyed by every citizen, and in connection with which a thousand persons were daily employed, is taken away and vested exclusively for twenty-five years, for an extensive district and a large population, in a single corporation, or its exercise is for that period restricted to the establishments of the corporation, and there allowed only upon onerous conditions.

If exclusive privileges of this character can be granted to a corporation of seventeen persons, they may, in the discretion of the legislature, be equally granted to a single individual. If they may be granted for twenty-five years they may be equally granted for a century, and in perpetuity. If they may be granted for the landing and keeping of animals intended for sale or slaughter they may be equally granted for the landing and storing of grain and other products of the earth, or for any article of commerce. If they may be granted for structures in which animal food is prepared for market they may be equally granted for structures in which farinaceous or vegetable food is prepared. They may be granted for any of the pursuits of human industry, even in its most simple and common forms. Indeed, upon the theory on which the exclusive privileges granted by the act in question are sustained, there is no monopoly, in the most odious form, which may not be upheld.

The question presented is, therefore, one of the gravest importance, not merely to the parties here, but to the whole country. It is nothing less than the question whether the recent amendments to the Federal Constitution protect the citizens of the United States against the deprivation of their common rights by State legislation. In my judgment the fourteenth amendment does afford such protection, and was so intended by the Congress which framed and the States which adopted it. . . .

The amendment was adopted to obviate objections which had been raised and pressed with great force to the validity of the Civil Rights Act, and to place the common rights of American citizens under the protection of the National government. It first declares that "all persons born or naturalized in the United States, and subject to the jurisdiction thereof, are citizens of the United States and of the State wherein they reside." It then declares that "no State shall make or enforce any law which shall abridge the privileges or immunities of citizens of the United States, nor shall any State deprive any person of life, liberty, or property, without due process of law, nor deny to any person within its jurisdiction the equal protection of the laws."

The first clause of this amendment determines who are citizens of the United States, and how their citizenship is created. Before its enactment there was much diversity of opinion among jurists and statesmen whether there was any such citizenship independent of that of the State, and, if any existed, as to the manner in which it originated. With a great number the opinion prevailed that there was no such citizenship independent of the citizenship of the State. Such was the opinion of Mr. Calhoun and the class represented by him. In his celebrated speech in the Senate upon the Force Bill, in 1833, referring to the reliance expressed by a senator upon the fact that we are citizens of the United States, he said: "If by citizen of the United States he means a citizen at large, one whose citizenship extends to the entire geographical limits of the country without having a local citizenship in some State or Territory, a sort of citizen of the world, all I have to say is that such a citizen would be a perfect nondescript; that not a single individual of this description can be found in the entire mass of our population. Notwithstanding all the pomp and display of eloquence on the occasion, every citizen is a citizen of some State or Territory, and as such, under an express provision of the Constitution, is entitled to all privileges and immunities of citizens in the several States; and it is in this and no other sense that we are citizens of the United States."

In the Dred Scott case this subject of citizenship of the United States was fully and elaborately discussed. The exposition in the opinion of Mr. Justice Curtis has been generally accepted by the profession of the country as one containing the soundest views of constitutional law. And he held that, under the Constitution, citizenship of the United States in reference to natives was dependent upon citizenship in the several States, under their constitutions and laws.

The Chief Justice, in that case, and a majority of the court with him, held that the words "people of the United States" and "citizens" were synonymous terms; that the people of the respective States were the parties to the Constitution; that these people consisted of the free inhabitants of those States; that they had provided in their Constitution for the adoption of a uniform rule of naturalization; that they and their descendants and persons naturalized were the only persons who could be citizens of the United States, and that it was not in the power of any State to invest any other person with citizenship so that he could enjoy the privileges of a citizen under the Constitution, and that therefore the descendants of persons brought to this country and sold as slaves were not, and could not be citizens within the meaning of the Constitution.

The first clause of the fourteenth amendment changes this whole subject, and removes it from the regime of discussion and doubt. It recognizes in express terms, if it does not create, citizens of the United States, and it makes their citizenship dependent upon the place of their birth, or the fact of their adoption, and not upon the constitution or laws of any State or the condition of their ancestry. A citizen of a State is now only a citizen of the United States residing in that State. The fundamental rights, privileges, and immunities which belong to him as a free man and a free citizen, now belong to him as a citizen of the United States, and are not dependent upon his citizenship of any State. The exercise of these rights and privileges, and the degree of enjoyment received from such exercise, are always more or less affected by the condition and the local institutions of the State, or city, or town where he resides. They are thus affected in a State by the wisdom of its laws, the ability of its officers, the efficiency of its magistrates, the education and morals of its people, and by many other considerations. This is a result which follows from the constitution of society, and can never be avoided, but in no other way can they be affected by the action of the State, or by the residence of the citizen therein. . . .

In the *Mayor of the City of Hudson* v. *Thorne*, an application was made to the chancellor of New York to dissolve an injunction restraining the defendants from erecting a building in the city of Hudson upon a vacant lot owned by them, intended to be used as a hay-press. The common council of the city had passed an ordinance directing that no person should erect, or construct, or cause to be erected or constructed, any wooden or frame barn, stable, or hay-press of certain dimensions, within certain specified limits in the city, without its permission. It appeared, however, that there were such buildings already in existence, not only in compact parts of the city, but also within the prohibited limits, the occupation of which for the storing and pressing of hay the common council did not intend to restrain. And the chancellor said: "If the manufacture of pressed hay within the compact parts of the city is dangerous in causing or promoting fires, the common council have the power expressly given by their charter to prevent the carrying on of such manufacture; but as all by-laws must be reasonable, the common council cannot make a by-law which shall permit one person to carry on the dangerous business and prohibit another who has an equal right from pursuing the same business."

In all these cases there is a recognition of the equality of right among citizens in the pursuit of the ordinary avocations of life, and a declaration that all grants of exclusive privileges, in contravention of this equality, are against common right, and void.

This equality of right, with exemption from all disparaging and partial enactments, in the lawful pursuits of life, throughout the whole country, is the distinguishing privilege of citizens of the United States. To them, everywhere, all pursuits, all professions, all avocations are open without other restrictions than such as are imposed equally upon all others of the same age, sex, and condition. The State may prescribe such regulations for every pursuit and calling of life as will promote the public health, secure the good order and advance the general prosperity of society, but when once prescribed, the pursuit or calling must be free to be followed by every citizen who is within the conditions designated, and will conform to the regulations. This is the fundamental idea upon which our institutions rest, and unless adhered to in the legislation of the country our government will be a republic only in name. The fourteenth amendment, in my judgment, makes it essential to the validity of the legislation of every State that this equality of right should be respected. How widely this equality has been departed from, how entirely rejected and trampled upon by the act of Louisiana, I have already shown. And it is to me a matter of profound regret that its validity is recognized by a majority of this court, for by it the right of free labor, one of the most sacred and imprescriptible rights of man, is violated. As stated by the Supreme Court of Connecticut, in the case cited, grants of exclusive privileges, such as is made by the act in question, are opposed to the whole theory of free government, and it requires no aid from any bill of rights to render them void. That only is a free government, in the American sense of the term, under which the inalienable right of every citizen to pursue his happiness is un-restrained, except by just, equal, and impartial laws.

23.   BLATCHFORD
Judicial Defense of Economic Liberty

The extent of Justice Stephen J. Field's conservative triumph became fully clear when the Supreme Court handed down its decision in the case of *Chicago, Milwaukee and St. Paul Railway Company* v. *Minnesota,* from which this selection* is taken. The words of the majority are those of Mr. Justice Samuel Blatchford (1820–1893), a New York Republican appointed to the Court in 1882 by President Chester A. Arthur, but the ideas are those of Justice Field. In this decision, and in others of a similar nature, the Court erected a judicial bulwark against legislative actions which might injure the rights of property. The "due process" clause of the Fourteenth Amendment was interpreted in such a way as to place the Supreme Court in a position to review the decisions of administrative bodies such as the Interstate Commerce Commission, which had been created to regulate the nation's railroads, and to declare unconstitutional legislative acts which violated the Amendment.

In 1890 the Supreme Court considered the constitutionality of a Minnesota Rail Rate Statute of 1887. The act set up a rail and warehouse commission with power to examine railway passenger and freight rates and to revise those it found unreasonable or unequal. Justice Blatchford, writing for the majority, stated that the statute was unconstitutional because the question of whether a rate is reasonable "is eminently a question for judicial investigation, requiring due process of law for its determination," thus denying the rate-making authority of state administrative agencies. Justice Samuel Miller wrote a concurring opinion, supporting Justice Blatchford but amplifying on the judicial nature of rate-making.

The opinion of the Supreme Court of Minnesota is reported in 38 Minnesota, 281. In it the court in the first place construed the statute on the question as to whether the court itself had jurisdiction to entertain the proceeding, and held that it had. Of course, we cannot review this decision.

* 134 U.S. 418, 452–61 (1890).

It next proceeded to consider the question as to the nature and extent of the powers granted to the commission by the statute in the matter of fixing the rates of charges. On that subject it said: "It seems to us that, if language means anything, it is perfectly evident that the expressed intention of the legislature is that the rates recommended and published by the commission (assuming that they have proceeded in the manner pointed out by the act) should be not simply advisory, nor merely *prima facie* equal and reasonable, but final and conclusive as to what are lawful or equal and reasonable charges; that, in proceedings to compel compliance with the rates thus published, the law neither contemplates nor allows any issue to be made or inquiry had as to their equality and reasonableness in fact. Under the provisions of the act, the rates thus published are the only ones that are lawful, and therefore, in contemplation of law, the only ones that are equal and reasonable; and, hence, in proceedings like the present, there is, as said before, no fact to traverse, except the violation of the law in refusing compliance with the recommendations of the commission. Indeed, the language of the act is so plain on that point that argument can add nothing to its force."

It then proceeded to examine the question of the validity of the act under the constitution of Minnesota, as to whether the legislature was authorized to confer upon the commission the powers given to the latter by the statute. It held that, as the legislature had the power itself to regulate charges by railroads, it could delegate to a commission the power of fixing such charges, and could make the judgment or determination of the commission as to what were reasonable charges final and conclusive.

The Chicago, Milwaukee and St. Paul Railway Company is a corporation organized under the laws of Wisconsin. The line of railroad owned and operated by it in the present case extends from Calmar, in Iowa, to LeRoy, in Minnesota, and from Leroy, through Owatonna and Faribault, to St. Paul and Minneapolis, the line from Calmar to St. Paul and Minneapolis being known as the "Iowa and Minnesota Division," and being wholly in Minnesota from the point where it crosses the state line between Iowa and Minnesota. It was constructed under a charter granted by the Territory of Minnesota to the Minneapolis and Cedar Valley Railroad Company, by an act approved March 1, 1856, Laws of 1856, c. 166, p. 325, to construct a railroad from the Iowa line, at or near the crossing of said line by the Cedar

River, through the valley of Strait River to Minneapolis. Section 9 of that act provided that the directors of the corporation should have power to make all needful rules, regulations and by-laws touching "the rates of toll and the manner of collecting the same;" and section 13, that the company should have power to unite its railroad with any other railroad which was then, or thereafter might be, constructed in the Territory of Minnesota, or adjoining States or Territories, and should have power to consolidate its stock with any other company or companies.

By an act passed March 3, 1857, c. 99, (11 Stat. 195,) the Congress of the United States made a grant of land to the Territory of Minnesota to aid in constructing certain railroads. By an act of the legislature of the Territory, approved May 22, 1857, (Laws of 1857, extra session, p. 20,) a portion of such grant was conferred upon the Minneapolis and Cedar Valley Railroad Company. Subsequently, in 1860, the State of Minnesota, by proper proceedings, became the owner of the rights, franchises and property of that company. By an act approved March 10, 1862, c. 17, (Special Laws of 1862, p. 226,) the State incorporated the Minneapolis, Faribault and Cedar Valley Railroad Company, and conveyed to it all the franchises and property of the Minneapolis and Cedar Valley Railroad Company which the State had so acquired; and by an act approved February 1, 1864, (Special Laws of 1864, p. 164,) the name of the Minneapolis, Faribault and Cedar Valley Railroad Company was changed to that of the Minnesota Central Railway Company. That company constructed the road from Minneapolis and St. Paul to LeRoy, in Minnesota; and the road from LeRoy to Calmar, in Iowa, and thence to McGregor, in the latter State, was consolidated with it. In August, 1867, the entire road from McGregor, by way of Calmar, LeRoy, Austin, Owatonna and Faribault, to St. Paul and Minneapolis, was conveyed to the Chicago, Milwaukee and St. Paul Railway Company, which succeeded to all the franchises so granted to the Minneapolis and Cedar Valley Railroad Company.

It is contended for the railway company that the State of Minnesota is bound by the contract made by the Territory in the charter granted to the Minneapolis and Cedar Valley Railroad Company; that a contract existed that the company should have the power of regulating its rates of toll; that any legislation by the State infringing upon that right impairs the obligation of the contract, that there was no provision in the charter or in any general statute reserving to the Territory or to the State the right to alter or amend the charter; and that no subsequent legislation of the Territory or of the State could deprive the directors of the company of the power to fix its rates of toll, subject only to the general provision of law that such rates should be reasonable.

But we are of opinion that the general language of the ninth section of the charter of the Minneapolis and Cedar Valley Railroad Company cannot be held to constitute an irrepealable contract with that company that it should have the right for all future time to prescribe its rates of toll, free from all control by the legislature of the State.

It was held by this court in *Pennsylvania Railroad Co.* v. *Miller*, 132 U. S. 75, in accordance with a long course of decisions both in the state courts and in this court, that a railroad corporation takes its charter, containing a kindred provision with that in question, subject to the general law of the State, and to such changes as may be made in such general law, and subject to future constitutional provisions and future general legislation, in the absence of any prior contract with it exempting it from liability to such future general legislation in respect of the subject matter involved; and that exemption from future general legislation, either by a constitutional provision or by an act of the legislature, cannot be admitted to exist unless it is given expressly, or unless it follows by an implication equally clear with express words.

There is nothing in the mere grant of power, by section 9 of the charter, to the directors of the company, to make needful rules and regulations touching the rates of toll and the manner of collecting the same, which can be properly interpreted as authorizing us to hold that the State parted with its general authority itself to regulate, at any time in the future when it might see fit to do so, the rates of toll to be collected by the company.

In *Stone* v. *Farmer's Loan and Trust Co.*, 116 U. S. 307, 325, the whole subject is fully considered, the authorities are cited, and the conclusion is arrived at, that the right of a State reasonably to limit the amount of charges by a railroad company for the transportation of persons and property within its jurisdiction cannot be granted away by the legislature unless by words of positive grant or words equivalent in law; and that a statute which grants to a railroad company the right "from time to time to fix, regulate and receive the tolls and charges by them to be received for transportation," does not deprive the State of its power, within the limits of its general authority, as controlled by the Constitution of the United States, to act upon the reasonableness of the tolls and charges so fixed and regulated. But, after reaching this conclusion, the court said (p. 331): "From what has thus been said, it is not to be inferred that this power of limitation or regulation is itself without limit. This power to regulate is not a power to destroy, and limitation is not the equivalent of confiscation. Under pretence of regulating fares and freights, the State cannot require a railroad corporation to carry persons or property without reward; neither can it do that which in law amounts to a taking of private property for public use without just compensation, or without due process of law."

There being, therefore, no contract or chartered right in the railroad company which can prevent the legislature from regulating in some form the charges of the company for transportation, the question is whether the form adopted in the present case is valid.

The construction put upon the statute by the Supreme Court of Minnesota must be accepted by this court, for the purposes of the present case, as conclusive and not to be reëxamined here as to its propriety or accuracy. The Supreme Court authoritatively declares that it is the expressed intention of the legislature of Minnesota, by the statute, that the rates recommended and published by the commission, if it proceeds in the manner pointed out by the act, are not simply advisory, nor merely *prima facie* equal and reasonable, but final and conclusive as to what are equal and reasonable charges; that the law neither contemplates nor allows any issue to be made or inquiry to be had as to their equality or reasonableness in fact; that, under the statute, the rates published by the commission are the only ones that are lawful, and, therefore, in contemplation of law the only ones that are equal and reasonable; and that, in a proceeding for a mandamus under the statute, there is no fact to traverse except the violation of law in not complying with the recommendations of the commission. In other words, although the railroad company is forbidden to establish rates that are not equal and reasonable, there is no power in the courts to stay the hands of the commission, if it chooses to establish rates that are unequal and unreasonable.

This being the construction of the statute by which we are bound in considering the present case, we are of opinion that, so construed, it conflicts with the Constitution of the United States in the particulars complained of by the railroad company. It deprives the company of its right to a judicial investigation, by due process of law, under the forms and with the machinery provided by the wisdom of successive

ages for the investigation judicially of the truth of a matter in controversy, and substitutes therefor, as an absolute finality, the action of a
railroad commission which, in view of the powers conceded to it by
the state court, cannot be regarded as clothed with judicial functions
or possessing the machinery of a court of justice.

Under section 8 of the statute, which the Supreme Court of Minnesota
says is the only one which relates to the matter of the fixing by the
commission of general schedules of rates, and which section, it says,
fully and exclusively provides for that subject, and is complete in itself,
all that the commission is required to do is, on the filing with it by a
railroad company of copies of its schedules of charges, to "find" that
any part thereof is in any respect unequal or unreasonable, and then it
is authorized and directed to compel the company to change the same
and adopt such charge as the commission "shall declare to be equal
and reasonable," and, to that end, it is required to inform the company
in writing in what respect its charges are unequal and unreasonable.
No hearing is provided for, no summons or notice to the company
before the commission has found what it is to find and declared what
it is to declare, no opportunity provided for the company to introduce
witnesses before the commission, in fact, nothing which has the
semblance of due process of law; and although, in the present case,
it appears that, prior to the decision of the commission, the company
appeared before it by its agent, and the commission investigated the
rates charged by the company for transporting milk, yet it does not
appear what the character of the investigation was or how the result
was arrived at.

By the second section of the statute in question, it is provided that
all charges made by a common carrier for the transportation of
passengers or property shall be equal and reasonable. Under this
provision, the carrier has a right to make equal and reasonable charges
for such transportation. In the present case, the return alleged that
the rate of charge fixed by the commission was not equal or reasonable,
and the Supreme Court held that the statute deprived the company of
the right to show that judicially. The question of the reasonableness of
a rate of charge for transportation by a railroad company, involving
as it does the element of reasonableness both as regards the company
and as regards the public, is eminently a question for judicial investigation, requiring due process of law for its determination. If the
company is deprived of the power of charging reasonable rates for the

use of its property, and such deprivation takes place in the absence of an investigation by judicial machinery, it is deprived of the lawful use of its property, and thus, in substance and effect, of the property itself, without due process of law and in violation of the Constitution of the United States; and in so far as it is thus deprived, while other persons are permitted to receive reasonable profits upon their invested capital, the company is deprived of the equal protection of the laws.

It is provided by section 4 of article 10 of the constitution of Minnesota of 1857, that "lands may be taken for public way, for the purpose of granting to any corporation the franchise of way for public use," and that "all corporations, being common carriers, enjoying the right of way in pursuance to the provisions of this section, shall be bound to carry the mineral, agricultural and other productions and manufactures on equal and reasonable terms." It is thus perceived that the provision of section 2 of the statute in question is one enacted in conformity with the constitution of Minnesota.

The issuing of the peremptory writ of mandamus in this case was, therefore, unlawful, because in violation of the Constitution of the United States; and it is necessary that the relief administered in favor of the plaintiff in error should be a reversal of the judgment of the Supreme Court awarding that writ, and an instruction for further proceedings by it not inconsistent with the opinion of this court.

In view of the opinion delivered by that court, it may be impossible for any further proceedings to be taken other than to dismiss the proceeding for a mandamus, if the court should adhere to its opinion that, under the statute, it cannot investigate judicially the reasonableness of the rates fixed by the commission. Still, the question will be open for review; and

The judgment of this court is, that the judgment of the Supreme Court of Minnesota, entered May 4, 1888, awarding a peremptory writ of mandamus in this case, be reversed, and the case be remanded to that court, with an instruction for further proceedings not inconsistent with the opinion of this court.

24. BREWER

Defense of Judicial Independence

David Brewer (1837–1910) was the nephew of Stephen J. Field, and he studied law in the office of David Dudley Field, the eminent legal reformer and brother of the Supreme Court justice. Brewer was appointed associate justice of the Supreme Court by President Benjamin Harrison in 1889, serving together with his uncle until Field's retirement in 1897. Justice Brewer remained on the Court until his death in 1910. He was a moderate conservative who believed that the Constitution protected both personal rights and property rights, and he viewed with concern the centralization of power in the hands of the federal government. Further, Brewer feared the power of labor organizations, electoral majorities, and state regulatory bodies. He believed that only a strengthened judiciary could resist these unfortunate political developments. This selection* is taken from an address entitled "The Nation's Safeguard," which he delivered on January 17, 1893, at the sixteenth annual meeting of the New York State Bar Association held at Albany, New York.

I am not here this evening to defend the eighth commandment, or to denounce its grosser violators. I do not propose to discuss the foot-pad or the burglar; they are vulgar and brutal criminals, in whose behalf there has as yet been organized no political party. I wish rather to notice that movement which may be denominated the movement of "coercion," and which by the mere force of numbers seeks to diminish protection to private property. It is a movement which in spirit, if not in letter, violates both the eighth and tenth commandments, a movement, which seeing that which a man has attempts to wrest it from him and transfer it to those who have not. It is the unvarying law, that the wealth of a community will be in the hands of a few, and the greater the general wealth, the greater the individual accumulations. The large majority of men are unwilling to endure that long self-denial and

* *Proceedings* of the New York State Bar Association for 1893, pp. 37–46.

saving which makes accumulation possible; they have not the business tact and sagacity which brings about large combinations and great financial results; and hence it always has been, and until human nature is remodeled always will be true, that the wealth of a nation is in the hands of a few, while the many subsist upon the proceeds of their daily toil. But security is the chief end of government; and other things being equal, that government is best which protects to the fullest extent each individual, rich or poor, high or low, in the possession of his property and the pursuit of his business. It was the boast of our ancestors in the old country, that they were able to wrest from the power of the king so much security for life, liberty and property. Indeed, English history is the long story of a struggle therefor. The greatest of English orators opposing a bill which seemed to give power to the government to enter the homes of the individual, broke forth in this most eloquent eulogy of that protection and security which surrounded an English home, even against the king: "The poorest man in his cottage may bid defiance to all the forces of the crown. It may be frail; its roof may shake; the wind may blow through it; the storm may enter it, but the king of England cannot enter it. All his power dares not cross the threshold of that ruined tenement!"

Here, there is no monarch threatening trespass upon the individual. The danger is from the multitudes—the majority, with whom is the power; and if the passage quoted is the grandest tribute to the liberty which existed in England, I would thus paraphrase it to describe that which should prevail under this government by the people: The property of a great railroad corporation stretches far away from the domicile of its owner, through State after State, from ocean to ocean; the rain and the snow may cover it; the winds and the storms may wreck it; but no man or multitude dare touch a car or move a rail. It stands as secure in the eye and in the custody of the law, as the purposes of justice in the thought of God.

This movement expresses itself in two ways: First, in the improper use of labor organizations to destroy the freedom of the laborer, and control the uses of capital. I do not care to stop to discuss such wrongs as these—preventing one from becoming a skilled laborer, by forbidding employers to take more than a named number of apprentices; compelling equal wages for unequal skill and labor; forbidding extra hours of labor to one who would accumulate more than the regular stipend. That which I particularly notice, is the assumption of control over the employer's property, and blocking the access of laborers to it. The common rule as to strikes is this: Not merely do the employees quit the employment, and thus handicap the employer in the use of his property, and perhaps in the discharge of duties which he owes to the public; but they also forcibly prevent others from taking their places. It is useless to say that they only advise—no man is misled. When a thousand laborers gather around a railroad track, and say to those who seek employment that they had better not, and when that advice is supplemented every little while by a terrible assault on one who disregards it, every one knows that something more than advice is intended. It is coercion, force; it is the effort of the many, by the mere weight of numbers, to compel the one to do their bidding. It is a proceeding outside of the law, in defiance of the law; and in spirit and effect an attempt to strip from one that has, that which of right belongs to him—the full and undisturbed use and enjoyment of his own. It is not to be wondered at, that deeds of violence and cruelty attend such demonstrations as these; nor will it do to pretend that the wrong-doers are not the striking laborers, but lawless strangers who gather to look on. Were they strangers who made the history of the "Homestead" strike one of awful horror? Were they women from afar who so mal-treated the surrendered guards; or were they the very ones who sought to compel the owners of that property to do their bidding? Even if it be true that at such places the lawless will gather,—who is responsible for their gathering? Weihe, the head of a reputable labor organization may only open the door to lawlessness; but Beekman, the anarchist and assassin, will be the first to pass through; and thus it will be always and everywhere.

In the State of Pennsylvania, only last year, to such an extent was this attempt of an organization to control both employee and employer carried, that there is now pending in the courts of the State, upon the concurrent advice of all the justices of its supreme court, an inquiry as to whether this disturbance of social order did not amount to treason. And this is but one type of multitudes of cases all over the land. This is the struggle of irresponsible persons and organizations to control labor. It is not in the interest of liberty—it is not in the interest of individual or personal rights. It is the attempt to give to the many a control over the few—a step toward despotism. Let the movement succeed, let it once be known that the individual is not free to contract for his personal services, that labor is to be farmed out by organizations, as to-day by the Chinese companies, and the next step will be a direct effort on the part of the many to seize the property of the few.

The other form of this movement assumes the guise of a regulation of the charges for the use of property subjected, or supposed to be, to a public use. This acts in two directions: One by extending the list of those things, charges for whose use the government may prescribe; until now we hear it affirmed that whenever property is devoted to a use in which the public has an interest, charges for that use may be fixed by law. And if there be any property in the use of which the public or some portion of it has no interest, I hardly know what it is or where to find it. And second, in so reducing charges for the use of property, which in fact is subjected to a public use, that no compensation or income is received by those who have so invested their property. By the one it subjects all property and its uses to the will of the majority: by the other it robs property of its value. Statutes and decisions both disclose that this movement, with just these results, has a present and alarming existence. A switching company in Minneapolis had for eight years been operating under charges of $1.50 a car. With such charges it had not during that time paid off a floating debt incurred in construction, nor a dollar of interest or dividend to those who had invested in its stock or bonds. Without a hearing before any tribunal, the State of Minnesota, through its railroad commission, reduced these charges to $1 a car. Of what value would the ownership of that property be to its owners; and how soon would all semblance of title be swept away under foreclosure by the unpaid bondholders? Sometimes there is an appeal from a majority, and that effort at confiscation failed. And yet that the effort was made and that it did receive some judicial sanction is but a revelation of the spirit which lies behind and prompts the movement, and of the extent to which it has taken hold of the public mind.

There are to-day ten thousand million of dollars invested in railroad property, whose owners in this country number less than two million persons. Can it be that whether that immense sum shall earn a dollar, or bring the slightest recompense to those who have invested perhaps their all in that business, and are thus aiding in the development of the country, depends wholly upon the whim and greed of that great majority of sixty millions who do not own a dollar. It may be said that that majority will not be so foolish, selfish and cruel as to strip that property of its earning capacity. I say that so long as constitutional guarantees lift on American soil their buttresses and bulwarks against wrong, and so long as the American judiciary breathes the free air of courage, it cannot.

It must not be supposed that the forms in which this movement expresses itself are in themselves bad. Indeed the great danger is in the fact that there is so much of good in them. If the livery of heaven were never stolen, and all human struggles were between obvious right and conceded wrong, the triumph of the former would be sure and speedy. Labor organizations are the needed and proper compliment of capital organizations. They often work wholesome restraints on the greed, the unscrupulous rapacity which dominates much of capital; and the fact that they bring together a multitude of tiny forces, each helpless in a solitary struggle with capital, enables labor to secure its just rights. So also, in regulating the charges of property which is appropriated to a public use, the public is but exercising a legitimate function, and one which is often necessary to prevent extortion in respect to public uses. Within limits of law and justice labor organizations and State regulation of charges for the use of property which is in fact devoted to public uses are commendable. But with respect to the proposition that the public may rightfully regulate the charges for the use of any property in whose use it has an interest, I am like the lawyer who, when declared guilty of contempt, responded promptly that he had shown no contempt, but on the contrary had carefully concealed his feelings.

Now conceding that there is this basis of wisdom and justice, and that within these limits the movement in both directions will work good to society, the question is how can its excesses, those excesses which mean peril to the nation, be stayed? Will the many who find in its progress temporary and apparent advantages, so clearly discern the ultimate ruin which flows from injustice as voluntarily to desist; or must there be some force, some tribunal, outside, so far as possible, to lift the restraining hand? The answer is obvious. Power always chafes at but needs restraint. This is true whether that power be in a single monarch or in a majority. All history attests the former. We are making that which proves the latter. The triple subdivision of governmental powers into legislative, executive and judicial, recognizes the truth, and has provided in this last co-ordinate department of government the restraining force. And the question which now arises is whether, in view of this exigency, the functions of the judiciary should be strengthened and enlarged, or weakened and restricted. As might be expected, they who wish to push this movement to the extreme, who would brook no restraint on aught that seems to make for their gain, are unanimous in crying out against judicial interference, and are constantly seeking to minimize the power of the courts. Hence the demand for arbitrators to settle all disputes between employer and employees, for commissions to fix all tariffs for common carriers. The argument is that judges are not adapted by their education and training to settle such matters as these; that they lack acquaintance with affairs and are tied to precedents; that the procedure in the courts is too slow and that no action could be had therein until long after the need of action has passed. It would be folly to assert that this argument is barren of force. There are judges who never move a step beyond what has been; who would never adjudge the validity of the plan of salvation without a prior decision of the Master of the Rolls or the Queen's Bench in favor of the doctrine of vicarious sacrifice; and it is true that proceedings in the law courts do not anticipate the flight of time. But the great body of judges are as well versed in the affairs of life as any, and they who unravel all the mysteries of accounting between partners, settle the business of the largest corporations and extract all the truth from the mass of scholastic verbiage that falls from the lips of expert witnesses in patent cases, will have no difficulty in determining what is right and wrong between employer and employees, and whether proposed rates of freight and fare are reasonable as between the public and the owners; while as for speed, is there any thing quicker than a writ of injunction?

But the real objection lies deeper. Somehow or other men always link the idea of justice with that of judge. It matters not that an arbitrator or commissioner may perform the same function, there is not the same respect for the office nor the same feeling that justice only can be invoked to control the decision. The arbitrator and commission will be approached with freedom by many with suggestions that the public or the party, or certain interests demand or will be profited by a decision in one way; but who thus comes near to the court or offers those suggestions to the judge? There is the tacit but universal feeling that justice, as he sees it, alone controls the decision. It is a good thing that this is so; that in the common thought the idea of justice goes hand in hand with that of judge; and that when anything is to be wrought out which it is feared may not harmonize with eternal principles of right and wrong, the cry is for arbitration or commission, or something else whose name is not symbolical or suggestive. I would have it always kept so, and kept so by the very force of the work and life of him who is a judge. It is an Anglo-Saxon habit to pay respect to the judicial office; and it is also an Anglo-Saxon demand that he who holds that office shall so bear himself as to be worthy of respect.

So it is that the mischief-makers in this movement ever strive to get away from courts and judges, and to place the power of decision in the hands of those who will the more readily and freely yield to the pressure of numbers, that so-called demand of the majority. But the common idea of justice is that the judge should be indifferent between the litigants—as free as possible from the influence of either; and no temporary arbitrator or political commission can ever equal in these respects the established courts and regular judges.

And so it is, that because of the growth of this movement, of its development in many directions and the activity of those who are in it, and especially because of the further fact that, carrying votes in its hand, it ever appeals to the trimming politician and time-serving demagogue and thus enters into so much of legislation, arises the urgent need of giving to the judiciary the utmost vigor and efficiency. Now, if ever in the history of this country, must there be somewhere and somehow a controlling force which speaks for justice and for justice only. Let this movement sweep on with no restraining force, and it is the rule of all such movements that, unchecked they grow in violence, and Carlyle's "Shooting Niagara" will epitomize the story of the downfall and departure from this Western continent of government of the people, by the people and for the people.

What, then, ought to be done? My reply is, strengthen the judiciary. How? Permanent tenure of office accomplishes this. If a judge is to go out of office in a few months the litigant will be more willing to disobey and take the chances of finally escaping punishment by delaying the proceedings until a new judge shall take the place—one whom his vote may select and from whom, therefore, he will expect slight if any punishment; while if the incumbent holds office for life, the duration of that life being uncertain, whether one or thirty years, no litigant wants to take the risk of disobedience with a strong probability that a punishment, though it may be delayed, will come and come with a severity equal to the wrong of the disobedience. A striking illustration of the truth of this is found in the troubles that followed the election of 1876. The three States in which arose contests for the possession of the State government were Florida, Louisiana and South Carolina. In each of them an application was made to the highest court of the State and a decision announced by such court. In Florida the decision was accepted without question and the control of the State government passed safely in accordance therewith. In each of the other States it was an insignificant and disregarded factor in the strife. In Florida the judges held office for life; in the other States, for only short terms. The party having or believing it had a majority, was willing in these States to risk a contest with judges whose term of office would soon expire, for it hoped to place its own friends on the bench and thus be secured from all consequences of disobedience; but in the former State there was little safety in entering upon a contest with those who might remain in office for a generation and who could be disturbed in their position by nothing short of a revolution. So if you would give the most force and effect to the decisions of our courts, you must give to the judges a permanent tenure of office.

Again, it will give greater independence of action. Judges are but human. If one must soon go before the people for re-election, how loath to rule squarely against public sentiment! There is no need of imputing conscious dishonesty; but the inevitable shrinking from antagonizing popular feeling or the wishes or interests of some prominent leader or leaders tends to delay or modify the due decision, while the judge who knows nothing can disturb his position does not hesitate promptly and clearly to "lay judgment to the line and righteousness to the plummet." "Let the jury determine," is the motto of one tribunal; "The court must decide," is the rule of the other. Cases at law and a jury are favored in the one; equity and its singleness of responsibility is the delight of the other. Far be it from me to intimate aught against the character or ability of that larger number of elective judges in this country who secure continuation in office only through the well-earned confidence of the people. The bulk of my judicial life has been spent in such tribunals and under such experiences, and I know the worth and prize the friendship of these men. I am simply comparing system with system. It is a significant fact that some of the older States which have the elective system are lengthening the terms of judicial office. The judges of your highest court hold office for fourteen years, and in the sister State of Pennsylvania for twenty-one years. And this is almost equivalent to a life tenure, for it will be found that the term of office of a justice of the supreme court of the United States (taking all who have held that office, including the present incumbents), averages less than fifteen years.

It is said that the will of the people would often be delayed or thwarted, and that this is against the essential idea of government of and by the people. But for what are written constitutions? They exist, not simply to prescribe modes of action, but because of the restraints and prohibitions they contain. Popular government may imply, generally speaking, that the present will of the majority should be carried into effect; but this is true in no absolute or arbitrary sense, and the limitations and checks which are found in all written constitutions are placed there to secure the rights of the minority. Constitutions are generally, and ought always to be, formed in times free from excitement. They represent the deliberate judgment of the people as to the provisions and restraints which, firmly and fully enforced, will secure to each citizen the greatest liberty and utmost protection. They are rules prescribed by Philip sober to control Philip drunk. When difficulties arise, when the measures and laws framed by a majority are challenged as a violation of these rules and a trespass upon the rights of the minority, common justice demands that the tribunal to determine the question shall be as little under the influence of either as is possible. Burke says: "Society requires not only that the possessions of individuals should be subjected, but that even in the mass and body, as well as in the individuals, the inclinations of men should be thwarted, their wills controlled and their passions brought into subjection. This can only be done by a power out of themselves and not in the exercise of its functions subject to that will and those passions which it is his office to bridle and subdue. In this sense the restraints on men, as well as their liberties, are to be reckoned among their rights." And surely, if the judges hold office by a life tenure and with a salary which cannot be disturbed, it would seem as though we had a tribunal as far removed from disturbing influences as possible. Though if I were to perfect the judiciary system I would add a provision that they should also be ineligible to political office and to that extent free from political ambition.

It may be said that this is practically substituting government by the judges for government by the people, and thus turning back the currents of history. The world has seen government by chiefs, by kings and emperors, by priests and by nobles. All have failed, and now govern-

ment by the people is on trial. Shall we abandon that and try government by judges? But this involves a total misunderstanding of the
relations of judges to government. There is nothing in this power of
the judiciary detracting in the least from the idea of government of and
by the people. The courts hold neither purse nor sword; they cannot
corrupt nor arbitrarily control. They make no laws, they establish no
policy, they never enter into the domain of popular action. They do
not govern. Their functions in relation to the State are limited to
seeing that popular action does not trespass upon right and justice as
it exists in written constitutions and natural law. So it is that the
utmost power of the courts and judges works no interference with true
liberty, no trespass on the fullest and highest development of government of and by the people; it only means security to personal rights—
the inalienable rights, life, liberty, and the pursuit of happiness; it
simply nails the Declaration of Independence, like Luther's theses
against indulgences upon the doors of the Wittenburg church of
human rights and dares the anarchist, the socialist and every other
assassin of liberty to blot out a single word. . . .

VII

Opposition to the Welfare State

At various times in American history conservatives lost patience with democracy and directed their contempt and scorn at the American political system. James Russell Lowell, Charles Eliot Norton, and E. L. Godkin voiced these aristocratic preferences toward the end of the nineteenth century. In our own century Henry Adams, Ralph Adams Cram, Irving Babbitt, Paul Elmer More, and others have also rejected the assumptions of Lockean democracy. A distaste for capitalism, for industrialism, for mass movements, and for the common man marks their writings. To those interested in the minority pessimist view of American conservatism these thinkers may have much to say, but in terms of the mainstream of American conservatism they have trickled off into minor tributaries. Only the antiquarians of political thought will pursue their meanderings.

But the dilemma which these writers felt was a genuine one for mainstream conservatism. With the expansion of the suffrage and the growth of mass political parties the demands of the mass public grew. The political system provided the arena for competing groups seeking the benefits that government could bestow.

At first government attacked the serious abuses which unrestrained businessmen had created. Regulatory bodies were created in response to the outcries of enraged reformers. By the 1920's most of the obvious dangers to health and safety created by industrialism had come under some government scrutiny. Conservative Presidents Harding, Coolidge, and Hoover recognized that laissez-faire was neither possible nor inherently desirable, although they adopted probusiness attitudes. However, they felt that if carried too far, government intervention in the economic system would destroy individual liberty.

How much government intervention is too much? The answer to this question separated liberals from conservatives during and after the Depression of the 1930's. Unfortunately, there was no clear standard of measurement for the answer to this question. The New Deal of Franklin Roosevelt at first had no answer either. Later, in a series of pragmatic, experimental, and inconsistent reforms the scaffolding of the American welfare state was erected. In a policy without a design, enormous bureaucratic structures were created to support the machinery of welfare administration. Workers were forced to save a portion of their salaries, employers were forced to contribute to retirement plans and injury funds, collective bargaining was made official and binding, farmers were subsidized, and vast sums of other welfare subsidies were poured out of Washington and later from the state capitals and city governments.

To what extent the welfare state is a product of accident is unclear, but it is certain that it represents a reaction to the demands of special groups in the society. This process has been rationalized into a belief that government is primarily responsible for the economic security of the individual in an ever expanding network of new programs.

That individuals are economically more secure today than they were thirty or forty years ago is clearly true. But that this security has been bought at a price is equally beyond question. Only a few American conservatives have perceived the bargain as a bad one and stated their opposition to the welfare state. Obviously the argument is largely a negative one. It cannot be a popular argument since so many people are beneficiaries of the welfare system. The politician who attempted to repeal a portion of the system would run great risks. However, the risks to individualism created by the idea of the welfare state cannot be ignored. The status of dependency which it may induce could negate the very promise of democracy. The assumptions of the welfare state are not beyond challenge, although it is doubtful that conservatives can hope to change it materially.

25. PECKHAM
Freedom of Contract (1905)

Rufus W. Peckham (1838–1909), a Democrat and political reformer, had a long and distinguished career as a lawyer and a judge in New York State before being appointed to the United States Supreme Court by President Grover Cleveland in 1895. Justice Peckham served on the Court for thirteen years, and throughout his tenure he was a strong opponent of social and economic legislation. Although Peckham had some formal college training, it is interesting to note that he never received a college degree, having studied for the bar in his father's law office.

In 1905 a 5 to 4 majority declared unconstitutional a New York statute limiting hours of labor in bakery shops to sixty hours in one week or ten hours in any one day. In *Lochner* v. *New York*, from which the following selection* is taken, Justice Peckham expressed the sentiment of the majority of the Court when he stated that the state legislature had some power to limit the right of free contract but the determination of the hours of labor for bakery workers was not a matter concerning the safety, morals, or welfare of the public and hence not an area in which the legislature could exercise its authority.

. . . The indictment, it will be seen, charges that the plaintiff in error violated the 110th section of article 8, chapter 415, of the Laws of 1897, known as the labor law of the state of New York, in that he wrongfully and unlawfully required and permitted an employee working for him to work more than sixty hours in one week. There is nothing in any of the opinions delivered in this case, either in the supreme court or the court of appeals of the state, which construes the section, in using the word "required," as referring to any physical force being used to obtain the labor of an employee. It is assumed that the word means

* 198 U.S. 45, 53–65 (1905).

nothing more than the requirement arising from voluntary contract
for such labor in excess of the number of hours specified in the statute.
There is no pretense in any of the opinions that the statute was intended
to meet a case of involuntary labor in any form. All the opinions assume
that there is no real distinction, so far as this question is concerned,
between the words "required" and "permitted." The mandate of the
statute, that "no employee shall be required or permitted to work,"
is the substantial equivalent of an enactment that "no employee shall
contract or agree to work," more than ten hours per day; and, as there
is no provision for special emergencies, the statute is mandatory in all
cases. It is not an act merely fixing the number of hours which shall
constitute a legal day's work, but an absolute prohibition upon the
employer permitting, under any circumstances, more than ten hours'
work to be done in his establishment. The employee may desire to earn
the extra money which would arise from his working more than the
prescribed time, but this statute forbids the employer from permitting
the employé to earn it.

The statute necessarily interferes with the right of contract between
the employer and employés, concerning the number of hours in which
the latter may labor in the bakery of the employer. The general right
to make a contract in relation to his business is part of the liberty of
the individual protected by the Fourteenth Amendment of the Federal
Constitution. *Allgeyer* v. *Louisiana*, 165 U. S. 578. Under that provision
no State can deprive any person of life, liberty or property without
due process of law. The right to purchase or to sell labor is part of the
liberty protected by this amendment, unless there are circumstances
which exclude the right. There are, however, certain powers, existing
in the sovereignty of each State in the Union, somewhat vaguely termed
police powers, the exact description and limitation of which have not
been attempted by the courts. Those powers, broadly stated and without,
at present, any attempt at a more specific limitation, relate to the safety,
health, morals and general welfare of the public. Both property and
liberty are held on such reasonable conditions as may be imposed by
the governing power of the State in the exercise of those powers, and
with such conditions the Fourteenth Amendment was not designed to
interfere. *Mugler* v. *Kansas*, 123 U. S. 623; *In re Kemmler*, 136 U. S. 436;
Crowley v. *Christensen*, 137 U. S. 86; *In re Converse*, 137 U. S. 624.

The State, therefore, has power to prevent the individual from making
certain kinds of contracts, and in regard to them the Federal Constitution

offers no protection. If the contract be one which the State, in the legitimate exercise of its police power, has the right to prohibit, it is not prevented from prohibiting it by the Fourteenth Amendment. Contracts in violation of a statute, either of the Federal or state government, or a contract to let one's property for immoral purposes, or to do any other unlawful act, could obtain no protection from the Federal Constitution, as coming under the liberty of person or of free contract. Therefore, when the State, by its legislature, in the assumed exercise of its police powers, has passed an act which seriously limits the right to labor or the right of contract in regard to their means of livelihood between persons who are *sui juris* (both employer and employé), it becomes of great importance to determine which shall prevail —the right of the individual to labor for such time as he may choose, or the right of the State to prevent the individual from laboring or from entering into any contract to labor, beyond a certain time prescribed by the State.

This court has recognized the existence and upheld the exercise of the police powers of the States in many cases which might fairly be considered as border ones, and it has, in the course of its determination of questions regarding the asserted invalidity of such statutes, on the ground of their violation of the rights secured by the Federal Constitution, been guided by rules of a very liberal nature, the application of which has resulted, in numerous instances, in upholding the validity of state statutes thus assailed. Among the later cases where the state law has been upheld by this court is that of *Holden* v. *Hardy*, 169 U. S. 366. A provision in the act of the legislature of Utah was there under consideration, the act limiting the employment of workmen in all underground mines or workings, to eight hours per day, "except in cases of emergency, where life or property is in imminent danger." It also limited the hours of labor in smelting and other institutions for the reduction or refining of ores or metals to eight hours per day, except in like cases of emergency. The act was held to be a valid exercise of the police powers of the State. A review of many of the cases on the subject, decided by this and other courts, is given in the opinion. It was held that the kind of employment, mining, smelting, etc., and the character of the employés in such kinds of labor, were such as to make it reasonable and proper for the State to interfere to prevent the employés from being constrained by the rules laid down by the proprietors in regard to labor. The following citation from the observations of the Supreme Court of Utah in that case was made by the judge writing the opinion of this court, and approved: "The law in question is confined to the protection of that class of people engaged in labor in underground mines, and in smelters and other works wherein ores are reduced and refined. This law applies only to the classes subjected by their employment to the peculiar conditions and effects attending underground mining and work in smelters, and other works for the reduction and refining of ores. Therefore it is not necessary to discuss or decide whether the legislature can fix the hours of labor in other employments."

It will be observed that, even with regard to that class of labor, the Utah statute provided for cases of emergency wherein the provisions of the statute would not apply. The statute now before this court has no emergency clause in it, and, if the statute is valid, there are no circumstances and no emergencies under which the slightest violation of the provisions of the act would be innocent. There is nothing in *Holden* v. *Hardy* which covers the case now before us. Nor does *Atkin* v. *Kansas*, 191 U. S. 207, touch the case at bar. The *Atkin case* was decided upon the right of the State to control its municipal corporations and to prescribe the conditions upon which it will permit work of a public character to be done for a municipality. *Knoxville Iron Co.* v. *Harbison*, 183 U. S. 13, is equally far from an authority for this legislation. The employés in that case were held to be at a disadvantage with the employer in matters of wages, they being miners and coal workers, and the act simply provided for the cashing of coal orders when presented by the miner to the employer.

The latest case decided by this court, involving the police power, is that of *Jacobson* v. *Massachusetts*, decided at this term and reported in 197 U. S. 11. It related to compulsory vaccination, and the law was held valid as a proper exercise of the police powers with reference to the public health. It was stated in the opinion that it was a case "of an adult who, for aught that appears, was himself in perfect health and a fit subject for vaccination, and yet, while remaining in the community, refused to obey the statute and the regulation adopted in execution of its provisions for the protection of the public health and the public safety, confessedly endangered by the presence of a dangerous disease." That case is also far from covering the one now before the court.

Petit v. *Minnesota*, 177 U. S. 164, was upheld as a proper exercise of the police power relating to the observance of Sunday, and the case held that the legislature had the right to declare that, as a matter of law, keeping barber shops open on Sunday was not a work of necessity or charity.

It must, of course, be conceded that there is a limit to the valid exercise of the police power by the State. There is no dispute concerning this general proposition. Otherwise the Fourteenth Amendment would have no efficacy and the legislatures of the States would have unbounded power, and it would be enough to say that any piece of legislation was enacted to conserve the morals, the health or the safety of the people; such legislation would be valid, no matter how absolutely without foundation the claim might be. The claim of the police power would be a mere pretext—become another and delusive name for the supreme sovereignty of the State to be exercised free from constitutional restraint. This is not contended for. In every case that comes before this court, therefore, where legislation of this character is concerned and where the protection of the Federal Constitution is sought, the question necessarily arises: Is this a fair, reasonable and appropriate exercise of the police power of the State, or is it an unreasonable, unnecessary and arbitrary interference with the right of the individual to his personal liberty or to enter into those contracts in relation to labor which may seem to him appropriate or necessary for the support of himself and his family? Of course the liberty of contract relating to labor includes both parties to it. The one has as much right to purchase as the other to sell labor.

This is not a question of substituting the judgment of the court for that of the legislature. If the act be within the power of the State it is valid, although the judgment of the court might be totally opposed to the enactment of such a law. But the question would still remain: Is it within the police power of the State? and that question must be answered by the court.

The question whether this act is valid as a labor law, pure and simple, may be dismissed in a few words. There is no reasonable ground for interfering with the liberty of person or the right of free contract, by determining the hours of labor, in the occupation of a baker. There is no contention that bakers as a class are not equal in intelligence and capacity to men in other trades or manual occupations, or that they are not able to assert their rights and care for themselves without the protecting arm of the State, interfering with their independence of judgment and of action. They are in no sense wards of the State. Viewed in the light of a purely labor law, with no reference whatever to the question of health, we think that a law like the one before us involves neither the safety, the morals nor the welfare of the public, and that the interest of the public is not in the slightest degree affected by such an act. The law must be upheld, if at all, as a law pertaining to the health of the individual engaged in the occupation of a baker. It does not affect any other portion of the public than those who are engaged in that occupation. Clean and wholesome bread does not depend upon whether the baker works but ten hours per day or only sixty hours a week. The limitation of the hours of labor does not come within the police power on that ground.

It is a question of which of two powers or rights shall prevail—the power of the State to legislate or the right of the individual to liberty of person and freedom of contract. The mere assertion that the subject related though but in a remote degree to the public health does not necessarily render the enactment valid. The act must have a more direct relation, as a means to an end, and the end itself must be appropriate and legitimate, before an act can be held to be valid which interferes with the general right of an individual to be free in his person and in his power to contract in relation to his own labor.

This case has caused much diversity of opinion in the state courts. In the Supreme Court two of the five judges composing the Appellate Division dissented from the judgment affirming the validity of the act. In the Court of Appeals three of the seven judges also dissented from the judgment upholding the statute. Although found in what is called a labor law of the State, the Court of Appeals has upheld the act as one relating to the public health—in other words, as a health law. One of the judges of the Court of Appeals, in upholding the law, stated that, in his opinion, the regulation in question could not be sustained unless they were able to say, from common knowledge, that working in a bakery and candy factory was an unhealthy employment. The judge held that, while the evidence was not uniform, it still led him to the conclusion that the occupation of a baker or confectioner was unhealthy and tended to result in diseases of the respiratory organs. Three of the judges dissented from that view, and they thought the occupation of a baker was not to such an extent unhealthy as to warrant the interference of the legislature with the liberty of the individual.

We think the limit of the police power has been reached and passed in this case. There is, in our judgment, no reasonable foundation for holding this to be necessary or appropriate as a health law to safeguard the public health or the health of the individuals who are following the trade of a baker. If this statute be valid, and if, therefore, a proper case is made out in which to deny the right of an individual, *sui juris*, as employer or employé, to make contracts for the labor of the latter under the protection of the provisions of the Federal Constitution, there would seem to be no length to which legislation of this nature might not go. The case differs widely, as we have already stated, from the expressions of this court in regard to laws of this nature, as stated in *Holden* v. *Hardy* and *Jacobson* v. *Massachusetts, supra.*

We think that there can be no fair doubt that the trade of a baker, in and of itself, is not an unhealthy one to that degree which would authorize the legislature to interfere with the right to labor, and with the right of free contract on the part of the individual, either as employer or employé. In looking through statistics regarding all trades and occupations, it may be true that the trade of a baker does not appear to be as healthy as some other trades, and is also vastly more healthy than still others. To the common understanding the trade of a baker has never been regarded as an unhealthy one. Very likely physicians would not recommend the exercise of that or of any other trade as a remedy for ill health. Some occupations are more healthy than others, but we think there are none which might not come under the power of the legislature to supervise and control the hours of working therein, if the mere fact that the occupation is not absolutely and perfectly healthy is to confer that right upon the legislative department of the Government. It might be safely affirmed that almost all occupations more or less affect the health. There must be more than the mere fact of the possible existence of some small amount of unhealthiness to warrant legislative interference with liberty. It is unfortunately true that labor, even in any department, may possibly carry with it the seeds of unhealthiness. But are we all, on that account, at the mercy of legislative majorities? A printer, a tinsmith, a locksmith, a carpenter, a cabinetmaker, a dry goods clerk, a bank's, a lawyer's or a physician's clerk, or a clerk in almost any kind of business, would all come under the power of the legislature, on this assumption. No trade, no occupation, no mode of earning one's living, could escape this all-pervading power, and the acts of the legislature in limiting the hours of labor in all employments would be valid, although such limitation might seriously cripple the ability of the laborer to support himself and his family. In our large cities there are many buildings into which the sun penetrates for but a short time in each day, and these buildings are occupied by people carrying on the business of bankers, brokers, lawyers, real estate, and many other kinds of business, aided by many clerks, messengers, and other employés. Upon the assumption of the validity of this act under review, it is not possible to say that an act, prohibiting lawyers' or bank clerks, or others, from contracting to labor for their employers more than eight hours a day, would be invalid. It might be said that it is unhealthy to work more than that number of hours in an apartment lighted by artificial light during the working hours of the day; that the occupation of the bank clerk, the lawyer's clerk, the real estate clerk, or the broker's clerk in such offices is therefore unhealthy, and the legislature in its paternal wisdom must, therefore, have the right to legislate on the subject of and to limit the hours for such labor, and if it exercises that power and its validity be questioned, it is sufficient to say, it has reference to the public health; it has reference to the health of the employés condemned to labor day after day in buildings where the sun never shines; it is a health law, and therefore it is valid, and cannot be questioned by the courts.

It is also urged, pursuing the same line of argument, that it is to the interest of the State that its population should be strong and robust, and therefore any legislation which may be said to tend to make people healthy must be valid as health laws, enacted under the police power. If this be a valid argument and a justification for this kind of legislation, it follows that the protection of the Federal Constitution from undue interference with liberty of person and freedom of contract is visionary, wherever the law is sought to be justified as a valid exercise of the police power. Scarcely any law but might find shelter under such assumptions, and conduct, properly so called, as well as contract, would come under the restrictive sway of the legislature. Not only the hours of the employés, but the hours of employers, could be regulated, and doctors, lawyers, scientists, all professional men, as well as athletes and artisans, could be forbidden to fatigue their brains and bodies by prolonged hours of exercise, lest the fighting strength of the State be impaired. We mention these extreme cases because the contention is extreme. We do not believe in the soundness of the views which uphold this law. On the contrary, we think that such a law as this, although passed in the assumed exercise of the police power, and as relating to the public health, or the health of the employés named, is not within that power, and is invalid. The act is not, within any fair meaning of the term, a health law, but is an illegal interference with the rights of individuals, both employers and employés, to make contracts regarding labor upon such terms as they may think best, or which they may agree upon with the other parties to such contracts. Statutes of the nature of that under review, limiting the hours in which grown and intelligent men may labor to earn their living, are mere meddlesome interferences with the rights of the individual, and they are not saved from condemnation by the claim that they are passed in the exercise of the police power and upon the subject of the health of the individual whose rights are interfered with, unless there be some fair ground, reasonable in and of itself, to say that there is material danger to the public health or to the health of the employés, if the hours of labor are not curtailed. If this be not clearly the case the individuals, whose rights are thus made the subject of legislative interference, are under the protection of the Federal Constitution regarding their liberty of contract as well as of person; and the legislature of the State has no power to limit their right as proposed in this statute. All that it could properly do has been done by it with regard to the conduct of bakeries, as provided for in the other sections of the act, above set forth. These several sections provide for the inspection of the premises where the bakery is carried on, with regard to furnishing proper wash-rooms and water-closets, apart from the bakeroom, also with regard to providing proper drainage, plumbing and painting; the sections, in addition, provide for the height of the ceiling, the cementing or tiling of floors, where necessary in the opinion of the factory inspector, and for other things of that nature; alterations are also provided for and are to be made where necessary in the opinion of the inspector, in order to comply with the provisions of the statute. These various sections may be wise and valid regulations, and they certainly go to the full extent of providing for the cleanliness and the healthiness, so far as possible, of the quarters in which bakeries are to be conducted. Adding to all these requirements, a prohibition to enter into any contract of labor in a bakery for more than a certain number of hours a week, is, in our judgment, so wholly beside the matter of a proper, reasonable and fair provision, as to run counter to that liberty of person and of free contract provided for in the Federal Constitution.

It was further urged on the argument that restricting the hours of labor in the case of bakers was valid because it tended to cleanliness on the part of the workers, as a man was more apt to be cleanly when not overworked, and if cleanly then his "output" was also more likely to be so. What has already been said applies with equal force to this contention. We do not admit the reasoning to be sufficient to justify the claimed right of such interference. The State in that case would assume the position of a supervisor, or *pater familias*, over every act of the individual, and its right of governmental interference with his hours of labor, his hours of exercise, the character thereof, and the extent to which it shall be carried would be recognized and upheld. In our judgment it is not possible in fact to discover the connection between the number of hours a baker may work in the bakery and the healthful quality of the bread made by the workman. The connection, if any exists, is too shadowy and thin to build any argument for the interference of the legislature. If the man works ten hours a day it is all right, but if ten and a half or eleven his health is in danger and his bread may be unhealthful, and, therefore, he shall not be permitted to do it. This, we think, is unreasonable and entirely arbitrary. When assertions such as we have adverted to become necessary in order to give, if possible, a plausible foundation for the contention that the law is a "health law," it gives rise to at least a suspicion that there was some other motive dominating the legislature than the purpose to subserve the public health or welfare. . . .

It is impossible for us to shut our eyes to the fact that many of the laws of this character, while passed under what is claimed to be the police power for the purpose of protecting the public health or welfare, are, in reality, passed from other motives. We are justified in saying so when, from the character of the law and the subject upon which it legislates, it is apparent that the public health or welfare bears but the most remote relation to the law. The purpose of a statute must be determined from the natural and legal effect of the language employed; and whether it is or is not repugnant to the Constitution of the United States must be determined from the natural effect of such statutes when put into operation, and not from their proclaimed purpose. *Minnesota* v. *Barber*, 136 U. S. 313; *Brimmer* v. *Rebman*, 138 U. S. 78. The court looks beyond the mere letter of the law in such cases. *Yick Wo* v. *Hopkins*, 118 U. S. 356.

It is manifest to us that the limitation of the hours of labor as provided for in this section of the statute under which the indictment was found, and the plaintiff in error convicted, has no such direct relation to and no such substantial effect upon the health of the employé, as to justify us in regarding the section as really a health law. It seems to us that the real object and purpose were simply to regulate the hours of labor between the master and his employés (all being men, *sui juris*), in a private business, not dangerous in any degree to morals or in any real and substantial degree, to the health of the employés. Under such circumstances the freedom of master and employé to contract with each other in relation to their employment, and in defining the same, cannot be prohibited or interfered with, without violating the Federal Constitution.

The judgment of the Court of Appeals of New York as well as that of the Supreme Court and of the County Court of Oneida County must be reversed and the case remanded to the County Court for further proceedings not inconsistent with this opinion.

26.   SUTHERLAND

Freedom of Contract Reasserted (1923)

George Sutherland (1862–1942) grew up in Utah and represented that state in the United States Senate from 1905 to 1917. He served as president of the American Bar Association in 1917 and as Warren G. Harding's principal adviser in the campaign of 1920. A member of the conservative wing of the Republican Party, he opposed Theodore Roosevelt's proposal for recall of judicial opinions and Woodrow Wilson's nomination of Louis Brandeis to the Supreme Court. Sutherland's appointment in 1922 helped form a new conservative coalition, along with Justices James C. McReynolds and Pierce Butler, which led the Court's battle against government economic regulation and specifically against President Franklin Roosevelt's New Deal. In addition, Sutherland spoke out strongly against strict majority rule, regarding the judiciary as a needed check upon legislative excesses.

Justice Sutherland wrote the majority opinion in the 1923 case of *Adkins* v. *Children's Hospital* from which this selection* is taken. At issue was the constitutionality of a District of Columbia minimum wage law, enacted by Congress in 1918. The statute had established a District Wage Board and given it the power to fix minimum wages for women and children. A 5 to 3 majority declared the statute void, and Justice Sutherland found that "liberty of contract" had been violated by this minimum wage legislation.

The judicial duty of passing upon the constitutionality of an act of Congress is one of great gravity and delicacy. The statute here in question has successfully borne the scrutiny of the legislative branch of the government, which, by enacting it, has affirmed its validity; and that determination must be given great weight. This Court, by an unbroken line of decisions from Chief Justice Marshall to the present day, has steadily adhered to the rule that every possible presumption

* 261 U.S. 525, 544–62 (1923).

is in favor of the validity of an act of Congress until overcome beyond rational doubt. But if by clear and indubitable demonstration a statute be opposed to the Constitution we have no choice but to say so. The Constitution, by its own terms, is the supreme law of the land, emanating from the people, the repository of ultimate sovereignty under our form of government. A congressional statute, on the other hand, is the act of an agency of this sovereign authority and if it conflict with the Constitution must fall; for that which is not supreme must yield to that which is. To hold it invalid (if it be invalid) is a plain exercise of the judicial power—that power vested in courts to enable them to administer justice according to law. From the authority to ascertain and determine the law in a given case, there necessarily results, in case of conflict, the duty to declare and enforce the rule of the supreme law and reject that of an inferior act of legislation which, transcending the Constitution, is of no effect and binding on no one. This is not the exercise of a substantive power to review and nullify acts of Congress, for no such substantive power exists. It is simply a necessary concomitant of the power to hear and dispose of a case or controversy properly before the court, to the determination of which must be brought the test and measure of the law.

The statute now under consideration is attacked upon the ground that it authorizes an unconstitutional interference with the freedom of contract included within the guaranties of the due process clause of the Fifth Amendment. That the right to contract about one's affairs is a part of the liberty of the individual protected by this clause, is settled by the decisions of this Court and is no longer open to question. *Allgeyer* v. *Louisiana*, 165 U. S. 578, 591; *New York Life Insurance Co.* v. *Dodge*, 246 U. S. 357, 373–374; *Coppage* v. *Kansas*, 236 U. S. 1, 10, 14; *Adair* v. *United States*, 208 U. S. 161; *Lochner* v. *New York*, 198 U. S. 45; *Butchers' Union Co.* v. *Crescent City Co.*, 111 U. S. 746; *Muller* v. *Oregon*, 208 U. S. 412, 421. Within this liberty are contracts of employment of labor. In making such contracts, generally speaking, the parties have an equal right to obtain from each other the best terms they can as the result of private bargaining.

In *Adair* v. *United States*, *supra*, Mr. Justice Harlan (pp. 174, 175), speaking for the Court, said:

"The right of a person to sell his labor upon such terms as he deems proper is, in its essence, the same as the right of the purchaser of labor to prescribe the conditions upon which he will accept such labor from the person offering to sell. . . . In all such particulars the employer and employé have equality of right, and any legislation that disturbs that equality is an arbitrary interference with the liberty of contract which no government can legally justify in a free land."

In *Coppage* v. *Kansas*, *supra* (p. 14), this Court, speaking through Mr. Justice Pitney, said:

"Included in the right of personal liberty and the right of private property—partaking of the nature of each—is the right to make contracts for the acquisition of property. Chief among such contracts is that of personal employment, by which labor and other services are exchanged for money or other forms of property. If this right be struck down or arbitrarily interfered with, there is a substantial impairment of liberty in the long-established constitutional sense. The right is as essential to the laborer as to the capitalist, to the poor as to the rich; for the vast majority of persons have no other honest way to begin to acquire property, save by working for money.

"An interference with this liberty so serious as that now under consideration, and so disturbing of equality of right, must be deemed to be arbitrary, unless it be supportable as a reasonable exercise of the police power of the State."

There is, of course, no such thing as absolute freedom of contract. It is subject to a great variety of restraints. But freedom of contract is, nevertheless, the general rule and restraint the exception; and the exercise of legislative authority to abridge it can be justified only by the existence of exceptional circumstances. Whether these circumstances exist in the present case constitutes the question to be answered. It will be helpful to this end to review some of the decisions where the interference has been upheld and consider the grounds upon which they rest.

(1) *Those dealing with statutes fixing rates and charges to be exacted by businesses impressed with a public interest.* There are many cases, but it is sufficient to cite *Munn* v. *Illinois*, 94 U. S. 113. The power here rests upon the ground that where property is devoted to a public use the owner thereby, in effect, grants to the public an interest in the use which may be controlled by the public for the common good to the extent of the interest thus created. It is upon this theory that these statutes have been upheld and, it may be noted in passing, so upheld even in respect of their incidental and injurious or destructive effect upon preëxisting contracts. See *Louisville & Nashville R. R. Co.* v. *Mottley*, 219 U. S. 467. In the case at bar the statute does not depend

upon the existence of a public interest in any business to be affected, and this class of cases may be laid aside as inapplicable.

(2) *Statutes relating to contracts for the performance of public work.* *Atkin* v. *Kansas*, 191 U. S. 207; *Heim* v. *McCall*, 239 U. S. 175; *Ellis* v. *United States*, 206 U. S. 246. These cases sustain such statutes as depending, not upon the right to condition private contracts, but upon the right of the government to prescribe the conditions upon which it will permit work of a public character to be done for it, or, in the case of a State, for its municipalities. We may, therefore, in like manner, dismiss these decisions from consideration as inapplicable.

(3) *Statutes prescribing the character, methods and time for payment of wages.* Under this head may be included *McLean* v. *Arkansas*, 211 U. S. 539, sustaining a state statute requiring coal to be measured for payment of miners' wages before screening; *Knoxville Iron Co.* v. *Harbison*, 183 U. S. 13, sustaining a Tennessee statute requiring the redemption in cash of store orders issued in payment of wages; *Erie R. R. Co.* v. *Williams*, 233 U. S. 685, upholding a statute regulating the time within which wages shall be paid to employees in certain specified industries; and other cases sustaining statutes of like import and effect. In none of the statutes thus sustained, was the liberty of employer and employee to fix the amount of wages the one was willing to pay and the other willing to receive interfered with. Their tendency and purpose was to prevent unfair and perhaps fraudulent methods in the payment of wages and in no sense can they be said to be, or to furnish a precedent for, wage-fixing statutes.

(4) *Statutes fixing hours of labor.* It is upon this class that the greatest emphasis is laid in argument and therefore, and because such cases approach most nearly the line of principle applicable to the statute here involved, we shall consider them more at length. In some instances the statute limited the hours of labor for men in certain occupations and in others it was confined in its application to women. No statute has thus far been brought to the attention of this Court which by its terms, applied to all occupations. In *Holden* v. *Hardy*, 169 U. S. 366, the Court considered an act of the Utah legislature, restricting the hours of labor in mines and smelters. This statute was sustained as a legitimate exercise of the police power, on the ground that the legislature had determined that these particular employments, when too long pursued, were injurious to the health of the employees, and that, as there were reasonable grounds for supporting this determination on the part of

the legislature, its decision in that respect was beyond the reviewing power of the federal courts.

That this constituted the basis of the decision is emphasized by the subsequent decision in *Lochner* v. *New York*, 198 U. S. 45, reviewing a state statute which restricted the employment of all persons in bakeries to ten hours in any one day. The Court referred to *Holden* v. *Hardy, supra,* and, declaring it to be inapplicable, held the statute unconstitutional as an unreasonable, unnecessary and arbitrary interference with the liberty of contract and therefore void under the Constitution. . . .

Subsequent cases in this Court have been distinguished from that decision, but the principles therein stated have never been disapproved.

In *Bunting* v. *Oregon*, 243 U. S. 426, a state statute forbidding the employment of any person in any mill, factory or manufacturing establishment more than ten hours in any one day, and providing payment for overtime not exceeding three hours in any one day at the rate of time and a half of the regular wage, was sustained on the ground that, since the state legislature and State Supreme Court had found such a law necessary for the preservation of the health of employees in these industries, this Court would accept their judgment, in the absence of facts to support the contrary consideration. The law was attacked on the ground that it constituted an attempt to fix wages, but that contention was rejected and the law sustained as a reasonable regulation of hours of service.

Wilson v. *New*, 243 U. S. 332, involved the validity of the so-called Adamson Law, which established an eight-hour day for employees of interstate carriers for which it fixed a scale of minimum wages with proportionate increases for overtime, to be enforced, however, only for a limited period. The act was sustained primarily upon the ground that it was a regulation of a business charged with a public interest. The Court, speaking through the Chief Justice, pointed out that regarding "the private right and private interest as contradistinguished from the public interest the power exists between the parties, the employers and employees, to agree as to a standard of wages free from legislative interference" but that this did not affect the power to deal with the matter with a view to protect the public right, and then said (p. 353):

"And this emphasizes that there is no question here of purely private right since the law is concerned only with those who are engaged in a business charged with a public interest where the subject dealt with as to all the parties is one involved in that business and which we have seen comes under the control of the right to regulate to the extent that the power to do so is appropriate or relevant to the business regulated."

Moreover, in sustaining the wage feature, of the law, emphasis was put upon the fact (p. 345) that it was in this respect temporary "leaving the employers and employees free as to the subject of wages to govern their relations by their own agreements after the specified time." The act was not only temporary in this respect, but it was passed to meet a sudden and great emergency. This feature of the law was sustained principally because the parties, for the time being, could not or would not agree. Here they are forbidden to agree.

The same principle was applied in the *Rent Cases* (*Block* v. *Hirsh*, 256 U. S. 135, and *Marcus Brown Holding Co.* v. *Feldman*, 256 U. S. 170), where this Court sustained the legislative power to fix rents as between landlord and tenant upon the ground that the operation of the statutes was temporary to tide over an emergency and that the circumstances were such as to clothe "the letting of buildings . . . with a public interest so great as to justify regulation by law." The Court said (p. 157):

"The regulation is put and justified only as a temporary measure [citing *Wilson* v. *New, supra*]. A limit in time, to tide over a passing trouble, well may justify a law that could not be upheld as a permanent change."

In a subsequent case, *Pennsylvania Coal Co.* v. *Mahon*, 260 U. S. 393, 416, this Court, after saying "We are in danger of forgetting that a strong public desire to improve the public condition is not enough to warrant achieving the desire by a shorter cut than the constitutional way of paying for the change," pointed out that the *Rent Cases* dealt with laws intended to meet a temporary emergency and "went to the verge of the law."

In addition to the cases cited above, there are the decisions of this Court dealing with laws especially relating to hours of labor for women: *Muller* v. *Oregon*, 208 U. S. 412; *Riley* v. *Massachusetts*, 232 U. S. 671; *Miller* v. *Wilson*, 236 U. S. 373; *Bosley* v. *McLaughlin*, 236 U. S. 385.

In the *Muller Case* the validity of an Oregon statute, forbidding the employment of any female in certain industries more than ten hours during any one day was upheld. The decision proceeded upon the theory that the difference between the sexes may justify a different rule respecting hours of labor in the case of women than in the case of men. It is pointed out that these consist in differences of physical structure, expecially in respect of the maternal functions, and also in the fact that historically woman has always been dependent upon man, who has established his control by superior physical strength. The cases of *Riley*, *Miller* and *Bosley* follow in this respect the *Muller Case*. But the ancient inequality of the sexes, otherwise than physical, as suggested in the *Muller Case* (p. 421) has continued "with diminishing intensity." In view of the great—not to say revolutionary—changes which have taken place since that utterance, in the contractual, political and civil status of women, culminating in the Nineteenth Amendment, it is not unreasonable to say that these differences have now come almost, if not quite, to the vanishing point. In this aspect of the matter, while the physical differences must be recognized in appropriate cases, and legislation fixing hours or conditions of work may properly take them into account, we cannot accept the doctrine that women of mature age, *sui juris*, require or may be subjected to restrictions upon their liberty of contract which could not lawfully be imposed in the case of men under similar circumstances. To do so would be to ignore all the implications to be drawn from the present day trend of legislation, as well as that of common thought and usage, by which woman is accorded emancipation from the old doctrine that she must be given special protection or be subjected to special restraint in her contractual and civil relationships. In passing, it may be noted that the instant statute applies in the case of a woman employer contracting with a woman employee as it does when the former is a man.

The essential characteristics of the statute now under consideration, which differentiate it from the laws fixing hours of labor, will be made to appear as we proceed. It is sufficient now to point out that the latter as well as the statutes mentioned under paragraph (3), deal with incidents of the employment having no necessary effect upon the heart of the contract, that is, the amount of wages to be paid and received. A law forbidding work to continue beyond a given number of hours leaves the parties free to contract about wages and thereby equalize whatever additional burdens may be imposed upon the employer as a result of the restrictions as to hours, by an adjustment in respect of the amount of wages. Enough has been said to show that the authority to fix hours of labor cannot be exercised except in respect of those occupations where work of long continued duration is detrimental to health. This Court has been careful in every case where the question has been raised, to place its decision upon this limited authority of the legislature to regulate hours of labor and to disclaim any purpose to uphold the legislation as fixing wages, thus recognizing an essential difference between the two. It seems plain that these decisions afford no real support for any form of law establishing minimum wages.

If now, in the light furnished by the foregoing exceptions to the general rule forbidding legislative interference with freedom of contract, we examine and analyze the statute in question, we shall see that it differs from them in every material respect. It is not a law dealing with any business charged with a public interest or with public work, or to meet and tide over a temporary emergency. It has nothing to do with the character, methods or periods of wage payments. It does not prescribe hours of labor or conditions under which labor is to be done. It is not for the protection of persons under legal disability or for the prevention of fraud. It is simply and exclusively a price-fixing law, confined to adult women (for we are not now considering the provisions relating to minors), who are legally as capable of contracting for themselves as men. It forbids two parties having lawful capacity—under penalties as to the employer—to freely contract with one another in respect of the price for which one shall render service to the other in a purely private employment where both are willing, perhaps anxious, to agree, even though the consequence may be to oblige one to surrender a desirable engagement and the other to dispense with the services of a desirable employee. The price fixed by the board need have no relation to the capacity or earning power of the employee, the number of hours which may happen to constitute the day's work, the character of the place where the work is to be done, or the circumstances or surroundings of the employment; and, while it has no other basis to support its validity than the assumed necessities of the employee, it takes no account of any independent resources she may have. It is based wholly on the opinions of the members of the board and their advisers—perhaps an average of their opinions, if they do not precisely agree—as to what will be necessary to provide a living for a woman, keep her in health and preserve her morals. It applies to any and every occupation in the District, without regard to its nature or the character of the work.

The standard furnished by the statute for the guidance of the board is so vague as to be impossible of practical application with any reasonable degree of accuracy. What is sufficient to supply the necessary cost of living for a woman worker and maintain her in good health and protect her morals is obviously not a precise or unvarying sum— not even approximately so. The amount will depend upon a variety of circumstances: the individual temperament, habits of thrift, care, ability to buy necessaries intelligently and whether the woman live alone or with her family. To those who practice economy, a given sum will afford comfort, while to those of contrary habit the same sum will be wholly inadequate. The coöperative economies of the family group are not taken into account though they constitute an important consideration in estimating the cost of living, for it is obvious that the individual expense will be less in the case of a member of a family than in the case of one living alone. The relation between earnings and morals is not capable of standardization. It cannot be shown that well paid women safeguard their morals more carefully than those who are poorly paid. Morality rests upon other considerations than wages; and there is, certainly, no such prevalent connection between the two as to justify a broad attempt to adjust the latter with reference to the former. As a means of safeguarding morals the attempted classification, in our opinion, is without reasonable basis. No distinction can be made between women who work for others and those who do not; nor is there ground for distinction between women and men, for certainly, if women require a minimum wage to preserve their morals men require it to preserve their honesty. For these reasons, and others which might be stated, the inquiry in respect of the necessary cost of living and of the income necessary to preserve health and morals, presents an individual and not a composite question, and must be answered for each individual considered by herself and not by a general formula prescribed by a statutory bureau.

This uncertainty of the statutory standard is demonstrated by a consideration of certain orders of the board already made. These orders fix the sum to be paid to a woman employed in a place where food is served or in a mercantile establishment, at $16.50 per week; in a printing establishment, at $15.50 per week; and in a laundry, at $15 per week, with a provision reducing this to $9 in the case of a beginner. If a woman employed to serve food requires a minimum of $16.50 per week, it is hard to understand how the same woman working in a printing establishment or in a laundry is to get on with an income lessened by from $1 to $7.50 per week. The board probably found it impossible to follow the indefinite standard of the statute, and brought other and different factors into the problem; and this goes far in the direction of demonstrating the fatal uncertainty of the act, an infirmity which, in our opinion, plainly exists.

The law takes account of the necessities of only one party to the contract. It ignores the necessities of the employer by compelling him to pay not less than a certain sum, not only whether the employee is capable of earning it, but irrespective of the ability of his business to sustain the burden, generously leaving him, of course, the privilege of abandoning his business as an alternative for going on at a loss. Within the limits of the minimum sum, he is precluded, under penalty of fine and imprisonment, from adjusting compensation to the differing merits of his employees. It compels him to pay at least the sum fixed in any event, because the employee needs it, but requires no service of equivalent value from the employee. It therefore undertakes to solve but one-half of the problem. The other half is the establishment of a corresponding standard of efficiency, and this forms no part of the policy of the legislation, although in practice the former half without the latter must lead to ultimate failure, in accordance with the inexorable law that no one can continue indefinitely to take out more than he puts in without ultimately exhausting the supply. The law is not confined to the great and powerful employers but embraces those whose bargaining power may be as weak as that of the employee. It takes no account of periods of stress and business depression, of crippling losses, which may leave the employer himself without adequate means of livelihood. To the extent that the sum fixed exceeds the fair value of the services rendered, it amounts to a compulsory exaction from the employer for the support of a partially indigent person, for whose condition there rests upon him no peculiar responsibility, and therefore, in effect, arbitrarily shifts to his shoulders a burden which, if it belongs to anybody, belongs to society as a whole.

The feature of this statute which, perhaps more than any other, puts upon it the stamp of invalidity is that it exacts from the employer an arbitrary payment for a purpose and upon a basis having no causal connection with his business, or the contract or the work the employee engages to do. The declared basis, as already pointed out, is not the value of the service rendered, but the extraneous circumstance that the employee needs to get a prescribed sum of money to insure her subsistence, health and morals. The ethical right of every worker, man or woman, to a living wage may be conceded. One of the declared and important purposes of trade organizations is to secure it. And with that principle and with every legitimate effort to realize it in fact, no one can quarrel; but the fallacy of the proposed method of attaining it is that it assumes that every employer is bound at all events to furnish it. The moral requirement implicit in every contract of employment, viz, that the amount to be paid and the service to be rendered shall bear to each other some relation of just equivalence, is completely ignored. The necessities of the employee are alone considered and these arise outside of the employment, are the same when there is no employment, and as great in one occupation as in another. Certainly the employer by paying a fair equivalent for the service rendered, though not sufficient to support the employee, has neither caused nor contributed to her poverty. On the contrary, to the extent of what he pays he has relieved it. In principle, there can be no difference between the case of selling labor and the case of selling goods. If one goes to the butcher, the baker or grocer to buy food, he is morally entitled to obtain the worth of his money but he is not entitled to more. If what he gets is worth what he pays he is not justified in demanding more simply because he needs more; and the shopkeeper, having dealt fairly and honestly in that transaction, is not concerned in any peculiar sense with the question of his customer's necessities. Should a statute undertake to vest in a commission power to determine the quantity of food necessary for individual support and require the shopkeeper, if he sell to the individual at all, to furnish that quantity at not more than a fixed maximum, it would undoubtedly fall before the constitutional test. The fallacy of any argument in support of the validity of such a statute would be quickly exposed. The argument in support of that now being considered is equally fallacious, though the weakness of it may not be so plain. A statute requiring an employer to pay in money, to pay at prescribed and regular intervals, to pay the value of the services rendered, even to pay with fair relation to the extent of the benefit obtained from the service, would be understandable. But a statute which prescribes payment without regard to any of these things and solely with relation to circumstances apart from the contract of employment, the business affected by it and the work done under it, is so clearly the product of a naked, arbitrary exercise of power that it cannot be allowed to stand under the Constitution of the United States.

We are asked, upon the one hand, to consider the fact that several States have adopted similar statutes, and we are invited, upon the other hand, to give weight to the fact that three times as many States, presumably as well informed and as anxious to promote the health and morals of their people, have refrained from enacting such legislation. We have also been furnished with a large number of printed opinions approving the policy of the minimum wage, and our own reading has disclosed a large number to the contrary. These are all proper enough for the consideration of the lawmaking bodies, since their tendency is to establish the desirability or undesirability of the legislation; but they reflect no legitimate light upon the question of its validity, and that is what we are called upon to decide. The elucidation of that question cannot be aided by counting heads.

It is said that great benefits have resulted from the operation of such statutes, not alone in the District of Columbia but in the several States, where they have been in force. A mass of reports, opinions of special observers and students of the subject, and the like, has been brought before us in support of this statement, all of which we have found interesting but only mildly persuasive. That the earnings of women now are greater than they were formerly and that conditions affecting women have become better in other respects may be conceded, but convincing indications of the logical relation of these desirable changes to the law in question are significantly lacking. They may be, and quite probably are, due to other causes. We cannot close our eyes to the notorious fact that earnings everywhere in all occupations have greatly increased—not alone in States where the minimum wage law obtains but in the country generally—quite as much or more among men as among women and in occupations outside the reach of the law as in those governed by it. No real test of the economic value of the law can be had during periods of maximum employment, when general causes keep wages up to or above the minimum; that will come in periods of depression and struggle for employment when the efficient will be employed at the minimum rate while the less capable may not be employed at all.

Finally, it may be said that if, in the interest of the public welfare, the police power may be invoked to justify the fixing of a minimum wage, it may, when the public welfare is thought to require it, be invoked to justify a maximum wage. The power to fix high wages connotes, by like course of reasoning, the power to fix low wages. If, in the face of the guaranties of the Fifth Amendment, this form of legislation shall be legally justified, the field for the operation of the police power will have been widened to a great and dangerous degree. If, for example, in the opinion of future lawmakers, wages in the building trades shall become so high as to preclude people of ordinary means from building and owning homes, an authority which sustains the minimum wage will be invoked to support a maximum wage for building laborers and artisans, and the same argument which has been here urged to strip the employer of his constitutional liberty of contract in one direction will be utilized to strip the employee of his constitutional liberty of contract in the opposite direction. A wrong decision does not end with itself; it is a precedent, and, with the swing of sentiment, its bad influence may run from one extremity of the arc to the other.

It has been said that legislation of the kind now under review is required in the interest of social justice, for whose ends freedom of contract may lawfully be subjected to restraint. The liberty of the individual to do as he pleases, even in innocent matters, is not absolute. It must frequently yield to the common good, and the line beyond which the power of interference may not be pressed is neither definite nor unalterable but may be made to move, within limits not well defined, with changing need and circumstance. Any attempt to fix a rigid boundary would be unwise as well as futile. But, nevertheless, there are limits to the power, and when these have been passed, it becomes the plain duty of the courts in the proper exercise of their authority to so declare. To sustain the individual freedom of action contemplated by the Constitution, is not to strike down the common good but to exalt it; for surely the good of society as a whole cannot be better served than by the preservation against arbitrary restraint of the liberties of its constituent members.

It follows from what has been said that the act in question passes the limit prescribed by the Constitution, and, accordingly, the decrees of the court below are *affirmed.*

27. HOOVER

The Role of the President

Herbert C. Hoover (1874–1964) was President of the United States from 1929 to 1933. He had been chairman of the Commission for Relief in Belgium from 1915 to 1919 and Secretary of Commerce from 1921 to 1928, and he had gained a national reputation as both a humanitarian and a political leader. Hoover's writings and speeches represent important defenses of the right of the businessman to conduct his affairs with a minimum of government interference. Hoover viewed the freedom of the businessman in a "free economy" as a vital part of the sum total of American freedom, as the main avenue of American progress. He feared the harmful consequences of attacks directed at it, whether they were driven by dislike for the business system or by a desire for "social justice." Hoover warned Americans of the dangers of the bureaucratic state which restricts individual liberty by social planning. The selections which follow show the thinking of President Hoover during his brief tenure as a practicing conservative President.

The first selection* is taken from an address given before the Gridiron Club in Washington, D.C., December 14, 1929.

In the Middle Ages it was the fashion to wear hair shirts to remind one's self of trouble and sin. Many years ago I concluded that a few hair shirts were part of the mental wardrobe of every man. The President differs only from other men in that he has a more extensive wardrobe. We have had tonight an indication of the great variety of persons and organizations who cheerfully and voluntarily insist on acting as hair shirts for the President. I am not complaining; I am only explaining one of the things that train his soul and his public conduct in urbanity. Incidentally, you could discover from these proceedings why Presidents seldom worry about anything. They have so many

* William Starr Myers, ed., *The State Papers and Other Public Writings of Herbert Hoover* (New York: Doubleday, Doran & Company, Inc., 1934), pp. 187–93. By permission.

troubles in the closet or stowed away in the ice box that when one of them gets tiresome they can always send for another, and by great variety maintain interest and a high cheerfulness of spirit.

You have from time to time during this meeting heard mention of the Senate, and you listened to observations upon the relations of the Executive with this great coördinate arm of the Government. I have for some time also been an interested observer of these relations. I have even searched through the intimate history of my predecessors since George Washington, endeavoring earnestly to discover remedies, antidotes, sedatives, irritants, stimulants, and experience. The important thing I have observed from an inspection of thirty administrations is that there is nothing new on this subject. Presidents have long since learned that one of the undisclosed articles in the Bill of Rights is that criticism and digging of political graves are reserved exclusively to members of the legislative arm. But presidents have also learned that they have one privilege not extended to members of the legislative arm— they have the option on when to talk and when not to talk.

There is always a minority of the Members of Congress who hope that the President will fail in his task, and who make the same unkind remarks in every administration in exactly the same phrases. Those who say the sensational things necessarily command the attention of the press. They do not represent the great majority of that body. The oppositions in Congress developed the same strategies even in Washington's day as those they now employ. Never has there been a session of Congress when somebody did not waste vast energy building a Scylla and a Charybdis for the President to navigate, or did not elaborately spread those old traps known as the devil and the deep blue sea. At various points in every important debate the opposition never fails to call vigorously upon the Executive to exert leadership, to give direction, to use the big stick. If he yields to these temptations, he is immediately discovered to be meddling in the responsibilities of the independent arm of the Government. This is the oldest form of the devil-and-deep-blue-sea trap. The Republican Party has no right to complain; it has been the preoccupation of the opposition with this sort of deep and subtle political strategy over many decades that wins us national elections for our party.

Some people become impatient with the length of debate. But let us not forget that any legislation that involves the safety and the welfare of the United States must be probed to the bottom. It is the safety and the vitalizing force of all legislation. In some ways legislatures are much like the old-fashioned rail fences. Some rails are perfect, others are rough. Many of them point in the wrong direction. There are some with sharp splinters. It covers a lot of ground. Yet the fence itself marches straight and performs its function in an effective and lasting manner. Those of us who have had opportunity to observe legislative bodies in other countries, and at the same time to understand some of the varied human motives of men, make no apologies for the Senate of the United States. Together with the House of Representatives it has for over 150 years not only served the American people, but they have time and again proved themselves the greatest of all legislatures of the world.

One of your anxieties this evening has been my appointment of commissions and committees. You have been misled into the impression that I shall soon appoint one every day. That is wrong—I shall probably need to appoint two a day. My conception of government leads me to the firm conviction that we have arrived at a time in our history, because of the increasing complexity of our civilization and the delicacy of its adjustments, when we must make doubly certain that we discover the truth. It is necessary that we make the fullest use of the best brains and the best judgment and the best leadership in our country before we determine upon policies which affect the welfare of a hundred and twenty million people. And I propose to do it.

The President of the United States is obliged to determine a multitude of questions and policies. By the Constitution he must recommend to Congress such measures as he shall deem necessary and expedient, and he is required to finally pass upon every act of Congress. He is the Chief Executive of the greatest business in the world, which at some point touches upon every single activity of our people.

By his position he must, within his capacities, give leadership to the development of moral, social, and economic forces outside of government which make for betterment of our country.

If we are to curtail the extension of the arm of government into the affairs of our people, we must do it by inspiration of individuals, by coöperation with voluntary organizations, that they through their own initiative, through their own action should remedy abuse and initiate progress. Self-government comprises more than political institutions. It is more than municipal governments and state governments, legislatures, and executive officers.

The safeguard against oppressive invasions of government into the lives and liberties of our people is that we shall cure abuse and forward progress without the government action. That is self-government in the highest form of which democracy has yet given conception—that is self-government outside of government.

The committees of Congress are themselves commissions for the investigation and the determination of legislative policies. But Congress cannot longer encompass the entire human field. Congress cannot determine administrative policies; it cannot inspire or lead voluntary forces.

The most dangerous animal in the United States is the man with an emotion and a desire to pass a new law. He is prolific with drama and the headlines. His is not the road to the fundamental advance of the liberty and the progress of the American people at this time in our history. The greatest antidote for him is to set him upon a committee with a dozen people whose appetite is for facts. The greatest catastrophe that could come to our country is that administration policies or legislation or voluntary movements shall be encouraged or enacted upon the basis of emotion, not upon facts and reason.

The President has open to him many governmental agencies in search for fact and for the determination of conclusion from them. He receives the largest measure of assistance from the executive departments and congressional committees. But over and beyond all these agencies there are a thousand problems; where the truth must be searched from a multitude of facts; where individual and regional experience must be had; where new ideas must be recruited from the kaleidoscope of a great shifting mass of humanity; where judgment must be distilled from many minds; where common agreement must be secured from conflicting forces; where assurance must be given to the people of the correctness of conclusions; and where their exposition must be secured.

These subjects cover the whole range of human thought, and I do not arrogate to myself the combined knowledge or judgment of the technologists, the philosophers, the scientists, the social thinkers, the economists, and the thousand callings of our people.

In these matters commissions and committees of our citizens can be made to add to the security of our steps and the certainty of acceptance of our policies. There is no worse agency of government than commissions and committees for executive action. Action requires undivided mind and undivided responsibility. But for the purpose of these special determinations I shall need more and more commissions, and more and more conferences, and I am grateful for the willingness our citizens have shown to give their time and service upon them.

And it is my belief that this is a vital means of government by the people and for the people, now that the people have ceased to live the simple life.

Those who have responsibility have but little to complain of and much to be grateful for from the press. If they were to complain it would be not against the representatives of the press but against the appetite of the American people as to the form of news. The human animal gets most of his thrills out of Washington from accounts of rivalry, conflict, fight, and combat, both actual and prospective. The press must cater to this and most of the news must be projected in this form, whether it be a stage fight or mere difference of opinion. Obviously, such accounts create and intensify enmities and thus increase combats and generate more news.

But when national interest requires it, the press does not fail to shift from combat to coöperation.

The Nation has passed through a trying period during the past month. Fear, alarm, pessimism, and hesitation swept through the country, which, if unchecked, would have precipitated absolute panic throughout the business world with untold misery in its wake. Its acute dangers were far greater than we are able to disclose at the present time. But the Washington correspondents and the press not only sensed that danger but gave a whole-hearted coöperation which contributed in large degree to smothering that conflagration. We shall feel after-effects. But the outstanding contribution of the press was the entire abandonment of the search for conflict. The search was for the points of agreement, the word of men of good will, the spread of coöperation.

I am wishing that the press could join in another demonstration of national solidarity in the face of national danger. We have for years seen the steady growth of friction between great naval powers arising from competitive armament. I don't hold that it meant inevitable war, but certainly the continuing pouring of its poison into public mind does not make for peace. The steady arming of Europe before the Great War by the same competitive processes was not the perfection of peace on that occasion.

We have inaugurated conferences designed to bring this competition to an end. The success of those conferences will depend as much upon the press as upon the abilities and character of the negotiators. If the press goes to London resolved that the differences which will inevitably develop shall be painted as fights, campaigns, and combats, rather than earnest effort to find the area of agreement, if the conference is to be represented to the people of the world as an international war of words and intrigue, it will fail. If it fails, the poison flowing from the failure will be a thousandfold more potent in suspicion and hate than ever before.

Never in our history has the press played so large a part or incurred so great a responsibility in our foreign relations as at present. The reasoned public opinion and the example of the American people have become the most powerful influences for peace and orderly progress of the world. Its mobilization at home and the coöperation in its use with other nations abroad is our contribution to peace, entirely within our time-honored refusal to become entangled in such engagements as might involve us in the use of military force.

America has always occupied that mission in the world. Here was lifted the first banner of the right of men to govern themselves, and that voice resounded through the revolutionary drums of the world for a century. It was Americans who first gave effective voice that controversies between nations should be settled by arbitration and judicial determination. It was the public opinion of America which intervened that the results of the World War should not repeat the aftermath of the Thirty Years' War, when one-third of the population of Europe died. It was the voice of America that led to the renunciation of war as an instrument of national policy. It is the United States that successfully summoned the public opinion of the world against the first violation of the Kellogg pact. It was the public opinion of the United States that enacted the call for a reduction of naval arms.

Recently I made the suggestion that the time had come when men should renounce starvation of women and children as a weapon of war, not alone for humane considerations but to remove a constant impulse to increasing arms. I have suggested that its enforcement must rest upon the public opinion of the world. There has been an almost universal approbation from our own countrymen of that proposal because it represents the spirit of America. From abroad has come its approval by the leaders of a score of nations. There are discordant notes and discordant nations. The old fallacy has been again produced that making war more terrible will frighten nations to peace. War has become more terrible every year since the invention of gunpowder, and every half century has seen more and more men sacrificed upon the battle field. Human courage rises far above any terror yet invented. I have been told that one cannot furnish food to civilians without furnishing it to armies, but no body of armed men ever did starve when food existed. There was no army in the World War that did not feed in full up to the last hour of the armistice, no matter when rows of pinched faces and emaciated children stood by the roadsides and ransacked their offal for wasted bread.

I am instructed by some that by putting the screws on the civil population we get war over with more quickly and it is thus more humane; the last war proved that attempts at starvation only sharpen hate; it hardens resolution. I have been told that no advance rules made in peace can be made binding in war; that public opinion of the neutral world is futile to restrain belligerents when the war is once launched. That is partly true, unless the subject is one on which public opinion can instantly react as to right and wrong. Public opinion of the neutral world does not react on the legalistic question of whether doormats are contraband or non-contraband. That is the main reason why all the agreements providing for the so-called freedom of the seas have never become a reality. But public opinion can and will react against forced starvation of nations. I have seen it stated that public opinion of neutrals had no effect in the last war. On the contrary, when the final verdict of history is given, it will be found that the loser lost, not for lack of efficiency, or valor, or courage, or from starvation, but by failure to heed the public opinion of what were originally neutral nations.

Public opinion against the use of starvation as a weapon once created will never be downed. The voice of America on behalf of humanity requires no agreement among nations to give it force. It needs no alliances, no leagues, no sanctions. That voice when raised in human cause is the most potent force in the world today.

28.   HOOVER

Defense of Private Initiative

On February 3, 1931, with the Depression worsening, President Hoover issued a press statement* that emphasized the preservation of self-help and the encouragement of individual generosity, rather than the use of government to solve the nation's economic crisis.

Certain senators have issued a public statement to the effect that unless the President and the House of Representatives agree to appropriations from the Federal Treasury for charitable purposes they will force an extra session of Congress.

I do not wish to add acrimony to a discussion, but would rather state this case as I see its fundamentals.

This is not an issue as to whether people shall go hungry or cold in the United States. It is solely a question of the best method by which hunger and cold shall be prevented. It is a question as to whether the American people on one hand will maintain the spirit of charity and mutual self help through voluntary giving and the responsibility of local government as distinguished on the other hand from appropriations out of the Federal Treasury for such purposes. My own conviction is strongly that if we break down this sense of responsibility of individual generosity to individual and mutual self help in the country in times of national difficulty and if we start appropriations of this character we have not only impaired something infinitely valuable in the life of the American people but have struck at the roots of self-government. Once this has happened it is not the cost of a few score millions but we are faced with the abyss of reliance in future upon Government charity in some form or other. The money involved is indeed the least of the costs to American ideals and American institutions.

* William Starr Myers, ed., *The State Papers and Other Public Writings of Herbert Hoover* (New York: Doubleday, Doran & Company, Inc., 1934), pp. 496–99. By permission.

President Cleveland, in 1887, confronted with a similar issue stated in part:

> "A prevalent tendency to disregard the limited mission of this power and duty should, I think, be steadfastly resisted, to the end that the lesson should be constantly enforced that though the people support the Government, the Government should not support the people.
>
> "The friendliness and charity of our countrymen can always be relied upon to relieve their fellow-citizens in misfortune. This has been repeatedly and quite lately demonstrated. Federal aid in such cases encourages the expectation of paternal care on the part of the Government and weakens the sturdiness of our national character, while it prevents the indulgence among our people of that kindly sentiment and conduct which strengthens the bonds of a common brotherhood."

And there is a practical problem in all this. The help being daily extended by neighbors, by local and national agencies, by municipalities, by industry and a great multitude of organizations throughout the country today is many times any appropriation yet proposed. The opening of the doors of the Federal Treasury is likely to stifle this giving and thus destroy far more resources than the proposed charity from the Federal Government.

The basis of successful relief in national distress is to mobilize and organize the infinite number of agencies of self help in the community. That has been the American way of relieving distress among our own people and the country is successfully meeting its problem in the American way today.

We have two entirely separate and distinct situations in the country; the first is the drought area; the second is the unemployment in our large industrial centers—for both of which these appropriations attempt to make charitable contributions.

Immediately upon the appearance of the drought last August, I convoked a meeting of the governors, the Red Cross and the railways, the bankers and other agencies in the country and laid the foundations of organization and the resources to stimulate every degree of self help to meet the situation which it was then obvious would develop. The result of this action was to attack the drought problem in a number of directions. The Red Cross established committees in every drought county, comprising the leading citizens of those counties, with instructions to them that they were to prevent starvation among their neighbors and, if the problem went beyond local resources, the Red Cross would support them.

The organization has stretched throughout the area of suffering, the people are being cared for today through the hands and with sympathetic understanding and upon the responsibility of their neighbors who are being supported in turn by the fine spirit of mutual assistance of the American people. The Red Cross officials whose long devoted service and experience are unchallenged, inform me this morning that except for the minor incidents of any emergency organization, no one is going hungry and no one need go hungry or cold.

To reinforce this work at the opening of Congress I recommended large appropriations for loans to rehabilitate agriculture from the drought and provision of further large sums for public works and construction in the drought territory which would give employment in further relief to the whole situation. These Federal activities provide for an expenditure of upward of $100,000,000 in this area and it is in progress today.

The Red Cross has always met the situations which it has undertaken. After careful survey and after actual experience of several months with their part of the problem they have announced firmly that they can command the resources with which to meet any call for human relief in prevention of hunger and suffering in drought areas and that they accept this responsibility. They have refused to accept Federal appropriations as not being consonant either with the need or the character of their organization. The Government Departments have given and are giving them every assistance. We possibly need to strengthen the public health service in matters of sanitation and to strengthen the credit facilities of that area through the method approved by the Government departments to divert some existing appropriations to strengthen agricultural credit corporations.

In the matter of unemployment outside of the drought areas important economic measures of mutual self help have been developed such as those to maintain wages, to distribute employment equitably, to increase construction work by industry, to increase Federal construction work from a rate of about $275,000,000 a year prior to the depression to a rate now of over $750,000,000 a year; to expand state and municipal construction—all upon a scale never before provided or even attempted in any depression. But beyond this to assure that there shall be no suffering, in every town and county voluntary agencies in relief of distress have been strengthened and created and generous funds have been placed at their disposal. They are carrying on their work efficiently and sympathetically.

But after and coincidently with voluntary relief, our American system requires that municipal, county and state governments shall use their own resources and credit before seeking such assistance from the Federal Treasury.

I have indeed spent much of my life in fighting hardship and starvation both abroad and in the southern states. I do not feel that I should be charged with lack of human sympathy for those who suffer but I recall that in all the organizations with which I have been connected over these many years, the foundation has been to summon the maximum of self help. I am proud to have sought the help of Congress in the past for nations who were so disorganized by war and anarchy that self help was impossible. But even these appropriations were but a tithe of that which was coincidently mobilized from the public charity of the United States and foreign countries. There is no such paralysis in the United States and I am confident that our people have the resources, the initiative, the courage, the stamina and kindliness of spirit to meet this situation in the way they have met their problems over generations.

I will accredit to those who advocate Federal charity a natural anxiety for the people of their states. I am willing to pledge myself that if the time should ever come that the voluntary agencies of the country together with the local and state governments are unable to find resources with which to prevent hunger and suffering in my country, I will ask the aid of every resource of the Federal Government because I would no more see starvation amongst our countrymen than would any senator or congressman. I have the faith in the American people that such a day will not come.

The American people are doing their job today. They should be given a chance to show whether they wish to preserve the principles of individual and local responsibility and mutual self help before they embark on what I believe is a disastrous system. I feel sure they will succeed if given the opportunity.

The whole business situation would be greatly strengthened by the prompt completion of the necessary legislation of this session of Congress and thereby the unemployment problem would be lessened, the drought area indirectly benefitted and the resources of self help in the country strengthened.

29. HOOVER
False Liberalism

This selection* is taken from a campaign speech given by President Hoover at Madison Square Garden, New York City, October 31, 1932. In the speech Hoover expressed his view that the campaign then being waged for the Presidency was a conflict between two philosophies of government, and he presented and compared these philosophies.

. . . I challenge the whole idea that we have ended the advance of America, that this country has reached the zenith of its power, the height of its development. That is the counsel of despair for the future of America. That is not the spirit by which we shall emerge from this depression. That is not the spirit that made this country. If it is true, every American must abandon the road of countless progress and unlimited opportunities. I deny that the promise of American life has been fulfilled, for that means we have begun the decline and fall. No nation can cease to move forward without degeneration of spirit.

I could quote from gentlemen who have emitted this same note of pessimism in economic depressions going back for 100 years. What Governor Roosevelt has overlooked is the fact that we are yet but on the frontiers of development of science, and of invention. I have only to remind you that discoveries in electricity, the internal-combustion engine, the radio—all of which have sprung into being since our land was settled—have in themselves represented the greatest advances in America. This philosophy upon which the Governor of New York proposes to conduct the Presidency of the United States is the philosophy of stagnation, of despair. It is the end of hope. The destinies of this country should not be dominated by that spirit in action. It would be the end of the American system.

* William Starr Myers, ed., *The State Papers and Other Public Writings of Herbert Hoover* (New York: Doubleday, Doran & Company, Inc., 1934), pp. 423–28. By permission.

I have recited to you the progress of this last generation. Progress in that generation was not due to the opening up of new agricultural land; it was due to the scientific research, the opening of new invention, new flashes of light from the intelligence of our people. These brought the improvements in agriculture and in industry. There are a thousand inventions for comfort in the lockers of science and invention which have not yet come to light; all are but on their frontiers. As for myself I am confident that if we do not destroy this American system, if we continue to stimulate scientific research, if we continue to give it the impulse of initiative and enterprise, if we continue to build voluntary coöperative action instead of financial concentration, if we continue to build it into a system of free men, my children will enjoy the same opportunity that have come to me and to the whole 120,000,000 of my countrymen. I wish to see American Government conducted in this faith and in this hope.

If these measures, these promises, which I have discussed; or these failures to disavow these projects; this attitude of mind, mean anything, they mean the enormous expansion of the Federal Government; they mean the growth of bureaucracy such as we have never seen in our history. No man who has not occupied my position in Washington can fully realize the constant battle which must be carried on against incompetence, corruption, tyranny of government expanded into business activities. If we first examine the effect on our form of government of such a program, we come at once to the effect of the most gigantic increase in expenditure ever known in history. That alone would break down the savings, the wages, the equality of opportunity among our people. These measures would transfer vast responsibilities to the Federal Government from the states, the local governments, and the individuals. But that is not all; they would break down our form of government. Our legislative bodies can not delegate their authority to any dictator, but without such delegation every member of these bodies is impelled in representation of the interest of his constituents constantly to seek privilege and demand service in the use of such agencies. Every time the Federal Government extends its arm, 531 Senators and Congressmen become actual boards of directors of that business.

Capable men can not be chosen by politics for all the various talents required. Even if they were supermen, if there were no politics in the selection of the Congress, if there were no constant pressure for this and for that, so large a number would be incapable as a board of directors of any institution. At once when these extensions take place by the Federal Government, the authority and responsibility of state governments and institutions are undermined. Every enterprise of private business is at once halted to know what Federal action is going to be. It destroys initiative and courage. We can do no better than quote that great statesman of labor, the late Samuel Gompers, in speaking of a similar situation:

"It is a question of whether it shall be government ownership or private ownership under control. If I were a minority of one in this convention, I would want to cast my vote so that the men of labor shall not willingly enslave themselves to government in their industrial effort."

We have heard a great deal in this campaign about reactionaries, conservatives, progressives, liberals, and radicals. I have not yet heard an attempt by any one of the orators who mouth these phrases to define the principles upon which they base these classifications. There is one thing I can say without any question of doubt—that is, that the spirit of liberalism is to create free men; it is not the regimentation of men. It is not the extension of bureaucracy. I have said in this city before now that you can not extend the mastery of government over the daily life of a people without somewhere making it master of people's souls and thoughts. Expansion of government in business means that the Government in order to protect itself from the political consequences of its errors is driven irresistibly without peace to greater and greater control of the Nation's press and platform. Free speech does not live many hours after free industry and free commerce die. It is a false liberalism that interprets itself into Government operation of business. Every step in that direction poisons the very roots of liberalism. It poisons political equality, free speech, free press, and equality of opportunity. It is the road not to liberty but to less liberty. True liberalism is found not in striving to spread bureaucracy, but in striving to set bounds to it. True liberalism seeks all legitimate freedom first in the confident belief that without such freedom the pursuit of other blessings is in vain. Liberalism is a force truly of the spirit proceeding from the deep realization that economic freedom can not be sacrificed if political freedom is to be preserved.

Even if the Government conduct of business could give us the maximum of efficiency instead of least efficiency, it would be purchased at the cost of freedom. It would increase rather than decrease abuse and corruption, stifle initiative and invention, undermine development of leadership, cripple mental and spiritual energies of our people, extinguish equality of opportunity, and dry up the spirit of liberty and progress. Men who are going about this country announcing that they are liberals because of their promises to extend the Government in business are not liberals, they are reactionaries of the United States.

And I do not wish to be misquoted or misunderstood. I do not mean that our government is to part with one iota of its national resources without complete protection to the public interest. I have already stated that democracy must remain master in its own house. I have stated that abuse and wrongdoing must be punished and controlled. Nor do I wish to be misinterpreted as stating that the United States is a free-for-all and devil-take-the-hindermost society.

The very essence of equality of opportunity of our American system is that there shall be no monopoly or domination by any group or section in this country, whether it be business, sectional or a group interest. On the contrary, our American system demands economic justice as well as political and social justice; it is not a system of laissez faire.

I am not setting up the contention that our American system is perfect. No human ideal has ever been perfectly attained, since humanity itself is not perfect. But the wisdom of our forefathers and the wisdom of the 30 men who have preceded me in this office hold to the conception that progress can only be attained as the sum of accomplishments of free individuals, and they have held unalterably to these principles.

In the ebb and flow of economic life our people in times of prosperity and ease naturally tend to neglect the vigilance over their rights. Moreover, wrongdoing is obscured by apparent success in enterprise. Then insidious diseases and wrongdoings grow apace. But we have in the past seen in times of distress and difficulty that wrongdoing and weakness come to the surface and our people, in their endeavors to correct these wrongs, are tempted to extremes which may destroy rather than build.

It is men who do wrong, not our institutions. It is men who violate the laws and public rights. It is men, not institutions, which must be punished.

In my acceptance speech four years ago at Palo Alto I stated that—

"One of the oldest aspirations of the human race was the abolition of poverty. By poverty I mean the grinding by under-nourishment, cold, ignorance, fear of old age to those who have the will to work."

I stated that—

"In America today we are nearer a final triumph over poverty than in any land. The poorhouse has vanished from amongst us; we have not reached that goal, but given a chance to go forward, we shall, with the help of God, be in sight of the day when poverty will be banished from this Nation."

Our Democratic friends have quoted this passage many times in this campaign. I do not withdraw a word of it. When I look about the world even in these times of trouble and distress I find it more true in this land than anywhere else under the traveling sun. I am not ashamed of it, because I am not ashamed of holding ideals and purposes for the progress of the American people. Are my Democratic opponents prepared to state that they do not stand for this ideal or this hope? For my part, I propose to continue to strive for it, and I hope to live to see it accomplished.

One of the most encouraging and inspiring phases of this whole campaign has been the unprecedented interest of our younger men and women. It is in this group that we find our new homes being founded, our new families in which the children are being taught those basic principles of love and faith and patriotism. It is in this group that we find the starting of business and professional careers with courageous and hopeful faces turned to the future and its promise. It is this group who must undertake the guardianship of our American system and carry it forward to its greater achievements.

Inevitably in the progress of time, our country and its institutions will be entirely in their hands. The burdens of the depression have fallen on the younger generation with equal and perhaps greater severity than upon the elders. It has affected not only their economic well-being, but has tended also to shatter many illusions. But their faith in our country and its institutions has not been shaken. I am confident that they will resist any destruction to our American system of political, economic and social life.

It is a tribute to America and its past and present leaders and even more a tribute to this younger generation that, contrary to the experience of other countries, we can say tonight that the youth of America is more staunch than many of their elders. I can ask no higher tribute from my party for the maintenance of the American system and the program of my administration than the support being given by the younger men and women of our country. It has just been communicated to me that tonight at this time, in every county and almost every precinct of our country, 3,000,000 members of the Young Republican League are meeting for the support of a Republican victory November 8th—a victory for the American system.

My countrymen, the proposals of our opponents represent a profound change in American life—less in concrete proposal, bad as that may be, than by implication and by evasion. Dominantly in their spirit they represent a radical departure from the foundations of 150 years which have made this the greatest nation in the world. This election is not a mere shift from the ins to the outs. It means deciding the direction our Nation will take over a century to come.

My conception of America is a land where men and women may walk in ordered liberty, where they may enjoy the advantages of wealth not concentrated in the hands of a few but diffused through the lives of all, where they build and safeguard their homes, give to their children full opportunities of American life, where every man shall be respected in the faith that his conscience and his heart direct him to follow, where people secure in their liberty shall have leisure and impulse to seek a fuller life. That leads to the release of the energies of men and women, to the wider vision and higher hope; it leads to opportunity for greater and greater service not alone of man to man in our country but from our country to the world. It leads to health in body and a spirit unfettered, youthful, eager with a vision stretching beyond the farthest horizons with an open mind, sympathetic and generous. But that must be builded upon our experience with the past, upon the foundations which have made our country great. It must be the product of our truly American system.

VIII

Conservatism
Since World War II

While opposition to the spread of the welfare state has continued as a theme of traditional conservatism, it has been unable to attract new adherents because of its negative tone. Instead, a positive conservatism has appeared, although its contours are not yet distinct or its supporters unified. At this moment, when liberalism seems to predominate, a fresh variety of American conservatism is being formed.

Today both liberalism and conservatism are undergoing change. The issues that once divided them are again shifting. There are signs that the liberal impetus which started in the New Deal and carried through Lyndon Johnson's Great Society has been slowed. On the other hand, the marriage between business and conservatism is less secure than in the past. Many businessmen welcome government as a partner and willingly accept more government activity. Some see benefits in welfare politics, while others are attracted by government spending for research and development.

One important new phenomenon has affected the prevailing practices of business—the tendency for modern corporations to become virtually miniature private welfare states. Supported by writers such as Adolf A. Berle (1895–   ), many businessmen see the corporation as an alternative to government collectivization. Yet many other social critics have noted the potential danger that the corporation itself poses to traditional views of individual liberty.

The political parties are now largely nonideological vote-gathering mechanisms, and conservatives may find a safe haven in either of the major political parties. This development has added to the confusion of contemporary ideological labels. A Republican President, Dwight D. Eisenhower, called himself a "progressive conservative," while his Democratic rival, Adlai Stevenson, maintained that his was the "truly conservative party of this country."

New conservatism has been a post-World War II development. Instead of drawing upon aristocratic conservatives like Brooks Adams or Irving Babbitt, many of the new conservatives have turned to

Edmund Burke, whose influence until recently had been largely confined to Europe. The new conservatives have attempted to reconcile Burke with the American tradition. The flavor of Burke's writings is especially appealing to many modern conservatives because of his distrust of abstract reasoning, theoretical analyses, and universal claims of truth. Burke's adherence to tradition rather than to naked human reason does not indicate an opposition to change as much as a prejudice in favor of existing and time-honored institutions.

The conversion of American conservatism from Locke to Burke is by no means complete: many new conservatives reject Burke because of his aristocratic posture; others claim to find Burke irrelevant to American conditions. Nonetheless, American conservatism may be ready to replace Locke with Burke as its patron saint. Burke did defend the American Revolution because it seemed to him to justify the ancient rights of Englishmen. Locke and his social contract were, however, more appropriate to the condition of a new nation forming new social and political institutions. Perhaps, now that our institutions have matured, a philosopher who is practical, traditional, and less prone to assert unprovable generalizations is a better source of conservative ideals.

At the moment the movement of modern conservative thought is led by men who are closer to Locke than to Burke. Intellectuals such as Russell Kirk seem closer to Europe than to America, but the new leadership of conservative thought also includes thinkers like William Buckley who are in the process of creating a new and meaningful American conservatism. Though there remains much disagreement within the ranks of the conservative movement, there is general optimism about the future for American conservatism.

30. TAFT

Opposition to the
North Atlantic Treaty

Robert A. Taft (1889–1953) was the son of William Howard Taft, the twenty-seventh President of the United States. The young Taft quickly rose to political prominence after a brilliant law career. He served in the Ohio legislature for seven years and in the United States Senate from 1939 until his death in 1953. Taft was twice a serious contender for the Republican Presidential nomination, but he was twice rebuffed by his party.

His Senate speeches reveal an original conservative mind, especially in the area of foreign affairs. His views on the North Atlantic Treaty Organization, the cornerstone of most post-World War II American foreign policy, reveal this originality. Although an anti-Communist, Taft feared the novelty of NATO and felt it inconsistent with our desire for peace. On July 11, 1949, Senator Taft delivered a speech in the United States Senate, from which this selection* is taken, in opposition to the ratification of the proposed North Atlantic Treaty. Taft feared the financial, political, and military consequences of this vast new American commitment. At the conclusion of his speech six of his fellow Republicans stood and applauded, but unfortunately for Taft, Senators John Foster Dulles and Arthur Vandenberg had obtained support for the treaty from most other Republican members of the Senate.

MR. TAFT. Mr. President, I listened with great interest to the speech made today by the distinguished Senator from Iowa [Mr. Gillette]. I wish to assure the Senate that I have not consulted with the Senator from Iowa; but the arguments I shall make against the Atlantic Pact are very similar to the ones he made, and I agree thoroughly with the very effective argument and very effective speech he made on that subject.

* *Congressional Record* (81st Congress, 2d Session), Vol. 95, pp. 9383, 9392.

However, the same arguments have led me to the conclusion that I must vote against the pact, rather than for it, as he has announced he intends to do.

It is with great regret that I have come to my conclusion, but I have come to it because I think the pact carries with it an obligation to assist in arming, at our expense, the nations of western Europe, because with that obligation I believe it will promote war in the world rather than peace, and because I think that with the arms plan it is wholly contrary to the spirit of the obligations we assumed in the United Nations Charter. I would vote for the pact if a reservation were adopted denying any legal or moral obligation to provide arms. . . .

I have come reluctantly to the conclusion, therefore, that the arms program now presented to Congress must be considered an integral part of the Atlantic Treaty.

If that is the fact, we have a very different problem from the one which is urged upon us by the Committee on Foreign Relations, by its distinguished chairman, by the State Department, and by the distinguished Senator from Michigan.

First. With the arms in the pact it is even more clear that the pact is a military alliance, a treaty by which one nation undertakes to arm half the world against the other half, and in which all the pact members agree to go to war if one is attacked. It cannot be described otherwise than a military alliance. Of course, it is not like some of the alliances in the past, although many of them, such as the Franco–British Alliance prior to World War I, were entirely defensive in character, or purported to be. Others were offensive and defensive alliances. I quite agree that the purpose of this alliance is not offensive, and that we have no offensive purpose in mind. But it is exactly like many defensive military alliances of the past.

Second. The pact standing by itself would clearly be a deterrent to war. If Russia knows that if it starts a war it will immediately find itself at war with the United States, it is much less likely to start a war. I see and believe in the full force of that argument. That is why I would favor the extension of the Monroe Doctrine to Europe. But if Russia sees itself ringed about gradually by so-called defensive arms, from Norway and Denmark to Turkey and Greece, it may form a different opinion. It may decide that the arming of western Europe, regardless of its present purpose, looks to an attack upon Russia. Its view may be unreasonable, and I think it is. But from the Russian standpoint it may not seem unreasonable. They may well decide that if war is the certain result, that war might better occur now rather than after the arming of Europe is completed. In 1941, Secretary Hull sent a message to Japan in the nature of an ultimatum which said, in effect, that if Japan did not withdraw from China, sooner or later they would face a war with the United States. The Japanese appear to have concluded that if ultimately there was to be such a war, it was to their interest to have it occur at once.

Third. The pact with the arms obligation, I believe, violates our obligations under the United Nations. The pact apparently is not made under articles 52 to 54 inclusive, because we do not propose to consult the Security Council as there contemplated, we do plan to take enforcement action without the authorization of the Security Council, and we do not plan to keep them fully informed. The pact must, therefore, be supported under article 51, which says:

> Nothing in the present Charter shall impair the inherent right of individual or collective self-defense if an armed attack occurs against a member of the United Nations, until the Security Council has taken the measures necessary to maintain international peace and security. . . .

Fourth. The obligation to furnish arms is either a mere token obligation, or it is one of vast extent. I do not know enough about modern military equipment to make any estimate. I have heard that to provide sixty divisions, which is said to be the very minimum necessary and perhaps completely inadequate against Russian attack, would cost a total of $24 billion. We are entering on a new lend-lease. The history of these obligations has been that once begun, they cannot be easily brought to an end. Furthermore if the Russian threat justifies arms for all of western Europe, surely it justifies similar arms for Nationalist China, for Indochina, for India, and ultimately for Japan; and in the Near East for Iran, for Syria, and for Iraq. There is no limit to the burden of such a program, or its dangerous implications.

Fifth. The justification for the arms aid rests on the necessity of defense against Russia, but remember that once these arms are provided they are completely within the control of the nation receiving them. They are subject to the orders of those who, at the time, control the government of the country. Those governors may be Communists or Fascists, they may be peace loving, or they may be aggressors. In

future years, these arms may be used against us instead of on our side.
If Russia should choose to go to war within the next year or two, they
might easily be captured by the Russians and turned against us. We
would be playing a dangerous game if we encouraged every country
in Europe to arm itself to the teeth. Modern arms are not toys.

Sixth. By approving this pact with the arms program, I believe we
are committing ourselves to a particular course of action in war which
may be unwise at the time when a war may actually develop. It is one
thing to agree to go to war with Russia if it attacks western Europe.
It is another to send American ground troops to defend Norway or
Denmark or Holland or Italy or even France and England. I cannot
assert positively that we are committing ourselves to a particular type
of war, but I am inclined to think that we are. Thus, General Bradley
testified before the committee:

> Finally, after studied appraisal of the future security provisions for our
> country, the Joint Chiefs of Staff are in unanimous agreement that our
> strategy, in case we are attacked—

And that means if any member country is attacked, if we ratify this
pact—

> must rely on sufficient integrated forces of land, sea, and air power to carry
> the war back to the aggressor, ultimately subjugating the sources of his
> military and industrial power. Plans for the common defense of the existing
> free world must provide for the security of western Europe without
> abandoning these countries to the terrors of another enemy occupation.
> Only upon that premise can nations closest to the frontiers be expected to
> stake their fortunes with ours in the common defense.

This appears to contemplate a land war with Russia on the continent
of Europe. It appears to contemplate an invasion along the lines which
Napoleon and Hitler found to be impossible. It asserts clearly that the
nations which signed this pact expect us to send American troops to
defend their frontiers.

If this is their expectation, I think we are promising something we
cannot do, as I said earlier. I see no way in which we could defend Italy,
for it is not even permitted to have an army of its own. The defense of
Norway and Denmark would probably be impossible and, if we are
bound to do it, may result in the loss of thousands of American lives.

It may be that we should conduct a war on the Continent of Europe, even though it involves again the sending of millions of American boys to fight Russians who, on land, will outnumber them four to one. But I do not think we should commit ourselves at the present time to any such program or make any such promise to our allies. We may find, if war ever comes, that our part in the war should be conducted from the air alone. We may find that the occupation of an enemy country is vain and useless if the war can be won otherwise, by the destruction of all of their military potentials. We should not commit ourselves by the ratification of this pact to the military assistance program and the plan of campaign which has apparently been promised the members of the pact.

Seventh. Finally, Mr. President, it is becoming increasingly apparent that England, at least, intends to trade extensively with Russia, and inevitably the same thing will be true of other western European nations. They have provided airplane engines for Russia, heavy machinery and other equipment which can aid the Russians' war-making potential. The more we take off their shoulders the burden of providing for their own defense, the more free they will be to ship steel and heavy machinery to the east. As a matter of fact, trade between eastern and western Europe has prevailed for thousands of years, and it is going to go on, no matter what we say about it. Of course, the recent agreement between Russia and England is very clear evidence of that fact. We are providing extensive economic assistance. To a large extent, economic assistance and aid for arms will go into the same pot. I do not think that the American people at this time desire to increase the over-all aid we are giving to western Europe with its tremendous burden on the American taxpayer.

Mr. President, since I feel that this pact is inextricably linked with the arms program, and since I believe that, so linked, the program is a threat to the welfare of the people of the United States, I shall vote against the treaty.

I am quite willing to consider the providing of assistance to particular countries, at particular times, if such aid seems at that time a real deterrent to war, and on that principle I voted for aid to Greece and Turkey. But that is a very different thing from an obligation to build up the armed forces of eleven countries, and a commitment on the American taxpayer for twenty years to give continued aid under circumstances of which we have not the slightest conception today.

It is a very different thing from arming half the world against the other half.

My conclusion has been reached with the greatest discomfort. When so many disagree with that conclusion, I must admit that I may be completely wrong. I do not claim to be an expert in questions of foreign policy. I would like to be able to vote for a policy that will commit us to war if Russia attacks western Europe. I would be glad to join in an agreement to occupy Germany indefinitely to guard against a third attack from that quarter. I would waive my other objections to the Atlantic Pact if I did not feel that it was inextricably involved with the arms program. But I cannot escape the logic of the situation as I see it, and therefore I cannot vote for a treaty which, in my opinion, will do far more to bring about a third world war than it will ever do to maintain the peace of the world.

31. TAFT

The Basis of American Foreign Policy

In the following selection,* his Senate speech of January 5, 1951, Senator Taft, at that time a strong contender for the Republican Presidential nomination, spoke out against assumptions about the Cold War that were then widespread in the country.

Mr. President, I wish to thank the majority leader for his action in opening the floor of the Senate for debate before the President's State of the Union message. In view of the crisis in which we find ourselves today, the President may well take longer for the preparation of his message, but certainly that should not prevent discussion of vital national issues on the floor of the Senate.

During recent years a theory has developed that there shall be no criticism of the foreign policy of the administration, that any such criticism is an attack on the unity of the nation, that it gives aid and comfort to the enemy, and that it sabotages any idea of a bipartisan foreign policy for the national benefit. I venture to state that this proposition is a fallacy and a very dangerous fallacy threatening the very existence of the nation.

In very recent days we have heard appeals for unity from the administration and from its supporters. I suggest that these appeals are an attempt to cover up the past faults and failures of the administration and enable it to maintain the secrecy which has largely enveloped our foreign policy since the days of Franklin D. Roosevelt. It was a distinguished Democrat, President Woodrow Wilson, who denounced secret diplomacy and demanded open covenants openly arrived at. The administrations of President Roosevelt and President Truman have repudiated that wise democratic doctrine and assumed complete authority to make in secret the most vital decisions and commit this country to the most

* *Congressional Record* (82d Congress, 1st Session), Vol. 97, pp. 58–72.

important and dangerous obligations. As I see it, members of Congress, and particularly members of the Senate, have a constitutional obligation to reexamine constantly and discuss the foreign policy of the United States. If we permit appeals to unity to bring an end to that criticism, we endanger not only the constitutional liberties of the country but even its future existence.

I may say that I hope the debate will occur on the floor of the Senate. I was invited to speak over the radio tonight following the speeches by former President Hoover and Mr. Dulles, and I declined because I felt that a statement of foreign policy by a Senator ought to be made on the floor of the Senate. I think there ought to be a continuous discussion of that policy during this session of the Senate.

Certainly when policies have been determined, unity in execution is highly desirable, and in the preparation for and the conduct of war it is essential. During recent months, the Republican minority has joined in granting to the President those powers which may be necessary to deal with the situation. We have not hesitated to pass a draft law, a law granting extensive powers of economic control, and almost unlimited appropriations for the armed forces. No action of the minority can be pointed to as in any way blocking or delaying the mobilization of our resources and our armed forces. If there has been any delay in the rearming, it has been in the administrative branch of the government.

But it is part of our American system that basic elements of foreign policy shall be openly debated. It is said that such debate and the differences that may occur give aid and comfort to our possible enemies. I think that the value of such aid and comfort is grossly exaggerated. The only thing that can give real aid and comfort to the enemy is the adoption of a policy which plays into their hands as has our policy in the Far East. Such aid and comfort can only be prevented by frank criticism before such a policy is adopted.

Whatever the value of unity, it is also true that unity carried to unreasonable extremes can destroy a country. The Kaiser achieved unity in Germany. Hitler again achieved the same unity at the cost of freedom many years later. Mussolini achieved unity in Italy. The leaders of Japan through a method of so-called thought control achieved unity in Japan. In every case, policies adopted by these enforcers of unity led to the destruction of their own country. We have regarded ourselves as safe and a probable victor in every war. Today it is just as easy for us to adopt a false foreign policy leading to the destruction of our people as for any other nation to do so. The best safeguard against fatal error lies in continuous criticism and discussion to bring out the truth and develop the best program. . . .

We would be lacking in the fulfillment of our obligations and false to our oaths if we did not criticize policies which may lead to unnecessary war, policies which may wreck the internal economy of this country and vastly weaken our economic abilities through unsound taxation or inflation, policies which may commit us to obligations we are utterly unable to perform, and thus discredit us in the eyes of the world. Criticism and debate are essential if we are to maintain the constitutional liberties of this country and its democratic heritage. Under the present administration, at any rate, criticism and debate I think are essential to avoid danger and possible destruction of our nation.

The principal purpose of the foreign policy of the United States is to maintain the liberty of our people. Its purpose is not to reform the entire world or spread sweetness and light and economic prosperity to peoples who have lived and worked out their own salvation for centuries, according to their customs, and to the best of their ability. We do have an interest, of course, in the economic welfare of other nations and in the military strength of other nations, but only to the extent to which our assistance may reduce the probability of an attack on the freedom of our own people.

After liberty, peace must be the goal of our policy and of our leaders—more than it has been in recent years. In order to assure progress and happiness for our people, we must avoid war like poison, except when it is absolutely essential to protect our liberty. War not only produces pitiful human suffering and utter destruction of things worth while, but it actually may end our own liberty, certainly for the time being. From our experience in the last two world wars, it actually promotes dictatorship and totalitarian government throughout the world. It is almost as disastrous for the victor as for the vanquished. War is to be preferred only to the destruction of our liberty.

It seems to me most unwise ever to admit that war is inevitable until it has occurred, and it seems to me that today our policy and the thinking of too many Americans are based too much on the premise that war is inevitable. It is a possibility which we must face, and for which we must prepare, but the theory of a preventive war, so closely related to the acceptance of that thesis, is contrary to every American principle and every moral principle. . . .

What then should be our military policy in preparation for a possible attack by Russia on ourselves or on our allies? Our first consideration must be the defense of America. Whatever one may feel about the action of the United States in other parts of the world, no matter how much of an internationalist a man may be, he must recognize that this country is the citadel of the free world. The defense of the United States itself is, of course, the first goal of our own people, essential to protect our liberty; but it is just as important to the rest of the world that this country be not destroyed, for its destruction would mean an end to liberty everywhere and to the hope of restoring liberty where it has been lost. It seems obvious that the immediate problem of defending this country depends upon control of the sea and control of the air.

There is no question that we have the largest navy in the world, and certainly, while the British are our allies, complete control of the sea throughout the world, except as it may be hampered by Russian submarines. We have a powerful air force, but it seems to me vitally necessary that that air force be increased until we have control of the air over this country and over the oceans which surround our continent. It should be capable of expansion in time of war to secure as great control as possible over the rest of the world and over the enemy country. With our resources and with Great Britain as an ally, that is not impossible. By the end of the last war, we had practically complete control of the air over Germany and Japan, and it was the decisive factor in the winning of the war. Not only is the air force necessary for defense of America, but it is the one weapon which can damage the enemy bases from which air attacks upon us can be made, and which can drop atom bombs where they may be decisive.

The greatest question of policy before the country and before this Congress, however, relates to our undertakings in Europe. Under the general principles I have laid down, I would say that we had better commit no American troops to the European continent at this time. Some modification is required in that theory because, first, we are now occupying Germany with the obligations growing out of the Second World War, and second we have made certain promises under the Atlantic Pact, which we are bound to carry out.

It might be well first to consider just what our obligations are under the Atlantic Pact. One thing seems certain. There is no legal obligation to send American land soldiers to Europe. . . .

But it was only our military planners who discussed sending American land troops to Europe. Responsible officials of the government absolutely repudiated any idea that the Atlantic Pact contemplated any such aid. If the President in his conference with Mr. Attlee, or Secretary Acheson at Brussels, has undertaken to commit the United States to any such assistance before or during a war they are usurping the authority given by law and their program should be submitted to Congress for consideration before we become obligated. The President has no power to agree to send American troops to fight in Europe in a war between members of the Atlantic Pact and Soviet Russia. Without authority he involved us in the Korean War. Without authority he apparently is now attempting to adopt a similar policy in Europe. This matter must be debated and determined by Congress and by the people of this country if we are to maintain any of our constitutional freedoms. I note that, at his press conference yesterday, the President asserted that he had the right to send additional troops to Europe. Technically, of course, he can send troops to occupied Germany as long as the war status is in effect. But, in fact, no more troops are needed for the occupation of Germany. In fact those already there are a heavy burden on the German people. Also we hope that soon the war status may be ended by resolution. If the President has any technical right to send American troops to Europe, certainly Congress by resolution, such as the Coudert resolution, or by restriction in the appropriation bill providing the divisions required, may finally determine the policy to be pursued. . . .

The threat of communism is real. Those who are directing its affairs are brilliant and unprincipled. America must be the leader in the battle to prevent the spread of communism and preserve the liberty of the world. In the field of military operations our strongest position is in the air and on the sea, and we should not attempt to be also a controlling power on the land. We should not be a military aggressor or give the impression of military aggression or incite a war which might otherwise never occur. Operations on the continents of Europe and Asia, if any, should be undertaken only with the greatest care and under careful limitation. We must not so extend ourselves as to threaten economic collapse or inflation, for a productive and free America is the last bastion of liberty.

And finally the policy we adopt must be approved by Congress and the people after full and free discussion. The commitment of a land army to Europe is a program never approved by Congress, into which we should not drift. The policy of secret executive agreements has brought us to danger and disaster. It threatens the liberties of our people.

32.   ROSSITER
"The Two Conservatisms"

Clinton Rossiter (1917–   ), Senior University Professor of American Institutions at Cornell University, is the author or editor of numerous books, including a number of important works on American government and politics. Rossiter's *Conservatism in America* (1955; rev. 1962) is perhaps the best brief survey of American conservative thought, although his interpretations are personal and often controversial. The following selection,* his article "The Two Conservatisms," is an excellent brief evaluation of some developments in modern American conservatism.

A wonder of the postwar era is the revival of political conservatism. After generations of exile from the American lexicon, the word itself has been welcomed home with cheers and is flaunted alike by polite publicists and impolite politicians who a few years ago would sooner have acknowledged themselves arsonists than conservatives. The attitude it expresses has been openly avowed by magazines that make it their business to avow what Americans are currently thinking. The "old-fashioned liberal" is emerging at last in the dull but truthful colors of self-conscious conservatism. An overdose of reform and revolution has finally made him an honest man.

The belated decision of many American conservatives to confess their conservatism would be a semantic and political blessing except for the usual difficulty: no one knows what conservatism means, and no one can agree on the identity of the authentic conservative. There are almost as many ill-assorted individuals and groups now crowding together under the stout umbrella of conservatism as have always been gathered under the pleasant parasol of liberalism. The catalogue of those patriots who have rediscovered conservatism stretches from the lunatic right to the gradualist left. The prefixing of such adjectives as

* *South Atlantic Quarterly*, Vol. 50 (January, 1952), pp. 64–69. By permission.

"enlightened," "progressive," "positive," and even "liberal" makes the Babel only more confusing. Gerald L. K. Smith, Henry Hazlitt, George Sokolsky, Harry Byrd, Robert A. Taft, Ralph Flanders, August Hecksher, Clifford Case, Peter Viereck, Henry Luce, Thomas E. Dewey, John Snyder, and W. Averill Harriman cannot all be conservatives if conservatism is to have any meaning as the descriptive title of a well-defined body of attitudes and assumptions shared by millions of good Americans.

The fact is that there seem to be two general brands of present-day conservatism and thus two fairly inclusive breeds of American conservatives. This article, which will enter no judgments and call no names, is an attempt to distinguish between the two conservatisms. This division is based not on philosophical, psychological, or sociological terms and techniques, but on practical distinctions empirically observed. In March, 1950, I published an article in *Fortune* entitled "Wanted: An American Conservatism." In the year that followed the appearance of this plea for a "positive" conservatism, I received several hundred comments, criticisms, and queries about my point of view. With the article and these communications in hand, I proceeded to quiz, face-to-face and by mail, a representative group of some fifty businessmen, educators, professional men, and public officials. I made a conscious effort to seek out the political beliefs of all manner of men in these four socioeconomic groups in present-day American society. Some of these men were high-placed, others altogether modest in position and property. Some had three college degrees, others had none. Some were politically alert and active, others amazingly passive. Some lived in New York, some in Wisconsin, some in California.

In one important sense these men constituted a uniform group: they shared a fundamental antipathy for the dominant political theory and practice of the past eighteen years—for New Deal and Fair Deal, Roosevelt and Truman, service state and welfare state, reform and revolution. They were alike in their vigorous insistence on "the preservation of the American way of life" as our primary political task. In another, equally important sense, however, they split into two camps: they exhibited such clear-cut distinctions of temperament and intellectual method that I was able to establish, at least to my own satisfaction, the existence of two separate divisions of modern American conservatism. These two divisions for the most part ignored sectional, educational, and class lines.

Several sets of labels could be pinned on these two groupings, depending largely upon where each of us stood inside or outside them. In pursuit of my announced purpose to call no names, I will make use of the euphemistic designations *conservative* and *ultra-conservative*. There were, according to my analysis of the comments and assumptions of these fifty representative men, at least nine valid criteria by which to separate the great mass of American anti-reformers into the one or the other of these major camps.

First, in his thinking and talking about the present discontents the conservative remains generally optimistic, while the ultra-conservative has turned almost lugubriously pessimistic. For both of them the Golden Age is in the past; indeed, the ultra-conservative can date and describe his "state of nature" with astounding precision. But for the conservative the future, too, holds promise, even if the age can at best be silver. The distinction between the conservative's cautious optimism and the ultra-conservative's blatant pessimism is most clearly perceived when the two are asked to comment upon the average man's capacities for self-government. Ultra-conservatives simply cannot see how the Republic can save itself from internal collapse because of inefficiency and confusion, if not because of subsidies and socialism. The conservative, to be sure, has little of the sanguine spirit of the congenital reformer, but he rarely exhibits the despair that marks the genuine ultra-conservative.

Second, in his dealings with men and ideas, especially other-minded men and new ideas, the conservative retains a certain flexibility, a disposition toward conciliation and compromise; the ultra-conservative is so suspicious and dogmatic as to appear an unbending doctrinaire. The different attitudes toward the trend to governmental regulation of the economy provide the neatest example of this distinction. The conservative seems relatively untroubled by the mixed character of our economy, although he wants the mixing to go no further and prefers that a different group of men take control. The ultra-conservative thinks we are in the midst, or at best on the brink, of outright socialism. The notion that an economy can be mixed and still free he denies with vehemence. In any case, the conservative understands clearly what the ultra-conservative seems not even to suspect: that in a dynamic society it is often the business of the conservative actually to sponsor reform and always his business to insure that progress, in Lord Hugh Cecil's words, is "intelligent, efficient, and appropriate to circumstance."

Third, the conservative perceives more readily than the ultra-conservative that freedom and responsibility go always hand-in-hand. Let us call the American press to witness. The anti-Fair Deal newspapers and columnists fall with astounding precision into our two categories. The aversion of the Chicago *Tribune* and New York *Herald Tribune* (or of George Sokolsky and Mark Sullivan) to such proposed tinkerings with the machine as the Ewing and Brannan plans could not be more alike; their discussions of them could not be more different. Or consider for a moment the Senate and its privilege. The contrast between Margaret Chase Smith's Declaration of Conscience and Senator McCarthy's standard tirade leads many people to wonder if perhaps this question of responsibility and irresponsibility is not at the bottom one of good and bad taste.

Fourth, although the conservative and the ultra-conservative pride themselves equally on being "men who deal in facts," a disproportionate share of the latter's facts are so selected as to lose significance or so loaded as to lose credibility. The conservative, whose typical fact-gathering agency is the Committee of Economic Development, clings to the notion that statistics can and should be impartial expert witnesses. The ultra-conservative, some of whose uses of statistics can be examined in the pamphlets and broadsides of the National Economic Council and the Foundation for Economic Education, seems to look upon "cold facts" and "true figures" as variables that can be made to conform to predetermined decisions, all of which, he is sure, make them no less cold and true.

Fifth, the conservative has a much more pronounced disposition than the ultra-conservative to understand, aid, and pity his fellow man. He is certainly no quicker or more generous with his philanthropy than the ultra-conservative, but his charity of judgment as well as of donations has a quality of compassion or unstrained mercy that the ultra-conservative's more suspicious nature will not permit him to exhibit. Perhaps the reason is that the ultra-conservative does not always see the world as it actually exists, especially the pain and poverty that no society has ever eliminated sufficiently, and insists upon measuring all men by the high standards of performance he imposes upon himself.

Sixth, while both breeds of conservative are dedicated to individualism, the ultra-conservative puts more emphasis on the "rugged" variety. The conservative's flexibility and charity mark him as a person more suited to co-operation and association; his individualism has, therefore, a more fraternal or social flavor. This attitude may well be the key reason why the ultra-conservative, hardly coincidentally, has difficulty in breaking loose from the American tradition of isolation. He likes to act unilaterally in all his affairs and would prefer that his government act likewise. This country's typical internationalist, whether of the United Nations or United World Federation persuasion, is the conservative; its typical isolationist is the ultra-conservative.

Seventh, both conservative and ultra-conservative, like the good Americans they are, do a great deal of talking and writing about rights and liberties, but with this significant distinction: the conservative emphasizes political and social rights, while not forgetting economic; the ultra-conservative emphasizes economic, while occasionally forgetting social and political. One way to tell whether a man is conservative or ultra-conservative is to ask for his definition of a "police state."

Eighth, although both of them share the attitudes of anti-governmentalism characteristic of anti-reformers the free world over, the conservative looks upon government as a friendly enemy, the ultra-conservative, for whom it is always "the bureaucracy," looks upon it as an enemy pure and simple. *Our Enemy: The State* reads the title of a widely distributed piece of ultra-conservative literature. The reforms of the past eighteen years have hardened into dogma the American ultra-conservative's traditional distrust of political power and institutions. Although the conservative wants no more T.V.A.'s, he at least seems to have made peace with the one that exists. Not so the ultra-conservative, who still insists that it is unmitigated socialism.

Ninth, and most important, the conservative is thoroughly committed to the cause of democracy. Since he is conservative and therefore puts his special trust in tradition, continuity, and stability, he is inclined and indeed expected to be somewhat skeptical about the full flowering of the democratic dogma. Nevertheless, he is a stout soldier in that third force between Fascism and Communism upon which the future of Western civilization depends. Liberals who attempt to exclude him from the ranks of freedom are guilty of stupidity if not outright fratricide. The ultra-conservative, if we may take him at his word, has become so sour on democracy that he can be expected to soon come up with a new belief in political aristocracy. Those Americans who toy with home-grown Fascism or admire foreign tyranny are still in a small minority, but those who insist that "we are a republic, not a democracy," are ever growing more numerous and candid. It has apparently not occurred to them that we are both—a democratic republic, a republican democracy.

The reader may add criteria of his own or perhaps may challenge some of the nine brought forward here. He may wish to be harsher with the ultra-conservative by labeling him a reactionary or with the conservative by insisting that he is really a liberal sailing under false colors. The important thing is that he recognize two general species of modern American conservative at least as well defined as the traditional grouping on the left of liberals and radicals. One of these fellows is basically optimistic, flexible, conscious of his responsibilities, charitable, co-operative, and democratic. The other is pessimistic, dogmatic, irresponsible (at least in speech and print), truculent, ruggedly individualistic, and ever more skeptical of democracy. The differences between them are of course only relative, but they are marked and momentous differences nevertheless. It remains to be seen which brand of modern American conservatism will provide the stouter bulwark against threats of totalitarianism from without and of drift and tension from within.

33.   BUCKLEY
Failures of Conservatism

William F. Buckley (1925–   ) is the editor of the *National Review*, the intellectual journal which is the most prominent periodical of contemporary American conservatism. Buckley rapidly attained fame when, at the age of twenty-six, he wrote *God and Man at Yale* (1951), an attack upon the liberal intellectual establishment at that university. In 1965 he ran, unsuccessfully, for the mayorality of New York City in an effort to defeat the liberal Republican candidate, John V. Lindsay. Buckley has consistently maintained that there is a liberal establishment that dominates and degrades American life and defiles the nation's best traditional values. This selection is taken from the final chapter of his book *Up from Liberalism*.*

4.

. . . Bear in mind, I speak of the failure of the conservative demonstration. A society can be organized, as ours is, around immutable and highly explicit postulates; but it is, in practice, unlikely to submit to them when submission appears nonsensical. A libertarian theorist has no difficulty in cinching his theoretical case against the social security laws—he has merely to state simply that the program has the effect of abridging a freedom unnecessarily. But the flesh-and-blood dissident has earthier problems. John Stuart Mill, the muse of Pure Freedom of Opinion, maintained that so categorical is the right of dissent that the dissident must be protected even from the slightest suggestion of the "moral coercion of public opinion." That is the simon-pure theory. But try to prevent a community from expressing impatience with, let us say, a local Communist. For that matter, try to prevent John Stuart Mill Professors of Political Science from visiting a little genteel moral coercion on the thick skull of that perverse reactionary in their department who believes that.

The oppressed minority, if it is asking for relief by the majority,

* (New York: Macdowell, Obolensky, 1959), pp. 178–90. By permission.

must find a way of stating its case compellingly. Otherwise, the majority is not likely to inconvenience itself. If the majority, moreover, feels that the complaints of the minority are frivolous, it is not likely to go out of its way to accommodate us, however conclusively we establish our solidarity with such supra-constitutional deities as John Stuart Mill.

Why? The answer does not lie in the simple fact that very few people are opposed to the coercive character of social security. Very few people take advantage of the freedom of speech, is that not so? If a law were imposed limiting the right of free speech, how many people would be affected? I should guess thousands, not tens of thousands, for there are not so many of us engaged in writing, or speaking our heterodoxies in public. But all of us would rise, as one man, to protest the passage of any such law, because we are adequately trained to resist impingements on that freedom. We are not, however, adequately trained to resist other restrictions, even those that affect many more members of the community than an impingement of free speech would do. Pass a law levying an additional tax for social security, and millions are affected. The fact that they acquiesce in the appropriation of their pennies does not alter the fact that they have fewer pennies to spend, and that their freedom is, accordingly, diminished. Conservatives have failed to alert the community to the interconnection between economic freedom and—freedom. No government would dare be so abusive as ours is of our economic freedoms if we were alive to the relationship. It is a part of the conservative intuition that economic freedom is the most precious temporal freedom, for the reason that it alone gives to each one of us, in our comings and goings in our complex society, sovereignty—and over that part of existence in which by far the most choices have in fact to be made, and in which it is possible to make choices, involving oneself, without damage to other people. And for the further reason that without economic freedom, political and other freedoms are likely to be taken from us.

At the moment the nation is very much attracted by the sophism of Professor Galbraith, to which I have alluded before, namely that we are not as consumers really free, since we are pawns of the advertising agencies. To begin with, there is the factual exaggeration (the perverseness of the American buying public is the despair of advertising agencies); but even then, what meaning has the generalization for us? Of *course* we are influenced by others in what we do and think, and sometimes we are influenced in the direction of making choices that are hard to defend objectively. Professor Galbraith is horrified by the number of Americans who have bought cars with tail fins on them, and I am horrified by the number of Americans who take seriously the proposals of Mr. Galbraith. But whereas he would, by preempting the people's money, take the power from them to put tail fins on their cars, I should be hesitant (though I would prefer the society with lots of tail fins to the society with lots of Dr. Galbraith's proposals running around dangerously) to preempt the people's money, even though part of it is due to be spent on purchasing books by Dr. Galbraith—which, by the way, have been very well advertised.

Let the individual keep his dollar—however few he is able to save— and he can indulge his taste (and never mind who had a role in shaping it) in houses, in doctors, in education, in groceries, in entertainment, in culture, in religion; give him the right of free speech or the right to go to the polling booth, and at best he contributes to a collective determination, contributes as a general rule an exiguous voice. Give me the right to spend my dollars as I see fit—to devote them, as I see fit, to travel, to food, to learning, to taking pleasure, to polemicizing, and, if I must make the choice, I will surrender you my political franchise in trade, confident that by the transaction, assuming the terms of the contract are that no political decision affecting my sovereignty over my dollar can be made, I shall have augmented my dominance over my own affairs.

That is the demonstration, surely, that the conservatives need to make, before we are overwhelmed; but how pitiful have been our efforts, how tragic our failure. How vulnerable our desire for economic freedom to the devastating indictment of materialism. It is widely felt that the right of property is a rich-man's concern, that the Cadillac he hungers after is the fullest expression of that freedom. How widely it is assumed that societies can, without damage to the metaphysical base of freedom, do away with Cadillacs. Thus have they framed the argument: you have nothing to lose, by our depredations on economic freedom, but a few Cadillacs. It is as if we asked them to prove the value of free speech even to the few who exercise it, by citing only the works of Gerald L. K. Smith.

It follows why conservatism has failed to hold the line for freedom, whether in behalf of dissident social security subscribers, farmers at loggerheads with Agriculture Department bureaucrats, workers conscripted into labor unions, or businessmen struggling against the massive harassment of regulatory agencies. Conservatives have not "proved" to the satisfaction either of the public or of the academy that the moderate* welfare state has paralyzing economic or political consequences for the affluent* society. Our insistence that the economic comeuppance is just around the corner (not *this* corner, *that* one. No, not *that* one, *that* one over *there* . . .) has lost to conservatism public confidence in its economic expertise. And on the matter of liberty, conservatives have not been persuasive (because of the failure I speak of) in their contention that the freedoms they have been forced by the welfare state to do without add up to humiliation, let alone privation.†

The individual who proclaims it an impingement upon his freedom to be required to pay two per cent of his salary into a social security fund will be fretted over by the community about as much as the community, left to its own devices, would worry about the professors who pronounce it an affront on their dignity to be required to sign a non-Communist oath. At the latter's disposal there are great echo chambers (the highly mobilized civil liberties lobby, the professional academic associations, and so on) which if they do not succeed in persuading the majority to be on their side, give the impression that they have, which is almost as good; and so they have their way, with state and national legislatures. But there is no significant lobby to go into action to defend the rights of the libertarian when concern is with property rights, because of the elementary failure to establish the nexus between individual freedom and property rights. Until the objec-

---

* Vague adjectives—dangerous, I concede, in this kind of analysis. I understand a "moderate" welfare state to be one that addresses itself to the physical necessities of life (as distinct from the kind of omniconcerned welfarism that, e.g., Professor J. K. Galbraith would visit upon us); and by "affluent" I mean the society that can relieve physical distress out of earned surplus, without doing organic damage to the society's economic mechanism.

† The obvious exception is the rich man, whose problem is distinctive and, I use the word deliberately, pathetic. The rich man is unmistakably the victim of ideology. In an affluent society, we do not need to tax the millionaire 90 per cent, or his estate 70 per cent. The money that comes in to the treasury, at these levels, is negligible, measured against the budget. If the federal individual income tax were cut to a 50 per cent top, the U.S. would have lost in revenue in 1955, a total of $734 million. In America the rich man is no longer the natural antagonist of the people. The demagogues and egalitarians need to work hard to keep lit the fires of egalitarianism and envy. A recent (Gallup) poll indicates that the majority of Americans a) believe the income tax goes no higher than 35 per cent, and b) believe the tax *should* go no higher than 25 per cent.

tion to involuntary participation in social security reifies in the public mind as something more than a ritualistic exercise in libertarian crankiness, we are not going to set the nation marching to our rescue.

5.

The temptation is to measure freedom subjectively. But it is very dangerous indeed to cede to a society the right to declare what are and what are not the freedoms worth exercising. To be sure, one man may not feel free unless he can render his political views without let or hindrance. Another may put the highest value on his freedom to walk through the streets late at night. A third may care principally about his freedom to shoot ducks. Freedom belongs also to the eccentric—that much we should be quite firm about. It may be eccentric to complain about being docked a few dollars a week for social security; but how far can we go, if we deal thus cavalierly with the minority's freedoms, without changing the very nature of the voluntarist society?

What all conservatives in this country fear, and have plenty of reason to fear, is the loss of freedom by attrition. It is therefore for the most realistic reasons, as well as those of principle, that we must resist every single accretion of power by the state, even while guarding our rhetoric against such exaggerations as equating social security with slavery. The conservative rhetoric has here and there run ahead of events. Even though I myself take the gloomy view that our society is marching toward totalitarianism, I should not go so far as to say that America is not now, as societies go, free—howeverly gravely I view the restrictions on freedom implicit in, e.g., the progressive income tax, the ban on religious teaching in public schools, the union shop, the FEPC's, the farm laws, etc. Freedom is *not* indivisible. The more freedom the better, which means that some freedom is better than none at all, and more than some is better still. The conservative must, therefore, guard against the self-discrediting generalization that our society is no longer "free," while insisting, as implacably as the Liberal does every time a Communist is harassed by a disciplinary law, that not an appropriation is passed by the legislatures, but that our freedom is diminished.

The failure of the conservative demonstration in political affairs rests primarily on our failure to convince that the establishment of the welfare state entails the surrender, bit by bit, of minor freedoms which, added together, can alter the very shape of our existence.

The tendencies of Liberalism are every day more visibly coercive, as the social planners seek more and more brazenly to impose their preferences upon us. Here, I believe, is a practical distinction at which conservatives should hammer hard—the distinction between the kind of welfarism that turns dollars over to people, and that which turns services over to him. The former kind is embodied in such legislation as social security, unemployment compensation, and old age assistance. The latter in federal aid to education, to housing, to rural electrification, small business, etc.; and the proposed "insurance" programs, e.g., health, accident, etc.

In the first instance, the recipient of the money is free to allocate it according to his own lights, to satisfy his own needs and pleasures according to his own estimate of their priority. There are the obvious perils, that he will stress whiskey rather than milk, television over education; but these are the perils of liberty, with which conservatives are prepared to live. In making money grants, as distinguished from the other kind (for instance public housing subsidies), the government is prevented from taking active control of industries or social services, or from having the deciding hand in the creation or development of social or service institutions. I judge this to be significant, because as long as one is free to spend the money with reference to one's desires, the government's control is at least once removed. And then at the tactical level, the longer one can hold off or slow down such grandiose ambitions of the welfarists as free health services, expanded public housing, government aid to airports, highways, schools, Olympic game sites, the more difficult it will be to establish the necessity for the government's undertaking such enterprises. The arguments of the affluent society work in two ways: as we become richer we can indeed devote more attention to economic non-essentials. But as the people become richer we can also leave more and more to them to do out of their own resources, can we not? Surely the argument for socialized medicine in India is more compelling than the argument for socialized medicine in America. That is to say, if the relevant standard is, How many Indians, as opposed to Americans, can afford to pay their own medical bills? Granted, the question is left begging. Where is the government of India going to raise the money to pay for the hospitals, health centers, doctors, nurses and equipment we can all agree are urgently needed in India? The problem having been pondered over in the context of economic realities, the wise man will conclude that the best way to make medicine widely available is to make wealth widely available, and in turn the best way to do that is to liberate the economic system from statist impositions.*

I think the conservative has the best of the argument when he maintains that security does not equal freedom, even though he admits that freedom is also for the eccentric. Objective standards of freedom must not be lost sight of, in our indulgence of the eccentric. If a man feels free in prison, we must simultaneously acknowledge his right to feel free, and declare that he is not free. If the people announce that they feel freer by virtue of the securities extended by the welfare state, we must be prepared to concede what they authoritatively tell us about their state of mind—yet insist, doggedly, that we strive after an objectively free society. If the people are willing to accept substitutes for freedom, that may be styled as their "right." There is no effective means of disputing man's right to self-deception, and certainly there is no questioning his capacity for it; but spinach remains spinach, and on this point one must speak plainly. The conservative must struggle to impart to the popular imagination the great insight into the nature of freedom which, because it was kept vividly in mind in the early years of our nation, preserved the climate of freedom.

I add a note of caution: though the conservative must say that freedom is freedom, not anything else that suits someone just as well, he must guard against saying that the kind of security purchased by, e.g., the social security laws, is an "illusory" security. That is an observation that makes men and women who are subjected to it very impatient, and rightly so. To be sure, all "security" is illusory; but unless we have more specific things in mind, we surely do not want to trouble to make the point that that which is illusory is illusory. As far as state welfare is concerned, there is a long enough historical record of it to establish that relatively affluent societies given to a measure of state welfarism *can* extend their economic lives over an impressive period of time without collapsing from exhaustion. The social security law and related welfare laws have been in operation for about twenty

---

* J. K. Galbraith seems to agree, though he says it in a roundabout way: "An affluent society, that is also both compassionate and rational, would, no doubt, secure to all who needed it the minimum income essential for decency and comfort . . . When poverty was a majority phenomenon [as it now is in, e.g., India—W.F.B.] such action could not be afforded. A poor society . . . *had* [my emphasis—W.F.B.] to enforce the rule that the person who did not work could not eat. And possibly it was [even] justified in the added cruelty of applying the rule to those who could not work or whose efficiency was far below par."

years, and in them many people have in fact found security. (I am not of course suggesting these same people would not have found security elsewhere, had the government stayed out of the picture.) During those twenty years we spent 650 billion dollars on national defense, so that the coordinate economic strain on our society was enormous and, let us hope, unusual.

Even so, our economy has not collapsed—though it almost certainly has been damaged. It is quite possibly true that through such measures as federal social security we sow seeds that could lead to economic destruction, but then it is also true that being born with Original Sin is a poor way to start out in life. Social security will *not* necessarily bring economic collapse—it is merely a step in the wrong direction; a departure from sound principles of government. To insist doctrinally that it will bring disaster is to weaken the case for conservatism, and make difficult the conservative demonstration.

6.

Mr. Peregrine Worsthorne of England, who wrestles eloquently with the problem of conservative leadership in his own country, had made known his position on the welfare state,* and it is in line with that of our own New Conservatives. He writes of the necessity of strengthening England's middle class, but warns that any move to do so must be "only a part of a wider program with a national appeal. Essential to such a program . . . is loyalty to the basic features of the Welfare State which, by reducing class antagonisms, creates precisely the right climate of opinion for strengthening the middle class. Those conservatives who would dismantle the Welfare State overlook the fact that a secure working class, far from being a challenge to the middle class, is its indispensable condition. For only if the many are spared economic hardship can the few expect to enjoy economic and social privilege . . . the concept of welfare must be staunchly defended. Nor, given an expanding economy, will this impose a crippling economic burden, and those conservatives who pretend it will are doing their own cause unnecessary damage."

I am not absolutely sure I know what Mr. Worsthorne is saying. Is he telling us—perhaps it is true—that the working class will hereinafter lay down the conditions of life in England? The class question in

* "Conservative Thoughts Out of Season," *Encounter*, London, August, 1958.

this country is not so tidy, but the problem is there. Universal suffrage broke up the conservative society. And since the enlargement of the electorate tends to be an irreversible political process, the means are not visible by which the voters can be estopped from substituting political for economic means of self-aggrandizement; from redistributing. But we are not to *look* for the means?

And does Mr. Worsthorne mean by "loyalty" what others mean by it? I should think conservatives should be loyal in their *opposition* to the welfare state, for the reasons I have touched upon; even while recognizing that for the time being, at least, political opposition to deeply imbedded welfarist carbuncles is futile. But how is the conservative politician of tomorrow going to oppose the *next* suggested federal enterprise, if not by adducing reasons of a principled kind— which apply with equal cogency to existing measures, whose justification he is supposed to be loyal to? How oppose free false teeth (I almost said compulsory false teeth) or free psychoanalysis (compulsory?) without making a case against social security?

Mr. Worsthorne is correct in suggesting that whatever tactical opportunities the welfare state accidentally delivers to conservatives (e.g., a pacified lower class), we should proceed to exploit. And it may be, even, that he senses correctly the mood in England: that so long as conservatives inveigh against the existing welfare state as though they would, given the opportunity, dismantle it, the working class will see to it that they are never given the power. But Mr. Worsthorne must not ask us to suppress the critical intelligence—and nothing less than that will do, to instill in us a loyalty to the welfare state. And, of course, we have dreams to dream.

34.   GOLDWATER
Civil Rights and the Welfare State

Barry Goldwater (1909–   ), United States Senator from
Arizona, has long been a leading spokesman for contemporary American
conservatism. A member of a prominent Arizona business family, Goldwater
has devoted large sums of money and a great deal of personal time and
energy to Republican Party affairs. In 1964 he was rewarded with the party's
Presidential nomination, only to suffer a serious defeat in the November
election. That the loss was also a setback for conservatism itself is doubtful.
His book *The Conscience of a Conservative** is a basic text used by many
American conservatives to define the nature of their political thought. The
following selection is taken from Chapters Four and Eight of the book,
dealing with civil rights and the welfare state.

AND CIVIL RIGHTS

An attempt has been made in recent years to disparage the principle
of States' Rights by equating it with defense of the South's position on
racial integration. I have already indicated that the reach of States'
Rights is much broader than that—that it affects Northerners as well
as Southerners, and concerns many matters that have nothing to do
with the race question. Still, it is quite true that the integration issue
is affected by the States' Rights principle, and that the South's position
on the issue is, today, the most conspicuous expression of the principle.
So much so that the country is now in the grips of a spirited and
sometimes ugly controversy over an imagined conflict between States'
Rights, on the one hand, and what are called "civil rights" on the other.

I say an imagined conflict because I deny that there *can* be a conflict
between States' Rights, properly defined—and civil rights, properly
defined. If States' "Rights" are so asserted as to encroach upon

* (New York, Hillman Books, 1960, copyright Victor Publishing Co.), pp. 32-38,
70-77. By permission.

individual rights that are protected by valid federal laws, then the exercise of state power is a nullity. Conversely, if individual "rights" are so asserted as to infringe upon valid state power, then the assertion of those "rights" is a nullity. The rights themselves do not clash. The conflict arises from a failure to define the two categories of rights correctly, and to assert them lawfully.

States' Rights are easy enough to define. The Tenth Amendment does it succinctly: "The powers not delegated to the United States by the Constitution nor prohibited by it to the States are reserved to the States respectively, or to the people."

Civil rights should be no harder. In fact, however—thanks to extravagant and shameless misuse by people who ought to know better—it is one of the most badly understood concepts in modern political usage. Civil rights is frequently used synonymously with "human rights"—or with "natural rights." As often as not, it is simply a name for describing an activity that someone deems politically or socially desirable. A sociologist writes a paper proposing to abolish some inequity, or a politician makes a speech about it—and, behold, a new "civil right" is born! The Supreme Court has displayed the same creative powers.

A *civil* right is a right that is asserted and is therefore protected by some valid law. It may be asserted by the common law, or by local or federal statutes, or by the Constitution; *but unless a right is incorporated in the law, it is not a civil right and is not enforceable by the instruments of the civil law.* There may be some rights—"natural," "human," or otherwise—that *should* also be civil rights. But if we desire to give such rights the protection of the law, our recourse is to a legislature or to the amendment procedures of the Constitution. We must not look to politicians, or sociologists—or the courts—to correct the deficiency.

In the field of racial relations, there are some rights that are clearly protected by valid laws and are therefore "civil" rights. One of them is the right to vote. The Fifteenth Amendment provides that no one shall be denied the franchise on account of race, color or previous condition of servitude. Similarly with certain legal privileges enforced by the Fourteenth Amendment. The legislative history of that amendment makes it clear (I quote from the Civil Rights Act of 1866 which the Amendment was designed to legitimize) that people of all races shall be equally entitled "to make and enforce contracts, to sue, be parties, and give evidence, to inherit, to purchase, lease, sell, hold and convey real and personal property and to full and equal benefit of all laws and proceedings for the security of persons and property." After the passage of that Act and the Amendment, all persons, Negroes included, had a "civil" right to these protections.

It is otherwise let us note, with education. For the federal Constitution does *not* require the States to maintain racially mixed schools. Despite the recent holding of the Supreme Court, I am firmly convinced—not only that integrated schools are not required—but that the Constitution does not permit any interference whatsoever by the federal government in the field of education. It may be just or wise or expedient for negro children to attend the same schools as white children, but they do not have a civil right to do so which is protected by the federal constitution, or which is enforceable by the federal government.

The intentions of the founding fathers in this matter are beyond any doubt; *no powers regarding education were given the federal government.* Consequently, under the Tenth Amendment, jurisdiction over the entire field was reserved to the States. The remaining question is whether the Fourteenth Amendment—concretely, that amendment's "equal protection" clause—modified the original prohibition against federal intervention.

To my knowledge it has never been seriously argued—the argument certainly was not made by the Supreme Court—that the authors of the Fourteenth Amendment intended to alter the Constitutional scheme with regard to education. Indeed, in the famous school integration decision, *Brown* v. *Board of Education* (1954), the Supreme Court justices expressly acknowledged that they were not being guided by the intentions of the amendment's authors. "*In approaching this problem,*" Chief Justice Warren said "*we cannot turn the clock back to 1868 when the amendment was adopted . . . We must consider public education in the light of its full development and in its present place in American life throughout the nation.*" In effect, the Court said that what matters is not the ideas of the men who wrote the Constitution, but the *Court's* ideas. It was only by engrafting its own views onto the established law of the land that the Court was able to reach the decision it did.

The intentions of the Fourteenth Amendment's authors are perfectly clear. Consider these facts. 1. During the entire congressional debate on the Fourteenth Amendment it was never once suggested by any proponent of the amendment that it would outlaw segregated schools. 2. At the same time it approved the Fourteenth Amendment, Congress established schools in Washington in Georgetown "for the sole use of . . . colored children." 3. In all the debates on the amendment by the State Legislatures there was only one legislator, a man in Indiana, who thought the amendment would affect schools. 4. The great majority of the States that approved the amendment permitted or required segregated schools at the very time they approved the amendment. There is not room here for exhaustive treatment of this evidence, but the facts are well documented, and they are all we have to know about the Fourteenth Amendment's bearing on this problem. The amendment was not intended to, and therefore it did not outlaw racially separate schools. It was not intended to, and therefore it did not, authorize *any* federal intervention in the field of education.

I am therefore not impressed by the claim that the Supreme Court's decision on school integration is the law of the land. *The Constitution, and the laws "made in pursuance thereof," are the "supreme law of the land."* The Constitution is what its authors intended it to be and said it was—not what the Supreme Court says it is. If we condone the practice of substituting our own intentions for those of the Constitution's framers, we reject, in effect, the principle of Constitutional Government; we endorse a rule of men, not of laws.

I have great respect for the Supreme Court as an institution, but I cannot believe that I display that respect by submitting abjectly to abuses of power by the Court, and by condoning its unconstitutional trespass into the legislative sphere of government. The Congress and the States, equally with the Supreme Court, are obliged to interpret and comply with the Constitution according to their own lights. I therefore support all efforts by the States, excluding violence of course, to preserve their rightful powers over education.

As for the Congress, I would hope that the national legislature would help clarify the problem by proposing to the States a Constitutional amendment that would reaffirm the States' exclusive jurisdiction in the field of education. This amendment would, in my judgment, assert what is already provided unmistakably by the Constitution; but it would put the matter beyond any further question.

It so happens that I am in agreement with the *objectives* of the Supreme Court as stated in the *Brown* decision. I believe that it *is* both wise and just for negro children to attend the same schools as whites, and that to deny them this opportunity carries with it strong implications of inferiority. I am not prepared, however, to impose that judgment of mine on the people of Mississippi or South Carolina, or to tell them what methods should be adopted and what pace should be kept in striving toward that goal. That is their business, not mine. I believe that the problem of race relations, like all social and cultural problems, is best handled by the people directly concerned. Social and cultural change, however desirable, should not be effected by the engines of national power. Let us, through persuasion and education, seek to improve institutions we deem defective. But let us, in doing so, respect the orderly process of the law. Any other course enthrones tyrants and dooms freedom. . . .

THE WELFARE STATE

Washington—The President estimated that the expenditures of the Department of Health, Education and Welfare in the fiscal year 1961 (including Social Security payments) would exceed $15,000,000,000. Thus the current results of New Deal legislation are Federal disbursements for human welfare in this country second only to national defense.

The *New York Times*, January 18, 1960, p. 1.

For many years it appeared that the principal domestic threat to our freedom was contained in the doctrines of Karl Marx. The collectivists—non-Communists as well as Communists—had adopted the Marxist objective of "socializing the means of production." And so it seemed that if collectivization were imposed, it would take the form of a State owned and operated economy. I doubt whether this is the main threat any longer.

The collectivists have found, both in this country and in other industrialized nations of the West, that free enterprise has removed the economic and social conditions that might have made a class struggle possible. Mammoth productivity, wide distribution of wealth, high standards of living, the trade union movement—these and other factors have eliminated whatever incentive there might have been for the "proletariat" to rise up, peaceably or otherwise, and assume direct ownership of productive property. Significantly, the bankruptcy of doctrinaire Marxism has been expressly acknowledged by the Socialist Party of West Germany, and by the dominant faction of the Socialist Party of Great Britain. In this country the abandonment of the Marxist approach (outside the Communist Party, of course) is attested to by the negligible strength of the Socialist Party, and more tellingly perhaps, by the content of left wing literature and by the programs of left wing political organizations such as the Americans For Democratic Action.

The currently favored instrument of collectivization is the Welfare State. The collectivists have not abandoned their ultimate goal—to subordinate the individual to the State—but their strategy has changed. They have learned that Socialism can be achieved through Welfarism quite as well as through Nationalization. They understand that private property can be confiscated as effectively by taxation as by expropriating it. They understand that the individual can be put at the mercy of the State—not only by making the State his employer—but by divesting him of the means to provide for his personal needs and by giving the State the responsibility of caring for those needs from cradle to grave. Moreover, they have discovered—and here is the critical point—that *Welfarism is much more compatible with the political processes of a democratic society.* Nationalization ran into popular opposition, but the collectivists feel sure the Welfare State can be erected by the simple expedient of buying votes with promises of "free" hospitalization, "free" retirement pay and so on . . . The correctness of this estimate can be seen from the portion of the federal budget that is now allocated to welfare, an amount second only to the cost of national defense.*

I do not welcome this shift of strategy. Socialism-through-Welfarism poses a far greater danger to freedom than Socialism-through-Nationalization precisely because it *is* more difficult to combat. The evils of Nationalization are self-evident and immediate. Those of Welfarism are veiled and tend to be postponed. People can understand the consequences of turning over ownership of the steel industry, say, to the State; and they can be counted on to oppose such a proposal. But let the government increase its contribution to the "Public Assistance" program and we will, at most, grumble about excessive government spending. The effect of Welfarism on freedom will be felt later on—after its beneficiaries have become its victims, after dependence on government has turned into bondage and it is too late to unlock the jail.

But a far more important factor is Welfarism's strong emotional appeal to many voters, and the consequent temptations it presents the average politician. It is hard, as we have seen, to make out a case for

* The total figure is substantially higher than the $15,000,000,000 noted above if we take into account welfare expenditures outside the Department of Health, Education and Welfare—for federal housing projects, for example.

State ownership. It is very different with the rhetoric of humanitarianism. How easy it is to reach the voters with earnest importunities for helping the needy. And how difficult for Conservatives to resist these demands without appearing to be callous and contemptuous of the plight of less fortunate citizens. Here, perhaps, is the best illustration of the failure of the Conservative demonstration.

I know, for I have heard the questions often. Have you no sense of social obligation? the Liberals ask. Have you no concern for people who are out of work? for sick people who lack medical care? for children in overcrowded schools? Are you unmoved by the problems of the aged and disabled? Are you *against* human welfare?

The answer to all of these questions is, of course, no. But a simple "no" is not enough. I feel certain that Conservatism is through unless Conservatives can demonstrate and communicate the difference between being concerned with these problems and believing that the federal government is the proper agent for their solution.

The long range political consequences of Welfarism are plain enough: as we have seen, the State that is able to deal with its citizens as wards and dependents has gathered unto itself unlimited political and economic power and is thus able to rule as absolutely as any oriental despot.

Let us, however, weigh the consequences of Welfarism on the citizen.

Consider, first, the effect of Welfarism on the donors of government welfare—not only those who pay for it but also the voters and their elected representatives who decide that the benefits shall be conferred. Does some credit redound on them for trying to care for the needs of their fellow citizens? Are they to be commended and rewarded, at some moment in eternity, for their "charity"? I think not. Suppose I should vote for a measure providing for free medical care: I am unaware of any moral virtue that is attached to my decision to confiscate the earnings of X and give them to Y.

Suppose, however, that X approves of the program—that he has voted for welfarist politicians with the idea of helping his fellow man. Surely the wholesomeness of his act is diluted by the fact that he is voting not only to have his own money taken but also that of his fellow citizens who may have different ideas about their social obligations. Why does not such a man, instead, contribute what he regards as his just share of human welfare to a private charity?

Consider the consequences to the recipient of welfarism. For one thing, he mortgages himself to the federal government. In return for benefits—which, in the majority of cases, he pays for—he concedes to the government the ultimate in political power—the power to grant or withhold from him the necessities of life as the government sees fit. Even more important, however, is the effect on him—the elimination of any feeling of responsibility for his own welfare and that of his family and neighbors. A man may not immediately, or ever, comprehend the harm thus done to his character. Indeed, this is one of the great evils of Welfarism—that it transforms the individual from a dignified, industrious, self-reliant *spiritual* being into a dependent animal creature without his knowing it. There is no avoiding this damage to character under the Welfare State. Welfare programs cannot help but promote the idea that the government *owes* the benefits it confers on the individual, and that the individual is entitled, by right, to receive them. Such programs are sold to the country precisely on the argument that government has an *obligation* to care for the needs of its citizens. Is it possible that the message will reach those who vote for the benefits, but not those who receive them? How different it is with private charity where both the giver and the receiver understand that charity is the product of the humanitarian impulses of the giver, not the due of the receiver.

Let us, then, not blunt the noble impulses of mankind by reducing charity to a mechanical operation of the federal government. Let us, by all means, encourage, those who are fortunate and able to care for the needs of those who are unfortunate and disabled. But let us do this in a way that is conducive to the spiritual as well as the material well-being of our citizens—and in a way that will preserve their freedom. Let welfare be a private concern. Let it be promoted by individuals and families, by churches, private hospitals, religious service organizations, community charities and other institutions that have been established for this purpose. If the objection is raised that private institutions lack sufficient funds, let us remember that every penny the federal government does *not* appropriate for welfare is potentially available for private use—and without the overhead charge for processing the money through the federal bureaucracy. Indeed, high taxes, for which government Welfarism is so largely responsible, is the biggest obstacle to fund raising by private charities.

Finally, if we deem public intervention necessary, let the job be done by local and state authorities that are incapable of accumulating the vast political power that is so inimical to our liberties.

The Welfare State is *not* inevitable, as its proponents are so fond of telling us. There is nothing inherent in an industrialized economy, or in democratic processes of government that *must* produce de Tocqueville's "guardian society." Our future, like our past, will be what we make it. And we can shatter the collectivists' designs on individual freedom if we will impress upon the men who conduct our affairs this one truth: that the material and spiritual sides of man are intertwined; that it is impossible for the State to assume responsibility for one without intruding on the essential nature of the other; that if we take from a man the personal responsibility for caring for his material needs, we take from him also the will and the opportunity to be free.

Suggestions for Further Reading

Readers curious to know more about American conservatism should consult the following listed books. In addition, for contemporary affairs, attention should be given the *National Review, Modern Age*, and the *Intercollegiate Review*, leading conservative journals. Beyond these the *Freeman, Human Events*, the *University Bookman*, and the *New Guardsman* should be examined.

IRVING BABBITT, *Democracy and Leadership* (Boston: Houghton, Mifflin, 1924).
 Babbitt provides an aristocratic critique of mass democracy, calling for a form of more indirect democracy. The book is representative of an intellectual conservatism that was popular in the 1920's.

DANIEL BELL, ed., *The Radical Right* (New York: Anchor, 1964).
 This collection of articles by leading academics helps explain the emergence of the radical right in the 1950's and 1960's. The book shows that many of these radicals found Eisenhower too "liberal" and doubted the loyalty of numerous American political leaders because of the sense of social displacement and psychological danger they felt.

WILLIAM BUCKLEY, *Rumbles Left and Right* (New York: G. P. Putnam's Sons, 1963).
 Although sympathetic to the rising demands for majority recognition of minority rights, Buckley is fearful of national government intervention. The preservation of local community responsible for the solution of these problems may be less dangerous than massive federal action, and it may be more responsive to individual needs.

JAMES BURNHAM, *The Managerial Revolution* (New York: John Day, 1941).
The idea that the contemporary world is in the grip of a conservative revolution was proposed by Burnham in 1941. A new class of governmental and corporate managers would gradually receive power, until capitalism and democracy were both destroyed by a virtual technical dictatorship of the "experts."

ALLEN GUTTMANN, *The Conservative Tradition in America* (New York: Oxford University Press, 1967).
Professor Guttmann maintains that conservatism has very little significance in American politics but is still alive in American literature. The argument is rather disjointed, but by labeling followers of Edmund Burke as "conservatives" and followers of John Locke as "liberals" Guttmann has stacked the deck. It turns out that almost no one is a conservative.

FREDERICK HAYEK, *The Constitution of Liberty* (Chicago: University of Chicago Press, 1960).
This is a highly successful scholarly explanation of modern conservatism. Although economic in outlook, the analysis is wide in scope and rather convincing for the uncommitted.

WILMOORE KENDALL, *The Conservative Affirmation* (Chicago: H. Regnery, 1962).
This is one of the best-reasoned presentations of modern American conservatism. Professor Kendall separates the necessary from the dispensable and the dangerous in recent public policies.

WILMOORE KENDALL, *John Locke and the Doctrine of Majority Rule* (Urbana: University of Illinois Press, 1941).
Few modern American conservatives have had the audacity to attack both John Locke and John Stuart Mill. Professor Kendall prefers Plato to both. The relativism of liberal thought is the real enemy.

RUSSELL KIRK, *The Conservative Mind* (Chicago: H. Regnery, 1960).
This standard historical analysis of American conservative thought must be read by all concerned students of this field. It tends, however, to relate the English and American developments in a manner which might confuse many readers. The emphasis is placed upon literary figures and Edmund Burke.

RUSSELL KIRK, *A Program for Conservatives* (Chicago: H. Regnery, 1954).
Like Edmund Burke, Professor Kirk insists that men are essentially unequal and have the duty to accept their divinely appointed social position. In a civilized nation a few choice individuals are the natural rulers. These men, who usually hold inherited property, can alone be depended upon to conserve the best in the social order against the revolutionary and innovative tendencies of the masses.

MELVIN R. LAIRD, ed., *The Conservative Papers* (Chicago: Quadrangle Books, 1964).
Congressman Laird has collected a group of essays, addresses, and lectures into a useful package. The book is timely and highly political. It may, at times, equate conservatism with the Republican Party.

DAVID E. LILIENTHAL, *Big Business: A New Era* (New York: Harper, 1953).
Lilienthal frankly expresses his faith in big business, which he regards as the hope of the future. Only capitalism can save the Western ideals of democracy and freedom. Antitrust prosecutions are undesirable, while big government and big business are natural, and desirable, products of our age.

WALTER LIPPMANN, *The Public Philosophy* (Boston: Little, Brown, 1955).
Lippmann, the most esteemed columnist of the century, is an unusual kind of conservative. Although he had accepted collectivism at one time, Lippmann became disillusioned with majoritarian democracy. He fears the new irresponsible democratic politician and calls for a return to the "public philosophy," which includes the Magna Charta, the Declaration of Independence, the English and American Bills of Rights, and certain "traditions of civility."

FRANK S. MEYER, *In Defense of Freedom* (Chicago: H. Regnery, 1962).
Denying the relevance of Burke for modern America, Meyer is critical of some fellow conservatives. He prefers to emphasize the heritage of individual liberty, which he believes has been threatened by liberals and misunderstood by Burkean conservatives who have a yearning for outmoded institutions.

PAUL ELMER MORE, *Aristocracy and Justice* (Boston: Houghton Mifflin Co., 1915).
More offers a scholarly criticism of fundamental democratic ideas. Social reform and economic amelioration are rejected in favor of the strengthening of character and the recognition of America's natural leaders, who would lead the masses.

Ayn Rand, *Capitalism: The Unknown Ideal* (New York: New American Library, 1967).
 This collection of essays presents an extreme defense of the right of property as found in the ideas of classic capitalism. Government is seen to be in need of sharp curtailment in the interest of individual rights. The book represents a powerful attack upon welfare state policies. The *National Review* does not approve.

Clinton Rossiter, *Conservatism in America* (New York: A. Knopf, 1962).
 This is the best introduction to the subject of American conservatism. Unfortunately, Professor Rossiter adopts a definition of conservatism which is on the European model, so that he tends to underrate the significance of American conservatism since the decline of the Federalist Party. Curiously, Rossiter has been a foremost spokesman for modern American conservatism.

George Santayana, *Dominations and Powers* (New York: Scribner, 1951).
 The great American philosopher describes his distaste for American liberalism in this outstanding, but difficult, book. Preferring a "timocracy," a rule of merit, Santayana admits that it cannot be achieved. The best we can do is to support timocratic institutions against liberal dissolution and conformity.

Alexis de Toqueville, *Democracy in America* (New York: Vintage, 1954).
 Originally written in 1835 and 1840, this work has become a modern classic. A French aristocrat, Toqueville admitted that democracy was the wave of the future but warned that in America a "tyranny of the majority" might evolve which could produce a pressure toward conformity. He warned that the drive for equality could endanger individual liberty.

John G. Tower, *A Program for Conservatives* (New York: MacFadden, 1962).
 A conservative Texas Senator places the doctrines of conservatism into the context of current American political problems.

Peter Viereck, *Conservatism Revisited* (New York: Scribner, 1949).
 Unlike Russell Kirk, Peter Viereck does not prefer aristocratic leadership within our democratic system. Viereck's heroes are Hamilton, Calhoun, and John Stuart Mill. Although willing to accept the changes wrought by F.D.R.'s New Deal, Viereck admires the free market system and the stabilizing force of habit.

GARY WILLS, *Politics and Catholic Freedom* (Chicago: H. Regnery, 1964).

For American conservatives who happen to be Catholics, this book provides a criticism of "liberalizing" tendencies within the Church. Even Pope John XXIII is not spared criticism for these changes in Catholicism.